KANT'S LIFE
AND THOUGHT
ERNST CASSIRER

Translated by JAMES HADEN

Introduction by STEPHAN KÖRNER

NEW HAVEN AND LONDON : YALE UNIVERSITY PRESS

Published with assistance from the foundation
established in memory of James Wesley Cooper
of the Class of 1865, Yale College.

Designed by James J. Johnson
and set in Palatino Roman type.
Printed in the United States of America by
Edwards Brothers Inc., Ann Arbor, Michigan.

Library of Congress Cataloging in Publication Data

Cassirer, Ernst, 1874–1945.
   Kant's life and thought.

   Translation of: Kants Leben und Lehre.
   Includes index.
   1. Kant, Immanuel, 1724–1804.   I. Title.
B2797.C313   193   81–3354
ISBN 0–300–02358–8   AACR2
(pbk.) 0–300–02982–9

10   9

CONTENTS

INTRODUCTION TO THE
ENGLISH EDITION

Ever since its first publication in 1918 Ernst Cassirer's book on Kant's life and teaching has been widely and, I believe, rightly regarded as a classic of its kind. The aim of this introduction to the English translation is not so much to justify this estimate as to indicate the relevance of Cassirer's Kant interpretation to contemporary philosophy in its renewed endeavor to understand Kant's position and in its varied reactions to it. If this aim is to be achieved, it is necessary, however briefly (1) to consider some recent or still influential interpretations and modifications of Kant's central theses; (2) to characterize Cassirer's version of transcendental idealism; and (3) to draw attention to some of Cassirer's distinctive exegetic points in the light of his historical and philosophical ideas.

1

Kant's Copernican revolution in philosophy consists in asking and answering two kinds of questions which, borrowing terms from the Roman jurists, he calls "questions of fact" *(quid facti)* and "questions of legality" *(quid iuris)*.[1] The former concern factual claims to the effect that all rational beings in their thinking—theoretical, practical, aesthetic, or teleological—accept certain judgments or employ certain concepts. The latter questions concern the justification of the factual

---

1. See, for example, *Critique of Pure Reason*, B 116.

claims. The Copernican revolution is based on an entirely new conception of philosophy and philosophical method which Kant describes as critical or transcendental.

Within the theoretical sphere, that is to say, mathematics, natural science, and commonsense thinking about what is the case, Kant's factual claims include three theses about synthetic judgments a priori—a judgment being synthetic if, and only if, its negation is not self-contradictory and a priori if, and only if, it is logically independent of any judgment describing a sense experience. He claims (1) that there are synthetic judgments a priori; (2) that there is one and only one internally consistent set of them; and (3) that it has been completely exhibited in the *Critique of Pure Reason*. (It comprises all axioms and theorems of Euclidean geometry, all true arithmetical propositions, and certain assumptions of Newtonian physics, such as the principles of causality, of the conservation of substance, and of continuity.)

Kant's attempted justification of these three claims—of existence, uniqueness, and completeness—is a characteristic and important instance of a transcendental justification. It presupposes that we have objective experience or experience of objects and that within it we can distinguish what is given to the senses (its sensory or a posteriori content) from what, although not so given, is yet ascribed by us to the objects (its nonsensory or a priori form). And it consists in producing, or trying to produce, a cogent argument to the effect that the a priori features of objective experience are necessary conditions of its objective character. Transcendental arguments are thus based on the twofold conviction that an experience without—or deprived of— these features is not "a possible objective experience";[2] and that, in another succinct, if rather metaphorical, Kantian phrase "we can have a priori knowledge only of those features of the things which we ourselves put into them."[3]

The fundamental tasks of the *Critique of Pure Reason*, namely the factual exposition and transcendental justification of the system of

2. See, for example, ibid., B 810.
3. Ibid., B xviii.

(theoretical) a priori judgments in its uniqueness and completeness, involve the subsidiary tasks of expounding and transcendentally justifying the system of the Categories, which Kant also regards as unique and complete. The Categories, for example, causality and substance, are concepts which occur in nonmathematical, synthetic a priori judgments; which are a priori in the sense of being applicable to, but not abstracted from, sense experience; and which in being applied to what is given to the senses confer objectivity upon it. Kant calls the transcendental justification of the Categories their transcendental "deduction." In doing so he again adopts and adapts a technical legal term from those jurists who mean by "deduction" the demonstration that what has been established as being *de facto* the case is also appropriate *de jure*.[4] In this sense of the term a deduction may, but need not, coincide with a logical deduction.

The theses of Kant's First Critique which have just been outlined have all been subjected to various—in some cases very different—interpretations, criticisms, and modifications. In considering them it is advisable to observe the Kantian distinction between questions of fact and factual claims on the one hand and questions of legality and transcendental justification on-the other. As regards the interpretation of Kant's factual claims to have expounded the unique and complete system of synthetic a priori judgments and Categories, there is hardly any disagreement among the commentators. There is, on the other hand, sharp disagreement about the correctness of these factual claims—even among philosophers who accept Kant's distinctions between synthetic a posteriori and synthetic a priori judgments and between a posteriori and a priori concepts.

The main reason for their disagreement lies in their different reactions to post-Kantian developments in mathematics and physics. These are on the one hand the discovery of non-Euclidean geometries, together with the incorporation of one of them into the general theory of relativity, and on the other hand the discovery of quantum mechanics, which—at least in its dominant interpretation—is incompatible with the Kantian a priori principles of causality and con-

4. See, for example, B 116, above.

tinuity. According to these reactions we may distinguish between Kantian absolutists who accept Kant's factual claims in their original form (e.g., Leonard Nelson and the so-called Göttingen school); neo-Kantian absolutists who accept Kant's uniqueness claim, but replace his system of synthetic a priori judgments and Categories by a different one (e.g., some Anglo-American analytical philosophers); and neo-Kantian pluralists who reject his claims of uniqueness and, hence, of completeness (e.g., Hermann Cohen and the so-called Marburg school, of which Cassirer was a prominent member).

Turning to Kant's transcendental justification of his factual claims, especially his transcendental deduction of the Categories, one is immediately struck by exegetic divergences which are radical and irreconcilable. For the pluralists, who deny Kant's uniqueness claim, a transcendental deduction of a unique system of Categories and, hence, of universally and necessarily true synthetic a priori judgments is impossible—whatever the alleged nature of such a "deduction" may be. To express the matter in accordance with Kant's quasi-legal terminology, the pluralists hold that since the *quaestio facti* has to be answered in the negative, that is to say, since the factual claim has to be rejected, the *quaestio iuris* does not arise (or, in a phrase of the Roman jurists, *cadit quaestio*).

In the most common contemporary interpretation, Kant's transcendental deduction of the Categories is seen as an attempted logical inference from 'x is capable of objective experience' to 'x is capable of objectifying (transforming, unifying, organizing, into an objective phenomenon) a spatiotemporally ordered, subjectively given manifold by applying *the* Categories to it.' Of Kantian and neo-Kantian absolutists, who accept the uniqueness claim for Kant's or some other system of Categories, some consider this logical inference to be valid, others consider it invalid but remediably so, while still others consider it irremediably invalid. Thus many analytical philosophers with Kantian sympathies argue that the logical inference can be validly reconstructed if the Kantian set of Categories is replaced by another.[5]

---

5. See, for example, J. Bennett, "Analytic, Transcendental Arguments," Bieri et al., eds., *Transcendental Arguments and Science* (Dordrecht, 1979), pp. 45–64.

An exception is C. D. Broad, who suggests that the invalid logical inference can at best be replaced by a more modest probabilistic argument.[6] Lastly, Leonard Nelson and his followers, though accepting Kant's factual claims, regard his transcendental deduction as an instance of the irremediably invalid logical fallacy of a vicious infinite regress. According to Nelson, Kant's correct factual claims can be justified only by showing that the Categories are applicable to an originally obscure, nonpropositional cognition, in the same way that the a priori concepts of arithmetic and geometry are applicable to the nonpropositional intuition of time and space.[7]

In order to understand Kant's thought and influence it is important to separate his fundamental conviction that "we can have a priori knowledge only of those features of the things which we ourselves put into them" from his absolutist claim that what we so put into them is determined for all times and for all rational beings. For, although the fundamental conviction, which is common to all versions of transcendental idealism, may well have inspired the absolutist claim, it is compatible with a pluralistic assumption of alternative and even changeable systems of a priori concepts and judgments.

To the distinctions drawn by the *Critique of Pure Reason* within the sphere of theoretical thinking between the a posteriori and merely subjectively given features, which are its matter, and the a priori, objective features, which are its form, there correspond analogous distinctions drawn by the *Critique of Practical Reason* within the sphere of practical thinking and by the *Critique of Judgment* within the spheres of aesthetic and teleological thinking. Within the practical sphere the difference between a posteriori matter and a priori imposed and organizing form manifests itself in the contrast—and conflict—between desires and inclinations on the one hand and the moral will and moral duties on the other. In the sphere of aesthetic experience it manifests itself in the contrast between the pleasant and the beautiful. Like the factual claims and justifications of the First Critique, Kant's factual

6. See *Kant—An Introduction* (Cambridge, 1978), pp. 183 ff.

7. See "Die Kritische Methode und das Verhältnis der Psychologie zur Philosophie" (1904), reprinted in *Ges. Schriften,* ed. Paul Bernays et al., vol. 1 (Hamburg, 1970), pp. 4–78.

claims about the a priori features of morals, aesthetics, and teleology have been subjected to very different interpretations and criticisms. And these have again suggested proposals for various reforms, ranging from versions of neo-Kantian absolutism, over versions of a pluralistic neo-Kantian pluralism, to outright rejections of the transcendental approach in these fields.

Kant's transcendental or critical method is his most distinctive contribution to philosophy, a discipline which has always been very conscious of its dependence on "the correct method." But many of his other original ideas have proved hardly less influential. Examples of Kantian themes in recent philosophy that stem from the First Critique are the antilogicist analysis of arithmetic and the identification of physics with Newtonian physics. The former has not only become a central topic in the philosophy of mathematics but has, through its acceptance by Hilbert and Brouwer, influenced the course of mathematics itself. The latter has become important in the philosophy of science, in particular in the discussion of quantum physics, for example, Einstein's rejection of its indeterministic implications. An example of a Kantian theme stemming from the Second Critique is the discussion and rejection of utilitarianism in ethics, and hence in political philosophy, where—possibly under the influence of new developments in welfare economics—the conflict between utilitarian and antiutilitarian analyses of justice has again become central.

Kant's Third Critique has been comparatively neglected by contemporary philosophers, even by those whose main concern is with aesthetics. A probable reason for this neglect is the widely accepted view that Kant's *Critique of Judgment* owes its existence less to his philosophical insight and originality than to his idiosyncratic devotion to philosophical architectonics. It is one of the great merits of Cassirer's commentary to have shown this view to be mistaken, or at least extremely doubtful.

2

Although Cassirer's own philosophical position and approach to the history of ideas developed under the continuous influence of Kant's work, they in turn, as is to be expected, influenced his judgment of Kant's achievement and life. Cassirer very early on accepted—and never abandoned—the fundamental guiding principle of Kant's transcendental philosophy, namely that the objectivity of phenomena is not given to the senses or otherwise passively received by the mind, but is the result of the mind's imposing an a priori form on the manifold given to it. An example, indeed the prototype, of such imposition of form and objectivity on a given manifold is the mind's creation of the a priori structure of Newtonian physics by the application to sense experience of the (Kantian) Categories. This application is, as Cassirer sometimes puts it, the "making of a world"—the world of Newtonian physics in which all physical objects exist and are related to each other.

Yet Cassirer rejects the identification of physics with Newtonian physics, which he regards as constituting one physical world rather than the only possible one. He holds, moreover, that man is the maker of not only one type of world, but of worlds of different types, including, apart from the world or worlds of physics, the world or worlds of language, myth, religion, and art. In a lecture given in 1921 and in the introduction to the *Philosophy of Symbolic Forms*, he quotes with approval a passage by Heinrich Hertz which sees mathematical physics as resulting from a symbolic representation of experience.[8] In commenting on it he argues that Hertz's theory of the role of symbolic representation is merely a special case of his own general theory of the function of symbols in the constitution of a world.

According to Hertz it is the main task of science to "derive the future from the past"—a task which we perform by making for ourselves "inner, apparent pictures *(Scheinbilder)* or symbols" in such a manner that "the necessarily thought *(denknotwendigen)* consequences of the pictures are also pictures of the naturally necessary *(naturnotwendigen)* consequences of the represented objects." This account of the function of symbolic representation in the service of

8. See "Der Begriff der symbolischen Form im Aufbau der Geisteswissenschaften," in *Wesen und Wirkung des Symbolbegriffs* (Oxford, 1956), p. 186, and *Philosophie der Symbolischen Formen*, vol. 1 (Berlin, 1923–25), p. 5; Hertz, *Prinzipien der Mechanik* (Leipzig, 1894), p. 1.

scientific prediction was in the first place intended to explain and
justify Hertz's own reconstruction of classical mechanics by eliminat-
ing the concept of force from it. But, as Cassirer points out, it equally
explains and justifies much more radical modifications which break
through the constraints of classical physics accepted by Newton and
exhibited by Kant. It moreover confirms that, "as we must recognize
ever more clearly," the building of science "does not progress by
rising on a foundation which is firm and fixed forever."[9]

Lastly, as has been mentioned already, Hertz's account may be
taken as admitting or suggesting that since man does not live by
scientific prediction alone, the symbolic formation of worlds extends
beyond the world or worlds of science. It is this suggestion which for
Cassirer is the most important. For in pursuing it one comes to see
that science, language, and the mystical-religious world are all symbolic forms, each being "an energy of the mind by which a mental
content of meaning *(ein geistiger Bedeutungsgehalt)* is tied to a concrete
sensible sign and is internally incorporated into it *(ihm innerlich
zugeeignet wird)*."[10]

Although this definition of the concept of a symbolic form and the
necessarily brief characterization of Cassirer's idea of a general theory
or "grammar" of symbolic forms may help to throw some light on his
understanding and interpretation of Kant's philosophy, they cannot
do justice to his own thought unless they are supplemented by detailed applications of his theory. In fairness it should, moreover, be
noted that he regarded his philosophy of symbolic forms not as a
finished theory but as a theory *in statu nascendi*.[11]

Cassirer's approach to the history of ideas is closely related to his
philosophy; here the philosophy of history plays an important role,
since "the synopsis of the mental cannot realize itself anywhere except in its history."[12] For our purposes it is not necessary to explain
this statement in detail. Instead, it may be useful to mention two

9. "Zur Logik des Symbolbegriffs," *Theoria*, vol. 2 (1938), reprinted in *Wesen und
Wirkung des Symbolbegriffs*, p. 230.

10. *Wesen und Wirkung des Symbolbegriffs*, p. 175.

11. Ibid., p. 229.

12. Ibid., p. 171.

guiding ideas which characterize Cassirer not so much as a philosopher of history but as a historian of philosophy. They are, first, a general view about the direction and the progress of philosophy from Descartes to Kant and beyond; second, a general view about the relation between a philosopher's personality and his philosophy.

Cassirer agrees with those who regard as progressive the tendency of modern philosophy from Descartes to Kant to replace ontology by epistemology. He approves of Descartes's program "to determine the whole domain and limits of the mind," but rejects as impossible the Cartesian and, more generally, the rationalist attempt at "deducing . . . the concrete totality of the mind from a single logical principle."[13] He sees in Kant's epistemology, which conceives the object of experience as "the correlate of the synthetic unity of the understanding," a decisive step in the right direction.[14] But he also holds that further progress was made—by Herder and von Humboldt among others—in rejecting the limits of epistemology as too narrow and in trying to replace it by a philosophy of culture on the lines of his own philosophy of symbolic forms.

In explaining his view of the relation between a philosopher's work and his life Cassirer frequently appeals to Goethe. Thus in his essay "Goethe and the Kantian Philosophy" he quotes with approval a passage from the *Xenien* which implies that the philosopher cannot, any more than the poet, be separated from his work, since "alle Wahrheit zuletzt wird nur gebildet, geschaut" (all truth is ultimately shaped, intuited), that is to say, not just passively apprehended.[15] And at the very beginning of *Kant's Life and Thought* he expresses his full agreement with Goethe's conviction that "the philosophers cannot present us with anything but forms of life" (*Lebensformen*).[16] For Cassirer the essential task in interpreting a philosopher's work is to understand and present the interaction of his form of life and his form of doctrine (*Lehrform*). A person's form of life is his manner of dealing

13. *Philosophie der Symbolischen Formen*, vol. 1, pp. 14 ff.
14. Ibid., pp. 9–10.
15. See *Rousseau, Kant and Goethe* (Princeton, 1945), p. 84.
16. *Kant's Life and Thought*, p. 5. Unless otherwise indicated, all subsequent page references in the introduction refer to this work.

with the world in which he finds himself, not the sum of his man-nerisms and trivial habits. There is for example, as Cassirer shows, a deep similarity between the form of life of a Kant, by whose daily habits the citizens of Königsberg were able to set their watches, and the form of life of a Rousseau, who threw away his watch so that he would "no longer find it necessary to know what time of day it is."[17]

3

In trying to determine what is central and still alive in Kant's philoso-phy and what is peripheral and now of merely historical interest, Cassirer is naturally influenced both by his own philosophy and by his judgment of Kant's personality and form of life. As a neo-Kantian pluralist Cassirer sees Kant's main achievement in the discovery of the transcendental method or point of view, conceived as "the ex-pression of the enduring and continuing tasks of philosophy" rather than as "a complete historical whole" (p. 3). As an interpreter of Kant's form of life Cassirer distinguishes between Kant's devotion to "the objective necessity of his subject matter" and his delight in a "surveyable architectonic" of thought structures (p. 171).

Kant's absolutism and his love of architectonic perfection reinforce each other. This is particularly so in the theoretical sphere, where the inconceivability to Kant of a non-Newtonian physics and his aversion from unstable foundations combine to support his firm belief that there is—and can be—only one system of synthetic a priori judg-ments expressing the condition of any possible objective experience and only one set of Categories the application of which to the sensory manifold confers objectivity upon it. In distinguishing between Kant's fundamental insight into the nature of objective experience and his often highly artificial elaboration of a unique categorical framework, Cassirer is, of course, not alone among the commen-tators. But, unlike many of them, he not only objects to the alleged finality of the Kantian categorical framework, but to any uniqueness claim for such a framework.

Another important exegetic point, which conforms to Cassirer's

17. *Rousseau, Kant and Goethe*, p. 57.

thesis that objectivity is always the result of a symbolic making, concerns the Kantian distinction between phenomena and noumena (or things in themselves). According to Cassirer this distinction must not be understood as a distinction between knowable objects and unknowable objects which, though not subject to the conditions of possible objective experience, nevertheless exist independently of it. The concept 'x is a thing in itself' is merely the negative concept 'x is not an object of possible experience.' Kant, as Cassirer argues, does not make it clear enough that the positive meaning which the concept of a noumenon acquires in the practical sphere is not that of an objective *thing*, but that of an objective *value* which belongs not to the "range of empirical existence" but to a wholly different domain of being (p. 215).

Kant's exploration of this domain—the domain of human actions rather than natural events—finds an early expression in two essays, published in 1784 and 1785 (p. 223). Cassirer regards them not only as marking an important stage in the development of Kant's thought, but also as being crucial to the development of German idealism and, consequently, of European thought. History, according to Kant, differs from the natural sciences in that it reflects not on "a sequence of mere events, but on a sequence of actions." And since "the thought of action includes the thought of freedom," Kant's essays on the philosophy of history anticipate his ethical theory (p. 227).

For Cassirer these essays represent the culmination of the philosophy of the Enlightenment by clearly expressing its fundamental conviction that the historical progress of mankind coincides with "the ever-more-exact apprehension and the ever-deepening understanding of the thought of freedom" (p. 227). He illuminates the historical role of the essays by comparing the ideas contained in them with the ideas of Rousseau and Herder. Although Kant admired Rousseau as the Newton of moral and political thinking, and although in the essays he still speaks—as Cassirer points out—the language of Rousseau, he no longer accepts Rousseau's actual or metaphysical description of the presocial state of human happiness and innocence. For Kant had by then arrived at the conclusion that social organization is a possible means of educating man toward freedom (pp. 223 ff.).

Herder was a critical disciple who tried to develop his teacher's

thought in ways which Kant found wholly uncongenial. Cassirer, on
the other hand, regards some of Herder's ideas as a legitimate extension of Kant's doctrine. His philosophical and human sympathies
with both thinkers enable him to give an account of their intellectual
and personal relations which throws much light on their work, their
personalities, and their times. He shows in particular how deeply
Kant and Herder differed in their form of life, as expressed in the style
and substance of their works; and how, in spite of their respect for
each other, this difference tended to blind them to each other's principal merits. Thus Kant can feel little sympathy for a writer who, in
Cassirer's words, "is a poet as a philosopher and a philosopher as a
poet" (p. 230). And Herder is likely to be repelled by a philosophical
style which Kant likens to "engraving on copper for which an etching
needle is required" and opposes to "working on a piece of timber for
which chisel and mallet serve well enough" (p. 221). To the difference
in style there corresponds a profound difference of purpose. Just as
Kant's style is appropriate to, and required by, the task of criticism
and abstraction, so Herder's style is rooted in his aim of showing that
"whereas the philosopher must abandon one thread of perception
(*Empfindung*) in order to pursue another, in nature all these threads
are *one web*."[18]

In commenting on Kant's *Critique of Practical Reason* Cassirer emphasizes the crucial role in it of the transcendental approach which, as
in the *Critique of Pure Reason*, distinguishes between what is passively
received by the mind and what is spontaneously formed and thereby
made objective. What is passively received is in the theoretical sphere
an aggregate of impressions given to the faculty of sense, in the
practical sphere an aggregate of desires given to the "lower faculty of
desire." What spontaneously transforms these aggregates so as to
confer objectivity upon them is in the theoretical sphere the faculty of
the understanding, in the practical sphere the spontaneous and autonomous will. The result of this transformation is in the theoretical
sphere a world of objects of experience, in the practical sphere a
world of objective values (p. 239 ff.).

18. Herder, *Über den Ursprung der Sprache*, quoted in *Philosophie der Symbolischen
Formen*, vol. 3, p. 39.

By comparing the transcendental approach in the First and Second Critiques Cassirer reveals some misinterpretations of Kant's aim and method in ethics, in particular the charge of an empty formalism—a charge which is particularly inappropriate when linked with praise for the transcendental approach to theoretical thinking. Another charge, for the rejection of which Cassirer gives good reasons, is the accusation that the Kantian concept of freedom (as opposed, for example, to the empiricist concept, which means no more than the absence of specific constraints in a wholly deterministic universe) is internally inconsistent or in some other sense absurd. He shows in particular that there is no inconsistency between Kant's thesis that the will is free to conform to or to violate the categorical imperative and his claim that the nature of this freedom cannot be understood or that, in Kant's words, even though we do not comprehend the practical and unconditioned necessity of the categorical imperative, "we nevertheless comprehend its incomprehensibility" (p. 263).

An important, perhaps the most important, part of Cassirer's commentary is his treatment of Kant's *Critique of Judgment.* It is there that Cassirer's own philosophy and approach to the history of ideas are most in evidence. He argues first of all that, as has been mentioned earlier, this work is not just the fairly obvious concluding bit in the mapping of the a priori features of the world or worlds which have been investigated in the First and Second Critiques. He next shows convincingly that "the domains of art and of the organic forms of nature" which are the subject matter of the Third Critique constitute for Kant "a different world from those of mechanical causality and of norms" and that this world is subject to "its own characteristic form of laws" (p. 285).

He lastly argues that Kant's conception of these laws and their objectifying function implies "nothing less than a change in the mutual systematic position of all the fundamental, critical concepts so far acquired and determined" (p. 287). There arises, therefore, the task of showing in detail the extent to which the earlier foundations are left unaltered and the extent to which they have been replaced. In undertaking it Cassirer is well served by his historical and scientific knowledge and by his ability to consider philosophical problems as an independent thinker rather than as a dogmatic follower of Kant or any other philosopher.

At the very outset of his discussion of the Third Critique Cassirer warns against giving way to the temptation of seeing it as anticipating Darwin's theory of evolution or of modern biology in general. Such an interpretation would among other things obscure the connection between Kant's analysis of "being harmonious" (*zweckmässig* as used by eighteenth-century German writers) and of "having a purpose" (*zweckhaft*). According to Cassirer, in the Third Critique Kant is not investigating the conditions for the *existence* of harmonious structures in nature and art but "the peculiar direction taken by our cognitive faculty when it *judges* an entity as harmonious, as expressing an inner form" (p. 284). He advances weighty textual evidence to show that the Third Critique has indeed widened and deepened Kant's original concept of the a priori by including "pleasure"—which so far he had considered as absolutely and irradicably empirical—in the "domain of what is determinable a priori and a priori knowable" (p. 303).

Cassirer's interpretation of the Third Critique as constituting an important advance beyond Kant's earlier works is supported by drawing attention to its effect on Kant's contemporaries, notably Goethe. To show the deep impression it made on Goethe one can hardly do better than quote the following passage from Goethe's *Einwirkung der neueren Philosophie*, in which he says of the *Critique of Judgment* that he owes to it "one of the happiest periods of his life" because in it he saw his "most diverse thoughts brought together, artistic and natural production handled the same way; the powers of aesthetic and teleological judgment mutually illuminating each other."[19]

Throughout his book Cassirer tries to see Kant's work in the context of his life and his life and works in the context of his time. He draws attention to often surprising affinities and contrasts between Kant and other creators of Western culture, including—apart from Newton, Rousseau, Goethe, and Herder—Leibniz, Schiller, Lessing, and many others. And he corrects a popular picture of Kant's personality, based on a one-sided view of his regular habits and the alleged

---

19. Weimar Edition, vol. 11, p. 50, quoted in *Rousseau, Kant and Goethe*, p. 64.

rigorous formalism of his moral philosophy. He quotes Charlotte von Schiller as saying that Kant would have been one of the greatest human beings if he had been capable of feeling love, but he finds in Kant's character a "courtesy of the heart" which is close to love as well as to the true spirit of Kant's ethics (pp. 413 ff.).

The commentary contains many illuminating anecdotes which reveal Kant as the very opposite of a pedantic, provincial, and professorial professor. A characteristic example is a remark made in the year 1764 by Hamann, who said about the young Kant that although he carried quite a number of lesser and major works in his head he was so involved in the "whirl of social diversions" that he was "quite unlikely ever to finish any of them" (p. 52).

In concluding these remarks on Cassirer's book, it seems proper to emphasize once again that they are meant to hint at its exegetic and philosophical value and to indicate its relevance to contemporary philosophy and scholarship, and at best can do no more. If they induce some potential readers to study the book, without deterring others from doing so, they will have fulfilled their purpose.

New Haven   STEPHAN KÖRNER
1981

NOTE ON THE
TRANSLATION

Kants Leben und Lehre was first published in 1918, by Bruno Cassirer in Berlin, as a supplementary volume to the edition of Kant's works of which Ernst Cassirer was both general editor and also sole or coeditor of four individual volumes. The edition, entitled *Immanuel Kants Werke*, began appearing in 1912 and was completed with the eleventh, supplementary volume in 1918. An essentially unchanged second edition of *Kants Leben und Lehre* was published in 1921, also by Bruno Cassirer. The present translation has been made from the second edition.

Cassirer's notes have been translated and notes have been added where clarification was called for or a citation was missing. Any mistakes in citations that were found in Cassirer's notes have been silently corrected and missing publication information supplied. Notes added in their entirety in the English edition appear in square brackets. References in the notes consisting of a roman and an arabic numeral only are to volume and page of *Immanuel Kants Werke*, edited by Ernst Cassirer et al. References to the edition of the Prussian Academy of Sciences have in most cases been added in the English edition; following standard practice, these are indicated by the abbreviation "*Ak.*," followed by volume and page number.

The following English translations of Kant's works have been used for quotations in the text, with modifications: *Critique of Pure Reason*, tr. Norman Kemp Smith (London, 1929); *Critique of Practical Reason and Other Writings in Moral Philosophy*, tr. Lewis White Beck (Chicago,

1949); *Kant's Critique of Aesthetic Judgment,* tr. James Creed Meredith (Oxford, 1911); *Kant's Critique of Teleological Judgment,* tr. James Creed Meredith (Oxford, 1928); *First Introduction to the Critique of Judgment,* tr. James Haden (Indianapolis, 1965); *Kant's Political Writings,* ed. Hans Reiss, tr. H. B. Nisbet (Cambridge, 1970); *Kant's Inaugural Dissertation and Early Writings on Space,* tr. John Handyside (Chicago, 1929); *Philosophical Correspondence, 1759–99,* ed. and tr. Arnulf Zweig (Chicago, 1967); *Prolegomena to Any Future Metaphysics,* tr. Lewis White Beck (Indianapolis, 1950); *Dreams of a Spirit-Seer, Illustrated by Dreams of Metaphysics,* ed. Frank Sewall, tr. E. F. Goerwitz (London, 1900); *Kant's Cosmogony as in His Essay on the Retardation of the Rotation of the Earth and His Natural History and Theory of the Heavens,* ed. and tr. W. Hastie (Glasgow, 1900).

I would like to mention here with great appreciation and respect Charles Hendel, by whose suggestion and encouragement I originally undertook this translation. Hendel has been to a large extent the moving force behind the Yale University Press's publication of Cassirer's works in English; a friend of Cassirer and a colleague during the latter's years at Yale University, Hendel shares to a rare degree Cassirer's breadth of philosophical outlook and interests. His services in support of knowledge and study of Cassirer's thought in English-speaking countries should be neither underestimated nor forgotten.

Wooster, Ohio   JAMES HADEN
1981

Kant's Life and Thought

FROM THE FOREWORD TO
THE FIRST EDITION

The work I publish here is intended to serve as a commentary on and supplement to the complete edition of Kant's works, of which it forms the conclusion. Therefore it is not addressed to those readers who consider themselves in any sense "finished" with Kant and his philosophy; rather it is for readers still in the midst of studying Kant's works. This book aims to show them a path leading from the periphery of the critical system to its center, from the host of particular questions to an open and comprehensive view of the entirety of Kant's thought. As a result, I have tried from the very beginning not to become lost in the multitude of special problems which Kant's doctrine continually presents, but, by rigorous concentration, to bring out only the plan of his system and the major, essential outlines of the Kantian intellectual edifice. The value of the detailed work done by the Kant-Philologie of the last few decades is not to be underestimated, and the results it has led to in the historical and systematic sense naturally demanded careful consideration in the present book. Yet it seems to me as though this trend toward detailed research has frequently hindered rather than furthered a living insight into the meaning of Kant's philosophy in its unity and totality. Confronted by a school of research and activity which seems to preen itself above all on the detection of Kant's "contradictions," and which in the end threatens to reduce the entire critical system to a mass of such contradictions, we may and must strive to regain the kind of synoptic view of Kant and his doctrine possessed by Schiller or Wilhelm von

Humboldt. With this aim in mind, the constant concern of the following study is to turn back from the multiplicity and almost immeasurably complex involution of particular problems to the natural and self-subsistent character, the noble simplicity and universality, of the basic formative ideas of the Kantian system. Given the limitation put on this exposition by the overall plan of the edition, this goal could, of course, only be reached by dispensing with a complete presentation of the sheer bulk of Kant's thought and its detailed explication for the reader. And for the biographical portion of the book I had to impose the same restriction on myself as for the systematic portion. Here, too, I have consciously ignored the wealth of details and anecdotal embroidery which has been handed down by the earliest biographers of Kant, and which since then has entered into all the accounts of his life. I have tried to bring out only those major and enduring characteristics of Kant's career that in the course of his human and philosophical development emerged more and more clearly as this career's consistent "meaning." Knowledge of Kant as a person has not, I hope, suffered accordingly. For Kant's characteristic and genuine individuality can be sought for only in the same basic traits of his mode of thought and character on which his objective and philosophically creative originality rests. This originality does not consist in any peculiarities and quirks of personality and the externalities of his life, but in the orientation and tendency toward the universal revealed in the shaping of both his life and his philosophy. I have tried to show how both aspects condition and complement each other, how they point to an identical origin and finally join in a single outcome, and thus how Kant's personality and work are in fact from one and the same mold. On the other hand, as far as the external circumstances of Kant's life are concerned, the intention here was to present them only insofar as they reveal and express the peculiarly distinctive content of Kant's actual existence—the essence and the growth of his fundamental ideas.

The manuscript of this book was ready for the press in the spring of 1916; only the delay inflicted by the war on the progress of the edition of the complete works is to blame for the fact that it is appearing now, more than two years after its completion. I regret this postponement of printing all the more deeply because I can no longer place the book in the hands of the man who followed it from its inception with the warmest and most helpful interest. Hermann Cohen died on April 4, 1918. The significance of his works for the renewal and the development of Kantian philosophy in Germany I have tried to state elsewhere, and I do not want to return to that here.[1] But I must mention with deep gratitude the personal impact which I myself, more than twenty years ago, received from Cohen's books on Kant. I am conscious that I was first introduced to the full earnestness and the depth of Kant's teaching through these books. Since that time, I have returned again and again to the problems of Kantian philosophy in ever-renewed studies of my own and in the context of a variety of concrete tasks, and my conception of these problems has in many respects diverged from that of Cohen. But all along I have found the underlying methodological idea which guided Cohen, and on which he founded his interpretation of the Kantian system, to be fruitful, productive, and helpful. For Cohen himself this idea—the unavoidable necessity of the "transcendental method"— became the essence of scientific philosophy. And because he construed the Kantian teaching in this way, not as a closed historical entity but as the expression of the permanent *tasks* of philosophy itself, it became for him not only an influence in history but a force which directly affects life. He experienced it and taught it as that sort of power, and in this same sense he understood the close connection between the Kantian philosophy and the general problems of the German spirit. He had suggested this connection in many of his writings, but its complete and comprehensive presentation was the project he had set himself for the present edition of Kant's complete works. Now, however, this long-planned book on Kant's significance for German culture, whose outline and structure he unfolded to me a few days before his death, can no longer be written. But even though it was not granted to us to have Cohen himself as one of the collaborators on this edition, his name is ever to be linked with it. For

1. "Hermann Cohen und die Erneuerung der Kantischen Philosophie," *Festheft der "Kant-Studien" zu Cohens 70. Geburtstag. Kantstudien* 17 (1912): 253 ff.

just as he himself remained until the end close to each individual collaborator on the edition, as friend and as teacher, so his mode of thinking shaped a unity of ideals and indicated the basic conviction concerning materials and method which they shared and which has continued to define and guide their labors.

Schierke i. Harz   Ernst Cassirer
August 14, 1918

INTRODUCTION

Goethe once uttered the dictum with respect to Kant that all philosophy must be both loved and lived if it hoped to attain significance for
life. "The Stoic, the Platonist, the Epicurean, each must come to terms
with the world in his own fashion; indeed, precisely that is the task of
life from which no one is exempted, to whatever school he may belong. The philosophers, for their part, can offer us nothing but patterns of life. The strict moderation of Kant, for example, required a
philosophy in accordance with his innate inclinations. Read his biography and you will soon discover how neatly he blunted the edge of
his stoicism, which in fact constituted a striking obstacle to social
relationships, adjusted it and brought it into balance with the world.
Each individual, by virtue of his inclinations, has a right to principles
which do not destroy his individuality. Probably the origin of all
philosophy is to be sought for here or nowhere. Every system succeeds in coming to terms with the world in that moment when its true
champion appears. Only the acquired part of human nature ordinarily founders on a contradiction; what is inborn in it finds its way
anywhere and not infrequently even overcomes its contrary with the
greatest success. We must first be in harmony with ourselves, and
then we are in a position, if not to eliminate, at least in some way to
counterbalance the discords pressing in on us from outside."[1]

1. Goethe's conversation with J. D. Falk. *Goethes Gespräche*, newly edited by F.
Frhr. v. Biedermann, Leipzig, 1909–11, vol. 4, p. 468.

These words epitomize one of the essential goals toward which exact investigation and presentation of Kant's life must be directed. This aim rules out mere narration of external vicissitudes and events; the peculiar fascination and the peculiar difficulty of the task consist rather in discovering and illuminating the *Lebensform,* the form of life, corresponding to his form of thinking. As regards the latter, it has its own history, transcending all personal boundaries, for the problems of the Kantian philosophy, if one traces their origin and development, cannot be confined within the sphere of his personality. On the contrary, in those problems an independent logic of facts emerges; there dwells in them a theoretical content which, detached from all temporal and subjectively personal bonds, possesses an objective existence grounded in itself alone.

And yet, on the other hand, with Kant the relation between form of thought and form of life cannot be understood to mean that the latter came to be only the basis and passive receptacle for the former. In Kant's actual existence, as Goethe—doubtless correctly—says, thought, in its objective content and its objective "truth," not only rules life but also receives in return the characteristic stamp of the life to which it imparts its form. Here that peculiar reciprocal relationship prevails in which each of the two moments that influence each other appears simultaneously as determining and determined. What Kant is and means, not in the context of the whole history of philosophy, but as an individual intellectual personality, is manifest only in this twofold relation. How this relationship is forged, and how the unity it creates is then outwardly revealed ever more lucidly and purely, forms the basic spiritual theme of his life and therefore the focal point of his biography. For in the last analysis the essential task of every biography of a great thinker is to trace how his individuality blends ever more closely with his work and seemingly vanishes entirely, and how its spiritual outlines yet remain embedded in the work and only thus become clear and apparent.

At the threshold of modern philosophy stands a work which affords a classic exposition of this connection. The intent of Descartes's *Discourse on Method* is to develop a radical technique by means of which all the special sciences are to be deduced and demonstrated from their primary and universal "grounds"; but how clearly this objective explanation, by an inner necessity, fuses with our information on Descartes's own development, from the initial universal doubt to the unshakable certainty given him by the idea of a "universal mathematics" and by the axioms and basic propositions of his metaphysics! A rigorous deduction of objective propositions and truths is the aim of the treatise, but at the same time, unintentionally and as it were accidentally, the modern type of philosophical personality is here achieved and clearly delineated. It is as if the new unity of the "subjective" and the "objective" which composes the systematic underlying idea of the Cartesian theory were to be presented again from a completely different aspect and in a different sense.

The second masterpiece of Descartes, his *Meditations on First Philosophy*, also reveals this characteristic style. In these meditations we encounter the highest abstractions of Cartesian metaphysics, but we see them, as it were, growing out of a particular, concrete situation which is maintained in its full detail and specific coloring. The ego, the "cogito," is distilled out as the universal principle of philosophy; at the same time, however, in bold relief against this objective background, there stands out the image of the new life Descartes created for himself in his seclusion in Holland, consciously turning away from tradition and all social constraints and conventions. The literary form of the soliloquy may here point back to older prototypes, especially to Augustine's *Soliloquies* and Petrarch's philosophical confessions; the inner content, however, is nonetheless new and unique. For the confession here is not wrung from a moral or a religious emotion but springs from the pure and indomitable energy of thinking itself. Thought exhibits itself in its objective structure, as a systematic linkage of concepts and truths, or premises and consequents—but in the process the total act of judging and reasoning comes alive for us at the same time. And in this sense the personal *Lebensform* is explicated simultaneously with the form of his system. It can scarcely be asked any longer in this connection whether the former is dependent on the latter, or the latter on the former; ideal and real, world view and process of individual life, have become moments of one and the same indivisible spiritual growth.

If one tries to maintain a similar standpoint in the consideration of Kant's life and philosophy, one in fact immediately finds oneself faced with a special difficulty. For even in a superficial sense, the biographical material we possess seems totally insufficient to arrive at such a comprehensive view. The eighteenth century, more than almost any other, is characterized by its compulsion toward introspection and confession. This drive constantly draws new sustenance from the most varied sources: the trend toward psychological empiricism, toward "experiential study of the soul," joins with the religious motivations that stem from Pietism and the new cult of feeling that originated with Rousseau. Kant is intimately affected by all these spiritual and intellectual currents. His rearing as a child bears the stamp of Pietism; in his youth and manhood he turns to psychological analysis, in order to discover in it a new basis for metaphysics; and for him Rousseau is the Newton of the moral world who has uncovered its most secret laws and animating forces. But in spite of all this, what we possess in the way of personal testimony by Kant is just as meager in extent as it is thin in content. We know next to nothing of actual diary entries, unless one were to include in this category the remarks and observations he was wont to add to the text of books on which he lectured. In an age that sought and valued, above all, sentimental outpourings of the heart in correspondence with friends, he takes a coolly sceptical attitude toward all such spasms of emotion. His letters merely augment and extend the thoughts he set down in his scientific and philosophical treatises. As such, they are of extraordinary importance for knowledge of his system and its development, but they give way only occasionally and, as it were, grudgingly to a personal mood and a personal interest.

The older Kant grows, the more inveterate this basic trait becomes. His first essay, the *Thoughts on the True Estimation of Living Forces* (*Gedanken von der wahren Schätzung der lebendigen Kräfte*), does indeed begin with a number of purely personal observations, in which he appears to be seeking an initial definition of the standpoint from which he proposes to judge the material at hand. Here, on a theme that belongs purely to abstract mathematics and mechanics, not only do we hear the scientific researcher, but in addition in his youthful self-confidence the thinker and writer ventures beyond the strict confines of the particular task toward greater subjective vividness of treatment and exposition. And this tone is echoed even in the writings of his mature years; in the objective critique of metaphysics contained in the *Dreams of a Spirit-Seer (Träume eines Geistersehers)* one senses everywhere expressions of the personal liberations Kant is experiencing at the time. But from the moment the foundation of the critical system has been definitively laid, Kant's style also undergoes an inner change. The phrase "De nobis ipsis silemus" [of ourselves, we say nothing], which he takes from Bacon to serve as a motto for the *Critique of Pure Reason (Kritik der reinen Vernunft)*, gathers more and more force. The more definitely and clearly Kant conceives his great objective, the more laconic he becomes about everything concerning his own person. For the biographer of Kant, the source for the systematic investigation and exposition of his work seems to have run dry at the very point where it really begins to broaden.

Yet in itself this difficulty cannot and should not constitute any crucial hindrance, for the part of Kant's life that goes on outside his work cannot in any case be of decisive importance for the more profound task that confronts philosophical biography. Whatever the work itself does not reveal to us at this stage cannot be compensated for by any knowledge, however extensive, of the inner and outer life of its author. This lack, then, is not what we feel to be the actual barrier to our understanding of Kant's nature here, but rather— however paradoxical this may sound—it is the very reverse that interferes at this point with the freedom and breadth of our view. An adequate grasp of Kant's personality suffers not from too few but from too many facts and stories handed down to us about him. The earliest biographers of Kant, from whom we derive all our knowledge of his life, have no object other than the most exact reproduction of all those petty details which constitute his external life. They thought they had grasped Kant as a human being when they described him exhaustively and faithfully in all the particulars of his actions, in the division and organization of his daily life, in his most minute inclinations and habits. They extended this description to what he wore, ate, and drank. With the help of their reports, we can calculate, watch in hand, Kant's daily activity down to the hour and minute; we know about every detail of his household furnishings and economy; we are instructed in the minutest way about all the maxims of his physical and moral regimen. And Kant's image has passed over into tradition and popular memory exactly as they sketched it. Who could ever think of him without remembering one of the peculiarities and oddities, one of the thousand anecdotes born of his habits, so zealously assembled by this tradition?

But, on the other hand, whoever labors to depict Kant's spiritual and intellectual integrity purely on the basis of a knowledge of his philosophy must at once sense an inherent contradiction. For how can one comprehend the fact that the further this philosophy develops, the more thoroughly it is permeated with a tendency toward the purely general, toward the objectively necessary and universally valid—while simultaneously the individual in shaping his life seems to fall prey more and more to sheer particularity, idiosyncrasy, and crotchetiness? Are we faced here with a truly ineradicable contradiction between the form of the critical system and Kant's own form of life, or does this contradiction perhaps disappear as soon as we indicate a different basis for our biographical considerations and deliberately redirect them?

This is the first question the biographer of Kant faces. His task could only be deemed fulfilled if he were to succeed in organizing and interpreting the chaotic mass of notes and information we possess about Kant's person and his way of life, in such a way that this conglomeration of individual details is recast into a truly unified spiritual whole, not merely into the unity of a characteristic type of behavior. The first biographers of Kant, however charming at times their naive and literal portrayals, never attained this goal; indeed, they had virtually no systematic awareness of it. Their mode of observation remained in the true sense "eccentric"; they were satisfied with selecting and assembling discrete peripheral characteristics without seeking or even suspecting the true vital and intellectual center from which they emanated, directly or indirectly. If much of what we know or think we know about Kant's personality seems to us queer and paradoxical today, we should ask ourselves whether this oddness is founded objectively in Kant's life as such or in the subjective observation to which this life was from the beginning frequently exposed; whether, in other words, the appearance of eccentricity in Kant cannot be blamed primarily on eccentricity of understanding and interpretation.

But even so it is not solely the fault of the superficial standpoint from which observation has customarily proceeded if we believe we detect one final unresolved dualism between Kant's inward and outward life, however simple that life may appear. This contradiction is not just an illusion, but is rooted in the very conditions to which this life was subjected, and from which even its steady upward course failed to release it. The complete and symmetrical unfolding of life and of creative work granted to the most fortunate of great men was not allotted to Kant. He molded his whole life with the strength and purity of an indomitable will and infused it with a single ruling idea; but this will, which in the formation of his philosophy proved itself to be a maximally positive and creative element, affects his personal life with a restrictive and negative cast. All the stirrings of subjective feeling and subjective emotion comprise for him only the material which he strives with ever-growing determination to subject to the authority of "reason" and of the objective dictates of duty.

If Kant's life lost something of its richness and harmony in this struggle, on the other hand it was through this alone that it gained its genuinely heroic nature. Nevertheless, even this process of inner self-development can be disclosed only by conceiving Kant's life history and the systematic evolution of his philosophy as one. The characteristic integrity and wholeness expressed in Kant's being cannot be made manifest if one attempts to assemble it from its separate "parts"; one must think of it as something primary and fundamental underlying both his work and his life. How this originally indeterminate substratum unfolds and becomes equally manifest in his sheer intellectual energy and in the energy with which he molded his personal life forms the essential content of the story of Kant's development.

1 YOUTH AND EDUCATION

1

The story of Kant's childhood and schooling can be briefly told. Immanuel Kant was born on April 22, 1724, in the cramped circumstances of a German workingman's house, as the fourth child of the master saddler Johann Georg Kant. Concerning the origins of his family Kant says, in a letter written in his old age, that his grandfather, whose final residence was Tilsit, came from Scotland; that he had been one of the great number of those who emigrated from there toward the close of the seventeenth and at the beginning of the eighteenth centuries, some settling in Sweden and some in East Prussia.[1] Objective scrutiny has not substantiated this testimony, at least in the form in which Kant gives it; it has since been established that Kant's great-grandfather was already living as an innkeeper in Werden, near Heydekrug.[2] The statement by Borowski, his first biographer, that the family name originally read "Cant," and that Kant himself first introduced the now customary spelling of the name, has also proved incorrect; as far as the name can be traced through documentary evidence, we encounter it in the version "Kant" or

1. To Bishop Lindblom, October 13, 1797 (X, 326 f.) (*Ak.* XII, 204).

2. On this point, cf. Johann Sembritzki, *Altpreussische Monatsschrift* 36:469 ff. and 37:139 ff. In addition, see Emil Arnoldt, "Kants Jugend und die fünf ersten Jahre seiner Privatdozentur im Umriss dargestellt," *Gesammelte Schriften*, ed. Otto Schöndörffer, vol. 3, pp. 105 ff.

"Kandt." It is possible, therefore, that the statement concerning Scottish descent, which Kant must have received from an old family tradition, is wholly without foundation. In any case, no one has so far been able to prove it with any adequate degree of certainty.

About Kant's parents we know hardly more than what little their son subsequently related from his own scanty childhood recollections. His mother's image seems to have impressed him more strongly than did his father's. Even as an old man he spoke of her with deeply felt love and emotion, although he lost her when he was only thirteen. He was conscious of having experienced through her the spiritual influences that remained decisive for his entire concept and conduct of life. "I shall never forget my mother," he once expressed himself to Jachmann, "for she implanted and nurtured the first seed of the good in me; she opened my heart to the influence of Nature; she awakened and broadened my ideas, and her teachings have had an enduring, beneficent effect on my life."[3] His mother also seems to have been the first to recognize the boy's intellectual gifts, and she decided, on the advice of her spiritual counselor, the theology professor and preacher Franz Albert Schultz, to guide him toward an academic education.

With Schultz there entered into Kant's life a man who became decisively important for the entire formative period of his youth. In his fundamental religious orientation he was a Pietist, as were Kant's parents. But as a former pupil of Wolff, one whom the latter is said to have particularly esteemed, he was at the same time thoroughly familiar with the substance of contemporary German philosophy, and hence with the tendencies of secular culture in general. In the autumn of 1732, as a boy of eight, Kant entered the Collegium Fridericianum, whose direction Schultz took over in the following year. What this school offered him was solely information, and even in this respect it remained narrowly restricted. The ideal of the old Latin and academic school still reigned, especially in Prussia, and the aim of its instruction was almost exclusively directed toward the

---

3. Reinhold Bernhard Jachmann, *Immanuel Kant geschildert in Briefen an einen Freund* (Königsberg, 1804), Eighth Letter, pp. 99 ff.

knowledge and skillful use of Latin. Even in Pomerania in 1690, an old ecclesiastical order dating from 1535 that expressly forbade the use of the German language during classes had been reinvoked: "The preceptors shall on all occasions address the pupils in Latin and not in German, as that is frivolous and in children is scandalous and disgraceful."[4]

If one disregards the specifically theological orientation, the condition and the internal organization of the Fridericianum in the period when Kant attended it recalls in many respects the Latin school in Stendal, in which Winckelmann, who was about seven years Kant's senior, grew up. In both schools grammatical and philological teaching composed the framework of the instruction, and while mathematics and logic were indeed included in the curriculum, they were presented in only the sketchiest way. All of natural science, history, and geography was as good as totally excluded.[5] It can be calculated how little significance the instruction imparted to him at the Fridericianum had for his deeper intellectual orientation if one considers that it is precisely these fields to which Kant later feels drawn almost exclusively during the entire initial period of his creative work and to which he dedicates himself with his first youthful zest for knowledge as soon as freedom of choice is granted to him. Kant retained a friendly memory only of the Latin teacher in the *Prima*, the philologist Heydenreich, since through him he discovered a method of elucidating classical authors that depended not merely on the grammatical and formal elements, but also on the content, and that insisted on clarity and precision of concepts. He later expressly said of the other teachers, however, that they were probably incapable of fanning into flame the spark of philosophical or scientific study that lay in him. Thus his most individual, fundamental aptitude at this time remained completely shrouded in darkness; even those of Kant's boyhood

4. See Karl Biedermann, *Deutschland im achtzehnten Jahrhundert*, vol. 2, *Deutschlands geistige, sittliche und gesellige Zustände im achtzehnten Jahrhundert*, 2d ed. (Leipzig, 1880), pt. 1, p. 480.

5. Concerning Winckelmann's schooldays, cf. Karl Justi, *Winckelmann. Sein Leben, seine Werke und seine Zeitgenossen* (Leipzig, 1866–72), vol. 1, pp. 223 ff.

friends who thought they perceived in him the earmarks of future
greatness saw then only the eminent philologist-to-be. What the
school did give him as a genuine contribution to his later intellectual
development is confined to a respect for and an exact acquaintance
with the Latin classics, which he retained into his old age. He seems
to have been affected hardly at all by the spirit of Greek, which was
taught exclusively by use of the New Testament.

From the earliest childhood and youthful memories of most great
men there radiates a peculiar glow, illuminating them from inside as
it were, even in cases where their youth was oppressed by need and
harsh external circumstances. This magic is, as a rule, especially
characteristic of great artists. To Kant, on the contrary, his youth
appears in retrospect neither in the light of phantasy nor idealized by
memory; rather, with the judgment of mature understanding, he sees
in it merely the period of his intellectual tutelage and lack of moral
freedom. As thoroughly as he afterwards became imbued with Rousseau's theoretical principles, he was never able to arouse in himself
the sentiment for childhood and youth that is alive in Rousseau. Rink
relates one of Kant's sayings, that he who as a man yearns for the
time of his childhood must himself have remained a child,[6] and it is
even more indicative and moving when Hippel recounts that this
man, who was so reticent in all expressions of emotion, was accustomed to say that terror and apprehension overwhelmed him as soon
as he reflected on his former "child slavery."[7] It can be seen in these
bitter words that Kant's upbringing left on him a mark he could never
fully efface from his life. The decisive factor here was not the external
pressure of his social status and the exertions and privations it imposed on him, for all this he bore throughout his life with such composure that it seemed to him almost incomprehensible and offensive
when others later spoke of it. The value of life, when it is reckoned
according to the sum of pleasure, is "less than nothing":[8] this is no
isolated theorem of Kant's philosophy, but precisely the pervasive

6. Cf. F. T. Rink, *Ansichten aus Immanuel Kants Leben* (Königsberg, 1805), pp. 22 ff.
7. Theodor Gottlieb von Hippel the Elder's biography (Gotha, 1801), pp. 22 ff.
8. *Critique of Teleological Judgment*, §83 (V, 514) (*Ak.* V, 434).

motto of his outlook on the world and of his conduct of life. From the very beginning, the goal of his life was not "happiness" but self-sufficiency in thinking and independence of will.

At this very point, however, there was interference from the spiritual discipline to which Kant was subjected in his youth. It did not end with the concrete fulfillment of definite prescriptions and duties, but strove for possession of the *whole* human being, of his opinions and convictions, of his feeling and his will. This scrutiny of the "heart," in the pietistic sense, was practiced incessantly. There was no inner stirring, be it ever so hidden, that could escape or elude this examination, and that perpetual supervision did not attempt to control. Even after thirty years, David Ruhnken, at that time a famous teacher of philology at the University of Leiden, who had attended the Fridericianum with Kant, speaks of the "pedantic and gloomy discipline of fanatics" to which their life at the school was subjected.[9] A mere glance at the curriculum of the institution, filled with uninter-rupted prayers and devotional exercises, with periods of edification, sermons, and catechizations, confirms this judgment. All this gave the instruction not only its moral but also its intellectual imprint, for even the theoretical classes were expressly designed to remind one of their relation to religious and theological questions.

If we wish to form a clear picture of the spirit of this instruction, we must supplement the scanty reports we possess as to the teaching activity of the Fridericianum with the many characteristic testimonials that inform us about the growth and development of the pietistic spirit in Germany. In this context, the individual differences are of little weight, for it was the fate of Pietism that, whereas it originally aimed purely at the revivification of an inward, personal religion, as it evolved it hardened almost entirely into a common stereotype. What individuals tell of their conversion takes on little by little the marks of a fixed pattern repeated with only slight variations. And this pattern was more and more explicitly made into a sine qua non for the at-tainment of salvation. One of Susanna von Klettenberg's feminine correspondents detects even in the former's truly profound religious

9. Ruhnken to Kant, March 10, 1771 (IX, 94) (*Ak.* X, 112).

nature no "formal penitential struggle," without which, she claims, the inner transformation forever remains uncertain and dubious.[10] A definite religio-psychological *technique* now emerged more and more consciously and ostentatiously, in contrast to the original religious content of Pietism. One can scarcely open one of the biographies of this period without meeting its traces everywhere. Not only was the general theological education of young people at that time influenced by this technique—as has been vividly and impressively shown by Semler in his autobiography, for example—even men like Albrecht von Haller, who represent the entire scope and substance of contemporary German culture, sought vainly throughout their lives for inward liberation from it.

In Kant's critical mind, however, this emancipation seems to have been completed quite early. Even in his boyhood and youth, the dissociation that later comprises one of the essential and basic moments of his system is in preparation—the divorce of the ethical meaning of religion from all those surface manifestations that take the shape of dogma and ritual. As yet this dissociation did not involve any abstract conceptual knowledge; it was rather a feeling that grew ever firmer in him when he compared and weighed against each other the two religious attitudes he saw before him in his parental house and in the academic life of the Fridericianum. If juxtaposed purely superficially, the judgments Kant passed on Pietism in his later years sound at first remarkably discordant and contradictory, but their meaning becomes completely unambiguous when one reflects that Kant is thinking of entirely disparate forms of pietistic thought and behavior. The first, which he found embodied in his parents' home, he continued to value and praise even after he had dissociated his personal viewpoint from it. "Even though," as he once said to Rink, "the religious ideas of that time and the concepts of what they called virtue and piety were anything but clear and adequate, still they really got hold of the basic thing. You can say

10. General information on the history of Pietism can be found in A. B. Ritschl, *Geschichte des Pietismus*, 2 vols. (Bonn, 1880–86); Julian Schmidt, *Geschichte des geistigen Lebens in Deutschland von Leibniz bis auf Lessings Tod 1681–1781*, (Leipzig, 1862–64); Biedermann, *Deutschland im achtzehnten Jahrhundert*, vol. 2, part 1.

what you want about Pietism—the people who were serious about it were outstanding in a praiseworthy respect. They possessed the highest thing men can possess, that calm, that serenity, that inner peace, undisturbed by any passion. No trouble, no persecution put them in a bad humor, no dispute was able to incite them to anger and enmity. In short, even the mere observer was involuntarily compelled to respect them. I still remember how there once broke out between the harness and saddler trades quarrels over their respective privileges, from which my father suffered rather directly; regardless of that, this rift was treated by my parents, even in household conversation, with such consideration and love toward their opponents . . . that, although I was a boy at the time, still the thought of it will never leave me."[11]

Even more intense was the aversion Kant always felt toward the regulation and mechanization of religious life, for which Pietism likewise served him as the prototype. Not only did he condemn every self-tormenting dissection of one's own inner life (with express reference to Haller), because to him this was the direct path to "the mental disorder of alleged supernatural inspirations . . . illuminatism or terrorism,"[12] but in later years he also rejected and branded as hypocritical all public displays of religious feelings of any kind. His opinion of the worthlessness of prayer, which he revealed both in personal conversation and in his writings, is well known, and in all his expressions of this opinion a suppressed emotion can be sensed in which a recollection of the "fanatical discipline" of his youth still seems to echo.[13] Here for the first time we see how a fundamental tenet of Kantian philosophy, the contrast it makes between the religion of morality and the religion of "ingratiation," has its roots in one of the thinker's earliest and deepest life experiences.[14]

11. Rink, *Ansichten aus Immanuel Kants Leben*, pp. 13 ff. Cf. a similar remark to Kraus in Rudolf Reicke, *Kantiana* (Königsberg, 1860), p. 5.

12. *Anthropologie*, §4 (VIII, 17–18) (*Ak.* VII, 133).

13. See the biography of Hippel, p. 34. Cf. especially the essay "Vom Gebet" (IV, 525 ff.).

14. There is no doubt that Kant's own ideal of the religious education of youth was developed as it were *per antiphrasin* from the experiences of his childhood. He writes to Wolke, the director of the Philanthropin at Dessau, when he recommends his friend

When Kant's *Anthropology (Anthropologie in pragmatischen Hinsicht)* appeared, Schiller complained in a letter to Goethe that even this "serene and Jove-like spirit" had not quite been able to rid his wings of the "contamination of life," and that certain dark impressions from his youth had remained indelibly stamped on him. This judgment rests on a correct intuition, but it is one-sided because it retains only the negative aspect of this situation. The conflict into which Kant was thrown signifies both the first and the formative discipline of his character and will. By resolving it in harmony with his own disposition and view of life, he crystallized a basic trait of both his own nature and of his future development.

Kant's initial years at the university, to judge by the slight information about them that has been preserved, are also significant more for this education of the will than for the knowledge furnished him in the regular course of lectures. In Prussia at this time, school and university supervision were still barely distinct from each other. As late as 1778, under the reign of Frederick the Great, a ministerial edict was promulgated to the professors of the University of Königsberg expressly forbidding the free organization of academic instruction and demanding the closest adherence to prescribed textbooks, on the grounds that the worst compendium was better than none at all. The professors might, if they possessed sufficient wisdom, emend the

---

Motherby's son to him as a pupil: "In respect to religion, the spirit of the Philanthropin is actually quite in harmony with the thinking of the boy's father—so much so that he wishes that even the natural knowledge of God, to the degree that the boy gradually achieves it with increase of years and understanding, should not immediately be directed to devotional activities, save only after he has learned to realize that all of these have value only as a means of quickening a daily fear of God and a conscientiousness in the pursuit of one's duties, as divine commands. For the idea that religion is nothing but a kind of ingratiation and fawning before the Highest Being—arts in which men differ only by the variety of their opinions as to the way which might be the most pleasing to Him—is an illusion which, whether based on dogmas or free from dogmas, makes all moral thinking uncertain and ambiguous. For this illusion assumes, in addition to a good life, something else as a means of obtaining—surreptitiously as it were—the favor of the Most High and occasionally exempting oneself thereby from the most scrupulous care in respect of the good life, and yet having a sure refuge in readiness for an emergency." To Wolke, March 28, 1776 (IX, 149) (*Ak.* X, 178). [Cf. below, chap. 7.—Tr.]

author, but the reading of their own *dictata* was totally abolished. Moreover, the syllabus for each subject was laid down in detail, and particular value was put on the institution of regular examinations by the lecturers, "partly to learn how their *auditores* have grasped this and that, partly to arouse their zeal and attention and thus to become acquainted with the able and industrious."[15] Hence the area in which academic study on the part of teachers and students was constrained to move was narrowly circumscribed, to say the least.

Kant, who by a basic trait of his nature habitually adapted himself to the existing order of life and was content with it, at first seems hardly ever to have intentionally overstepped these narrow confines. It is all the more significant, therefore, that from the start he nevertheless transgresses them, involuntarily as it were. Just as he later, as a *dozent*, expands the prescribed pattern of instruction (the previously mentioned ministerial order expressly excepts Professor Kant and his collegium on physical geography, since in this field no entirely suitable textbook was yet available), so as a student less than seventeen years old he already shows all the evidences of a precocious intellectual independence in selecting and organizing his studies.

"Choose one of the faculties!" was still the universal formula of direction and guidance for the organization of the universities of the time, and in Prussia, for example, this formula had just recently been enjoined once again by a decree of Friedrich Wilhelm I dated October 25, 1735. "And henceforth," this decree runs, "shall the objections be of no avail that many young persons, when they come to the academy, do not yet know whether they should settle on theology, law, or medicine, especially since *studiosi* must already know this, and little is to be hoped for from them if they conduct their affairs so badly that, when they go to the academy, they have not yet decided on what they wish to work on there. Also, the pretext that they wish to apply themselves only to philosophy or a part thereof is under no circumstances to be accepted; but each shall declare himself in addi-

15. Concerning the condition and regulations of the University of Königsberg, cf. D. H. Arnoldt, *Ausführliche und mit urkunden versehene Historie der Königsberger Universität* (Königsberg, 1746).

tion for one of the higher faculties, and make it his business to derive at least some profit from these."[16]

In contrast to this conception of Friedrich Wilhelm I, which regards the university only as a training ground for the future civil servant, who is to be made useful and competent for some particular branch of service, Kant was convinced from the very beginning, as far as we know, of a different basic view, which he held fast to and brought to fruition undisturbed by all external pressures. When he matriculated at the University of Königsberg on September 24, 1740, he was burdened by the most straitened and needy circumstances. According to an entry in the Königsberg church register, his mother had been interred three years before "poorly and quietly," that is, without the attendance of the clergy and with remission of fees, and the same notation is found for the burial of his father on March 24, 1746. But with the certainty and unconcern of genius, Kant seems even then to have spurned any thought of mere training for a profession. For a long time tradition stamped him, on uncertain evidence, as a student of theology, but since the exhaustive investigation of this question by Emil Arnoldt, it has been established that Kant did not, in any case, belong to the theological faculty, and hence probably did not intend to educate himself for a theological calling. The statement on this score which was found in Borowski was struck out by Kant himself in the course of the scrutiny to which he subjected Borowski's biographical sketch. Particularly crucial in this regard is the report of one of the most intimate of Kant's youthful friends, Heilsberg, later the councillor for war and crown lands in Königsberg, who explicitly testifes that Kant had never been an "advanced *studiosus theologiae.*" If he attended lectures on theology, he did so only because of a conviction he also continually impressed on his fellow students: one must seek knowledge from all fields of study and therefore dare neglect none of them, not even theology, "even if one did not thereby seek his daily bread." In connection with this, Heilsberg depicts how

16. See D. Arnoldt's history of the University of Königsberg. Cf. with this and with the following in particular, Emil Arnoldt, "Kants Jugend," pp. 115 ff.

Kant and he, together with a third young friend, Wlömer, had attended a lecture by Franz Albert Schultz, Kant's former teacher at the Fridericianum, and had so distinguished themselves through their interest and understanding that Schultz called them to him at the close of the last class and inquired about their personal situations and plans. When Kant replied that he wished to be a doctor,[17] while Wlömer confessed himself a jurist, Schultz further demanded to know why in that case they listened to theological lectures, a question Kant answered with the simple phrase: "out of intellectual curiosity." This answer has a genuinely unsophisticated force and pregnancy. It already contains the first consciousness of an intellectual orientation that could neither be expressed by nor satisfied by a single outward goal of study. An involuntary recognition of this state of affairs is signified by Jachmann's later acknowledgment in his biography of Kant that he had fruitlessly inquired about the "syllabus" Kant had followed at the university; even the one friend and intimate of Kant known to him, Doctor Trummer in Königsberg, had been unable to give him any information on this matter. Just this much is certain, that Kant principally studied *humaniora* at the university and devoted himself to no "positive" science.[18]

The predicament in which this biographer of Kant and his friends found themselves contains an element of unconscious irony: concealed in it is the complete opposition that exists between the tangible goals of ordinary mankind and that purposiveness without purpose which governs the life of even the most reflective and self-conscious genius. Kant's turning away from the traditional academic work and subject matter of the university of his day toward the *humaniora*, looked at from the standpoint of his life history, indicates one of the earliest seeds of just that freer, "humane" form of education to whose later acceptance and realization in Germany Kant's philosophy contributed so decisively. In the evolution of this new ideal of humanity

17. Whether this answer of Kant's—as Arnoldt hints—contained an "admixture of sly humor" is uncertain; it is safer to assume that in the then-existing pattern of the division of the faculties, this was the only answer by which Kant could express his ruling interest in natural science.

18. Jachmann, *Immanuel Kant*, Second Letter, pp. 10 ff.

the most individual and the most universal, the personal and the ideal, intertwine directly. In Kant's lectures the young Herder, who had just liberated himself from the constricting intellectual coercion of his childhood and school years, first discovered that new demand for the "education of mankind" that henceforth constituted the foundation and the impetus for his own creative work.

Moreover, for Kant himself the fruits of these years of study lay less in what theoretical knowledge and insights they afforded him than in the intellectual and moral discipline to which they educated him from the beginning. From all that we know about this period of his life, the privations in even the least things, which had to be overcome daily with the most unrelenting tenacity, never disturbed his inner equanimity; they merely deepened his innate disposition to stoicism. And precisely because this stoicism was never imposed on him from without, but stemmed from a fundamental orientation of his own nature, this phase of his life was marked by a certain innocent vigor and unconcern. Throughout the sketches by Kant's comrades of that period, especially in the memoirs which Heilsberg set down at eighty as material for Wald's memorial address on Kant, this trait emerges conspicuously. One sees how an intimate and common bond of a personal and intellectual kind springs up between Kant and the fellow students with whom he lives, a bond which at the same time takes on the external form of a primitive community of goods— as Kant assists the others with his advice and tutoring, while he receives help from them in the minor tribulations of his material affairs.[19] Thus within this circle there reigns a spirit of true comradeship, a free give-and-take, in which none becomes the debtor of the other.[20] On this point Kant was extremely stern with himself from his early youth. One of the basic maxims he had laid down from the start was to maintain his economic independence, because he saw in it a condition for the self-sufficiency of his mind and character. But although with advancing age Kant's uncompromising sense of independence gradually brought something rigid and negative into his

19. See Heilsberg's account in Reicke, *Kantiana*, pp. 48 ff.
20. See in this regard the description by Emil Arnoldt, "Kants Jugend," pp. 146 ff.

life, there is still visible in his youth a freer and unaffected flexibility in this regard, which was natural to his convivial character and sociable gifts. The harmony of these two tendencies, the impulse to companionship and living communication, and at the same time the positive assertion of inward and outward freedom, is what gave Kant's student life its balance.

The biographer of Winckelmann, whose school years bear a striking resemblance to Kant's in many details of his intellectual development and of the molding of his outer life,[21] has said that there was nothing juvenile in Winckelmann's character save the strength to endure quantities of work.[22] This description is applicable to Kant as well. Even the comradeship with his associates of his own age, about which many humorous details are told, basically developed out of a community of study and work wherein there are already recognizable in Kant, who always emerges as the preeminent intellectual leader, many traits foreshadowing the future university teacher. Just as Kant himself, as Heilsberg recounts, loved "no frivolities, and still fewer revelries," so he gradually converted his audience—a significant expression—to a similar attitude; the sole recreation he permitted himself and them consisted in playing billiards and ombre, which, with the great skill they acquired, sometimes furnished them with a welcome source of income.

Yet in reconstructing the spiritual and intellectual elements of this period we should be even less content to stop with the outward pattern of Kant's life than we generally are. Everything we are told about it is totally subordinate in its significance to the new domain of the mind that must have been first revealed to Kant at that time. In this period the concept of *science*, both in its abstract generality and in its specific embodiments, became truly vivid for him. What secondary

21. In this respect one should especially compare the account that Paalzow gives of Winckelmann's student years (in Justi, *Winckelmann*, vol. 1, pp. 46 ff.) with what Heilsberg (in Reicke, *Kantiana*, pp. 48 ff.) relates concerning Kant; it is especially typical that Winckelmann also opposed the requirement of enrollment in one of the three "higher faculties."

22. Justi, *Winckelmann*, vol. 1, p. 44.

school had proffered him as knowledge was at bottom no more than crude material for memorization, whereas now he encounters philosophy and mathematics as essentially interrelated and interacting. The professor who introduced him to them achieved in so doing a decisive influence on the entire future course of his studies. What we know about this teacher, Martin Knutzen, and of his activity as instructor and author, does not immediately account for the depth of this influence. To be sure, Knutzen does reveal himself in his writings as a serious and keen thinker, but the problems that concern him do not essentially transcend the horizons of the current academic philosophy. Within these limits he does not fully commit himself to any particular faction, striving for originality of judgment and independence of decision; however, even the closest scrutiny to which he has been subjected as Kant's teacher can scarcely discover any truly unusual ideas and definitely novel suggestions.[23] Although Christian Jacob Kraus—of all Kant's friends and pupils the one with the most profound understanding of the significance and the content of his philosophy—nonetheless did say of Knutzen that he was the sole person in Königsberg at that time able to affect Kant's genius, this relates less to the content of his teaching than to the spirit in which it was presented. Of the teachers at the University of Königsberg, Knutzen alone represented the European concept of universal science. He alone looked beyond the limitations of the conventional textbook learning; he stood in the midst of the universal discussions that were being carried on about the foundations of rational and empirical knowledge, and he devoted equal interest to Wolff's writings and to Newton's.

Through this teacher's lectures and exercises, Kant entered into a new intellectual atmosphere. The significance of the single fact that it was Knutzen who first lent him Newton's works can hardly be overestimated, since for Kant Newton was the lifelong personification of the concept of science. A sense that he had at last taken a first and permanent step into the world of the intellect must have been alive in

23. Cf. Benno Erdmann, *Martin Knutzen und seine Zeit* (Berlin, 1878).

Kant from the beginning. Borowski tells us that from now on he "attended Knutzen's lectures in philosophy and mathematics."[24] These covered logic as well as natural philosophy, practical philosophy as well as natural law, algebra and infinitesimal analysis as well as general astronomy. A new cognitive horizon was thus disclosed to Kant, one which for his mind, oriented from the start toward systematization and methodology as it was, was bound also to transform the substance and the meaning of knowing.

This trend in his inner development emerged with full clarity in Kant's first published paper, which marks the close of his student years. He must have written it while still a student; the proceedings of the philosophical faculty of the University of Königsberg for the summer semester of 1747 contain the notice that the *Thoughts on the True Estimation of Living Forces (Gedanken von der wahren Schätzung der lebendigen Kräfte)* by the "Studiosus Immanuel Kandt" has been submitted to the censorship of the dean. The printing of the treatise was long delayed; begun in 1746, it was only completed three years later. No detailed biographical data on the intellectual motives that led Kant to choose this theme can be discovered, but simply from the content we can hazard a guess at the path by which the young Kant arrived at the problem of the measurement of force. A survey of the literature on natural philosophy and physics of the early decades of the eighteenth century yields recognition of a general question underlying the controversy over measurement of force, as it was zealously waged in Germany in particular. The defenders of the Leibnizian *measure* of force attempted at the same time to uphold the Leibnizian *concept* of force. This concept was threatened from both sides, for on the one hand it was opposed by the Cartesian geometric outlook in which matter and motion are nothing but modifications of sheer extension, while on the other hand basic Newtonian mechanics, which totally rejects any conclusion as to the essence of force and sees the description and calculation of phenomena as the sole task of empirical

24. Ludwig Ernst Borowski, *Darstellung des Lebens und Charakters Immanuel Kants* (Königsberg, 1804), pp. 28 ff.

science, was asserted ever more strongly and uncompromisingly.[25]

As this controversy progressed, the roles of the individual opponents had gradually become oddly interchanged and confused. For
the "metaphysicians" no longer stood clearly and distinctly apart
from the "mathematicians"—as had seemed to be the case when the
discussion began—but both factions bring "metaphysics" into play,
then hurl recriminations at each other for using it. Newton and Clarke
see in Leibniz's concept of the monad a revival of the Aristotelian-
medieval concept of substance, which conflicts with the basic principles of the modern, mathematic-scientific mode of knowledge. Leibniz, on the other hand, never misses an opportunity for indignation
over the concept of forces acting at a distance, claiming that it resur-
rects the old "barbarism" of scholastic physics, with its substantial
forms and occult qualities. The issue thus began to shift more and
more from the purely physical realm to that of universal method. It
was precisely in virtue of this aspect of the problem that Kant felt
himself attracted to it.

Here the question was no longer the discovery and confirmation
of individual, definite facts, but rather a fundamental conflict in the
interpretation of the recognized and accepted phenomena of motion in
general; here not just isolated observations and data but the *principles*
on which the examination of nature is founded and their diverse areas
of jurisdiction had to be weighed against one another. Kant always
formulated his particular question in the light of this general task.
What is noteworthy in this maiden paper is that the first step Kant
takes into the realm of natural philosophy immediately turns into an
inquiry into its method. His entire critique of the Leibnizian conception is subordinated to this point of view; at one point he expressly
explains that he is not so much combating Leibniz's result as its foundation and derivations, "not actually the facts themselves, but the
modus cognoscendi."[26] This confident and deliberate focusing on the

25. For a fuller discussion of this, see my book *Das Erkenntnisproblem in der
Philosophie und Wissenschaft der neueren Zeit*, 2d ed. (Berlin, 1911), vol. 2, pp. 400 ff.

26. *Thoughts on the True Estimation of Living Forces* [*Gedanken von der wahren Schätzung der lebendigen Kräfte*, 1746], chap. 2, §50 (I, 60) (*Ak.*I, 60).

modus cognoscendi is what gives Kant's treatment of the complicated issue its characteristic stamp. "One must have a method by which he can invariably, through a general consideration of the basic principles on which a certain belief is constructed and through the comparison of them with their implications, infer whether the nature of the premises comprises everything requisite for the propositions deduced from them. This occurs when one notes clearly the qualifications involved in the nature of the conclusion and is careful in constructing the proof to select such basic propositions as are confined to the specific qualifications contained in the conclusion. If this is not found to be the case, then we may be certain that these conclusions, thus defective, prove nothing. . . . Briefly, this entire treatise is to be regarded solely and simply as a consequence of this method."[27] Kant called his first work in the philosophy of physics a "treatise on method," as he later, at the zenith of his creative life, termed the *Critique of Pure Reason* (*Kritik der reinen Vernunft*) a treatise on method; the change which the meaning of this designation had undergone for him comprises his whole philosophy and its development.

For Kant at this point is still far away from a "critical" view in the sense of his later doctrine, and it would be arbitrary to read it into this treatise. He had already begun to doubt whether academic metaphysics was firm and solid, but this doubt had its roots more in a general feeling than in conceptual precision and clarity. "Our metaphysics," he states in this paper, "is, like many other sciences, in fact only at the threshold of truly well-founded knowledge; God knows when we shall see it crossed. To see its weakness in many of its undertakings is not difficult. Nothing is more to blame for this than the prevailing inclination among those who seek after extension of human knowledge. They would like to have a great fund of wisdom concerning the world, but it would be desirable for it to be sound as well. Almost the sole return to a philosopher for his labors is, after a painstaking inquiry, to rest at last in the possession of really well-founded, exact knowledge. Hence, it is a great deal to require of him that he but seldom trust his own approval, that he not conceal

27. Ibid., §88 (I, 95 ff.) (*Ak*, I, 93 ff.).

the imperfections of his own discoveries when it is in his power to rectify them. The understanding is greatly inclined to self-approbation, and indeed it is quite difficult to restrain it for long; but one should keep oneself in check, so as to sacrifice for the sake of well-founded knowledge everything that has a diffuse seductive-ness."[28] But within Kant's own essay this considered and precocious renunciation collides continually with his élan and youthful speculative daring. Not only is the distinction between "living" and "dead" force, on which the whole treatise rests, itself far more "metaphysical" than "physical" in nature, but also the essay is dominated throughout by the effort to rise from sheer description of the particular and the actual to direct insight into the most universal "possibilities" of thinking. An especially characteristic example is the speculation that the given three-dimensional space of our empirical world is perhaps but a special case of a system of spatial forms, which may be diverse in their structure and their metrics. "A science of all these possible types of space would be," the treatise adds, "unquestionably the highest geometry which a finite mind could undertake." It would at the same time imply the idea that the various forms of space may correspond to an actual number of different worlds, which however are not related by any dynamic connection and interaction.[29] In general, the paper attempts to reconcile and unify mathematics and metaphysics. Kant himself is of course aware that this is contrary to the dominant scientific taste of the period, yet it was an indispensable endeavor for him because it was evident that the "primary sources of the events in Nature" must certainly constitute "a proper subject of metaphysics."[30]

From the standpoint of Kant's life history, however, the peculiar interest of the *Thoughts on the True Estimation of Living Forces* lies less in the content of the paper than in the tone in which it is written. Its content doubtless looks rather thin in purely scientific respects, especially if one compares it with earlier and with contemporary works on

28. Ibid., chap. 1, §19 (I, 29 ff.) (*Ak.* I, 30 ff.).
29. Ibid., §§8–11 (I, 20 ff.) (*Ak.* I, 22 ff.).
30. Ibid., chap. 2, §51 (I, 61) (*Ak.* I, 61).

classical mechanics, with Euler's *Mechanica sive motus scientia* of 1736 and d'Alembert's *Essai de Dynamique* of 1743. One can see that the twenty-two-year-old student, although he has absorbed an astonishing amount of knowledge from the literature of mathematics and physics, has not yet fully mastered the most fundamental content of the mathematical education of that age. Kant's mode of inquiry rests throughout on the distinctions between dead and living force, between the relations of "dead pressure" and "active motion," distinctions already undermined by the demand of modern mechanics for unambiguous definition of all basic concepts and for the exact mensurability of all relations. In this regard, Lessing's well-known caustic epigram to the effect that Kant in his estimation of living forces neglected the estimation of his own forces was not wrong. Yet even today, when almost all its conclusions are obsolete, the work radiates a peculiar charm, a charm that lies not in what it explicitly contains and offers us, but in what it aspires to and promises us. This is our first encounter with the idiosyncratic temper of Kant's thought in its full strength and clarity. This thinking is oriented exclusively toward *what is the case,* with respect to which every opinion is devoid of weight, though it seem thoroughly authenticated by tradition and by the luster of a famous name. "There was a time when there was much to fear in such an undertaking; but I fancy that this time is now past and the human understanding has happily thrown off the fetters which ignorance and awe had formerly imposed on it. Now one can venture boldly to disregard the prestige of *Newton* and *Leibniz,* if it blocks the discovery of truth, and to yield to no persuasion other than the force of the understanding." Thus viewed, the assessment of the doctrine of living forces takes on a new meaning. Its youthful critic no longer stands forth as advocate of the opinion of a particular faction, but as the partisan of the "understanding." The dignity of human reason is to be vindicated by reconciling its internal conflicts as personified by such astute men.[31] But this vindication does not remain on the purely eclectic plane; when Kant turns his special attention to a certain "mediating proposition," intended to reconcile the claims of

---

31. Foreword, §1, and chap. 3, §125 (I, 5, 152) (*Ak.* I, 7, 149).

both opponents,[32] the mediation thus enjoined is not supposed to represent a mere compromise between the substance of the opposing views, but is to be reached through exact testing and analysis of the conditions which govern both assertion and counterassertion and which bestow on each its basic validity.

Thus we can already sense here how the general style of Kant's mode of thought is, as it were, taking on shape and definition in every sentence, although this style still lacks a theme truly worthy of it. And consciousness of this individuality and originality is so strong in him that it compels direct self-declaration. "I imagine," he says in the foreword to the paper, "that it is sometimes useful to place a certain magnanimous reliance on one's own powers. Confidence of this sort quickens all our efforts and imparts to them a certain buoyancy which greatly assists the search for truth. If one's state of mind has the conviction of his ability to persuade himself, one is permitted the conviction that he may to some extent trust his own perceptiveness and that it is possible to detect a Herr von Leibniz in errors, thus one bends all his efforts toward verifying his suspicions. After one has gone astray a thousand times in such an undertaking, the gain accruing to our knowledge of truth will still be much more considerable than when one has only kept to the beaten path. Here I take my stand. I have already marked out the road ahead which I intend to follow. I shall embark on my course, and nothing shall hinder me from pursuing it."[33]

With such simplicity and vigor does the note of promise resound in the opening sentences of Kant's first paper. At the moment of his debut as a philosophical writer all constraint and poverty in his outward life is as though obliterated, and there emerges in almost abstract clarity only that decisive law governing his being and his mode of thought. From now on, that wonderful trait of consistency appears in his life and compensates for its lack of fullness and outer variety. He has discovered the form, not of a specific dogma, but rather of his own thinking and willing. With the limitless self-

32. Ibid., chap. 2, §20 (I, 31) (*Ak.* I, 32).
33. Ibid., foreword, §7 (I, 8) (*Ak.* I, 10).

confidence of genius, even the young man in his twenties is conscious
that this form will be preserved and fulfilled. He sets at the head of
the *Thoughts on the True Estimation of Living Forces* the motto from
Seneca: "Nihil magis praestandum est quam ne pecorum ritu
sequamur antecedentium gregem, pergentes non qua eundum est,
sed qua itur."[34] It remained to be demonstrated that this motto,
which Kant chooses as the maxim for his thinking, could also constitute the maxim for his life. Kant was able to achieve and ensure future
freedom in the exercise of his profession as writer only by first re-
nouncing it for a long while. Even before his first work is printed, he
leaves Königsberg, "forced by the state of his circumstances," as
Borowski tells us, to take a position as private tutor in the house of a
country preacher.[35] This exile in the role of *Hofmeister* lasted at least
seven years (if not nine); but during it Kant won the independence
from society and the free self-determination which comprised all that
he ever sought or expected for himself in the way of a happy life.[36]

2

In the years that follow, Kant's life recedes almost entirely into
shadow—so much so that even its superficial contours can no longer be
traced with certainty, and even the data concerning the places and
dates of the several phases of this period are dubious and flickering.
Most biographers agree that Kant initially took up residence as tutor
in the household of the reform minister Andersch in Judschen, and
from there removed to the von Hülsen estate in Gross-Arnsdorf near
Saalfeld. But the further information that he was also active as private
tutor in the house of Count Johann Gebhardt von Keyserling in

34. ["There is naught more important than that we should not follow like sheep the
herd that has gone before, going not where we should but where the herd goes."]
35. See Borowski, *Darstellung des Lebens und Charakters Immanuel Kants*, pp. 30 ff.
36. "Even as a youth the master desired to make himself self-sufficient and independent of everyone, so that he might live not for men but for himself and his duty. In
his old age he declared that this freedom and independence was the basis of all happiness in life, and asserted that it had always made him much happier to do without than
to allow indulgence to make him the debtor of another." (Jachmann, *Immanuel Kant*,
Eighth Letter, pp. 65 ff.).

Rautenburg near Tilsit is uncertain and ambiguous. Christian Jacob Kraus, at any rate, asserts flatly that Kant never entered into any relation of the sort; his testimony in this matter has special weight since it was Kraus who took over the post of private tutor and master in the Keyserling home in Königsberg following the marriage of Countess Keyserling to her second cousin Heinrich Christian Keyserling. In any event, judging by the ages of the Keyserling sons, any tutorial activity on Kant's part could hardly have taken place before 1753, and in the following year Kant must already have resumed residence in Königsberg, since a letter of that period is dated from there. Whatever the exact circumstances may have been,[37] it is obvious that such vague and uncertain data are no basis for a judgment that might shed the slightest degree of light for us on Kant's inner development in this period. Only Borowski has preserved a few scanty bits of information on this subject. "The placid rustic environment," he says, "served to foster his industry. His head already held the outlines of many undertakings, a large number of them already almost completely worked out, which he . . . in 1754 and the subsequent years, to the surprise of many . . . produced all at once in rapid succession. It was then that he assembled from all fields of learning in his commonplace books what seemed to him important in any way for human knowledge, and he still thinks back today to those years of his rural sojourn and labor with great contentment."[38]

If this account, as seems certain, rests on Kant's own statements—Kant at the very least indirectly corroborated it, since he left it unaltered in looking over Borowski's biographical sketch—the conclusion is that the new set of influences to which Kant was subjected by the pressures of his external situation had no power to destroy the calm continuity of his mental growth. Though in the recollections of Kant's old age this period appears as one totally devoid of struggle, still it was not a time that fostered harmony between his inner and outer life. The years as private tutor, to be sure a typical

37. All the materials bearing on the resolution of this question are compiled by Emil Arnoldt ("Kants Jugend," pp. 168 ff.); cf. also E. Fromm, "Das Kantbildnis der Gräfin K. Ch. A. von Keyserling," *Kantstudien* 2 (1898):145 ff.

38. Borowski, *Darstellung des Lebens und Charakters Immanuel Kants*, pp. 30 ff.

part of an intellectual's destiny in that age, invariably meant for any sensitive nature a stern school of spiritual deprivation. The social status of the *Hofmeister* was in every respect oppressive and troublesome. "They don't want to spend more than forty thalers for a tutor"; it is said in the letters of Frau Gottsched, "for that he is supposed to take care of the steward's accounts as well."[39] One can get a lively impression of what the situation was like, especially in East Prussia, if one pictures the conditions portrayed by Lenz, twenty-five years later, in his comedy *Der Hofmeister,* set at an estate at Insterburg. "Plague take it, Pastor!" says the Privy Councillor to the pastor who wants his son to become a tutor. "You didn't raise him to be a servant, and what is he except a servant when he sells his freedom as a private person for a handful of ducats? He's a slave, over whom his master has unlimited power, only he has to have learned enough at the academy to anticipate their heedless notions in advance so as to gloss over his servitude. . . . You complain so much about the nobility and its arrogance; those people consider a tutor one of the domestic servants. . . . But who makes you feed their arrogance? Who makes you turn servant when you have learned something and become the vassal of some numskull of a nobleman who all his life has been used to nothing but slavish obsequiousness from his household help?" The noblest and strongest characters, Fichte for example, always felt profoundly bitter about this serfdom of the private tutor. Kant, so far as we know, was completely spared experiences of this kind. He did sense mutual incompatibility between him and his occupation, and later he protested with a smile that he was perhaps the worst private tutor the world had ever known.[40]

Nonetheless, everything known to us of his relations with the families where he worked shows the high personal esteem in which he was held. Here too, within the circle in which he dwelt, intellectual leadership and a sort of moral ascendancy seem to have swiftly accrued to him. From his youth there flowed from his person, unpretentious though it was, a strength which flourished in every situation

---

39. *Letters of Frau Gottsched,* vol. 2, p. 97 (quoted in Biedermann, *Deutschlands geistige, sittliche und gesellige Zustände,* vol. 2, pt. 1, p. 522).

40. Cf. Jachmann, *Immanuel Kant,* Second Letter, pp. 11 ff.

of life in which he was put and which exacted respect from everyone. His self naturally shaped his environment and his relations with others. For a long time after he had departed, Kant remained in extremely friendly communication with the family of Count von Hülsen. The letters they sent him contained, by Rink's testimony, "the heartfelt expression of thanks, respect, and love, which thus reveals that they see to it that he participates in every interesting family event." "It is perhaps not entirely superfluous to note," Rink adds, "that the von Hüllesen family liberated their serfs during the reign of the then King of Prussia [Friedrich Wilhelm III], and, as is stated in the official notices, they were graciously favored by the humanitarian monarch by elevation to the rank of count."[41] When the Countess von Keyserling moved to Königsberg after her second marriage, Kant continued in an intimate personal and intellectual connection with the Keyserling household; Kraus has told us that since Kant customarily sat in the place of honor at table directly beside the Countess, "it was necessary for one to be a total stranger for this place to be yielded to him as a courtesy."[42]

If we put all this information together, one fact emerges, namely, that even these years as a household tutor, foreign and ill-suited to his true nature as that role appears to be, brought a deep and lasting effect for Kant himself and for others. Kant had originally been compelled to take a position as tutor, but this did not destroy his feeling of inner freedom, since his goal, for which he had risked this intrusion into the prime of his youth, stood fixed and unshakable. In the universal sweep of its view, in profundity and acuteness of conception, in the vigor and power of its language the *Universal Natural History and Theory of the Heavens (Allgemeine Naturgeschichte und Theorie des Himmels)*, which must have been largely written or drafted during Kant's days as tutor, is surpassed by but few of Kant's later works.[43]

41. Rink, *Ansichten aus Immanuel Kants Leben*, pp. 28 ff.

42. Cf. Kraus's account in Reicke, *Kantiana*, p. 60; see also the account of Elisabeth von der Recke, the daughter of Countess von Keyserling (excerpts from *Über C. F. Neanders Leben und Schriften* [Berlin, 1804], pp. 108 ff.). For further information concerning Countess Keyserling and her circle, see E. Fromm, *Kantstudien* 2 (1898):150 ff.

43. Arthur Warda (*Altpreussische Monatsschrift* 38:404) makes it plausible that Kant stayed in Judschen as tutor until 1750, and from 1750 until Easter of 1754 worked on the

It was more than mere scrapbooks of learning that Kant brought to fruition in these years; what he achieved was a free intellectual outlook and mature judgment on the whole realm of scientific problems, both of which the *Thoughts on the True Estimation of Living Forces* had lacked. Secure in both inward and outward matters, he could now return to the university. He succeeded in "assembling the means of advancing toward his future vocation less encumbered by cares,"[44] and he now also possessed a compass of knowledge that enabled him in his beginning years as instructor to lecture on logic and metaphysics, on physical geography and general natural history, and on problems of theoretical and practical mathematics and mechanics. On June 12, 1755, Kant became a doctor of philosophy on the strength of a treatise *De igne (On Fire)*; on September 27 of the same year, after the public defense of his work *Principiorum primorum cognitionis Metaphysicae nova dilucidatio (A New Explanation of the First Principles of Metaphysical Knowledge),* he was granted permission to hold a course of lectures. Thus Kant began his new career with both a physical and a metaphysical theme. But his mind, which invariably pressed forward to organization and critical structure, was unable to rest content with a simple juxtaposition of diverse sciences. From yet another standpoint he was set the problem of putting physics and metaphysics on firm principles and delimiting their respective modes of ordering problems and of acquiring knowledge. Only when this distinction was completed would it be possible to construct that bridge between philosophy and natural science, between "experience" and "thinking," on which the new concept of knowledge— itself inaugurated and confirmed by the critical philosophy—rests.

However, before we pass on to this development, as we look back at the whole course of Kant's youth yet once more a general observation forces itself upon us. The life of the great individual, seemingly running its course in complete detachment from the grand historical

estate of the von Hülsen family in Gross-Arnsdorf. Since the dedication of the *Universal Natural History and Theory of the Heavens* is dated March 14, 1755, and the work unquestionably required several years of preparation, the inference is that its conception and working out largely fall within Kant's years as tutor.

44. Rink, *Ansichten aus Immanuel Kants Leben,* p. 27.

movements of the age, also stands united at its heart with the collective life of the nation and of the age. The fundamental spiritual forces in Prussia in the eighteenth century are summed up in three names: Winckelmann, Kant, and Herder. The formative years of all three display a common direction despite the diversity that stems from the uniqueness of their basic outlooks and the detailed conditions of their development, a path reflecting the general spiritual and material situation of the Prussia of that day. Prussia's accomplishments under Friedrich Wilhelm I had been achieved through an iron discipline, through the power of self-restraint and renunciation. The forces from which the new political shape of the country was to be forged were brought together under a regime of harshest compulsion and extreme penury. As this compulsion permeated all the strictures of private life, it determined, through the institutions of child-rearing and education, the view of life which was to put its stamp thereon. The life of the great individual had first of all to be liberated from the emptiness, narrowness, and lack of freedom of the political and intellectual milieu. Winckelmann and Herder waged this battle with mounting bitterness. Winckelmann, after he discovered himself in Rome, looked back upon the serfdom of his youth and on "barbaric" Prussia with intense anger; and Herder too felt that his intellectual powers fully unfolded only at the very moment when he was on the point of leaving his homeland forever. His true nature first flowered in its entirety in contact with the breadth of the world and of life; his "Travel Diary" offered the first rounded picture of his personal and literary originality. He was no longer bound to his native country by sentiment; "the States of the King of Prussia," he coolly decrees, "will never be happy until they are split into brotherhoods."

If one compares Kant's way of thinking to that of Winckelmann and Herder, the fact that Kant dedicated the first work revealing him as a mature and universal thinker, the *Universal Natural History and Theory of the Heavens,* to Friedrich II assumes a general symbolic significance. It is—considering this trend throughout the whole of Kant's future life—as if he thereby had forever sworn allegiance to his homeland, in all its narrowness and limitation. Whatever his spiritual development, in comparison with that of Winckelmann and Herder, may have lost in so doing cannot be measured, but on the other hand the gain which from then on became an integral part of the evolution of his character and his will was infinitely significant. Kant remained on the soil where birth and the circumstances of life had placed him; but with the strength and self-restraint that form a specific characteristic of his intellectual and moral genius he wrested from this soil what mental fruits it contained. Having already learned in youth and adolescence to fulfill the duty of a man, he remained faithful to this duty to the end, and from the energy of this moral will there grew the critical philosophy's new theoretical perspective on the world and on life.

II THE EARLY TEACHING YEARS AND THE BEGINNINGS OF KANTIAN PHILOSOPHY

1. The Natural Scientific World-Picture—Cosmology and the Physics of the Universe

Kant held his first lecture in the autumn of 1755, in the house of Professor Kypke, where he was then living. The spacious lecture room this house possessed, the entrance hall, and even the steps were "packed with an almost incredible crowd of students." Kant was extremely nervous at this unexpected wealth of listeners. He lost almost all his composure, spoke even more softly than usual, and had to correct himself frequently. However, even these numerous errors in his presentation did not detract from the effect of the lecture on its sizable audience; rather they gave "only an even more lively warmth" to the admiration for this unassuming thinker. The "presumption of the most comprehensive erudition" on Kant's part had by now been permanently formed, and his expositions were followed patiently and expectantly. In the next lecture the picture had changed: Kant's presentation was not only thorough but also frank and winning, and it remained so from then on.

This portrait is drawn from the biography by Borowski,[1] who was himself present in the audience at Kant's first lecture. It is a typical testimony to the strong personal impression that the young Kant made on everyone. That "presumption of the most comprehensive

---

1. Ludwig Ernst Borowski, *Darstellung des Lebens und Charakters Immanuel Kants* (Königsberg, 1804), pp. 185 f.

erudition" Kant encountered in his auditors can hardly have been
founded on his literary reputation, since the very work that could
have been the foundation of his literary fame once and for all at this
period, the *Universal Natural History and Theory of the Heavens*, had by
a curious mischance remained completely unknown to the public.
The publisher had gone bankrupt while the work was in press; his
entire warehouse was sealed up, and therefore this book never came
onto the market.[2] What was known of Kant's scientific labors at the
time he began his lectures was therefore restricted—aside from his
initial publication in natural philosophy—to a few brief essays he had
published in the *Wochentliche Königsbergische Frag- und Anzeigungs-
Nachrichten* in 1754.[3] It could not have been from these few pages,
which treat specific questions of physical geography, that the expectations of the audience for the young instructor in logic and
metaphysics had been brought to such a pitch. Even when Kant received his master's degree on June 12, 1755, a throng of learned and
highly regarded men of the city was in attendance, which "revealed
its respect by the exceptional hush and attentiveness" with which he
was obliged.[4] It must have been the effect of Kant's conversation and
personal relationships that earned him this respect, just as later,
when all his major philosophical works had finally appeared, his
most intimate friends and pupils were adamant in their assertion that
in personal intercourse and in his lectures Kant "was far more genial
than in his books," that he "threw off ingenious ideas by the
thousands," and had squandered "an immeasurable wealth of
ideas." The special mark of his originality they found just here, for

2. Ibid., pp. 194 f.
3. "Untersuchung der Frage, ob die Erde in ihrer Umdrehung um die Achse,
wodurch sie die Abwechselung des Tages und der Nacht hervorbringt, einige Veränderung seit den ersten Zeiten ihres Ursprungs erlitten habe" ["Inquiry into the Question Whether the Axial Rotation of the Earth, Which Produces the Alternation of Day
and Night, Has Undergone Any Change since Its Earliest Period"], *Wochentliche
Königsbergische Frag- und Anzeigungs-Nachrichten*, June 8 and 15, 1724; "Die Frage ob die
Erde veralte physikalisch erwogen" ["Consideration of the Question Whether the
Earth Has Physically Aged"], ibid., August 10 and September 14. (See I, 189 ff., 199 ff.)
(*Ak.* I, 183 ff., 193 ff.).
4. Borowski, *Darstellung des Lebens und Charakters Immanuel Kants*, p. 32.

with the run-of-the-mill academician, the book is commonly more learned than its author, whereas the depth and special quality of the true "independent thinker" manifests itself precisely in that his writings do not rank above their author but remain subordinate to him.[5]

In any event, if anything could have destroyed the freshness and immediacy of Kant's mind, it would have been the life into which he now entered in the first years of teaching activity. Over and over he had to struggle with the uncertainty of his livelihood and often with worry about the immediate future. He had laid by twenty Friedrichsdor, as insurance against total destitution in the event of an illness. So as not to dip into this "hoard," he had, by Jachmann's account, "bit by bit to sell off his originally extensive and imposing library, because for several years he could not meet the costs of his most pressing needs from his wages."[6] Even some decades later, Kraus said to Poerschke that anyone who decided to attach himself to the University of Königsberg had taken a vow of poverty.[7] But the external privations, which Kant had long been accustomed to, were not the only pressures he faced. There was also the monstrous academic workload he now assumed under the compulsion of his situation, one which would have slain any other nature but his at the very outset. In the first semester, the winter of 1755–56, he lectured on logic, mathematics, and metaphysics; the next term added, along with the repetition of his previous lectures, a course on physical geography and on the foundations of general natural science. And from now on the scope of his academic activity grew wider and wider; the winter of 1756–57, which introduced ethics into the cycle of his lectures, shows twenty hours a week as compared with twelve and sixteen the preceding semesters. If we move some years further along, we find announced—for instance in the summer semester of 1761—as well as logic and metaphysics, mechanics and theoretical

5. See Karl Ludwig Poerschke's description and judgment, in his lecture on Kant's birthday celebration, April 22, 1812.

6. Reinhold Bernhard Jachmann, *Immanuel Kant geschildert in Briefen an einen Freund* (Königsberg, 1804), Second Letter, p. 13.

7. See Johannes Voigt, *Das Leben des Professors Christian Jacob Kraus* (Königsberg, 1819), p. 437.

physics; besides physical geography, arithmetic, geometry, and trigonometry, a "disputation" on these latter every Wednesday and Saturday morning, with the remaining class hours on both days "devoted partly to review and partly to solution of problems." In all, this announcement comprises no less than thirty-four to thirty-six hours a week, so one may question whether the whole compass of the program was ever carried through.[8] Is it any wonder that Kant often complained that he felt this activity, which he performed most conscientiously and scrupulously and without the least interruption, to be only laborious mental serfdom? "I sit daily," he writes to Lindner in October of 1759, "at the anvil of my lectern and keep the heavy hammer of repetitious lectures going in some sort of rhythm. Now and then an impulse of a nobler sort, from out of nowhere, tempts me to break out of this cramping sphere, but ever-present need leaps on me with its blustering voice and perpetually drives me back forthwith to hard labor by its threats—*intentat angues atque intonat ore* [he beholds the serpents and his mouth thunders forth]."[9]

This admission is truly unnerving, and yet one is almost inclined to forget it when one looks at Kant's writings from this period. For scanty as they are—his literary production from 1756 to 1763 comprises only a few pages—each of them displays a superior intellectual mastery of his theme and a fresh and original point of view in its treatment. In the *Monadologia Physica* [*Physical Monadology*], he posits a theory of the "simple" atom and of forces acting at a distance that probes the fundamental problems of the natural philosophy of that era, especially as they were being taken up and systematically presented at that very time by Boscovich; in the *New Notes on the Explanation of the Theory of the Winds (Neue Anmerkungen zur Erläuterung der Theorie der Winde)* he anticipates the explanation of Mariotte's law of

8. A list of all the lectures announced by Kant in the years 1755–96 has been assembled by Emil Arnoldt and supplemented by Otto Schöndörffer, the editor of Arnoldt's *Gesammelte Schriften*, through important research. On the foregoing, cf. *Gesammelte Schriften*, vol. 5, pt. 2, pp. 177 ff., 193 ff.

9. To Lindner, October 28, 1759 (IX, 17 ff.). At the time to which this letter pertains, Kant had—after finishing his "Versuch einiger Betrachtungen über den Optimismus" ["Some Experimental Reflections about Optimism"]—announced a lecture on logic (using Meier's textbook), on physical geography (using his own manuscript), and on pure mathematics and mechanics (using Wolff). (See II, 37) (*Ak.* II, 35).

rotation of the winds that Dove later gave in 1835; in the *New Theory of Motion and Rest (Neuer Lehrbegriff der Bewegung und Ruhe)* of 1758, he develops an insight into the relativity of motion completely opposed to the ruling conception, which stood under the aegis of Newton's name and authority. From all of this shines forth an intellectual power undimmed by daily academic drudgery, a universal active energy that allows itself to be only fleetingly confined within the narrow limits imposed on it by the conventional form of university work.

One should not look to this period for fundamental and ultimate philosophical judgments, for everything it contains shows it to belong to the process of intellectual *orientation* which Kant had first to work through for himself. In the later essay, "What Is Orientation in Thinking?" ("Was heisst: sich im Denken orientieren?") (1786), Kant, in analyzing the meaning of the words of the title, brought out three different fundamental meanings of the concept of orientation. The first, in which the sensory root of the word is still clearly recognizable, concerns orientation in *space;* it refers to the determination of the regions of the heavens, which we make by reference to the place where the sun rises. This geographical concept is then joined by the extended mathematical meaning, in which the question is to determine directions in a specific space as such, without requiring any given object and its locus (such as the place where the sun rises) as points of reference. In this sense we "orient" ourselves in a familiar dark room, if we are simply given the position of some object (any one at all, because with its place fixed, all the others can be ascertained by the known relationship of right and left). In both cases we make use of experience with a purely sensuous basis, since the opposition of the directions right and left itself rests on a felt distinction in the subject himself, namely between the right and the left hands. The last and highest stage is reached when we progress from geographical and mathematical orientation to *logical* orientation in the most general sense of that word, in which it is no longer a matter of the locus of a thing in space, but of fixing the place of a judgment or a cognition in the universal system of *reason.*[10]

The distinct stages and their sequence as Kant gives them here can

10. "Was heisst: sich im Denken orientieren?" ["What Is Orientation in Thinking?"] (IV, 351 ff.) (*Ak.* VIII, 134 ff.).

be applied to his own intellectual development. There too he starts
with a physical, geographical orientation: it is the plurality and origin
of the earth's formation, and equally its place in the cosmos, which
are the initial objects of his natural scientific interests. The "Inquiry
into the Question Whether the Axial Rotation of the Earth, Which
Produces the Alternation of Day and Night, Has Undergone Any
Change since Its Earliest Period" ("Untersuchung der Frage, ob die
Erde in ihrer Umdrehung um ihre Achse einige Veränderung seit den
ersten Zeiten ihres Ursprungs erlitten habe") and the solution of the
problem of whether we can speak of an aging of the earth in the
physical sense, constitute, in 1754, the beginning of his work as a
writer on natural science; it is extended by special studies on the
theory of the winds, as well as on the causes of earthquakes and on
volcanic phenomena. But all these individual questions are conceived
in relation to the one great basic theme of that period: the universal
problem of cosmogony, which receives its exhaustive exposition in
the *Universal Natural History and Theory of the Heavens.* Yet it appears
that even this attempt at a completely universal explanation of the
phenomena of nature remains insufficient so long as the *principles* and
the ultimate empirical and theoretical grounds of the processes of
nature are not clearly understood. The concern for orientation brings
these increasingly into prominence. Kant sees himself ever more decisively forced out of the realm of description of nature and of natural
history into that of natural philosophy. The *Monadologia physica* sets
up and defends a new form of atomism, while the *New Theory of
Motion and Rest* endeavors to remove an obscurity that had lodged in
the foundation of physics itself, in the definition of the basic concepts
of mechanics. And once again the analysis is broadened and
deepened, as it turns from the elements of physics to those of mathematics. Full light on the relations and laws of magnitudes, which
natural science deals with, can be expected only when the presuppositions of mathematical definition and measurement are completely
transparent. In this respect the "Attempt to Introduce the Concept of
Negative Magnitudes into Philosophy" ("Versuch den Begriff der
negativen Grössen in die Weltweisheit einzuführen") of 1763
achieves a first important result; in it the concepts of "direction" and

"opposite direction" are defined and used in a new and fruitful sense.

At the same time the conflict between syllogistic and mathematical thinking, between the logic of the schools and the logic of arithmetic, geometry, and natural science is rendered sharp and clear. The old question about the "boundaries" between mathematics and metaphysics thus is given a new substance. All the works of the next few years are related, directly or indirectly, to this central problem, which in the treatise *On the Form and Principles of the Sensible and the Intelligible World (De mundi sensibilis atque intelligibilis forma et principiis)* (1770) is finally given its complete systematic formulation. Once again it is shown that what is put forward here as a conclusive solution immediately dissolves into a complex of the knottiest questions, but the new general path is marked out once and for all, and will be confidently held to from now on. Determination of the spatial cosmos is replaced by determination of the "intellectual" cosmos; the empirical geographer is transformed into a "geographer of reason," who undertakes to map the circuit of its entire content under the guidance of definite principles.[11]

If we turn back from this preview of the general evolution of Kant's thinking to the particular tasks that are the mark and fulfillment of his work during his first decade as a teacher, a consideration of the extent of the world he had to conquer by thought is vital here. No other period in Kant's life is so highly defined and characterized by pure passion for substance. Now he begins a powerful labor aimed at mastering the material of intuition and studying what will provide the foundation for his new total conception of the world. To do this, secondary sources of all sorts have to make up for what Kant lacks in the way of firsthand impressions and experiences: geographical and scientific works, travel descriptions and reports of researches. Even the minutest detail in all this material does not escape his intense and lively notice. This way of assimilating material seems to bear with it all the dangers involved in passive reception of others' observations, but the lack of immediate sense perception is outweighed here by that

---

11. Cf. *Critique of Pure Reason*, Discipline of Pure Reason, second sect. A 759 = B 787 (III, 513).

gift for precise sensory imagination which is peculiar to Kant. By its means those individual strokes he gleaned from a wealth of scattered reports were composed into a unified, focused picture.

In this regard, what Jachmann has reported about his "astounding inner powers of intuition and imagination" is especially well known. "One day, for example, he described, in the presence of a born Londoner, Westminister Bridge, in its shape and orientation, length, breadth, and height and the specific masses of every particular part so precisely that the Englishman asked him how many years he had lived in London, and whether he was especially absorbed in architecture; whereupon he was assured that Kant had never gone outside Prussia and was not an architect by profession. He conversed in an equally detailed way with Brydone, so that the latter inquired how long he had stayed in Italy."[12] By virtue of this capacity of the mind he builds up—stroke by stroke, piece by piece—the whole of the visible cosmos; his inner powers of representation and thinking enlarge the scant data of the immediately given into a picture of the world that combines richness and systematic completeness. In this period, Kant's power of synthesis far outweighs that of analysis and criticism, contrary to the common notion about him. This urge toward wholeness is so strong in Kant's mind that his constructive imagination almost always outruns the patient study of particular data. The saying "Give me matter and I will build a world," which the preface to the *Universal Natural History and Theory of the Heavens* illustrates and works variations on, in this sense designates not only the special theme of Kantian cosmogony, but also the most general task under his consideration in this period. The astronomical cosmic construction is just the outcome and tangible expression of a specific fundamental power of his thinking. In two separate directions, with respect to space and time, this thinking inquires into the limits of what is empirically known and given. The seventh chapter of the *Universal Natural History and Theory of the Heavens*, which treats "Of the Creation in the Whole Extent of Its Infinitude in Space as Well as in Time," begins: "The universe, by its immeasurable greatness and the infinite variety

---

12. Jachmann, *Immanuel Kant,* Third Letter, pp. 18 f.

and beauty that shine from it on all sides, fills us with silent wonder. If the presentation of all this perfection moves the imagination, the understanding is seized by another kind of rapture when, from another point of view, it considers how such magnificence and such greatness can flow from a single law, with an eternal and perfect order. The planetary world in which the sun, acting with its powerful attraction from the center of all the orbits, makes the moving spheres of its system revolve in eternal circles, has been wholly formed . . . out of the originally diffused primitive stuff that constituted all the matter of the world. All the fixed stars which the eye discovers in the hollow depths of the heavens, and which seem to display a sort of prodigality, are suns and centers of similar systems. . . .

"If, then, all the worlds and systems acknowledge the same kind of origin, if attraction is unlimited and universal, while the repulsion of the elements is likewise everywhere active; if, in presence of the infinite, the great and small are small alike; have not all the universes received a relative constitution and systematic connection similar to what the heavenly bodies of our solar world have on the small scale—such as Saturn, Jupiter, and the Earth, which are particular systems by themselves, and yet are connected with each other as members of a still greater system? . . .

"But what is at last the end of these systematic arrangements? Where shall creation itself cease? It is evident that in order to think of it as in proportion to the power of the Infinite Being, it must have no limits at all. We come no nearer the infinitude of the creative power of God, if we enclose the space of its revelation within a sphere described with the radius of the Milky Way, than if we were to limit it to a ball an inch in diameter."[13]

And corresponding to this immeasurability in the duration of the world is the infinitude of its becoming. Creation is not the work of an instant; rather, after it has made a start by producing an infinity of substances and matter, it is active throughout the whole succession of eternity in ever-increasing degrees of fruitfulness. The formative principle can never cease working, and it will continuously be oc-

13. *Universal Natural History and Theory of the Heavens* (I, 309 ff.) (*Ak.* I, 306 ff.).

cupied with producing more natural events, new things, and new worlds. If thought, directed toward the past and the origin of things, must at last stop with formless matter, a "chaos," which is shaped progressively into a "world," namely a unified spatial composition and mechanical interrelation of the whole through the constructive forces of attraction and repulsion, the prospect into the future of becoming is unhampered for us, for "the remaining part of the succession of eternity is always infinite and that which has flowed is finite, the sphere of developed nature is always but an infinitely small part of that totality which has the seed of future worlds in itself, and which strives to evolve itself out of the crude state of chaos through longer or shorter periods."[14]

It is unnecessary to discuss here the significance of this theory, the so-called Kant-Laplace hypothesis, in natural science as a whole. So far as Kant's intellectual evolution is concerned, this work, which more than any other delves into the detail of empirical natural science, is significant less for its content than for its method. To reveal the essence of this method, one has at the outset to renounce labeling it by certain philosophical battle cries, such as the sectarian titles of "rationalism" and "empiricism." Whenever anyone has tried to use this schematic opposition as a plumb line for expounding Kant's intellectual development, it has confused the picture far more than it has clarified it. The original, fundamental orientation of Kant's research and thought is precisely that he has in view from the outset a deeper unity of the empirical and the rational than had heretofore been accomplished or recognized in the struggle between philosophical schools.

In this sense the *Universal Natural History and Theory of the Heavens* also asserts, as its title indicates, a thoroughgoing interrelation between the empirical and the theoretical, between experience and speculation. This work takes up the question of cosmogony at exactly the point where Newton had dropped it. Six planets, with their ten satellites, move jointly in the same direction around the sun as the central point and in fact in the selfsame direction in which the sun

14. [Ibid. (I, 317) (*Ak.* I, 314).]

itself rotates; and their orbits are so arranged that as a group they lie almost in one and the same plane, namely the equatorial plane of the sun as extended. If one takes this phenomenon as premise, one is led on to demand a cause of this complete agreement and to trace back the "unanimity of the direction and position of the planetary orbits" to it. Newton saw this problem but was unable to solve it, since he regarded (correctly, judged from the standpoint of the state of knowledge at that time) the space in which the planets moved as completely empty; thus there was no material cause discoverable which by its distribution throughout the space of the planetary bodies could have maintained the similarity of motion. Accordingly, Newton had to say that the hand of God executed this ordering directly without recourse to the forces of nature. He would have been unable to stop with this "conclusion grievous to a philosopher" if instead of seeking the physical bases of the system of astronomical phenomena exclusively in its present state he had turned his gaze backwards to the past of the system, if he had pushed forward from the consideration of the systematic *state* of the universe to its systematic becoming. The law of becoming is what first really accounts for the state of being and makes it thoroughly intelligible according to natural laws.

Thus while in Newton there is a unique blend of empiricism and metaphysics, because with him empirical causality reaches a point where it turns directly into and becomes metaphysical causality, Kant on the contrary returns to that demand for unity of method with which Descartes founded modern philosophy. This foundation itself is not alien to the astronomical problem in cosmology: the outline for an explanation of the world contained in Descartes's unpublished work *Le Monde* explicitly lays down the proposition that we can only comprehend the world in its actually given structure if we first cause it to come into being for ourselves. The *Universal Natural History and Theory of the Heavens* gives this thought the value of a general principle of the "philosophical" explanation of nature. That which for the physicist, for Newton, was the ultimate "given" in nature, must be unfolded before the mind's eye by a philosophical view of the cosmos and derived genetically. Here, hypothesis, even speculation itself, not only may but must go beyond the content of the given, under the assumption that it nonetheless submits to control by this content in that the theoretical results obtained must agree with the data of experience and observation.

In this connection it is clear that Kant, despite all his regard for the pursuit of empirical research, by no means exclusively acknowledged and applied himself to it. This becomes clearer still in the general tendency that wholly governs his own inquiries in this period. Not only the *Universal Natural History and Theory of the Heavens* but also the entire natural scientific orientation of the next decade is guided by an overall ethical and intellectual interest: it seeks nature in order to find man in it. "As I saw at the very beginning of my academic teaching," Kant wrote in his announcement of the schedule of his lectures for the year 1765–66, "that a great neglect among young people who are studying lies particularly in the fact that they learn to rationalize early, without possessing enough historical knowledge which can substitute for *experiences*, I therefore undertook the project of composing a pleasant and easy compendium of the history of the present state of the earth or geography in its broadest sense, which might prepare the way for *practical reason*, and kindle the desire to extend more and more the knowledge thus begun."[15] "Practical reason" is taken here in the widest sense of the term; it comprises the general moral vocation of man, like that totality of "knowledge of the world and of man" which plays so significant a role in every pedagogical program of the Enlightenment. In order to fulfill properly his place in creation, man must above all open his eyes to it; he must conceive himself to be part of nature and yet, by his final purpose, raised beyond it. Thus causal and teleological considerations are directly intertwined here. The way in which Kant, in the preface to the *Universal Natural History and Theory of the Heavens*, tries to reconcile the two with each other, striving to discover in the universal mechanical lawfulness of the cosmos itself the proof of its divine origin, does not as yet contain any original tendencies in comparison with the general outlook of the eighteenth century. The basic ideas of Leibniz's philos-

15. (II, 326) (*Ak.* II, 312).

ophy are merely repeated, namely, that the seamless causal order of everything is itself the highest and fully valid proof of its inner "harmony" and of its intellectual and moral "purposiveness." The world is full of miracles, but "miracles of reason": for the proof and seal of the divinity of being lies not in exceptions from the rules of nature, but in the universality and the inviolable validity of these laws themselves. Wherever the natural science of that time is philosophically oriented and grounded, it clings to this conception, which recurs not only in the scholastic doctrine of the Wolffians, but also in French philosophy with d'Alembert and Maupertuis. Since Kant unselfconsciously assumes this form of the teleological proof, all his intellectual and spiritual endeavors cohere in an unbroken unity. There is no talk of a dualism between the world of the is and the world of the ought, between physics and ethics, but his reflection moves back and forth between the two realms, without any feelings on Kant's part of any sort of shift or methodological leap.

This reflective stance is characteristically expressed also in his mood and outlook on life. Kant described this period of his *Magisterjahre* as the most peaceful of his life, when he later looked back at it.[16] Of course he still labored under the pressure of financial need and under the excess of academic work that was imposed on him, but the marvelous mental elasticity of these youthful years easily and completely overcame all constraints of this kind. Although in the later period of Kant's life, especially in the time when he was constructing and expounding the critical philosophy, concentration of every power of thought and life on a single point is characteristic of him, here, instead, there still reigns a free surrender to life and to experience in all its breadth. Just as Kant worked experiential material of the most diverse kinds and origins into his studies and lectures, so he seeks in this period the manifold stimulation of social intercourse. "Thus," Rink says, "Kant in his early years spent almost every midday and evening outside his house in social activities, frequently taking part also in a card party and only getting home around midnight. If he was

16. See the letter to Lagarde dated March 25, 1790 (X, 16) (*Ak.* XI, 142).

not busy at meals, he ate in the inn at a table sought out by a number of cultured people."[17] Kant gave himself to this mode of life in such an easy and relaxed way that even the most meticulous psychological observer among his intimates was occasionally puzzled about him; in 1764 Hamann says that Kant carries in his head a host of greater and lesser works, which he however probably will never finish in the "whirl of social distraction" in which he is now tossed.[18]

Kant's teaching at this time was also marked by this cosmopolitan urbanity, appropriate to the standards he had set for himself. His treatment of physical geography—"not with that completeness and philosophical exactitude in each part which is a matter for physics and natural history, but with the rational curiosity of a traveler who everywhere seeks out what is noteworthy, peculiar, and beautiful, collates his collection of observations, and reflects on its design"[19]—is not surprising because of the popular, encyclopedic character he gave to this discipline: he himself even declares about the teaching of the abstract scholarly disciplines that they ought to form in the hearer "first the man of *understanding*, then the man of *reason*," and only in the end the *learned* man. This inversion of the customary manner of instruction seems to him unavoidable for philosophy in particular, for one cannot learn "philosophy" but only "how to philosophize." Logic itself, prior to its emergence as "critique of and preface to true learnedness," must be employed as critique of and preface to "sound understanding," "just as this latter on the one hand touches crude concepts and ignorance, on the other science and learning." Ethics, too, may not start with abstract and formal prescripts of obligation, but must always reflect historically and philosophically on what *does* happen before it points out what *should* happen.[20] Thus it is in general an ideal of comprehensive practical human wisdom at which Kant aims in his own growth as well as in his teaching. Like the

17. F. T. Rink, *Ansichten aus Immanuel Kants Leben* (Königsberg, 1805), pp. 80 f.

18. *Hamanns Schriften*, ed. F. Roth (Augsburg, 1821–43), vol. 3, p. 213.

19. "Proposal for and Announcement of a College of Physical Geography" (1757) (II, 3) (*Ak.* II, 1).

20. See the announcement of the arrangement of his lectures during the winter term, 1765–66 (II, 319–28) (*Ak.* II, 303–13).

lectures on physical geography in the beginning, the later lectures on anthropology pursued this goal. The special, deeper basis for the congenial facility Kant's philosophy achieved in this period lies in the general relationship set up here between "experience" and "thinking," between "knowledge" and "life." No inner tension and contrast yet exists between these two poles. Thinking itself and its systematization, as it is here understood, is nothing but experience refined, freed of superstition and prejudice, and rounded out and extended through the power of analogy. It does not strive beyond this form.

Nowhere does Kant stand closer to the ruling eighteenth-century ideal of "philosophy," to the ideal of "popular philosophy," than at this point. Even if he does express and present this line of thought in a more clever, lively, and vital way than its other champions do, still by and large he gave it no perceptibly novel turn. He also seems to still expect the solution to basic philosophical problems from the sifting and refining of the concepts of common sense. In this sense, perhaps, his essay "Some Experimental Reflections about Optimism" ("Versuch einiger Betrachtungen über den Optimismus,") from the year 1759, aims to achieve a solution to the problem of the "best world," which however rather resembles a complete *petitio principii*. "If someone makes bold to assert," he says there, "that the Supreme Wisdom has preferred the worse to the best or that the highest Good has let itself love a lesser good rather than a greater one equally within its reach, I restrain myself no longer. One serves philosophy very ill if one uses it to overturn the principles of sound understanding and one does it little honor if one finds it necessary, in order to vanquish such efforts, to borrow their own weapons."[21]

Real radicalism is absent from his thinking and his life alike. This explains why Kant, even at a time when a complete change in his form of life and thought had been setting in for a long time, was still taken by those not close to him as the "worldly philosopher" whom they preferred to consult for decisions in questions of taste and style of life. Borowski tells us that his students were wont to ask of him,

---

21. "Versuch einiger Betrachtungen über den Optimismus" (II, 35 f.) (*Ak.* II, 27 ff.).

"straight from the shoulder," what they needed for life and for learning: they not only asked him, in 1759, for a course in "eloquence and German style," which Kant turned over to Borowski instead of doing himself, but they turned to him in 1764 also, at the funeral of a Königsberg professor, for help in "setting up the ceremonies."[22] Cultivated Königsberg society tried increasingly to draw him into its circle; "those who didn't even understand how to estimate his superiority," Rink remarks naively, "at least sought, each for himself, the honor of seeing so highly esteemed a man in his own circle of acquaintance."[23] Kant had a close personal relation with the officers of the Königsberg garrison, and for a long time ate almost every day with them; General von Meyer, a "clear mind," in particular liked it when the officers of his regiment were instructed by Kant in mathematics, physical geography, and fortification.[24] His connection with distinguished merchant families is well known, especially with the eccentric Green, the model for Hippel's *Clockwork Man (Der Mann nach der Uhr)*, and Green's crony Motherby. The most amiable traits of Kant's nature emerged in this friendship, which Kant's contemporaries loved to illustrate with a wealth of amusing anecdotes.[25] A noteworthy demonstration of the direction in which esteem for Kant was moving during his teaching years was eventually given even by the Prussian government, when, after the death of Professor Bock in 1764, it offered him the post of Professor of—Poetry, a post along with which went that of censor of all poems for official occasions and the obligation of composing German and Latin *carmina* for all academic celebrations.[26] If Kant had not, despite the hardships of his external circumstances (he shortly thereafter, when applying for the position

22. Borowski, *Darstellung des Lebens und Charakters Immanuel Kants*, pp. 189 f.; Hamann to Lindner, Easter Monday, 1764.

23. Rink, *Ansichten aus Immanuel Kants Leben*, p. 80.

24. Ibid., p. 32; Hamann to Lindner, February 1, 1764; Rudolf Reicke, *Kantiana* (Königsberg, 1860), p. 11.

25. On the friendship with Green and Motherby, cf. Jachmann, *Immanuel Kant*, Eighth Letter, pp. 75 ff.

26. The official acts in this connection are published in Friedrich Wilhelm Schubert's biography of Kant, *Sämmtliche Werke*, ed. K. Rosenkranz and F. W. Schubert (Leipzig, 1842), pp. 49 ff.

of a sublibrarian paying sixty-two dollars a year, spoke of his "very precarious subsistence at the local academy"),[27] possessed the resolution to resist this way of obtaining a livelihood, he would not have been spared the fate of acting in Königsberg as the successor to Johann Valentin Pietsch, Gottsched's renowned teacher.

Nonetheless it was just at this time that Kant's intellectual evolution took the path that in the end reversed his whole style of thought and life. The Berlin Academy of Sciences had proposed, for the year 1763, a topic that immediately attracted the attention of the entire German philosophical world. "Are the metaphysical sciences," it asked, "amenable to the same certainty as the mathematical?" Almost all the leading German thinkers—Lambert, Tetens, and Mendelssohn in particular, besides Kant—tried their hand at solving this problem. For the others it afforded them at most the chance to publicize and argue for the settled view they had already formed on the theme, through established opinion or by their own inquiries. For Kant, on the contrary, working out this task was the starting point for a movement of thought that continually advanced and gathered strength. The problem did not arise in the reply to the question he sent to the Academy but only really took hold of him after he had finished his answer. Outwardly, the circle of his interests and efforts seems hardly altered by this. Questions of natural science, psychology, and anthropology keep their grip on his thoughts,[28] and if the center of gravity of those reflections shifts gradually over from outer experience toward inner experience, only their object, not their principle, has changed. The essential novelty lies in the fact that now whenever Kant attends to a given subject, he is never occupied with it alone, but requires a justification of the essence of the *type of cognition* through which we are aware of it and which makes it knowable.

The *Universal Natural History and Theory of the Heavens* was far

---

27. To Friedrich II, October 24, 1765 (IX, 40) (*Ak.* X, 46).

28. Cf. "Versuch über die Krankheiten des Kopfes" ["Essay on Diseases of the Brain"], written in 1764 (II, 301 ff.) (*Ak.* II, 257 ff.); the review of Pietro Moscati's book *Von dem körperlichen wesentlichen Unterschiede zwischen der Struktur der Thiere und der Menschen* [*The Essential Physical Difference between the Structure of Animals and Men*] (Göttingen, 1771), (II, 437 ff.) (*Ak.* II, 421 ff.).

removed from this kind of analysis of the cognitive modes. It applied indiscriminately the procedures of scientific induction, of mathematical measurement and computation, and, finally, those of metaphysical thinking. The structure of the material world and the universal laws of motion that hold in it are made into the basis for a proof of God's existence, and Kant's mind leaps straight from a calculation of the different densities of the planets to speculation on the physical and mental differences of their inhabitants and to the prospects for immortality.[29] Since causal and teleological insights are so completely merged here, intuition of nature leads straight to a doctrine of the moral vocation of man, which then finds its conclusive expression in certain metaphysical propositions and requirements. "If one has satisfied his mind with such reflections," Kant concludes the *Universal Natural History and Theory of the Heavens*, "the contemplation of a starry heaven on a pleasant night affords a kind of enjoyment which is felt only by noble souls. Out of the universal stillness of Nature and the repose of the senses, the immortal soul's secret capacity for knowledge speaks an unnamed language and gives us implicit concepts which can be felt but not described. If there are among the thinking creatures of this planet base beings who, heedless of all the charms whereby so vast an object can allure them, are nevertheless able to linger firmly in the service of vanity, how unfortunate is this globe that it can produce such miserable beings! How fortunate it is, on the other hand, that amid all the constraints we must accept a way is opened to a happiness and sublimity which is exalted infinitely beyond the excellences attainable by the most advantageous course of Nature in every body in the universe."[30]

But the mind of a Kant could not dally with concepts that let themselves be "felt but not described." Where he set and acknowledged limits to conceptualizing, he demanded the proof and foundation of this "inconceivability." The need to translate the unnameable language of feeling into the precise and clear tongue of the understanding, and to make the "secret capacity for knowledge" itself man-

29. See the appendix to the *Universal Natural History and Theory of the Heavens* (I, 353 ff.) (*Ak.* I, 349 ff.).

30. Ibid. (I, 369 f.) (*Ak.* I, 367 f.).

ifest and lucid, became ever more imperative. Is the method of metaphysics—this is how the question must now be posed—interchangeable with that of mathematics and empirical science, or is there a fundamental opposition between them? And if the latter should be the case, have we in general any guarantee that thinking, purely logical concepts and logical deduction, is able to express fully the structure of "reality"? The final solution to this question still lies in the distant future for Kant, but having now been posed, it signifies a whole new orientation for the further evolution of his system.

2. The Problem of Metaphysical Method

The first step toward the gradual crumbling of the foundations on which the edifice of the *Universal Natural History and Theory of the Heavens* is raised lay in the direction of the problem of teleology. The basic intuitions that governed Kant as he worked out his thoughts on cosmology are through and through optimistic in nature. It is the Leibnizian system of "harmony" that Kant believes he recognizes in the form of Newtonian physics and mechanics. A secret plan underlies the mechanistic rise and fall of worlds, a plan we are unable to follow in detail, to be sure, but of which we are nonetheless certain that it will always lead the whole universe ever closer to its supreme goal: steadily increasing perfection. Even where this conviction is decked out in the traditional form of the teleological proof of God's existence, Kant makes no opposition. "I recognize the great value," he expressly remarks in the preface to the *Universal Natural History and Theory of the Heavens*, "of those proofs which are drawn from the beauty and perfect arrangement of the universe to establish the existence of a Supremely Wise Creator; and I hold that whoever does not obstinately resist all conviction must be won by those irrefutable reasons. But I assert that the defenders of religion, by using these proofs in a bad way, perpetuate the conflict with the advocates of Naturalism by presenting them unnecessarily with a weak side of their position."[31]

31. [Ibid. (I, 224) (*Ak.* I, 222).]

This weak side lies in confusing "material" and "formal" teleology, inner "purposiveness" and outward "intention." Not in every case where we observe the harmony of the parts within the whole and their cooperation toward a common end do we have the right to assume that that sort of agreement is only brought about through the artfulness of a mind standing outside and above the parts. For it might very well be that the nature of the object itself necessarily leads to such a harmony, that the original unity of a formative principle which unfolds itself little by little in a manifold of effects determines unaided such an internal organization of the details. We find a composition of this latter sort not only in all organic structures, but even in the pure forms through which the logical and geometrical lawfulness of space is known by us: for here a wealth of novel and surprising consequences flows from some kind of individual basic determination or relation, held together as though through a supreme "plan" and adapted to the solution of a wide variety of tasks.

Chiefly by dint of this distinction of formal and material, external and internal purposiveness, Kant is enabled to keep the idea of an end clear of any confusion with the trivial conception of utility. The *Universal Natural History and Theory of the Heavens* has already denounced this confusion and fought it with all the weapons of satire and mockery. Voltaire's *Candide*, which Kant later makes reference to,[32] could not in this regard teach him anything new. In the basic plan of nature and "providence" every creature, however insignificant, is on a par with man. For the infinity of creation embraces in itself as equally necessary all creatures which its superabundant riches bring forth: "From the most sublime sort of thinking beings to the humblest insect, no member is indifferent to her; and none can be taken away without rupturing the beauty of the whole, which consists in this interconnection."[33]

Yet it is more a personal reaction than a strict logical and systematic examination that Kant applies to the popular philosophical way of

32. See "The Only Possible Basis of Proof for a Demonstration of God's Existence," sect. II, Sixth Reflection, §4 (II, 138) (*Ak.* II, 131), and *Dreams of a Spirit-Seer*, pt. 2, chap. 3 (II, 390) (*Ak.* II, 373).
33. *Universal Natural History*, pt. 3 (I, 355 f.) (*Ak.* I, 354).

regarding teleology. Only gradually is keener critical analysis of the concepts and demonstrations brought to bear, probably receiving in this instance its first decisive impulse from outside. Much as Goethe, when a seven-year-old boy, was gripped by the "extraordinary event" of the Lisbon earthquake and for the first time felt moved to deeper spiritual reflection, and as the conflict between Rousseau and Voltaire over the "best of all possible worlds" was set ablaze by this same event, Kant likewise saw himself here summoned to the renunciation of intellectual justification. He tried to fulfill his obligation to inform and illuminate the public in three essays which he published in 1756, partly in the *Wochentliche Königsbergische Frag- und Anzeigungs-Nachrichten*, and partly separately,[34] but this did not silence the problem so far as he himself was concerned. "Some Experimental Reflections about Optimism" of 1759, which is no more than a hastily composed, academic occasional piece,[35] was also insufficient to settle it.

He took up the question yet again, four years later, in "The Only Possible Basis of Proof for a Demonstration of God's Existence" (Einzig möglichen Beweisgrund zu einer Demonstration des Daseins Gottes"), in order to present his view of teleology, in both the positive and the negative senses, systematically and exhaustively, and to give it a foundation. Here he finds the proof for the existence of the divine being, customarily drawn from the purposive arrangement of the world, largely proportioned "alike to the worth as to the weakness of human understanding." But this latter point he raises more acutely than before, and points out the fundamental defect clinging to the whole methodology of physico-teleology. The conviction that flows from it may be "exceedingly sensory and hence very lively and gripping and both accessible and comprehensible to the most ordinary understanding," but at no point can it stand up to the strict requirements of conceptual knowledge. For even supposing it were proved that order arose from disorder, a "cosmos" from "chaos," by specific divine actions, that primordial being which ought to be thought as infinite and all-sufficient will precisely thereby labor under a basic

34. See I, 427 ff., 439 ff., 475 ff. (*Ak.* I, 417 ff., 429, ff., 463 ff.).

35. There is information about the origin of this piece in a letter of Kant's to Lindner dated October 28, 1759 (IX, 16).

limitation laid on it from outside. If crude matter is the opponent which this being has to overcome and it displays its goodness and wisdom only in that victory, then if the proof is not to lose all its meaning and effectiveness this matter has to be recognized as something in itself, as a given stuff with which the purposeful power must occupy itself. Hence this procedure can only serve "to prove an originator of the connections and artful composition of the world, but not of matter itself and the creation of the elements of the universe." God will by this route always be shown only as master craftsman, not as creator of the world; the order and formation of matter appears as the work attributable to Him, but not its generation.

In this way that very idea of purposiveness of the world which is supposed to be established is put in extreme jeopardy. For there now enters into the world a basic dualism which, no matter how hard one may try to conceal it, is ultimately ineradicable. The shaping of the sheer stuff of being by intentional will is never absolute, but always something relative and conditioned: there is, in this mode of intuition, at least a definite substrate of being which as such does not carry the form of reason in itself but rather is opposed to it. The gap in the physico-theological proof is at this point clearly visible; it can be plugged only if we succeed in showing that what we have assumed to be the real and independent "essence" of matter and from which we can deduce its universal laws of motion is not alien to reason's regulation but rather is an expression and a particular manifestation of these very rules.[36]

This conception of the task now, however, transforms for Kant the whole aim and form of the proof of the existence of God. For now we no longer work from the configuration of the actual to discover in it testimony to a supreme will, which formed it according to its own wishes, but we take our stand on the validity of the highest truths and seek to win from them a passage to certitude concerning an absolute being. It is not in the realm of empirical, contingent things but in the realm of necessary laws, not in the territory of existence but in that of

36. On the whole of this, cf. "The Only Possible Basis of Proof," sect. II, Fifth and Sixth Reflections (II, 122–44) (*Ak.* II, 116–37).

sheer "possibilities," that we shall henceforth have to choose our starting point. In putting the problem in this way, Kant is indeed aware that he has overstepped the bounds of the popular mode of expounding philosophical ideas that he had followed in his writings up to this time. "I might also be fearful," he remarks, "of offending the sensibilities of those who complain most of all about dryness. But without being hampered by this charge, I must this time ask their indulgence on this score. For although I find as distasteful as anyone else the oversubtle wisdom of those who inflate, distill, and refine definite and useful concepts in their logical smelting shops until they burn away in vapors and volatile salts, yet the object of consideration before me is of a kind which one must either abandon totally the hope of demonstrating with certainty or else endure the analysis of its concepts into their atoms."[37] The process of abstraction cannot stop before it has pressed on to the pure and simple concept of "existence" on the one hand and the pure and simple concept of logical "possibility" on the other.

With this formulation of the opposition, Kant at the same time points back to the historical origin of the problem, which underlies it here. "The Only Possible Basis of Proof" uses the language of Leibnizian philosophy throughout. But in it the distinction between the actual and the possible goes back to the more profound methodological distinction between "contingent" and "necessary" knowledge, between "truths of fact" and "truths of reason." The latter, to which belong all propositions of logic and mathematics, are independent of the state of transient existing things, for they do not express the particular existent, occurring once, here and now, in a specific locus in space and at a determinate point of time, but rather they signify relations that are valid completely universally and are binding on any given content. That $7 + 5 = 12$, that the angle inscribed in a semicircle is a right angle, are "eternal truths," which do not depend on the nature of spatiotemporal, individual *things*, and which thus remain true even if there were no things of those sorts, even if there were no

---

37. "The Only Possible Basis of Proof," sect. I, First Reflection, §2 (II, 79) (*Ak.* II, 74-75).

matter and no physical world. In logic, in pure geometry and number science, and moreover in the principles of the pure theory of motion, it is thus a matter of cognitions that express a purely ideal dependence between substances in general, not of a connection between determinate empirical, actual objects or events. If we translate this logical insight into the terminology of Leibnizian metaphysics, it can be said that propositions of the first class, the pure truths of reason, are valid for all possible worlds that are comprehended in the divine understanding, while the mere truths of fact pertain only to specification of the one actual world that has been lifted out of this sphere of general possibilities by an act of the divine will and "permitted" actual existence.

From this point on, the particular form that Kant gives to the problem of the proof of God's existence is fully comprehensible. In the place of the "moral" dependence of things on God, which is the customary relation in this proof, he wishes to put "nonmoral" (or better, "extramoral") dependency, that is to say, he does not wish to seem to be drawing his arguments from the realm of particular phenomena, which the reference to a specific divine act of will seems to involve, but to take his stand on universal and necessary relations, which as such are irrefragable norms for every finite and infinite understanding alike.[38] He does not want to proceed from "things" as an already given order, but rather to go back to the universal possibilities that are the presupposition for the state of all ideal truths and hence mediately for the state of everything real as well. Therefore the proof that Kant attempts bears a thoroughly aprioristic character, for it follows not from the contingent, merely factual existence of a particular thing or even from the whole array of particular empirical things, but from an interconnection of concepts that, like the concepts of geometry and arithmetic, compose an unchanging, systematic structure, free of all arbitrariness.[39] Is it possible, Kant's question is now stated, to arrive at certainty concerning an absolute existent— that is, as will appear, at certainty about God—when on our part

38. Cf. ibid., sect. II, Second Reflection (II, 106) (*Ak.* II, 100).
39. Ibid., sect. I, conclusion (II, 96) (*Ak.* II, 90).

nothing but the certainty of ideal truths or "universal possibilities" is presupposed? Is God certain, not insofar as another kind of thing is certain or a specific contingent sequence of events is actual, but only insofar as the true and the false are differentiated, insofar as there are rules of any kind under which a correspondence between specific concepts holds apodictically while it is denied between others, equally evidently and necessarily?

Kant now believes that he can in fact give an affirmative answer to this latter question. For, he infers, if there were no absolute existent whatsoever, there could be no ideal relations, no agreement or contradiction between pure concepts. It was generally considered that such relations are in no way adequately grounded and certified by the purely formal unity expressed in the logical principle of identity and contradiction, but that they necessarily presuppose certain material conditions of thought. A rectangle is not a circle: of that I am certain by virtue of the principle of contradiction; but that there exist in general figures such as rectangle and circle, and that some kind of qualitative differentiation between substances can be made, I am taught not by the wholly general and formal logical principle, but by that specific lawful order which I designate by the name "space." If there were no such determinate things like space and the shapes in it, number and its differences, motion and its diversities of magnitude and direction—in other words, if these could not be distinguished from one another and contrasted simply as conceptual substances— then matter would also dwindle to "potentiality," and then it would be impossible not only to assert any empirical entity but even to assert any true proposition. Thought would thus be annihilated, not because its foundations are formally contradictory but because no data would be given to it any longer and hence in general nothing more would be posited to which it could be opposed. For possibility as such drops away, "not only if an internal contradiction is encountered as the logic of impossibility, but also if there is nothing material, no datum to think. For then nothing thinkable is given; but everything possible is something which can be thought and to which logical relationship according to the principle of contradiction applies"—not immediately but by way of this principle. And herein lies the nerve of

Kant's proof: it must be shown that in fact by the cancellation not only this or that existent, but all existents whatsoever and all "matter" of thought, in the sense just specified, would be destroyed. "If all existence is canceled out, nothing whatsoever is posited, in general nothing at all is given, no material for anything whatsoever thinkable, and all possibility falls away completely. There is, to be sure, no inner contradiction in the denial of all existence. For that would require something to be simultaneously asserted and canceled; here, however, nothing at all is posited, so one can not in fact say that this cancellation contains a self-contradiction. But that some sort of possibility exists and yet nothing actual, is self-contradictory, because if nothing exists, nothing is given which would be thinkable, and we are at odds with ourselves if we still want something to be possible."[40]

Yet it seems that in fact that Kantian proof does not end with this, for even if the foregoing argument is regarded as conclusive, it has in any event only shown that "something," some sort of substance in general, must exist absolutely and necessarily, but not that this substance is "God." But this portion of Kant's conclusion is given relatively briefly. If we are sure of an absolutely necessary existence in general, it can be demonstrated that this existence must be unique and simple, unchanging and eternal, that it comprises all reality in itself and that it must be of a purely spiritual nature—in short, that we must attribute to it all those characteristics which we normally combine in the name and concept of God.[41] Accordingly, the movement here does not *proceed from* the concept of God in order to exhibit in it the predicate of existence together with other predicates, since "existence" does not designate a conceptual predicate that might also belong to another thing, but comprises the simple and not further analyzable "absolute positing" of a thing.[42] The direction of proof is rather the reverse: when absolute being is attained and guaranteed, the effort is then to derive its determinations, its essential "what," more closely, and it is thus discovered and demonstrated that its nature exhibits all the characteristics that comprise the distinctive

40. Ibid., sect. I, Second Reflection, §2 (II, 82 f.) (*Ak.* II, 78).
41. Ibid., sect. I, Third Reflection (II, 86–95) (*Ak.* II, 81–87).
42. Ibid., sect. I, First Reflection (II, 76 ff.) (*Ak.* II, 72 ff.).

content of our concept of God. Thus the ontological argument is firmly adhered to, and the cosmological and the physico-theological proofs are referred back to it.

However, an alteration in ontological thinking occurs, which promises its complete supersession in the future. While the ontological proof, in the form given it by Anselm of Canterbury and revived by Descartes, starts with the concept of the most complete being so as to deduce its existence, while it infers "existence" synthetically from "essence," Kant begins instead with pure ideal possibilities, with the system of eternal truths as such, in order then to show by progressive analysis that an absolute being must be required as the condition of the possibility of this system. We have before us essentially a prelude to the transcendental method to come, since the ultimate justification for positing existence in an absolute sense resides in the fact that without this assertion the possibility of knowledge is inconceivable. Of course, however, judged from the standpoint of the later critical system all "positings" achieved by this route are relative, not absolute; they are restricted, both as to their validity and as to their application, to experience, which they make possible.

We can, though, for the time being abandon the more exact and detailed evaluation of the fundamental problem of "The Only Possible Basis of Proof," especially since Kant's own ongoing development of this problem will of itself bring ever greater clarity and definiteness. If we pause at the point to which this development has led us, the difference between "The Only Possible Basis of Proof" and all of Kant's previous writings is revealed primarily in the fact that it belongs to a higher stage of reflection and critical self-consciousness. It now no longer suffices for Kant to produce observations and proofs for the specific object he is considering, but at the same time he questions their logical origin and the specific sort of truth that belongs to them. Kant was girded and armed like no other thinker of this era to answer the question set by the Berlin Academy the year before. In fact, he did not seem directly stimulated to undertake the task by the announcement of the prize competition itself, but rather to have felt moved to it only after completing "The Only Possible Basis of Proof," by reason of the essential link he discovered between the problem of this essay and the Academy's question.[43] "It is desired to know," the question went, "whether metaphysical truths in general and the first principles of *Theologia naturalis* and of morals in particular are susceptible of clear and evident proofs like those of geometrical truths, and if they are not susceptible of the aforesaid proofs, what the peculiar nature of their certainty is, to what degree their stated certainty can be brought, and whether this degree is sufficient for complete conviction."

The decision on the essays submitted was reached in the session of the Academy in May, 1763. First prize was awarded to the treatise by Moses Mendelssohn, but it was expressly declared that Kant's essay "had come as closely as possible" to being the prize work "and merited the highest praise." Both papers, Kant's and Mendelssohn's, appeared together in the proceedings of the Academy.[44] A special historical irony was that Formey, as the permanent secretary of the Berlin Academy, was the first to congratulate Kant on his success in a letter dated July, 1763. This scientific eclectic owed his philosophical prestige to popularization of the Wolffian system, which he had attempted in a multivolumed, monotonous, and verbose work.[45] Had he been capable of appreciating the substance of Kant's treatise, he would necessarily have had a premonition that the paper which he printed on behalf of the Academy contained the seed of a revolution in philosophy, by which the "inflated pretentiousness of whole volumes of insights" of dogmatic metaphysics[46] would one day be destroyed.

So far as Kant was concerned, he was conscious from the start of

---

43. The Academy's announcement was published in June, 1761, while Kant set to work on the topic only at the end of 1762, shortly before the deadline for submission. He himself calls his treatise a "hastily composed work" (II, 322 [*Ak.* II, 308]; cf. also II, 202 [*Ak.* II, 301]). "The Only Possible Basis of Proof" appeared at the end of December, 1762; it was in Hamann's hands on December 21, as can be inferred from the latter's letter to Nicolai dated that day. The manuscript of the essay was therefore probably completed in the autumn of 1762 at the latest. Cf. the comments of Kurd Lasswitz and Paul Menzer in the Academy edition of Kant's works, vol. 2, pp. 470, 492 ff. See also Adolf von Harnack, *Geschichte der Königlich preussischen Akademie der Wissenschaften* (Berlin, 1901), p. 315.

44. Cf. II, 475 (*Ak.* II, 494).

45. Jean Henri Samuel Formey, *La belle Wolffienne*, (The Hague, 1741–53).

46. Cf. Kant's letter to Mendelssohn, April 8, 1766 (IX, 55) (*Ak.* X, 66).

what was at stake: "The question posed," his exposition begins, "is of the sort that, if it is properly solved higher philosophy will have to take on a definite form. If the method by which the utmost certainty in this sort of knowledge can be attained is established, and the nature of this conviction is well understood, an unchangeable methodological rule will necessarily unite thoughtful minds in similar endeavors, in the place of the everlasting instability of opinions and schools; just as Newton's method in the natural sciences transformed the confusion of physical hypotheses into a sure procedure guided by experience and geometry."

But what was the crucial idea by which Newton effected this revolution? What differentiates the physical hypotheses current before him from the rules and laws which he established? If we ask this question, we see that the manner in which the universal is related to the particular and united with it in modern mathematical physics has turned into something quite other than what it was in the speculative physics of Aristotle and the Middle Ages. Galileo and Newton do not begin with the general "concept" of gravity so as to "explain" the phenomena of weight; they do not infer from the essence and the nature of matter and motion what must occur in freely falling bodies; they occupy themselves first of all in ascertaining the data of the problem, as presented by experience. Fall toward the earth's center, projectile motion, the motion of the moon around the earth, ultimately the revolving of the planets around the sun in elliptical orbits: all these are phenomena which are examined at the outset and defined purely quantitatively. Only then do they ask the question whether this whole complex of facts which has been ascertained cannot be brought under a common concept, that is, whether there is not a mathematical relation, an analytic function, which contains and expresses all those particular relations. In other words, here one does not proceed from a "force" which is conceived or imagined, deducing specific motions from it (as, for instance, in the Aristotelian system the physics of falling bodies is "explained" by a natural striving that draws each part of matter to its "natural place"), but what we call "weight" is here but another way of expressing and unifying known and measurable relations of magnitude.

If we now apply what this relation tells us to metaphysics, we see that metaphysics is concerned with a different realm of facts from that of mathematical physics. For its object is not outer but inner experience; not bodies and their motions, but knowledge, acts of will, feelings, and inclinations make up its basic theme. The type of knowledge, however, is neither determined nor altered by this difference in the object. Here too it is solely a matter of analyzing given complexes of experience into simple basic relations, stopping with these as the ultimate data that cannot be traced further back. Here it is equally true that determinations enter into these data which, because they are unanalyzable into simpler parts, are not further susceptible of any scholastic definition (by *genus proximum* and *differentia specifica*). For there is a kind of determinacy and evidence—and here it occurs in basic concepts and relations—which cannot be increased by a logical definition in this sense, but only muddled. "Augustine says: I know very well what time is, but when someone asks me, I do not know." And thus in philosophy one can often recognize an object clearly and certainly, and derive sure conclusions from it, before possessing its definition, indeed even if one makes no effort to provide it. "I can be immediately certain of various predicates of any thing, even though I do not know it well enough to give the explicitly determined concept of it, that is to say, the definition. If I never explained what a desire is, I would still be able to say with surety that every desire presupposes a representation of what is desired, that this representation is an anticipation of the future, that the feeling of pleasure is connected with it, etc. Everyone is always aware of all this in the immediate consciousness of desire. From similar comparative observations one could probably at last arrive at the definition of desire. But as long as what is sought can be inferred from some immediately certain qualities of the thing itself, without a definition, it is needless to attempt so delicate an undertaking."[47] Thus in the natural sciences we no longer begin with the explication of the essence of force, but what we call "force" is at most the final analytic expression for known, measured relations of motions; so also the logical essence about which metaphysics inquires can only constitute the terminus of the inquiry, not its start.

47. "Inquiry into the Distinctness of the Principles of Natural Theology and Morals," Second Observation (II, 184) (*Ak.* II, 284).

Yet every compendium of metaphysics whatsoever reveals how strongly the conventional course of inquiry, hallowed by usage and tradition, contradicts this prescription. The account of what is most universal—here Alexander Baumgarten's *Metaphysica*, on which Kant customarily based his lectures, is particularly typical—the definitions of being, of essence, of substance, of cause or effect, and of appetite are here placed at the head, and the attempt is made to derive the particular by combining these definitions. But if one looks more closely at this supposed deduction, one recognizes that in truth it tacitly presupposes the knowledge of the particular which it claims to deduce, and makes use of it, so that the ostensible philosophical grounding is merely circular. If we want to achieve actual clarity as to what metaphysics is or is not suited to, only a return to the humbler but more honest experience of physics can be of assistance. It follows from this that in both instances we do not try to expand the content of our knowledge at any price, but that we strictly observe the boundaries of what is known and unknown, what is given and what is sought, and that neither we nor others transgress them. We arrive at "being" in both cases alike only through the painstaking and continuous analysis of appearances; in this we have to resign ourselves to the fact that, since—at least in the present state of metaphysics—we can never claim with certainty the completion of this analysis, all our determination of being in this realm is nothing absolute, but rather is relative and preliminary. "The genuine method of metaphysics," as the Prize Essay concisely and expressively summarizes these observations, "is fundamentally the same as that which Newton introduced into natural science and which had so many fruitful consequences. There it is said that one should seek out the rules by which certain phenomena proceed in Nature, by means of indubitable experiences, and if need be, with the aid of geometry. Even if one has no insight into their ultimate foundation in bodies, it is still certain that they act according to this law, and the complex data of Nature are explained when it is clearly shown how they are contained under these well-demonstrated rules. Similarly in metaphysics: seek out by secure inner experience, that is, immediately evident consciousness, those properties which unquestionably lie in the concept of any sort of universal state, and if you do not know the whole essence of the matter, you can still securely make use of them to infer much about the thing."[48]

There is one preeminent respect in which Kant now parts company both with conventional metaphysics and with the procedure he himself had initially employed. Metaphysics can discover nothing; it can only make plain the pure fundamental interconnections in experience. It brings clarity and intelligibility into what is given to us as an obscure and complex totality, makes its structure transparent to us. But of its own authority it adds no substantive factor whatsoever. Kant's thought in that previous period, wherein the *Universal Natural History and Theory of the Heavens* found expression, held that metaphysics stood squarely on the soil of experience, but where experiential data were insufficient, it did not hesitate to round out and go beyond what is empirically given by the synthetic power of imagination and inference. It started with the world, with the cosmos of the natural scientist, but it was led on, in a continuous and imperceptible line, to hypotheses about the First Being, the teleology of the world, and the survival and immortality of the human soul.

Now Kant becomes aware of just how problematical this whole mode of thinking is. Can metaphysics, he asks, proceed synthetically and constructively? And the instant the question is posed this clearly, it is equally clearly answered in the negative. For synthesis has a place where the concerns are the self-created products of the understanding, which therefore are subordinate to the law of the understanding purely and exclusively.

In this sense mathematics can and must above all pursue pure geometry synthetically, for the figures it treats only arise in and together with the act of construction. They are not abstractions from something given physically and they would retain their significance and truth even if nothing physical, nothing actually material, existed. What a circle or a triangle "is" exists only through the power of the intellectual and intuitive act in which we bring them into being by a composition of separate spatial elements, and there is not a single attribute of these forms, no determinant added from elsewhere, that

48. Ibid. (II, 186) (*Ak.* II, 286). For more on the historical connection of these statements with the methodology of Newton and his school, see *Das Erkenntnisproblem*, II, 402 ff., 590.

is not contained in this basic act and completely deducible from it. "A cone may elsewhere mean what it will; in mathematics it arises from the arbitrary representation of a right triangle which is rotated on one of its sides. The definition obviously originates, both here and in all other cases, through the synthesis."

It is clearly different with the concepts and definitions of philosophy. In mathematics, as has been shown, the specific object that is to be defined, such as an ellipse or a parabola, does not precede the genetic construction of the figure but instead arises from it; in contrast, metaphysics is confined from the outset to a definite, fixed material that is given to it. For it is not purely ideal determinations that it proposes to unfold to our minds, but the properties and relations of the "real." It has to create its object, therefore, no more than physics does, but it grasps only the actual nature of the object. It does not describe its object in the sense in which the geometer describes a certain figure, that is, by showing its construction, but rather it can only circumscribe it in the sense that it selects from it some distinctive characteristic and comprehends that in abstraction. A metaphysical concept obtains its relative validity only by the completeness of this relation to the "given" of inner and outer experience. Metaphysical thinking is not in the least entitled to be an invention; it is not prospective as is geometry, in which new conclusions are successively formed from an original definition, but rather retrospective, so that given a state of affairs it seeks out the conditions from which that state results; for a total phenomenon it seeks the possible "grounds of explanation."[49] These explanatory grounds are only hypothetical, but they become certain in proportion to the possibility of their embracing the totality of known appearances, and through them exhibiting it as a unity that is lawful and determinate. There is no doubt in Kant's mind that in the conception and execution of metaphysics to date this task has not been performed at all: "Metaphysics is without doubt the most difficult of all human inquiries; but no metaphysics has even been written."[50]

And in fact none could be written, so long as the tool available to

49. For the whole discussion, see the Prize Essay, First Observation, §§1 and 3 (II, 176 ff.) (*Ak.* II, 276 ff.).

50. Ibid., First Observation, §4 (II, 183) (*Ak.* II, 283).

thought for the task was the conventional method of logical deduction customary in school philosophy. For the means this procedure essentially, and moreover exclusively, uses is the syllogism: the world as known and conceived is validated when it is analyzed into a chain of rational conclusions. In this sense Wolff, in textbooks regarded as classics in his day, had developed his "rational thoughts" concerning God, the world and the soul, justice and the state and society, the activities of nature and the coherence of the life of the mind, in short, "concerning everything universally." Kant appreciated the methodical strictness and sobriety that imbues these works, and even at the height of his critical system he defended them against the objections by eclectic popular and fashionable philosophy. In the preface to the second edition of the *Critique of Pure Reason* Wolff is extolled as the "awakener of the spirit of thoroughness which is not extinct in Germany," because by the orderly establishment of principles, the clear definition of concepts, and by his avoidance of daring leaps in his inferences, he first tried to lead metaphysics into the sure path of a science.[51] Nonetheless, in Kant's whole philosophical development no indication can be found that he ever was intellectually dependent on the Wolffian system, as was the case with Mendelssohn and Sulzer. The artful technique of syllogistic proof never dazzled him, and in one of his own writings he attempted in 1762 to expose the "false sophistry" latent in it.[52]

More profound than this formal discussion is the charge that Kant now draws from his new conception of the tasks of metaphysics. The syllogistic procedure is "synthetic" in the specific sense given this term in the Prize Essay "Inquiry into the Distinctness of the Principles of Natural Theology and Morals" ("Über die Deutlichkeit der Grundsätze der natürlichen Theologie und Moral"). It moves from premises to conclusions, from general concepts and definitions laid down at the beginning to particular determinations. Yet, does such a cognitive procedure correspond to the one which, as we have seen, is

51. B xxxvi (III, 28 f.).

52. "Die falsche Spitzfindigkeit der vier syllogistischen Figuren erwiesen" ["The False Subtlety of the Four Syllogistic Figures Demonstrated"]. (See II, 49 ff.) (*Ak.* II, 45 ff.).

prescribed for us in every inquiry into what is real? Further, the principles on which all logical deductive procedure rests are the principle of identity and that of contradiction—the former, as Kant shows in a logical paper of 1755, the *Nova dilucidatio,* is the highest principle for all affirmative judgments, the latter for all negative ones.[53] Every inference aims at nothing but the identity of two terms, *A* and *B*; where this is not immediately obvious, it is shown mediately by inserting a series of concepts. The system of things and events, according to the basic principles of rationalism, is to be presented thus as an ever more exact and precise system of premises and conclusions. In this view of the task of philosophy, Wolff unmistakably goes back to Leibniz, but in the further elaboration of his system he erased the delicate methodological boundary that existed for the latter between the principle of contradiction and the principle of sufficient reason. According to Leibniz, the first of these is the principle of the necessary, the second that of contingent truths; the former gives rise to the propositions of logic and mathematics, while the latter is responsible specifically for the propositions of physics. Within the Wolffian scholastic system, however, the uniformity of the schema of proof constantly pushes toward uniformity among the principles themselves. Thus, the effort to overcome the separation between the material content of knowledge and the principles of knowledge dominates throughout, so that the attempt is to reduce them to the logical principle of identity and prove them from it. In this sense Wolff essayed a proof of the "principle of a ground," which was in fact circular: if there were something without a ground, he reasoned, then nothing must be the ground of something, which is self-contradictory. He even tried to deduce the necessity of the spatial order of appearances in this way, purely from the validity of the supreme logical principle: what we think as different from us, the inference ran, we must think as existing outside us, thus as spatially separated from us. The "other than us," *praeter nos,* was here directly translated into an "outside us," *extra nos,* the abstract concept of diversity into the concrete, intuitive externality of space.

53. *Principiorum primorum cognitionis metaphysicae nova dilucidatio* [*A New Explanation of the First Principles of Metaphysical Knowledge*], sect. I, Proposition II (I, 393) (*Ak*. I, 389).

The flaw in this manner of thinking had not gone unnoticed in German academic philosophy. In his criticism Crusius, the most important of Wolff's opponents, lays the utmost emphasis on the fact that the principle of contradiction, as a purely formal principle, can of itself alone yield no specific and concrete knowledge, but that a set of original and underivable, but nevertheless certain, "material principles" is unconditionally necessary for that.[54] Kant took his final, decisive step in this direction in the treatise that was probably finished immediately after the composition of the Prize Essay,[55] the "Attempt to Introduce the Concept of Negative Magnitudes into Philosophy." Here the source of the sharp distinction between logical and real opposition is directly expressed. The former occurs where two predicates are related to each other as A and non-A, thus where the logical affirmation of the one implies the logical denial of the other. The result of this opposition is hence pure nothingness; if I try to think a man as learned and as unlearned at the same time and in the same respect, or a body as simultaneously in motion and at rest, this thought is shown to be completely empty and impossible.

Matters stand otherwise in all cases of real opposition, in those cases where, popularly speaking, it is a matter not of an opposition of conceptual characteristics but of an opposition of forces. The velocity that a freely falling body, unhindered by any external factors, possesses can be canceled by another one that is equal but opposite; the result is not, as in the first case, a logical contradiction, but that quite definite and characteristic physical state which we designate by the expression "rest" or "equilibrium." If in the first case, the attempt to unite A and non-A conceptually, the outcome was an absurdity, here it is a determinate and completely unambiguous magnitude, since the magnitude "zero" is no less definite than any other quantity signified by a positive or negative number. Thus the way in which diverse real

---

54. See *Das Erkenntnisproblem in der Philosophie und Wissenschaft der neueren Zeit*, 2d ed. (Berlin, 1911), vol. 2, pp. 527–34, 587 ff.; cf. what Kant says about Crusius in the Prize Essay, Third Observation, §3 (II, 194 ff.) (*Ak.* II, 293 ff.).

55. The presentation of the treatise is recorded in the proceedings of the Königsberg faculty of philosophy on June 3, 1763, while the Prize Essay was finished at the end of 1762.

causes determine each other and combine into a unified fact, a relation best seen in the parallelogram of motions or forces, is not at all equivalent to the relation holding between merely logical predicates and judgments. The "real ground" is an independent, qualitatively distinct relation, which is not only inexhaustible by the logical relation of ground to consequent, of *antecedens* to *consequens*, but is never expressible through it. Hence metaphysical method is in the last analysis different from syllogistic, for metaphysics, in the sense Kant has given it, is the doctrine of real grounds. In metaphysics the analysis of complex events leads, as in natural science, to definite, ultimately simple basic relations, which can be grasped only in their pure factuality, but which, however, cannot be made comprehensible from concepts alone.

This is above all true of the causal relation, which we cannot doubt but which is nonetheless logically indemonstrable; indeed, the formal conceptual system of logic affords no means whatsoever to grasp and to think it determinately. It is easy to see how an inference is established through its conceptual ground, or a conclusion by the rule of identity, for in such cases we need only analyze the two concepts that are here related to each other to discover in them the selfsame property. But how something arises from something different, not according to the rule of identity, is a completely different question, about which Kant avows that no "real philosopher" has so far been able to make plain. The words "cause" and "effect," "force" and "action" are no solution, but merely restate the problem. All of them assert that because something is, another, different thing must exist, not that, in conformity with purely logical proof, because something is thought, something else must be thought as fundamentally identical with it.[56]

Here the first sharp dualism in the Kantian system emerges. The view that logic in its traditional form, as syllogistic, could suffice to "construct" the system of actuality crumbles once and for all, since it and its supreme principle, the principle of contradiction, are in-

---

56. See "Attempt to Introduce the Concept of Negative Magnitudes into Philosophy," third sect., General Remark (II, 240 ff.) (*Ak.* II, 201 ff.).

adequate to express the peculiarity of even the simplest real relation, that of cause and effect. But is thought to renounce the understanding of the composition and structure of being? Are we to abandon ourselves to an empiricism that is content to array impression with impression, fact with fact? Surely this cannot be Kant's intent, nor was it in any period of the evolution of his thought. The renunciation of syllogistic and its method, which imitates the synthetic proofs of geometry, in no way implies for him the renunciation of a rational foundation of philosophy as such, for the analysis of experience itself, which he now sees as the essential task of all metaphysics, is still for him through and through the work of reason.

If we survey Kant's view at this period of the capabilities of reason with respect to reality, a double relation is revealed. On the one hand, reason has to analyze the data of experience, until it has uncovered the ultimate simple fundamental relations of which experience is composed, relations which can then be shown purely as they exist but cannot be further deduced. But on the other hand, reason can ground and give evidence for the necessity of an absolute being, which is its characteristic task and prerogative, for from the pure, ideal possibilities that comprise its particular realm there follow, as "The Only Possible Basis of Proof" demonstrated, the existence and specification of the highest, most encompassing reality, which we designate by the concept of God. If these two functions are compared, we discover that they belong to two quite different orientations of thought. It is especially discordant for Kant on the one hand to consign reason in its determination of actuality completely to the data of experience, and on the other to entrust to it the power of bringing us to unconditional certainty regarding an infinite being lying beyond all possibility of experience. The analyst of inner experience, who tries to mold himself on the model of the Newtonian method, and the speculative philosopher, who clings to the central element of rational metaphysics, the ontological proof of God's existence, though in an altered form, here have not yet been clearly and sharply separated. In this opposition lay the seed and the conditioning factor of Kant's future philosophical development; once it was clearly grasped, it demanded a definite decision, which forced Kant further and further from the system of academic philosophy.

3. The Critique of Dogmatic Metaphysics:
Dreams of a Spirit-Seer

Kant established his reputation in the German literary and philosophical world by his writings of 1763. "The Only Possible Basis of Proof for a Demonstration of God's Existence" was reviewed in the *Literaturbriefe* by Mendelssohn, who was not wholly just to the essay's idiosyncratic ideas and method of proof, but who ungrudgingly and unstintingly acknowledged Kant as an "independent thinker," even where he could not follow him. Kant later said that this review first introduced him to the public. Further, the judgment made by the Berlin Academy on the "Inquiry into the Distinctness of the Principles of Natural Theology and Morals," and the fact that this essay appeared alongside Mendelssohn's prizewinning one in the proceedings of the Academy, made Kant's name known even beyond the borders of Germany. From now on literary acclaim numbers him among the leading minds of Germany, although his place in contemporary philosophy is not by any means clearly determined and staked out in the common judgment. Men like Lambert—who undoubtedly belongs among the most original minds of that epoch and whom Kant himself esteemed as the "foremost genius in Germany" in the field of metaphysics—enter into scientific correspondence with him and submit rough drafts of their philosophy to his judgment. Kant is now commonly seen as the future creator of a new system, which Mendelssohn urged him to work out in 1763 in the above-mentioned review in the *Literaturbriefe*, eighteen years before the appearance of the *Critique of Pure Reason*.

The phase that Kant's evolution as thinker and author entered after the writings of 1763 dashed the hopes of the world and of his friends most strikingly. What was expected and hoped for from him was the project of a new, deeper, and more tenable metaphysics—an abstract, analytic dissection of its presuppositions and a careful theoretical examination of its most general conclusions; what was received is a work which in its literary form and in its stylistic dress alike upset all the traditions of the literature of scientific philosophy. *Dreams of a Spirit-Seer, Illustrated by Dreams of Metaphysics (Träume eines Geistersehers erläutert durch Träume der Metaphysik)* is the title of this work, which appeared anonymously in Königsberg in 1766. Was the learned Magister Kant, was the author of the Academy's Prize Essay the author of this work? Inevitably there was doubt on that score, so jarring must have been the strange and unfamiliar tone in which it was written. For here it is no longer a matter of the theoretical scrutiny of metaphysics and its main propositions; rather, a reflective humor sports playfully with all its concepts and divisions, with its definitions and distinctions, with its categories and its logical chains of conclusions.

Yet, for all the exuberance of the satire, there conversely runs through the book a serious vein, which can be perceived clearly through all its mockery and self-irony. It is concerned with the doubts and reflections connected with the highest spiritual and religious problems of mankind, questions such as immortality and the endurance of the self, in which Kant had a crucial interest at every period of his thinking, whatever form his theoretical answers to them might take. "It will be said," we read at one place in the book, "that this is a very serious subject for so noncommittal an exercise as our discussion is, which deserves to be called a trifle rather than an earnest undertaking, and such a judgment would not be wrong. But although one need not make a great to-do over a trifle, one can do so given the opportunity. . . . I do not find that I have any sort of partisanship or that any unexamined bias has crept in to deprive my mind of its flexibility on all grounds pro or con, with one sole exception. The scales of the understanding are not quite impartial, and one arm of them, which bears the inscription: Hope of the future, has a mechanical advantage. . . . This is the sole error which I cannot set aside, and which in fact I never want to."[57]

But in this paradoxical mixture of jest and earnestness, which was

57. *Dreams of a Spirit-Seer*, pt. 1, chap. 4 (II, 365) (*Ak.* II, 349–50).

the decisive factor? Which was the author's true face and which the mask he had assumed? Was the book just a passing by-blow of free humor, or was there concealed behind this satyr play of the mind something resembling a tragedy of metaphysics? None of Kant's friends and critics was ever able to answer this question with certainty. The most sympathetic critics, such as Mendelssohn, were unrestrainedly amazed at this ambiguity. But Kant's reply to them was very like a riddle. "The unfavorable impression you express concerning the tone of my little book," he writes to Mendelssohn, "proves to me that you have formed a good opinion of the sincerity of my character, and your very reluctance to see that character ambiguously expressed is both valuable and pleasing to me. In fact, you shall never have cause to change this opinion. For though there may be flaws that even the most steadfast determination cannot eradicate completely, I shall certainly never become a fickle or fraudulent person, after having devoted the largest part of my life to studying how to despise those things that tend to corrupt one's honesty. Losing the self-respect that stems from a sense of honesty would therefore be the greatest evil that could, but most certainly shall not, befall me. Although I am absolutely convinced of many things that I shall never have the courage to say, I shall never say anything I do not believe."[58]

If one tries to approach the problem of intellect and life lurking mysteriously behind this work of Kant's, the outward story of the origin of the *Dreams of a Spirit-Seer* affords little help. Kant himself has brilliantly depicted, in a famous letter to Charlotte von Knobloch, how he first became aware of the marvelous tales surrounding the "visionary" Swedenborg, which led him to immerse himself deeper into Swedenborg's chief work, the *Arcana coelestia*. We use this account here not to repeat it, but are content to make reference to it.[59] Who will seriously believe that because he had bought the eight quarto volumes of Swedenborg's works, at a considerable outlay of trouble and expense, Kant would have decided to perform a literary analysis on the book? Or ought we to take the humorous preface to

58. To Mendelssohn, April 8, 1766 (IX, 55) (*Ak. X, 66*).
59. To Charlotte von Knobloch (1763) (see IX, 34) (*Ak. X, 40*).

the *Dreams of a Spirit-Seer* at face value in this regard? "The author," it says, "confesses with a certain humility that he was so simpleminded as to track down the truth of some tales of the sort mentioned. He found—as usual, where one has nothing to look for—he found nothing. Now this is in itself reason enough to write a book, but in addition there was that which has more than once wrung books out of reticent authors: the impetuous perseverance of known and unknown friends."

All this would hardly have influenced Kant, who was not easily led astray by any "author's itch,"[60] to occupy himself so intensely with the "arch-phantasist" Swedenborg, the "worst visionary of them all," if it were not that what he discovered in Swedenborg had a queer, indirect link with the crucial questions that his own inner development had led him to. Swedenborg is for Kant the caricature of all supersensible metaphysics, but precisely because of this distortion and exaggeration of all its distinctive features, he set himself to hold up a mirror to this metaphysics. If it failed to recognize itself in the gentle and objective analysis of the Prize Essay, it should now see itself in this caricature of it. For what in fact does distinguish the fantastic eccentricities of the visionary from the "architects of sundry airy thought-worlds" who were wont to call their creations "systems of philosophy"? Where is the line between the visionary's imaginings and that ordering of things "hewn less out of the stuff of experience than out of fraudulent concepts" by Wolff, or produced "by Crusius by the magical powers of some oracular utterances on the thinkable and the unthinkable" as out of nothing?[61] If the philosopher proposes to conjure up "experiences," the enthusiast will not lack for all sorts of instances of positively certified supersensible data and "facts," aside from the fact that scrutiny of this claim will very often lead one to vital gaps in its justification.

Or should the form of the system, the "rational connection" of concepts and conclusions, be crucial here? But his thorough study of

60. Compare his letter to Marcus Herz of the year 1773 (IX, 114) (*Ak.* X, 136).

61. *Dreams of a Spirit-Seer*, pt. 1, chap. 3 (II, 357) (*Ak.* II, 342); a passage in the Prize Essay, Third Observation, §3 (II, 196 f.) (*Ak.* II, 293 f.), explains what is meant by Crusius's "oracular utterances on the thinkable and the unthinkable."

the *Arcana coelestia* taught Kant once again just how far this systematization can be pushed, even in patent absurdities. Just as the upshot of the writings of 1763 is that no syllogistic is sufficient to give us knowledge of a single efficient cause, conversely the absence of true realities is no obstacle to verbalizing what seems to be a valid and continuous schema of deductions. The "dreams of reason" are in this respect no better than the "dreams of feeling"; the most cunning architectonic in the structure cannot overcome the lack of building materials. Even for the systematic philosopher there is no other criterion for the reality of his conclusions than the most scrupulous and patient testing of the data at his disposal for every particular question. But what an aspect traditional metaphysics takes on if we apply this yardstick to it! Everywhere we encounter problems that are revealed not only as uncomprehended but on closer look as incomprehensible, because the form in which the problem is put is infected by an ambiguous concept or a surreptitious assumption.[62] One talks about the "presence" of the soul in the body, one studies how the "spiritual" can act on the "material" or this on that, but fails to notice that the whole idea of the spiritual is due to habit and prejudice, rather than to exact scientific analysis. This is gross self-deception, but on the other hand it is understandable enough: "For whatever one knows a lot about as a child, he is certain later, as an adult, to be ignorant of, and the profound man in the end becomes the sophist of his youthful extravagance."

Kant had, however, at the conclusion of his treatise on negative magnitudes ironically referred to the "weakness of his insight," whereby he "customarily conceived least well what everybody believed easy to understand." Thanks to this weakness, the deeper he

62. Cf. Kant's letter to Mendelssohn of April 8, 1766: "My analogy between a spiritual substance's actual moral influx and the force of universal gravitation is not intended seriously; but it is an example of how far one can go in philosophical fabrications, completely unhindered, when there are no *data*, and it illustrates how important it is, in such exercises, first to decide what is required for a solution of the problem and whether the necessary *data* for a solution may be lacking. . . . Here we must decide whether there really are not limitations established by the bounds of our reason, or rather, the bounds of the experience that contains the *data* for our reason" (IX, 55) (*Ak.* X, 66).

goes into contemporary metaphysics "with its cursed fertility," the more it seems a book with seven seals. It envelops him in a web of opinions which, like Swedenborg's accounts of the spirit world, may be mastered historically, but which cannot be understood from first principles and brought to genuine conviction. There is but one firm standpoint left for him here: honest and open confession of ignorance. The whole problem of the spiritual realm, along with all other business relating to objects beyond all experience, is no longer a matter of theoretical speculation for him. What philosophy can accomplish at this point seems, impartially considered, trivial, but it is methodologically decisive for the whole conduct of cognition and life. It transforms grudging scepticism into something free and voluntary. "When science has made the circuit of its domain, it arrives in a natural way at the point of a modest distrust, and says to itself with irritation: How many things there are which I do not comprehend! But reason which has ripened through experience, and become wise, speaks joyfully through the mouth of Socrates, in the midst of the wares of the marketplace: How many things there are which I do not need! In this wise two highly diverse currents flow together, though they originated in quite different quarters, since the first is futile and malcontent but the second firm and temperate. For to choose rationally between them one must first know what is dispensable, indeed, impossible; but in the end science determines the limits set it by the nature of human reason. All baseless projects, however, not unworthy in themselves perhaps save that they lie outside the human sphere, empty into the limbo of futility. Then metaphysics becomes what at present it is rather far from being and what one ought least to presume of it: the handmaiden of wisdom."[63]

These sentences have a twofold interest for consideration of Kant's development as a whole. On the one hand, they show him to be still extremely closely connected with the substantive tendencies of the Enlightenment; on the other, however, they indicate that the spirit of this substance has been given a new form through a novel foundation. If the philosophy of the Enlightenment was naive in the

---

63. *Dreams of a Spirit-Seer*, pt. 2, chap. 3 (II, 385 f.) (*Ak.* II, 369).

way it rejected the supersensible and limited reason to the "here-and-now" and to what can be apprehended empirically, the same result appears in Kant as the product of a thought process that has gone through all the stages of critical reflection. He no longer stands on the soil of "experience" because he is wary or lazy, but he has consciously stationed himself there. Thus metaphysics is still science for him; however, it is no longer a science of things in a supersensible world, but of the limits of human reason.[64]

It directs man back to his proper and allotted sphere, because that is all that is necessary to man for his ethical vocation, for regulation of his action.

The whole moral voice of the Enlightenment, as it lived in the purest and greatest spirits, has here received its theoretical justification by Kant. "No; the time of fulfillment will come, will surely come," Lessing cries out at the end of the *Education of Mankind*, "since Man, the more convinced his understanding feels itself with respect to an ever better future, will have less need to borrow motivations for his actions from this future, for he will do the Good because it is good, not because arbitrary rewards are set up to bind and to strengthen his fickle gaze so as to recognize the better, inner rewards." Out of the same ethical insight and the same intellectual pathos Kant, a decade and a half prior to the *Education of Mankind*, had rendered his decision for and against metaphysics. "What? Is it then good to be virtuous only because there is a world beyond, or are actions no longer to be praised because they are in themselves good and virtuous?"[65] Whoever still needs the perspectives of metaphysics as a basis for ethics knows he is not yet in that pure autarchy and self-sufficiency which constitutes his genuine state. In this sense of ethical immanence the *Dreams of a Spirit-Seer* concludes with a reference to the words of the "honest Candide": "Let us take heed for our happiness, and go into the garden and work."

The new theoretical ideal at this point is directly transformed into a new ideal of life. We have in a well-known description by Herder, which cannot be omitted from any description of Kant's life, classic,

64. Ibid., pt. 2, chap. 2 (II, 384) (*Ak.* II, 368).
65. Ibid., pt. 2, chap. 3 (II, 389) (*Ak.* II, 372).

definitive witness as to how both ideals were stamped on Kant's entire mental stance and on the effect he had on others. "I have enjoyed the good fortune to know a philosopher, who was my teacher. In the prime of life he had the happy cheerfulness of a youth, which, so I believe, accompanied him even in grey old age. His forehead, formed for thinking, was the seat of indestructible serenity and peace, the most thought-filled speech flowed from his lips, merriment and wit and humor were at his command, and his lecturing was discourse at its most entertaining. In precisely the spirit with which he examined Leibniz, Wolff, Baumgarten, and Hume and pursued the natural laws of the physicists Kepler and Newton, he took up those works of Rousseau which were then appearing, *Émile* and *Héloïse*, just as he did every natural discovery known to him, evaluated them and always came back to unprejudiced knowledge of Nature and the moral worth of mankind. The history of nations and peoples, natural science, mathematics, and experience were the sources from which he enlivened his lecture and converse; nothing worth knowing was indifferent to him; no cabal, no sect, no prejudice, no ambition for fame had the least seductiveness for him in comparison with furthering and elucidating truth. He encouraged and engagingly fostered thinking for oneself; despotism was foreign to his mind. This man, whom I name with the utmost thankfulness and respect, was Immanuel Kant; his image stands before me to my delight."[66]

In his "Travel Diary" as well, Herder contrasts Kant's "living instruction" and pure "humane philosophy" with the dry, abstract, fragmented style of teaching he looks back on in his years as a child and youth. When he again and again stresses freedom and joyousness of soul as the foundation of Kant's nature, he does not seem fully aware that this harmonious balance was not for Kant a direct gift of nature and fate, but that it was won instead by hard intellectual struggles. These battles appear to have come to an end with the period of the *Dreams of a Spirit-Seer*. Kant has oriented himself toward pure "this worldiness" in the theoretical and ethical sense, in

---

66. Herder, *Letters on the Advancement of Humanity*, letter 79.

understanding as well as action. Now he believes himself planted ever more surely and firmly in the "human condition," and to be securely opposed to every deceptive enticement which might dislodge him from that stance.[67]

This tendency emerges in him so decisively that it is immediately communicated to everyone who came into close contact with him at that time. "He has given light to many an eye, simplicity of thought and naturalness of life," it is said in a poem composed in 1770 by a young man, Jakob Michael Reinhold Lenz, "in the name of all those from Courland and Livonia studying at Königsberg, presented to Professor Kant on his entry into his new post."[68] At this period there was realized in Kant the ideal of a life equally contemplative and active, which confined itself to the most immediate round of daily obligation and was capable of the widest prospects, which pronounced on the most universal mental and spiritual relationships and yet at every moment was conscious of the limits of human knowledge. Kant himself portrayed a life of that sort in a letter sent to Herder in Riga, in 1768: "In the early unfolding of your talents I foresee with divers pleasures the time when your fruitful spirit, no longer so sorely driven by the warm impulse of youthful feeling, attains that serenity which is peaceful yet full of feeling and is the contemplative life of the philosopher, just the opposite of that dreamed of by the mystics. From what I know of you, I confidently look forward to this epoch of your genius, of all states of mind the most advantageous to its possessor and to the world, one in which Montaigne occupies the lowest place and Hume so far as I know the highest."[69]

Among all the mental and spiritual influences on Kant in this period, the contribution of this state of mind is crucial—or more accurately, he views philosophic literature from the perspective of this psychic state and takes his stance toward it on that basis. Between Kant and Montaigne, between the "critical thinkers" and the "scep-

67. See the "Fragmente aus Kants Nachlass," *Immanuel Kants sämmtliche Werke*, ed. G. Hartenstein (Leipzig, 1867–68), vol. 8, p. 625.

68. The poem is printed in the "Stürmer und Dränger" collection edited by A. Sauer, vol. 2, pp. 215 f. (Kürschners Deutsche Nat.-Lit., vol. 80).

69. IX, 60 f. (*Ak.* X, 70).

tics," between the most strictly systematic thinker and the most un-
systematic thinker of all, there seems at first glance to be an unbridgeable chasm. And yet in this spiritual phase we are now considering,
there is a link between them, rooted in their common position with
respect to learnedness. Just as Montaigne warned over and over that
we enfeeble our power of comprehension when we demand that it
grasp too much, that we may become learned through others' knowledge but wise only through our own, similarly Kant's *Dreams of a
Spirit-Seer* is shot through with the belief that true wisdom is the
handmaiden of simplicity and that since in it the heart prescribes to
the understanding, it normally renders dispensable the immense apparatus of erudition and the whole clamorous estate of learning.[70]
Just as Montaigne elevates "Que sçais je?" to be the motto for his
philosophy of life, Kant sees in the "methodological prattle of the
toplofty schools often just an agreement to shirk a difficult question
by means of shifting word patterns, because the easy, and as a rule
reasonable: 'I do not know' is not readily heard in the academies."[71]
Just as Montaigne, as one of the first modern thinkers, wanted to
sever morality from all connections with religion, and demanded a
morality uncompelled by legal or religious prescriptions, one which
rather had grown "from its own root, from the seed of universal
reason," Kant indignantly asks whether the human heart does not
contain immediate ethical prescripts, and whether the machinery of
another world is needed to arouse one's vocation in this world.[72]

When he adds that the true and essential human goals ought not
to be thought dependent on such means, which forever lie beyond
human power, we encounter a different realm of thought and life; we
are transported into the mood of the confession of faith of the
Savoyard Vicar. To express what Rousseau's work meant to him from
the beginning, we do not need the famous anecdote which tells us
how, on reading in 1762 the newly published *Émile*, for the first time
Kant was unfaithful to his customary daily schedule, and to the
amazement of his fellow citizens did not take his afternoon walk. The

70. *Dreams of a Spirit-Seer*, pt. 2, chap. 3 (II, 389 ff.) (*Ak.* II, 368 ff.).
71. Ibid., pt. 1, chap. 1, (II, 333) (*Ak.* II, 319).
72. Ibid., pt. 2, chap. 3 (II, 389) (*Ak.* II, 372); cf. Montaigne, *Essays*, vol. 3, p. 12.

historical novelty of the phenomenon of Rousseau perhaps is seen most clearly in the total inadequacy of all the established standards decreed by that age when they are applied to him. As is the case with minds which have the special stamp of individuality, he exerted a completely opposite effect on those standards. As far as the characteristic philosophy of the Enlightenment is concerned, Rousseau remains a fundamentally incommensurable magnitude, though joined with it by many threads. Although the German Enlightenment did not unhesitatingly adopt a Voltairean tone, although the thoughtful and sober Mendelssohn strove to reach an equable and just evaluation, all vision of Rousseau's true originality was denied him. Mendelssohn's review of the *Nouvelle Héloïse* in the *Literaturbriefe*, in which he ranked Rousseau far below Richardson as regards "knowledge of the human heart," is indicative of a cross-section of the literary taste of that day; Hamann alone, in his *Chimärische Einfälle*, opposed it with his whole temperament and all the force of his bilious humor, and ridiculed it most effectively. Only the next generation, that of the young "geniuses," understood the artist in Rousseau. It was willingly captivated by the force of Rousseau's feeling and language; it thought that it heard in every word the voice of life and of "nature." But in this cult of feeling ignited by Rousseau, all the sharp distinctions, all the conceptual and dialectical problems which are no less essential to the whole of his personality and his historical mission were submerged.

In contrast to these two typical conceptions and estimations of Rousseau, Kant clings to a completely independent standpoint in his own judgment. If the Enlightenment upholds against Rousseau the rights of an intellectual culture grown old and rigid, sees him with the eyes of old age, if the "geniuses" see him with the eyes of youth, Kant confronts him from the start with the open-mindedness and the ripe judgment of a mature man. Only Lessing resembles him in this respect.[73] At the peak of his powers as an author in the years when he became acquainted with Rousseau—the *Observations on the Feeling*

73. See Lessing's notice on Rousseau's Dijon prize essay ("Das Neueste aus dem Reiche des Witzes," April, 1751) *Werke*, ed. K. Lachmann and F. Muncker (Stuttgart, 1886–1924), vol. 2, p. 388.

of the Beautiful and the Sublime[74] which appeared in 1764, is that work which next to the *Dreams of a Spirit-Seer* most clearly shows what Kant was capable of as a stylist—he has the liveliest sympathy for and interest in the new personal style Rousseau introduced into philosophic literature. But he is no prisoner of this charm. "I must," he commands himself, "read Rousseau until the beauty of expression no longer moves me, and then I can look at him rationally." But the aesthetic charm of Rousseau's writing is not the only thing that hampers reflective and temperate scrutiny; beyond that lies the no less dangerous charm of his dialectic. "The first impression which the reader who is not merely reading idly and passing time gets from the writings of J. J. Rousseau is that he is in the presence of an uncommonly acute mind, a noble sweep of genius, and a soul filled with a degree of feeling so high as to have been possessed all together by no other author, of whatever age or nationality. The succeeding impression is astonishment at the peculiar and nonsensical notions, so opposed to what is generally current, so that it readily occurs to one that the author, by his extraordinary talents and the sorcery of his eloquence, wanted to display himself as an eccentric fellow, who surpasses all his intellectual competitors through bewitching and startling novelty."

Kant does not stop with these two impressions, but seeks out the philosopher Rousseau behind the "sorcerer" Rousseau. Paradox in the man's manner of expression and in his very being does not blind him and lead him astray; he is convinced that this strange phenomenon, subject to no convention or mold, nonetheless must have its own inner law, which he endeavors to uncover. And here he arrives at a quite new and special view of it. If there was anything that the judgment of his contemporaries agreed on, it was that they saw in Rousseau the champion against the tyranny of "rules." As such, he was on the one hand attacked from the standpoint of popular "reason" and bourgeois morality, on the other hailed enthusiastically as a liberator. The return to "nature" seemed to be the return to freedom of personal, inner life, to the unchaining of subjective feeling and emotion.

74. *Beobachtungen über das Gefühl des Schonen und Erhabenen* (see II, 243 ff.) (*Ak.* II, 205 ff.).

For Kant, though, coming as he did from the side of Newton, the concept of nature had quite a different ring. He sees in it the expression of the highest objectivity, the expression of order and lawfulness. It is in this sense that he interprets Rousseau's tendency of thought as well. Just as Newton had done with the objective rules of the paths of the heavenly bodies, Rousseau sought for and laid down the objective ethical norm of human inclinations and actions. "Newton first saw order and lawfulness going hand in hand with great simplicity, where prior to him disorder and its troublesome partner, multiplicity, were encountered, and ever since the comets run in geometrical paths; Rousseau first discovered amid the manifold human forms the deeply hidden nature of man, and the secret law by which Providence is justified through his observations." This sturdy "nature," firmly at one with itself, is independent both of subjective inclination and of changes in theoretical notions. It is the autonomous moral law in its pure, unchangeable validity and obligation. All differences must vanish in the face of the simplicity and the grand unity and uniformity of this law, differences by which the individual believes himself to be exceptional through preeminence of birth and estate or through gifts of mind and learnedness. Kant himself asserts that he is "by inclination an inquirer," and says he traces in himself the thirst for knowledge and eager impatience to increase it. But he refuses to seek the essential moral worth and the "honor of mankind" in man's purely intellectual capacities and intellectual progress: Rousseau has "set him straight." "This delusive superiority disappears; I learn to respect mankind, and would find myself much more dispensable than a common laborer, if I did not believe that this reflection could give to everyone else a worth which restores to mankind its rights."[75]

Now it is understandable how in the very same letter to Mendelssohn in which he says that he views with disgust the inflated arrogance of entire volumes of metaphysical ideas as they currently

75. What Kant says here about Rousseau can be found in the remarks (first published by Friedrich Wilhelm Schubert) which he inserted into the manuscript of *Observations on the Feeling of the Beautiful and the Sublime* (1764). In most editions of Kant these are included under the title "Fragmente aus Kants Nachlass." Cf. Hartenstein's edition, vol. 8, pp. 618, 624, 630.

stand, indeed even with hatred, Kant also declares he is so far from taking metaphysics itself, objectively considered, to be unimportant or dispensable that he is convinced that the genuine and lasting well-being of the human race depends on it.[76] For the orientation and goal of metaphysics have now totally changed. One categorical demand for a new foundation of ethics has replaced the diverse problems treated in the schools under the headings of ontology, rational psychology, and theology. It is here, not in scholastic, logical concepts, that the true key to the signficance of the spiritual world is to be sought.

Did Kant derive this idea from Rousseau, or did he read it into him? This is a pressing question, for in just such subtle intellectual and ideal relationships the proposition Kant expressed concerning a priori theoretical knowledge holds: that we only know in things what "we ourselves put into them." Even as Schiller later could fathom the fully developed fabric of Kantian philosophy on brief acquaintance because he conceived it from the standpoint of his own center, the idea of freedom, which was the fundamental idea of his own life, similarly Kant has here, under the guidance of this idea so essential to him, read and understood Rousseau accordingly. Newton helped him to clarify the phenomenon of the world; Rousseau shows him the way to the deeper meaning of the noumenon of freedom. But significantly, in this very distinction there lies the germ of a new fundamental problem. Now it is necessary to show how it is possible to hold to the standpoint of pure "immanence" and yet to preserve the unconditionality of ethical norms, how we can keep the "intelligible" in ethics and still, or even for that very reason, reject the supersensible world of mystical twaddle and speculative metaphysics.

Given this question, which henceforth becomes more and more central and which governs the whole intellectual advance from the *Dreams of a Spirit-Seer* to *On the Form and Principles of the Sensible and the Intelligible World*, the position Kant adopts, both positively and negatively, toward Hume's theory becomes clear.[77] He says in his

---

76. Letter to Mendelssohn, April 8, 1766 (IX, 55) (*Ak*. X, 66).

77. I will not go into further detail here as to the vexed question of the direction, the extent, and the period of Hume's influence on Kant; to avoid repetition, reference is made to an earlier discussion of it (*Das Erkenntnisproblem*, 2d ed., vol. 2, 606 ff.).

letter to Herder dating from 1768 that he now feels closer to Hume in his entire intellectual orientation; Hume occupies the highest place among the teachers and masters of the true philosophical "state of mind."[78] And on the purely theoretical side, Kant assumes frankly and without reservations at least one crucial result of Hume's doctrine. That a mere conceptual analysis, carried out according to the principles of identity and contradiction, cannot afford the slightest knowledge of any sort of "basic reality"—this truth, already enunciated in the essay on negative magnitudes, is now for Kant further confirmed and deepened. "How something can be a cause or possess a power," he is convinced, can never be known through "reason," that is, by comparison of concepts according to the criterion of identity and contradiction; the knowledge of this basic relation can "be drawn solely from experience."[79]

But this agreement with Hume has limits in two respects. A completely different theoretical and ethical concern speaks in Kant and in Hume. Hume's scepticism is the full and adequate expression of his whole outlook and attitude. It is delight in doubting for the sake of doubting, delight in the unfettered activity of his superior analytical intelligence which totally rules and engrosses him. To be sure, the popular moral tendencies of the philosophy of the Enlightenment have some effect on him, especially in Hume's *Dialogues on Natural Religion,* but on the whole he turns a cool, half-ironic face of superiority toward ethical questions. Kant, in contrast, has become ever more sceptical toward all dogmatic religion and theology, to the extent that it presents itself as the foundation of ethics, but his position regarding the substance of ethics itself and his recognition of its unconditionally valid claims remained unchanged throughout his lifetime. In this regard, even the *Dreams of a Spirit-Seer* admits that the "scales of understanding" Kant uses are never wholly impartial, that they cannot do away with all ethical interest. The battle against metaphysics and its conception of God and a supersensible world means to him also the battle for a new positive foundation for autonomous morality.

Within the realm of pure logic as well, there is an analogous rela-

---

78. See above, pp. 85 f.
79. *Dreams of a Spirit-Seer,* pt. 2, chap. 3 (II, 387) (*Ak.* II, 370).

tion. Kant's conception of experience has a positive substantiality which no scepticism attains, for every genuine experiential cognition includes the application of mathematics. The experience Hume speaks of dissolves into the sheer play of representations, held together by the subjective rules of the imagination and the psychological mechanism of association. For Kant, the experience in which all our knowledge of basic reality must be rooted is rather the method of physical induction, as Newton built it up with the aid of a precise and specified experimental method and continuous application of mathematical analysis and calculation. Thus while Kant is aroused by Hume to struggle against metaphysics and to make war on all transcendence, his thinking immediately takes on a new and independent direction relative to Hume; for the more purely he now strives to cleave to the "fertile lowland of experience," the more clear it becomes to him that this depth of experience is itself founded in a factor which is rooted not in sensation as such but in mathematical concepts. Thus his keener grasp of the concept of experience itself leads him to distinguish more accurately the different conditions on which it rests, and to define their specific validity relative to each other.

4. The Separation of the Sensible and the Intelligible Worlds

One who has told the story of Kant's youth has noted that the conventional view that Kant's life unfolded in an extremely simple and disciplined way is less and less corroborated the more deeply familiar one is with the details of that life. Rather, in a perpetually surprising fashion it is shown that even the outward course of Kant's life is not measurable by everyday standards and rules. "Kant trod no ordinary way.... From the beginning of his independent development until his old age he never did what an ordinary man would have done in his place. Looked at closely, his life did not progress at all 'in perfect regularity,' but moved in a very irregular way toward its goals. It always ran counter to the common view of men and mystified the expectations of those observers around him. For what they had a right to expect of him, either he did not undertake, or else undertook it after they had given up hope, and then accomplished it so grandly and completely that his performance evoked amazement and thus again contradicted every expectation all the more."[80]

If this view has an air of paradox so far as it concerns the external course of Kant's life, it is entirely accurate as regards the intellectual labor that went into the formation of Kant's system. As methodical as this labor is in its deepest themes, it pursues its conclusions with little simplicity, regularity, and "linearity." Everywhere one comes upon places at which his thought, after it is just on the point of arriving at a definite solution, suddenly steps backwards. A problem is taken up, thought through, and its solution reached—but suddenly it is shown that the conditions under which it was first worked out were not appropriate and complete enough, and hence not one step of the solution is valid, but instead the whole way in which the question is put has to be framed anew. Reticent as they normally are about questions of his inner development, Kant's letters tell us again and again of reversals of this kind. A conceptual whole is not constructed bit by bit in a steady, unbroken progression, but new threads seem continually to be spun, only to be immediately severed. If Kant adhered to and defended every essential basic proposition of his critical doctrine once it had been constructed, it is characteristic of this preparatory period that he has a certain indifference toward everything that is a mere "result"; he feared premature termination of his intellectual process more than he sought it. "As for me," he writes to Herder in 1768, "since I depend on nothing and, with a profound impartiality toward the opinions of others and my own, often upend the whole structure and inspect it from a variety of points of view so as eventually to hit upon that in it which I can hope to subscribe to as true, I have, since we parted, inserted different ideas in many places."[81] And a later remark confirms the maxim of Kantian thinking even more definitely. "I am not of the view of a superior man who, once he has convinced himself of something, henceforward feels no doubt about it. That does not do in pure philosophy. The understanding

80. Emil Arnoldt, "Kants Jugend und die fünf ersten Jahre seiner Privatdozentur im Umriss dargestellt," *Gesammelte Schriften*, vol. 3, p. 205.

81. To Herder, May 9, 1768 (see IX, 59) (*Ak.* X, 70).

itself is naturally opposed to it. One must consider the propositions in all sorts of applications and even try to assume their contradictories, if they lack a special proof, and delay long enough so that the truth is illuminated from all sides."[82]

The moment one realizes this general procedure of Kant's, the primary, as it were subjective, basis of the totally surprising turn his doctrine took once again in the years between 1766 and 1770, the period between the *Dreams of a Spirit-Seer* and *On the Form and Principles of the Sensible and the Intelligible World,* is comprehensible. Yet once more the expectation the world attached to Kant's ongoing development was foiled most remarkably. We recall that in 1763, after the composition of "The Only Possible Basis of Proof" and the Prize Essay, knowledgeable philosophers saw in Kant the future creator of a new, more thorough metaphysics, a metaphysics with critically tested and examined foundations, but one which was to be constructed in general on the old "rational" model. Now, however, to their astonishment their experience was that Kant, whom they had numbered among their own, struck out on a path which seemed to cut him off from metaphysics forever. To be sure, he still confessed an old affection and weakness for it, but he did so with such an ironic air of superiority that the subjective liberation he believed he had now at last achieved could be felt all the more strongly. "Metaphysics, whom it is my lot to love though I can seldom boast of any favors from her,

---

82. *Reflexionen Kants zur kritischen Philosophie,* vol. 2: *Reflexionen zur Kritik der reinen Vernunft,* ed. Benno Erdmann (Leipzig, 1884), no. 5. I have thoroughly examined these reflections (which are marginal notations Kant made in the textbooks he read, especially Baumgarten's *Metaphysica*) and used them in an earlier exposition I did of the evolution of the critical philosophy; here they are deliberately introduced only when the date of their composition can be established with certainty, either because they contain definite evidence of a date, or when it is immediately and unambiguously apparent from their content. Where the dating is questionable, or where it can only be done indirectly by complex factual inferences, I have preferred to leave these documents aside rather than to burden a biographical exposition, which is dependent above all on accurate and unambiguous temporal evidence, with material which is not indispensable and is in many respects problematical. Presumably more exact tools for dating the *Reflexionen* will be supplied by the publication of Kant's entire *Handschriftliche Nachlass,* which Erich Adickes has begun for the Academy edition of Kant's writings.

provides two benefits. The first is to satisfy those tasks which arise in the inquiring mind when it delves rationally into the hidden properties of things. But here the outcome all too often plays our hopes false and evades our eager hands. . . . The other benefit is more proportioned to the nature of the human understanding; it consists in investigating whether the task can be decided from what man can know, and what relation the question may have to those empirical concepts on which all our judgments must always rest. In this respect metaphysics is a science of the limits of human reason. . . . I have not determined these limits with any precision here, but have indicated that the reader will find on further reflection that he can excuse himself from all vain inquiries with regard to a question the data for which are to be found in a world other than the one in which he perceives himself to be. I have thus wasted my time so that I might regain it. I have imposed on my reader, so that I might be of service to him, and if I did not afford him any new knowledge, I uprooted the folly and idle knowledge which bloats the understanding, and in its cramped space cleared a place which wise doctrines and useful instruction can occupy." Metaphysics conceived as a theoretical question and task seem thereby to be dismissed. Kant expressly declares that he lays aside the whole matter of spirits as settled and done with. It is of no future concern for him, since the foregoing considerations cut off all philosophical understanding of such beings, and henceforth there may be opinions about them but never knowledge. This assertion, he adds, may seem boastful, of course, but it is not, for the termination spoken of here is such only in a negative sense, which does not determine an object but only securely fixes the limits of our knowledge. On this basis the whole pneumatology of the human soul might be called a scientific system of our necessary ignorance regarding a supposititious species of being, and as such is easily equal to the task.[83]

After this confession, it must have been totally unforeseen that Kant, on assuming his new position as Professor of Logic and

83. *Dreams of a Spirit-Seer*, pt. 1, chap. 4 (II, 367 f.) (*Ak.* II, 348 f.), and pt. 2, chap. 2 (II, 384 f.) (*Ak.* II, 357 f.).

Metaphysics on August 20, 1770, would defend a treatise the very title of which promised to determine the form of the intelligible world and to distinguish its essential features from those of the sensible world. For what the comprehensive concept of the intelligible world here includes is in truth nothing other than that realm of immaterial substances, entry to which seemed to have been forbidden us. And in this instance it was not a matter of a literary pamphlet, sprung from a momentary mood; instead, a strict, systematic thinker here unfolded stroke by stroke, with the precision of a balance sheet, the entire program of his future work as teacher and scholar. We are now presented with a profound theory of the intelligible, founded on an inquiry into its principles and presuppositions and pursued through all the main areas of the familiar metaphysics. Kant never doubts for a moment that this whole investigation is prompted by questions the data for which lie in a world different from that in which we feel ourselves to be, but now he is far from scorning this inquiry as an "idle search." He strides forward, secure and undistracted, and if, as is natural in a preparatory work, he does not provide a picture of the intelligible world worked out to the last detail, still he is convinced that he has defined and clearly delineated its general outline. And nothing in this sketch points back to the earlier drafts and experiments; it is as though this new picture of the sensible and the intelligible worlds had sprung out of nothing before our eyes.

Yet we must seek out the connecting link for this work too, if not to the earlier answers, at least to the earlier problems of Kant's thought. What relation is there between the denial of the *Dreams of a Spirit-Seer* and the affirmation of *On the Form and Principles of the Sensible and the Intelligible World?* Are these both concerned with the same object, or has perhaps the theme of metaphysics undergone a change? And if the latter, what new tasks have quickened in Kant's mind in the interim and now occupy the center of his theoretical interest? There is no direct, or at least no complete, answer to all these questions in the testimony we have concerning Kant's development in the years from 1766 to 1770. But the substance of the Inaugural Dissertation itself fills in this gap, for it clearly and unmistakably points to the new region of thought that Kant has now entered. For

the first time, Leibnizian philosophy is shown to be a force that determines him inwardly. This assertion seems paradoxical, for did not
Kant's first work on the estimation of living forces treat a theme from
Leibniz's natural philosophy, and had not the totality of Leibniz's
doctrines—at least in the form they received at the hands of Wolff and
academic philosophy—from then on gone with him at every step? In
truth, however, Kant's frequent reference to the substance of these
doctrines shows that their most essential philosophic spirit remained
closed to him for the present. Even the *Monadologia Physica*, which
seems to hew most closely to Leibniz, is no exception, since as physical monadology it tries to reach the ultimate elements in the realm of
the corporeal. The monads are here conceived as centers of force,
from the mutual interaction, attraction, and repulsion of which matter, as extended mass, is constituted. This dynamic construction thus
consistently applies concepts which (like the concept of corporeal
atoms, the concept of action at a distance and physical influence)
were unqualifiedly designated as fictions in Leibniz's sense.

The concept of monads in its characteristic metaphysical meaning,
however, functions—in the "Inquiry into the Distinctness of the Principles of Natural Theology and Morals"—as a paradigm of that synthetic procedure of metaphysics Kant fought against, where the basic
concepts are not so much deduced through analysis of appearances
into their elements as rather arbitrarily "imagined."[84] This judgment
as well shows that Kant was at that time still completely unable to
survey and evaluate the monstrous analytical intellectual labor
through which Leibniz had, by contemplating phenomena, gained
his concept of substance as their "principle" and "foundation."[85] One
must have vividly in mind Kant's attitude toward Leibniz's doctrine
up until now to judge what a decisive change Leibniz's *Nouveaux
essais sur l'entendement humain* must have produced in Kant's overall
outlook when he first became acquainted with it. The manuscript of
this book had been buried in the library at Hanover for sixty years,

84. "Inquiry into the Distinctness of the Principles of Natural Theology and
Morals," First Reflection, §1 (II, 177) (*Ak.* II, 277).

85. More on this in my book *Leibniz' System in seinen wissenschaftliches Grundlagen*
(Marburg, 1902), esp. chap. 6.

until it was brought into print in 1765 by Raspe in his edition of the
Oeuvres philosophiques. Now, however, it inevitably affected the age
with all the force of a totally new impression. Leibniz once again
stood among them as a contemporary, as though raised from the
dead. Only now did the whole breadth and originality of his thought,
hitherto clouded by academic tradition, emerge. In this book, it was
universally felt, it was not a matter of an isolated learned artifact, but
of an event which was a decisive irruption into universal intellectual
history and all its problems and interests. This is the way in which
Herder and Lessing, who projected and made a start on a German
translation of the *Nouveaux essais,* understood and welcomed the
book.[86] And moreover it was just these years from 1765 to 1770 that
did the most for general knowledge and deeper understanding of the
Leibnizian philosophy in Germany, for with the appearance of Dutens's great edition in 1768, the whole of Leibniz's philosophical and
scientific labors, which till now had been scattered or unknown,
could be surveyed with some accuracy and completeness.

For Kant, too, an entire new source was opened up. His notes
from this period give abundant and unambiguous evidence that he
was intensively occupied with the *Nouveaux essais* in particular.[87] For
the first time he encountered Leibniz not only as philosopher of nature or as speculative metaphysician, but as epistemological critic.
Now he understood in what sense the doctrine of innate ideas and
truths cohered with the system of monadology, how it was on one
side the foundation of that system and on the other found only in it
full, concrete confirmation. Once more Kant sees himself face to face
with the great question about the relation between the methodology
of scientific knowledge and that of metaphysics. Leibniz leads him
back to his own fundamental problem, which now is freed of all ties
with particular, concrete questions and achieves its fully universal
expression.

86. See Lessing's *Werke,* ed. Lachmann and Muncker, vol. 15, pp. 521 f.
87. Cf. Kant's *Reflexionen,* nos. 513, 273–78; for the dating of these reflections, see
Erich Adickes, *Kant-Studien,* (Kiel and Leipzig, 1895) pp. 164 ff., and *Das Erkenntnisproblem,* 2d ed., vol. 2, pp. 622 f.

If we wish to visualize this process, we should not start with the actual historical meaning of Leibniz's system, but instead with how it presented itself to Kant's mind. Kant's interpretation of individual Leibnizian concepts and propositions is not free of misunderstandings and hardly could be, since, despite Dutens's collected edition, the most important sources for Leibniz's philosophy which are available to us—especially the major part of the philosophical and mathematical correspondence—were still undiscovered in the eighteenth century. But this is of little importance for the history of Kant's intellectual evolution, since it is not a matter of what Leibniz was, but of how Kant understood and saw him. When Kant later comprehensively surveyed Leibniz's system in the *Metaphysical Foundations of Natural Science (Metaphysische Anfangsgründe der Naturwissenschaften)* he laid all his emphasis on the point that the monadology ought not to be judged as an attempt to explain nature, but as a "Platonic concept of the world, correct in itself, insofar as the world is not an object of the senses but is regarded as a thing in itself, purely an object of the understanding, but one which is the foundation of sensory appearances."[88] In fact, this was the perspective from which he judged Leibniz's doctrine from the beginning. The monads are the "atoms" of things, but this atomicity in no way denotes that of a physical component which is an ingredient in the composition of bodies, but rather that ultimate, unanalyzable unity of which we are aware as the spiritual subject in the idea of the ego.[89] In the act of self-consciousness a unity is given us that is not derivable from something else, but that instead is the principle of all derivation. This unity is not the consequent of a more ultimate, deeper lying plurality, but forms the necessary presupposition for representing any plurality. For to think a plurality or to represent it to oneself, its diverse moments must be mutually interrelated and thought as an interconnected whole; this inclusive grasp, however, can be achieved only

88. *Metaphysical Foundations of Natural Science,* chap. 2, Proposition 4, note 2 (IV, 413) (*Ak.* IV, 507).

89. Cf. *Critique of Pure Reason,* note to the Second Antinomy, A 442 = B 470 (III, 318).

when we base it on that universal possibility of seeing the "one in the many" which we customarily signify by the name of "perception" or "consciousness."

Hence there are two views of the world opposed to one another in their principle and their origin, although they are united in the concrete whole of our experience. According to the one, we comprehend ourselves as spiritual substances, as a whole of psychic phenomena the entire manifold of which refers back to the same identical ego and only thus constitutes a single series of personal experiences, an integral "substance." According to the other, we regard ourselves, like the world around us, as a coherent corporeal whole governed by mechanical laws, those of pressure and impact. In the first form, the conception of what we call the "world" is that of a whole of purely inner states, an aggregate of representations and impulses; in the second, we contemplate the states as they might present themselves to an outside observer. For this the intensive manifold must be changed into an extensive one; the dependence of inner phenomena on one another, and their qualitative relationship of similarity must appear as an external order as we think it in the concepts of space and time.

But if we ask which of these two views of actuality possesses the higher truth, the answer cannot be in doubt. For in the former we comprehend ourselves as we are purely and simply for ourselves; the latter represents the viewpoint under which our being falls when seen from outside. In the one case a purely spiritual being is expressed and evidenced through purely spiritual concepts, such as that of the dynamic limitation of one state by another; in the other case we must transform what is in truth an inward relationship into the externality of space and time in order to make it publicly knowable. So on the one hand we have the picture of a world purely of the understanding: a community of diverse spiritual substances; on the other hand, the picture of a sense world, that is, a nexus of *appearances*, the coexistence and succession of which can be empirically observed and described. In this conception, as his comparison of Leibniz and Plato shows, Kant found the old opposition of the "phenomenon" and the "noumenon" pointed out and understood from a

fresh perspective. He now views the system of monadology in relation to this universal intellectual history, which Leibniz himself had
emphatically called attention to.[90] The classical division between the
intelligible and the sensible world[91] seems here to be deduced from
the fundamental laws of knowledge and only thus conceived as
necessary.

This also altered Kant's own stand regarding the question. In his
critique of metaphysics, from the Prize Essay to the *Dreams of a
Spirit-Seer*, he constantly asked for the data on which knowledge of a
supersensible world might rest, and he had not been able to unearth
these data in the received definition of academic metaphysics, not to
mention the theories and tales of a Swedenborg. Now, however, he
had discovered a new point of departure: the crucial datum, as Kant
only became fully aware on studying Leibniz, lies in the differing origin and the differing type of validity of the principles of our cognition.
It is here, if anywhere, that metaphysical reflection is to be rooted.
That which is truly spiritual is not the infinite, transcending every
form of our knowledge, but it is comprised in this very form of knowledge. The distinction between universally valid and particular, between necessary and contingent truth is "given," is indubitably certain; one may investigate whether it is possible to define the boundaries
of the sensible and the intelligible worlds without assuming anything
besides this distinction.

In the quarrel between Leibniz and Locke, Kant had come down
on the side of the former, and apparently without hesitation. The
Lockean derivation of the pure concept of the understanding from
experience always seemed to him to be a sort of *generatio aequivoca*; at
no point in his thinking was he content with this kind of "birth
certificate."[92] If Kant was an empiricist, that only meant for him the
demand that the validity of concepts be shown to be grounded in the
analysis of the *objective* contents of experience, but he never regarded

90. See the *Epistola ad Hanschium de Philosophia Platonica sive de Enthusiasmo
Platonico; Opera*, ed. L. Dutens (Geneva, 1768) vol. 2, p. 1.

91. Cf. *De mundi sensibilis atque intelligibilis forma et principiis*, §7 (II, 411) (*Ak*. II, 395);
also the *Critique of Pure Reason* A 235 ff. = B 294 ff. (III, 212 ff.).

92. Cf. *Critique of Pure Reason*, A 86 = B 119 and B 167 (III, 106 and 135).

the evidence of the subjective psychological origin of a concept and its being traceable back to simple sensations as the sufficient or necessary condition of its truth. That special concepts such as possibility, existence, necessity, substance, cause, and so on, together with everything related to them and following from them, are never to be obtained and inferred in this way is something about which he has now become totally clear. For since the relations which they express are not of a sensory nature, they can never be abstracted from the stuff of perceptions by a mere summation of particular sensations.[93]

If one wishes to say that these pure relational concepts are gotten "by abstraction" from the particular sensations of sight, hearing, and so forth, the ambiguity attaching to the concept of abstraction must first be put aside. A true logical or mathematical concept is not *abstracted* from sensory appearances (for then it would contain nothing which was not some kind of concrete component momentarily present in them), but rather it has an *abstractive relationship* to them, that is, it posits a universal relation regardless of whether such a relation is exemplified and presented in any particular sensory instances. Therefore it would be more accurately called a *conceptus abstrahens* than a *conceptus abstractus*.[94] In this sense Kant also called geometrical principles "ideas of pure reason" for some time, before he hit in the Inaugural Dissertation on the essential methodological designation of "pure intuitions" for space and time. For the latter, too, express relations which we need not have experienced particular instances of in order to know in general. In a certain sense we arrive at them "by abstraction," but the material from which the abstraction is taken is not sensations, but the activity of the mind itself, which we grasp in its immanent lawfulness and hence necessity.

"Some concepts," as it is said in a note from this period, "are abstracted from sensations, others purely from the law of the understanding, which compares abstract concepts so as to connect or to distinguish them. The origin of the latter is in the understanding; that of the former is in the senses. All concepts of such a kind are called

93. *De mundi sensibilis*, §8 (II, 411) (*Ak.* II, 395).
94. Ibid., §6 (II, 410) (*Ak.* II, 394).

pure concepts of the understanding: *conceptus intellectus puri*. To be
sure, on occasion sensations can evoke these activities of the understanding, and we become conscious of certain concepts of universal
relationships of abstract ideas according to laws of the understanding;
thus Locke's rule that without sensation we have no clear ideas holds
in this case. But although the *notiones rationales* arise through sensations and are thought only as applied to the ideas abstracted from
them, they are not contained in them nor abstracted from them, just
as in geometry we do not borrow the idea of space from the sensation
of extended things, though we can only make this concept (similarly)
clear when given the sensation of corporeal things. Hence the idea of
space is a *notio intellectus puri*, which can be applied to the abstracted
idea of mountains and casks. The philosophy of the concepts of *intellectus purus* is metaphysics; it is related to the rest of philosophy as
mathesis pura to *mathesis applicata*. The concepts of existence (reality),
possibility, necessity, ground, unity and plurality, part, whole, nothing, composite and simple, space, time, change, motion, substance
and accident, force and action, and everything else belonging to ontology proper are related to the rest of metaphysics as common arithmetic is to *mathesis pura*."[95]

The work *On the Form and Principles of the Sensible and the Intelligible*

95. *Reflexionen* on the *Critique of Pure Reason*, no. 513 (see above, n. 86, on the
dating). To see their historical connection with Leibniz vividly, one should put these
sentences side by side with the following from the preface to the *Nouveaux essais*:
"Perhaps our clever author (Locke) will not depart entirely from my feeling. For after
having occupied his whole first book in rejecting the inner light, taken in a certain
sense, he nonetheless affirms at the outset of the second, and in what follows, that
ideas which do not originate in sensation come from reflection. Now, reflection is
nothing but attending to what is within us, and the senses do not give us what we
already carry with us. That being so, can it be denied that there is already much innate
in our mind, since we are, so to speak, innate to ourselves? Or that there is in us: Being,
Unity, Substance, Duration, Change, Action, Perception, Pleasure, and a thousand
other objects of our intellectual ideas? And these objects being immediately and always
present to our understanding (although they are not always perceived by reason of our
distractions and desires), why be surprised that we say that these ideas, together with
all that depends on them, are innate in us?" For space and time, see especially
Nouveaux essais, II, 5: "Ideas ... such as that of space, figure, motion, rest are ... of the
mind itself, for they are ideas of the pure understanding, but which have a relation to
the external and to what the senses cause us to perceive."

World attaches to these thoughts the decisive terminological specification by which the ambiguous concept of "innate ideas" is bypassed. As regards the basic categories of the understanding, it is not a matter of innate ideas (*conceptus connati*), but of inherent laws of the mind (*leges menti insitae*), which we become conscious of by attending to their actions and also when experience occurs.[96] Here, too, Kant makes no material strides beyond Leibniz, but he has coined a new and significant expression for the fundamental ideas which the latter advocated, terminology which, in its pregnancy and incisiveness, leads on to a sharpening and deepening of the problem of the a priori.

But it was important first to hit upon yet another critical distinction, which necessarily led Kant into far more complex questions than the opposition between Leibniz and Locke. It was unthinkable to him to judge in Locke's favor, for he had always distinguished very definitely between "empiricism" and "empirism." But in building up pure intellectual knowledge, as he now undertook to do, by abandoning Locke did he have to abandon Newton also? And were there not between the latter and Leibniz the most severe unreconciled and seemingly irreconcilable contradictions? Since these contradictions had been given their most acute form in the polemical exchange of correspondence between Leibniz and Clarke, they had not been laid to rest. The whole philosophical and scientific literature of the eighteenth century is still full of them. Everywhere the metaphysicians' and ontologists' conceptions of the world are starkly and uncompromisingly contrasted. This division becomes a universal watchword, under which the intellectual battles of that time were fought. The greatest scientific genius of Germany, Leonhard Euler, discussed this conflict again very extensively in 1768, in a popular work, the *Letters to a German Princess.* While the metaphysician, he said, analyzes the world into ultimate, simple parts in order to understand it, the mathematician conversely must insist that the divisibility of matter, like that of space, is infinite and that therefore an unanalyzable simple entity is never reached. If the former resolves the actual into a sum of point substances which taken in their totality

96. *De mundi sensibilis*, §8 (II, 411) (*Ak.* II, 395).

manifest the phenomenon (or rather the appearance) of extension, the latter knows that a more complex spatial or temporal relation is reducible to another, simpler relation, but that extension can never be produced from points, the extensive from the intensive.

Further, while according to established metaphysical theories pure space and time are nothing in themselves but are to be regarded only as qualities or "accidents" of the bodies, which alone are actual, and their motions, the mathematician and physicist for their part are unconcerned with establishing the *sort* of reality that space and time possess. That some sort of reality is to be attributed to them, however, and that extension and duration, even apart from what is extended and enduring, have a substantial being are held to unconditionally, because without these assumptions it would be impossible to achieve a clear and determinate sense of the supreme laws of motion. The law of inertia, for example, cannot be definitely and precisely formulated if one does not differentiate pure or, as Newton called it, absolute space from all that it contains and recognize it as an independent whole, in relation to which the rest or motion of a material system can be spoken of.[97]

The keenest and most decisive objection against any encroachment of metaphysics in questions of the theory of nature was raised by a thinker for whom Kant had always felt the deepest respect, and whom he was accustomed to regard as the proper arbiter of all questions concerning the exact and empirical sciences. In the preface to the "Attempt to Introduce the Concept of Negative Magnitudes into Philosophy" Kant had already referred to Euler's procedure of taking the certain results of mathematics as the necessary touchstone of the truth or falsity of universal philosophical propositions; he relied on him in the treatise "On the First Ground of the Distinction of Regions

97. Leonhard Euler, *Lettres à une princesse d'Allemagne sur divers sujets de physiques et de philosophie* (Petersburg, 1768); *Theoria motus corporum solidorum seu rigidorum* (Rostock and Greifswald, 1765); "Réflexions sur l'espace et le temps," *Histoire de l'Académie des Sciences et Belles Lettres* (Berlin, 1748); *Mechanica sive motus scientia analytica exposita*, 2 vols. (Petersburg, 1736–42). See *Das Erkenntnisproblem*, 2d ed., vol. 2, pp. 472 ff., 501 ff., for more about Euler and his battle against the "metaphysical" theory of space and time.

in Space" ("Von dem ersten Grunde des Unterschiedes der Gegenden im Raume"), dating from 1768, which is explicitly advanced as a continuation of Euler's "Reflections on Space and Time," and in the book *On the Form and Principles of the Sensible and the Intelligible World* he is once more celebrated as *phaenomenorum magnus indagator et arbiter* ["great investigator and judge of phenomena"].[98]

Accordingly, one thing stood firm and indubitable for Kant, now that he was commencing a transformation of his doctrine which seemed to bring him closer to metaphysics once again, namely, that whatever validity might be attributed to metaphysical principles, mathematics, as pure and applied knowledge, had to be confirmed as unconditionally valid and guarded against all metaphysical "chicanery." How was this aim to be accomplished, however, if one held fast to the opposition between the sensible and the intelligible world, as Kant did from now on? Was it possible for mathematics to be completely applicable to the physical, unless both were declared to be of the same kind in their nature and essence? Here thought runs into a peculiar dilemma. If it decides to assert full correspondence between the mathematical and the physical, so that there is no proposition of pure mathematics which is not also completely valid in applied mathematics, then it seems that the origin and cognitive value of mathematical concepts are no different from those of empirical ones. On the other hand, if mathematical truths are regarded as truths of pure understanding, which derive not from things but from the laws and activities of the intellect itself, what guarantees do we have that things fully conform to pure concepts, that the sensible conforms to the intelligible? If we were to fall back on a "preestablished harmony" between the two realms, we would have mere verbiage, not a solution to the problem.[99]

And in fact the Leibnizian system of metaphysics runs aground on just this point. The basic flaw in this system, in Kant's judgment, is precisely that the sole form of the rational advanced and recognized in it can be affirmed only through its applicability to empirical being,

98. II, 206, 394, 431 (*Ak.* II, 167, 378, 414).
99. Cf. Kant's later verdict in his letter to Marcus Herz dated February 21, 1772 (IX, 102) (*Ak.* X, 123), and *De mundi sensibilis,* §22, Scholium (II, 426) (*Ak.* II, 409).

and that it introduces a false concept of this latter. For the form under which the empirically actual stands is space and time; these two, however, are not acknowledged in Leibniz's system to be specifically essential and pure means of cognition, but are only treated as "confused ideas." Strict, literal truth in this system belongs exclusively to the dynamic relations between substances, the relationships of the simple monads, while nothing that we express in the language of space and time ever gives us this truth, but always merely an indirect and clouded image of it.

If this view is valid, however, the doctrine of Leibniz and Wolff has foundered on this point. For if substances are primary and space and time secondary and derivative (indeed something derived that never fully matches its archetype), all the content of mathematics depends on the actuality of things. Thus, if we wished to think through the consequences and not turn arbitrarily aside, we would be brought back to the standpoint of an empirical foundation for mathematics, and it makes no material difference that the result is reached from premises quite different from Locke's. For generally speaking, where things determine concepts, not the reverse, only contingent knowledge is attainable, not knowledge which is universally valid and necessary. Hence, if the assumptions of the Leibnizian-Wolffian systems hold, and space and time express the structure of actuality, though not adequately, but in an obscure and confused fashion, that is the end of the exactitude and unconditional necessity of all mathematics. Mathematical propositions would then be entitled to claim merely relative and comparative, not absolute universality and truth, and the idea that geometrical axioms and propositions might be changed or contradicted by further experience would no longer be absurd. [100] Only one way is open to us to avoid all these difficulties: to grant mathematics its full freedom and independence from the empirical and actual, and conversely to guarantee its complete agreement with the latter. It would have to remain a part of the realm of pure

100. See esp. *De mundi sensibilis,* §15 (II, 420) (*Ak.* II, 403). It might be reiterated that here it naturally is not a matter of the actual view of space and time and the cognitive value of mathematics which Leibniz and Locke historically held, but of hypothetical inferences which Kant claims to be grounded in the premises of Leibniz's system.

intellectual forms, and yet be related to the sensible realm in a special and specific way true of no other mere "concept of the understanding." It would have to rest on a principle of knowledge which would be at once rational and sensory, general and individual, universal and concrete.

It is plain that we are not dealing here merely with an arbitrary and paradoxical demand, but that, if we now move on to an exact critical analysis of the forms of space and time, a genuine datum of knowledge corresponds to what is desired. For in these forms everything that was just previously asserted as a mere postulate finds its complete and precise fulfillment. Space and time are "general"; they are what all possibility of figure and place in general rest on, and hence they must be assumed in every statement about a determinate and particular form of being, and about an individual empirical structure. But at the same time they are "concrete," for we are not dealing with generic concepts in them, which might be exemplified in a number of particular instances, but if we wish to grasp them in their essential determinacy we must think them as both particular and "single." A generic concept contains its different species under it, as the concept of tree includes pines, lindens, oaks, etc. Here, though, with regard to space and time, there are no comparable subordinate classes. Analyze the whole of space and time as we will, we are led to nothing simpler in thought, no concept with a less complex content, but to conceive every foot and every yard, every minute and every second, we must also think the totality of spatial coexistence and temporal succession. The yard would not be thought "in" space nor the second "in" time were this requirement not met, for they must be marked off from all the other parts of space and time; therefore these latter must be thought together with them.

There now appears a new psychological and epistemological terminology for this peculiar way of relating the individual to the general and vice versa, and of conceiving the whole in every part and with every part. Wherever this kind of conception is needed and is possible, we have to do not with the form of a sheer concept, but with the form of intuition.[101] Now Kant has discovered the decisive idea that

---

101. See *De mundi sensibilis*, §§13–15 (II, 414–22) (*Ak.* II, 398–406).

contains the solution to all his former doubts. The intuition of space and time, which must be acknowledged as independent and peculiar givens for knowledge, in fact forms the true answer to the demands which till now must have seemed incompatible. In intuition, the moment of purity is combined with the moment of sensibility. Space and time are sensible, because coexistence and succession cannot be resolved into mere conceptual determinations by any analysis, however far it is pushed; both are "pure" because even without undertaking any sort of analysis into conceptual elements, we can comprehend the function they, as wholes, have of bringing us to full clarity, and we can grasp them in their unconditional validity, divorced from all that is merely factual and empirical. Only after we have progressed to this point do we have a science of the sensible, a strict and exact application of mathematics and its necessary determinations to phenomena and their change and cessation. We have differentiated two fundamental kinds of pure knowledge: that by which we determine the relations of the intelligible, and that by which we determine order in what is sensible. Only the first kind instructs us about things as they are, while the second, intuitive knowledge of space and time, makes the world of appearances accessible and meaningful to us, but within this its domain, full universality and necessity, unlimited precision and certainty, are conserved.[102]

In this way, Kant hit upon a final resolution of the opposition between Leibniz and Newton, though it could not be expressed as simply as in the case of the conflict between Leibniz and Locke. In the latter case, Kant could in every essential respect espouse Leibniz's judgment; if he rejected the label "innate" and substituted the affirmation of fundamental laws of the mind, which, however, are only recognized when they are exercised, this was more an improvement in terminology than a completely new substantial turn he gave to Leibnizian thought. But in the battle between Leibniz and Newton, it was no longer possible simply to declare himself for one side or the other, for in posing his problem this way he went as far beyond the one as the other. When Euler, in standing up for Newton, had defended the interests of empirical research, which were to be protected

102. See ibid., esp. §§11 and 12 (II, 413 ff.) (*Ak.* II, 397 ff.); §4 (II, 408 f.) (*Ak.* II, 392 f.).

against any encroachments from elsewhere, at this point a difficult and complex problem resulted for Kant's philosophical critique. It had to substitute a positive judgment for a negative one; it had not only to secure and confirm science within its own boundaries, but at the same time to determine with precision, as the proper domain of metaphysics, what lay beyond those boundaries.

Only thus could both the infringement of metaphysics on natural science and also the meddlings of the latter in the former successfully be warded off. The development of mathematical physics in the eighteenth century afforded many cautionary examples of the second kind of meddling. Kant had willingly allowed the geometer and the physicist the use of the concept of absolute space to derive their propositions, for in fact this use was exhausted in the assertion that the meaning of "space" in geometry and mechanics is not identical with what we call the whole of the material world, but stands over against it as something unmistakably all its own. Kant's own view agreed completely with this thesis, and he sought support for it from an examination of purely geometrical relations in his treatise of 1768, "On the First Ground of the Distinction of Regions in Space."[103] What he had no right to do, on the other hand, was this: from the nature of this pure mathematical space to draw conclusions on all sides concerning the basic problems of speculative cosmology and theology, touching the relation of God to the world, of creation to eternity. Newton had led the way here as well, subjoining to the calculations and experiments of the *Principia Mathematica* and the *Opticks* sections in which he had given his theory of space as God's "sensorium" and the organ of divine omnipresence, cautious and tentative in its form, to be sure, but nevertheless quite positive and dogmatic as regards its content.[104] And in the correspondence between Leibniz and Clarke questions of this kind had in the end overridden and pushed aside almost all others.

The dialectical contradictions into which one thus falls had, how-

103. See II, 391 ff. (*Ak.* II, 375 ff.).

104. Isaac Newton, *Philosophiae naturalis principia mathematica*, bk. 3, ed. Thomae Le Seur and Francisci Jacquier (Geneva, 1739), vol. 3, pp. 673 ff.; *Optice*, translated into Latin by Samuel Clarke (Lausanne, 1740), pp. 297 f.

ever, already been pointed out keenly and clearly by Leibniz. If one assumes, he had reasoned, that space and time are predicates which apply indifferently to all that is, thus identically to the mental and the physical, to God and the world, the Creation seems necessarily to be an act taking place in absolute space and absolute time. Thus its "where" and "when" are determinate, that is, there is a fixed moment of its inception and a fixed place, a delimited portion of infinite space, which serves as the original receptacle for matter.

But if one goes on to determine rationally, somehow or other, what this place and this time were, one is soon entangled in a net of antinomies. Since in empty space and empty time no place is to be preferred to any other nor manifests any essential difference from any other, any point that we might assume hypothetically as the "beginning" or the spatial locus of the Creation is arbitrarily interchangeable with any other. Therefore in this whole way of looking at the question it is impossible to posit any "here" without its immediately turning into a "there," or any "now" without its turning under our very hands into its opposite, an "earlier" or a "later."[105] Kant took the most active interest in all these problems—the Leibniz-Clarke correspondence had been freshly brought to his attention by its publication in Dutens's edition of Leibniz's works in 1768, and the notes he made in his personal copy of Baumgarten's *Metaphysica* show how deeply engrossed he was with it over a period of time—and he understood the question propounded here, but he gave it a far more universal meaning. The contradiction Leibniz has discovered here is not an isolated one; rather, it appears everywhere and anywhere sensory predicates are applied to intelligible objects or intelligible predicates to sensible objects. Whenever this is done, any proposition which we can assert is immediately confronted by its antithesis, and both can be demonstrated with apparently equal validity and necessity.

Kant himself tells us that in the period prior to the Inaugural Dissertation he worked out such antithetical proofs, and in doing so first became fully conscious of the distinctive features of the new

105 See the correspondence between Leibniz and Clarke (in my edition of Leibniz's main writings on the foundations of philosophy [Philosophische Bibliothek, vol. 107/8], vol. 1, pp. 134 f., 137 f., 188, 190).

theory, the separation of the substantive content of the sense world from that of the intelligible world with regard to principles and method. "At first I saw this theory only in shadow. I tried very seriously to prove propositions and their opposites, not in order to justify a dubious theory but because I suspected I might discover an illusion of the understanding with which it was involved. The year 1769 brought great light for me."[106] The illusion was destroyed as soon as it was recognized that in order for the object of any judgment to be completely determined, a specific mark stating the cognitive conditions under which it stands for us was required. If this is neglected, laws which are rooted in our subjective "aptitude" (indoles), and in fact are necessarily grounded in it, are erroneously taken to be conditions of things in general, which thus must pertain to them however we regard them; there then results a characteristic subreption of consciousness. Since the boundary lines of the mode of cognition are erased, all clarity and unambiguity of objects disappears; we no longer have any fixed subject of judgment, but wander back and forth between differing interpretations and meanings of our judgments with no sure guide. The human mind becomes a magic lantern which strangely alters and distorts the outlines of things by the semblance it projects onto them. The only protection against such a "deception of the mind" is the secure delimitation of the two spheres in which all our judgment moves. If this division is made, we can no longer blunder into the attempt to apply the predicate of "where" and "when" to objects in the pure world of the understanding, for example, God and immaterial substances, just as conversely we can no longer conceive sensible objects except under the specific conditions of sensibility, space and time as the pure forms of intuition.[107]

And two things are accomplished by this. The "infection," the contagium, of the intelligible by the sensible, which emerges so clearly in Newton's theory concerning God,[108] is avoided; on the other side, unconditional certainty and total applicability is guaranteed to the

106. *Reflexionen* on the *Critique of Pure Reason*, no. 4.
107. See *De mundi sensibilis*, sect. V: "On the Method of Dealing with the Sensitive and the Intellectual in Metaphysics" (II, 427 ff.) (*Ak.* II, 410 ff.).
108. See ibid., §§22 and 23 (II, 426, 428) (*Ak.* II, 409, 410–11).

forms of sensibility within their own field, thus for the whole sphere of objects of experience. Metaphysics as well as mathematics is satisfied in the same way; each has found in itself its center of gravity and its essential principle of certainty. It is here that the main theme and the proper center of the Inaugural Dissertation lie for Kant himself. On September 2, 1770, he writes to Lambert, to whom he is sending the book: "The first and fourth sections can be scanned without careful consideration; but in the second, third, and fifth, though my indisposition prevented me from working them out to my satisfaction, there seems to me to be material deserving more careful and extensive exposition. The most universal laws of sensibility play an unjustifiably large role in metaphysics, where, after all, it is merely concepts and principles of pure reason that are at issue. A quite special, though purely negative science, general phenomenology (*phenomenologia generalis*), seems to me to be presupposed by metaphysics. In it the principles of sensibility, their validity and their limitations, would be determined, so that these principles could not be confusedly applied to objects of pure reason, as has heretofore almost always happened. For space and time, and the axioms for considering all things under these conditions, are, with respect to empirical knowledge and all objects of sense, very real; they are actually the *conditions* of all appearances and of all empirical judgments. But extremely mistaken conclusions emerge if we apply the basic concepts of sensibility to something that is not at all an object of sense, that is, something thought through a universal or a pure concept of the understanding as a thing or substance in general, and so on. It seems to me, too (and perhaps I shall be fortunate enough to win your agreement here by means of my very inadequate essay), that such a *propaedeutic discipline*, which would preserve metaphysics proper from any admixture of the sensible, could be made usefully explicit and evident without great strain."[109] What Kant here regards as the object of an easy effort was to engross his most profound and taxing intellectual labor for a decade. Only the appearance of the *Critique of Pure Reason* almost eleven years after this letter to Lambert brought that propaedeutic to

109. IX, 73 (*Ak.* X, 92).

metaphysics which Kant has in mind to its true "explicitness and evidence."

But before we embark on this new path leading out of the Inaugural Dissertation, let us review again the development from which the conclusions of this book arose. There are relatively few external facts that can be established as to the period between the *Dreams of a Spirit-Seer* and the Dissertation, but if they are assembled, a clear picture of the philosophical advance of these years emerges. We know that Kant became acquainted with Leibniz's *Nouveaux essais* at this time, that in agreement with it he sketched out a theory of pure intellectual concepts in which space and time stand immediately alongside pure concepts of reason such as substance, cause, possibility and necessity, etc., and that his pathway to the sharp separating-off of the elementary concepts of sensibility, the pure concepts of intuition, was only gradually cleared. We can trace how he tried to resolve the conflict between the "mathematicians" and the "metaphysicians" on the problem of space and time for himself, bolstered in particular by Euler's writings and with reference to the discussion between Leibniz and Clarke; and how he becomes ever more deeply tangled in dialectical contradictions until at last, in 1769, he comes face to face with the decisive significance of the general problem of the antinomies.[110] He is given the new solution to the question along with this precise formulation of it. The thesis and the antithesis of the antinomies can only be reconciled if we understand that the two refer to different worlds. To establish the division between these two worlds, and thus to ground and secure each in itself, from now on comprises the proper task of metaphysics. Thus it is not valid in metaphysics for "practice to dictate method," for us to start, as in the other sciences, with particular inquiries and mental steps, and only later, when a certain quantity of knowledge has been accumulated, to seek the principles by which our thinking has been guided. Rather, here the question of method is the essential and the only justifiable starting point of all cognition: *methodus antevertit omnem scientiam.*[111]

110. For more on the significance of the problem of the antinomies for Kant's development, see Benno Erdmann's preface to his edition of the *Reflexionen*, pp. xxiv ff.

111. *De mundi sensibilis*, §23 (II, 427) (Ak. II, 411).

Any dogmatic judgment regarding which this basic preliminary question cannot be answered is to be rejected as an empty intellectual bagatelle.

At this point it is especially clear how Kant, while arriving at a new intellectual perspective, does not break with the previous evolution of his thought. Philosophy is still for him a "science of the boundaries of human thought," but a new datum, neither the whole scope nor bearing of which he has grasped so far, is now reached as a foundation for the determination of these boundaries. The system of a priori cognitions is the basis on which any division of the sensible and the intelligible worlds rests. Leibniz was the first to sketch out this system, but he did not see and make known its finer ramifications and convolutions, for beyond the common principle, rationality, which is equally proper to all its components, to logical and ontological concepts and to mathematical concepts alike, he overlooked the specific difference in validity that nonetheless holds. The Inaugural Dissertation took the first step toward illuminating this difference; now it was a matter of not stopping there, but of drawing the detailed boundary lines more and more sharply and precisely, until reason emerged as perfectly unified and at the same time as particularized and organized in all its individual moments.

5. The Discovery of the Critical Problem

When Kant, at the age of forty-six, entered into his new academic position with his work *On the Form and Principles of the Sensible and the Intelligible World*, it might have seemed as though his philosophical development had reached its true zenith and were on the verge of coming to an end. He had by now confronted all the major intellectual powers of the age and had won his own independent place among them. It seemed that nothing more was needed than to make the intellectual domain that he had struggled to achieve secure and to extend it on all sides. Kant himself believed that all his ensuing work would be devoted to this aim, merely more detailed fleshing-out and confirmation of the insights he had won. But just at this point occurs the decisive turn that gives his life and thought their true profundity.

What would have constituted the end for others, even for major philosophical talents, was for Kant's philosophical genius only the first step down a completely new road. Later, Kant himself located the beginning of his original achievements as thinker and writer in the year 1770, and in fact everything before this time, rich as its specific content was, seems of minor significance when measured by those standards set up by his development from the Inaugural Dissertation to the First Critique.

Before we launch on the study of this most important period of Kant's inner growth, though, some of the external facts about Kant's life and progress in his academic calling should be briefly recalled. His appointment as professor *ordinarius* of logic and metaphysics formed a significant stage in this, for it was that which first gave Kant leisure to carry out his philosophical work. Although he never complained in the slightest, the letters he addressed to the minister of education and to the king when applying for the professorship are instructive as to how heavily concern about the security of his future weighed on him. "This spring," he writes, "I enter the 47th year of my life, the course of which makes my apprehensions over future poverty ever more disquieting. . . . My years, and the scarcity of opportunities to make a living in the academy if one also has the scrupulousness to apply only for those posts which one can honorably hold, would, in the event that my humble request fails of its aim, necessarily extinguish and abolish any further hope I might have of remaining in my fatherland in the future."[112] Indeed, all the earlier steps Kant had made in this direction had remained fruitless. In his earliest years as teacher, the post of instructor in the Kneiphöfische Domschule in Königsberg, for which he applied, had been denied him; as Wald tells us in his memoir, it was taken by a "notorious ignoramus" by the name of Kahnert.[113] Kant's attempt to obtain the post of professor *extraor-*

---

112. To Minister von Fürst, March 16, 1770; to Friedrich II, March 19, 1770 (IX, 68, 70) (*Ak.* X, 86, 88).

113. See Reicke, *Kantiana*, p. 7; Borowski, *Darstellung des Lebens und Charakters Immanuel Kants*, p. 31. There are no remaining grounds to doubt these accounts since Arthur Warda ("Zur Frage nach Kants Bewerbung um eine Lehrerstelle an der Kneiphöfischen Schule," *Altpreussische Monatsschrift* 35:578 ff.) has shown from the

dinarius of logic and metaphysics, several years after Martin Knutzen's death, also came to grief; when Kant submitted his application
in April, 1756, war was just about to break out again, and the Prussian
regime left the post vacant for reasons of economy.[114] The next application, which Kant submitted two years later for the professorship of
logic and metaphysics, was made under even less favorable auspices.
The position became vacant with the death of Professor Kypke in
1758, at a time when all of East Prussia was occupied by the Russians
and under the control of their military government. So the application
had to be addressed not only to the philosophical faculty in
Königsberg, but also to the "Most Serene and Mighty Czarina and
Ruler of All Russia," the Czarina Elizabeth. Her representative, the
Russian governor of Königsberg, decided against Kant, however; instead of him, his colleague Buck received the appointment; he was
the primary candidate of the Senate of the university on the grounds
that he had more than twelve years' seniority over Kant.[115] But even
after Königsberg had reverted to Prussian control, and when at the
end of the Seven Years' War the affairs of higher education could be
more vigorously attended to, the Ministry of Justice, which at that
time had jurisdiction over higher education, had almost no opportunity to promote Kant. A rescript dated August 5, 1764, addressed to
the East Prussian administration in Königsberg, expressly notes that a
"certain instructor, Immanuel Kant by name," had come to their attention "by reason of several of his writings, which display very
thorough scholarship," but the only post which could be offered to
him at that time was a professorship of poetry in Königsberg. Though
Kant turned down this position, he at least had assurance that as soon
as another occasion arose he "would be placed," and a memorandum

---

records of the Kneiphöfische Domschule that Kahnert was a teacher there from 1757.
No positive evidence that Kant applied for the position has been discovered in the
records.

114. Kant's letter of application to King Friedrich II, April 8, 1756 (see IX, 2) (*Ak.* X, 3).

115. Kant's letters to the Rector and Senate, the philosophical faculty at Königsberg,
and to the Czarina Elisabeth of Russia were a formality explicitly required by the
Russian administration and had been enjoined by a specific ordinance. More information is given by Arthur Warda in the *Altpreussische Monatsschrift* 36:498.

expressly issued to the Senate of the University of Königsberg decreed "that the well-known and universally acclaimed teacher,
Magister Kant, is to be promoted at the first opportunity."[116] But six
more years elapsed before this chance presented itself.

Meanwhile, Kant had to be content with the fact that upon his
application, the position of sublibrarian in the royal castle library was
given to him, with an annual salary of sixty-two dollars, an amount
which, as he said in his application, as modest as it was "would serve
as some assistance to his highly uncertain academic subsistence."[117]
Thanks to the incompetence of his superior, the senior librarian Bock,
all the work to be done in the library fell almost entirely on his shoul-
ders, but he discharged the duties of the office for some years with
the care and accuracy he showed in all things, large and small. It was
only in April, 1772, two years after he had become a professor *ordinarius*, that he resigned from his position as sublibrarian, since this
division of his time was not compatible with his new academic obligations.[118] Further, Kant's concern over the financial security of his old
age during his last years as an instructor is most clearly shown by the
fact that when, in 1769, the prospect of a call to Erlangen presented
itself, he did not want to reject this "chance for a small but certain
prosperity" out of hand. But he took fright when the university,
wishing some sort of declaration, decreed his immediate nomination
and invited him, through the professor of mathematics and physics,
Simon Gabriel Suckow, to take up his duties shortly.

Only now did he feel the whole force of what the change in his
surroundings and his accustomed pattern of life would have meant to
him. "Renewed and very strong assurances," he wrote to Suckow,
"the growing likelihood of a perhaps imminent removal from this
place, attachment to my natal city and to a rather extensive circle of

116. On the plan to give Kant the professorship of poetry and the related rescripts
and decrees, see Schubert's biography of Kant, pp. 49 ff.

117. For the application to King Friedrich II and the Minister Freiherr von Fürst,
dated October 24 and 29, 1765, respectively, see IX, 40, 41 (*Ak.* X, 46, 47). Cf. also
Arthur Warda, *Altpreussische Monatsschrift* 35:477 ff.

118. To King Friedrich II, April 14, 1772 (IX, 109) (*Ak.* X, 130). For more information
on Kant's position and activities as sublibrarian, see Karl Vorländer, *Kants Leben* (Leipzig, 1911), pp. 79 ff.

friends and acquaintances, but most of all my enfeebled physical constitution are suddenly so powerfully opposed in my mind and heart to this plan, so that I look forward to peace of mind only there where I have so far always found it, though in burdensome circumstances. . . . I am very much afraid, dear sir . . . that I have brought your displeasure upon myself through a vain expectation to which I gave rise. But you, my dear sir, know the weaknesses of the human character too well not to forbearingly class a mind which is unreceptive to changes that seem trifling to others with those impediments over which one is as little master as he is of his fate, although their consequences are often detrimental."[119]

This way of thinking was confirmed still more in Kant during the succeeding years, when after becoming professor of logic and metaphysics he was no longer oppressed by financial worries. When Minister of Culture and Education von Zedlitz, who not only valued him as an academic instructor but revered him as a philosopher, attempted to convince him to accept the professorship in Halle, and when, at Kant's refusal, he not only reckoned up for him "the mathematically exact improvement" but also reminded him that for a man such as he it was his duty not to forgo the greater sphere of influence open to him, Kant nonetheless stood fast in his resolution. "I wish that persons with your knowledge and gifts were not so rare in your profession," Zedlitz wrote on that occasion; "I would not trouble you so. But I would like you to be not unmindful of your duty to be as useful as you could be, in the opportunity which is offered to you, and to consider that the 1,000 to 1,200 students at Halle have a right to further their education, which I do not want to be responsible for neglecting, through you."[120] Halle, where Wolff had worked for fourteen years after Frederick the Great called him back, enjoyed the reputation of being the first-ranking university in Germany in philosophy, and in the other faculties as well Zedlitz, who labored diligently to improve the university, could hold up to Kant some great names. Voltaire had said that to see the crown of German

---

119. To Suckow, December 15, 1769 (IX, 66) (*Ak.* X, 78).
120. Zedlitz to Kant, March 28, 1778 (IX, 171) (*Ak.* X, 212).

scholarship, one must go to Halle. Still, Kant withstood not only the seduction of vanity—Zedlitz had offered him the title of *Hofrat* (Councillor), in case "minor circumstances, from which even the philosopher cannot stand aloof," might be able to make this title attractive to him—but also what undoubtedly meant more to him, all the representations Zedlitz had made on the basis of his duties toward the world and toward young people in school. "Monetary gain and the excitement of a grand stage are, as you know, not much of an incentive for me," he wrote to Marcus Herz at this time. "A peaceful situation, nicely fitted to my needs, occupied in turn with work, speculation, and my circle of friends, where my mind, which is easily touched but otherwise free of cares, and my body, which is cranky but never ill, are kept busy in a leisurely way without strain, is all that I have wished for and had. Any change makes me apprehensive, even if it gives the greatest promise of improving my condition, and I am persuaded by this natural instinct of mine that I must take heed if I wish the threads which the Fates spin so thin and weak in my case to be spun to any length. My great thanks, then, to my well-wishers and friends, who think so kindly of me as to undertake my welfare, but at the same time a most humble request to protect me in my present situation from any disturbance."[121]

This decision has often been deplored; fun has also been poked at the philosopher's excessively tender sensibility and his anxiety regarding every question touching his external circumstances of life; but in both cases the judgment rests more on abstract and general grounds than on a weighing of the concrete life situation from which Kant came to his decision. At that time he was squarely facing the completion of his work, which in both the intellectual and the literary respect imposed on him a labor greater than which perhaps no other thinker had ever had to accomplish. From the moment Kant conceived this work, his life no longer had any independent and separate meaning; it was but the underpinning for that intellectual task which it was vital to accomplish. All the powers of his person were solely and simply applied to the process of thinking and put at its disposal.

121. To Marcus Herz, April 1778 (IX, 174) (*Ak.* X, 214).

During this time he continuously bemoaned his frail, "incessantly fitful" health, but his body withstood the intense strain, unprecedented even for Kant, thanks to a careful, scrupulously calculated diet. It is understandable how Kant, at this period, felt any change as nothing but perilous and upsetting, however much it might outwardly appear to be an improvement in his situation. Kant's letter to Marcus Herz recalls in many details, especially in its whole tenor, the correspondence Descartes carried on with Chanut, the French ambassador in Stockholm, when the latter invited him to the court of Christina of Sweden. Descartes, too, strongly resisted this invitation, which required him to abandon the pattern of life he had methodically chosen and so far adhered to strictly systematically—a resistance that in the end he gave up less through conviction than for external reasons. Kant, on the contrary, remained true to his inner law without hesitation, and we may believe that the "natural instinct" which he appeals to was the *daimon* of the great man who orders the external course of his life clearly and positively in accordance with the pure and essential demands of his work.

In his correspondence with Marcus Herz in the decade from 1770 to 1780, we have testimony of incomparable value as to how this work took shape through the steady progression of his thinking, despite all the inner difficulties and hindrances, testimony which must speak for itself, since other accounts of this period are almost completely lacking. For if one tries to infer from the accounts that we have of Kant's lectures on metaphysics a picture of his whole philosophical view at this time, the procedure is questionable in more than one respect. Aside from the fact that the dating of these reports cannot be established with sufficient certainty, so many extraneous things have gotten into them—partly the fault of the writer, partly from the textbook on which Kant based his lectures, as was customary—that their worth as sources for Kantian philosophy is problematical in the extreme. By contrast, the letters to Herz not only reflect the objective progress of Kant's thinking, but are also an accurate mirror of the shifting personal and intellectual moods that accompanied it. Marcus Herz participated as respondent in the public defense of Kant's book *On the Form and Principles of the Sensible and the Intelligible World* and under

Kant's personal tutelage was introduced to all the details of that work. Kant could expect from him, if from anyone, an understanding of the further intellectual development connected with that work. The exchanges of letters on this topic are quite spasmodic and seem to have ceased entirely for a while, but Kant, who was rendering in them an account to himself of how his thinking was progressing, seems always to have felt the need to begin them anew.

Even the personal relation between teacher and pupil took on an increasingly intimate and cordial form in this exchange of letters. "Chosen and inestimable friend," "Most worthy and prized friend," is the way Kant, who was always chary with the title "friend," saluted Herz in his letters. Feeling this way, he allowed Herz a deeper look into the workshop of his mind than anyone before. Even the first letter, of June, 1771, not only sketches out the new results he had achieved meanwhile, but also at the same time throws a clear light on the personal method of thinking he uses from now on. "You know that I examine reasonable criticisms," Kant writes to Herz when he is apologizing for the delay in his reply to the objections of Lambert and Mendelssohn to the Dissertation, "not merely as to how they might be refuted, but also upon reflection I always weave them into my judgments and allow them to overthrow all preconceived opinions that I have previously cherished. In this way I always hope to look at my judgments impartially, from the standpoint of someone else, so as to derive a third view which is better than the one I had. Moreover, simple absence of persuasion among men of such intelligence always proves to me that my theories must lack clarity, evidence, or even something essential. Long experience has taught me that insight into the matters we have in view cannot be forced and sped up by straining, but it takes a rather long while, since one must, with respites, look at divers concepts in as many different relationships and as broad a context as possible: above all, in doing this the sceptical mind should rouse itself and test whether what has been thought is proof against the keenest doubt. From this point of view, I think I have made good use of the time which I took at the risk of incurring a charge of discourtesy, but in fact out of respect for the judgment of both scholars. You know what a great influence sure and certain

knowledge of the distinction between what rests on subjective principles of the human soul, not only of sensibility but also of understanding, and that which concerns objects directly has on the whole field of
philosophy, indeed on the most important aims of mankind in general. If one is not bewitched by the passion for systems, inquiries into
this selfsame fundamental law in its widest application are mutually
confirmatory. I am therefore presently occupied with a work which,
under the title 'The Boundaries of Sensibility and Reason,' is to cover
basic, definite concepts and laws regarding the sense world as related
to a sketch of what constitutes the nature of the theory of taste,
metaphysics, and morals, something very detailed to carry out. During the winter I went through all the pertinent materials, sifted them
all, weighed them, fitted them together, but I finished the outline
only very recently."[122]

What was the new factor distinguishing this project from the
sketch given in the Inaugural Dissertation? It appears indubitable
from Kant's further remarks in the same letter to Herz that the Dissertation was also to form the basis for the forthcoming work Kant was
now contemplating, although he had already recognized its defects in
particular details. We must assume on his part an attitude both positive and negative, an insight that affirms the fundamental procedure
of On the Form and Principles of the Sensible and the Intelligible World and
that nonetheless denies the result with which it had concluded. We
obtain a clear indication of what this insight consisted in if we keep
clearly in mind those objections of Lambert and Mendelssohn that
were the starting point for Kant's further reflections and that served
to arouse his "sceptical mind." The objections of both men agree in
opposing the way in which the doctrine of the "ideality of space and
time" was expressed in the Dissertation. This doctrine, simply in
itself, contained nothing surprising or paradoxical for either of them,
for it was an established proposition of Leibnizian metaphysics that
space and time were only the orderings of "phenomena," a proposition that repeatedly was given the most diverse new twists in
eighteenth-century philosophical literature. Lambert and Men-

122. To Marcus Herz, June 7, 1771 (IX, 96) (Ak. X, 116).

delssohn took exception only to the fact that in the Dissertation this ideality of both space and time seemed to be interpreted once again into a mere subjectivity. "Time," Mendelssohn wrote, "is according to Leibniz a phenomenon, and has, like all appearances, something objective and something subjective." And Lambert, also, emphasized that he had not so far been able to convince himself of the assertion that time was "nothing real," for if change is real (as even an idealist must admit, since he is immediately aware of it in the alteration of his inner representations), time must be also, since all change is connected with time and not "thinkable" apart from it.[123]

Both objections failed to touch the essential, deeper sense of Kant's doctrine; they interchange "transcendental" idealism with "psychological" idealism, to put it in the language of the system to come. This is easy for us to see today, and Kant himself pointed it out in a well-known place in the Critique of Pure Reason.[124] But was not this misunderstanding excusable? Was it not almost inevitable, given the form in which the theory of space and time was presented? Must not the subjectivity of the forms of intuition, even though they were the basis of the certainty of mathematics and natural science, have nevertheless appeared to be a blot separating them from the pure concepts of the understanding, to their disadvantage? For it was the business of these latter to enable us to recognize things not only as they appear to us but also as they are in and for themselves. Though it might be insisted over and over that although space and time are not objects in the absolute sense, their concept is nonetheless "supremely true,"[125] still this truth always remained a second-order truth as long

123. See Mendelssohn's letter to Kant dated December 25, 1770 (IX, 90 ff.) (Ak. X, 108 ff.); Lambert's letter to him of October 13, 1770 (IX, 80 ff.) (Ak. X, 98 ff.).

124. See the Transcendental Aesthetic, §7, A 36–41 = B 53–58 (III, 67 ff.).

125. Cf. the Inaugural Dissertation, §14, no. 6 (II, 418) (Ak. II, 401): "Quanquam autem Tempus in se et absolute positum sit ens imaginarium, tamen, quatenus ad immutabilem legem sensibilium, qua talium pertinet, est conceptus verissimus et per omnia possibilia sensum objecta in infinitum patens intuitivae repraesentionis conditio." ["But though time, posited in itself and absolutely, is an imaginary being, yet so far as it is related to an immutable law of sensibles as such, it is a quite genuine concept, and a condition of intuitive representation, extending in infinitum through all possible objects of the senses."] See also the analogous statement concerning space, Dissertation, §15 E (II, 420) (Ak. II, 404).

as there were other concepts which could claim to relate "directly to things," not simply to appearances and their relations.

Kant's letter to Herz shows us how his reflections as they progress implant themselves at precisely this extremely difficult point. He adheres firmly to the separation of sensible from intellectual concepts as irreversibly certain, but at the same time he now extends the distinction between what rests on subjective principles and what pertains immediately to objects to the sphere thus far unaffected by critique. He now begins to see subjectivity, "not only of sensibility but of understanding as well," ever more definitely and distinctly, but instead of his being thereby enmeshed in a universal theory of doubt, the reverse is the case: the concepts of the understanding take on the same stamp of truth as the forms of pure intuition. Also, it is now the case that they are not true because they depict for us absolute objects, but because they are unavoidable conditions within the system of cognition, in the construction of experiential actuality, and hence are universally and necessarily valid. That this is so had already been recognized and said in the Dissertation, but only a relatively minor significance was granted to this purely logical use of the concepts of the understanding in contrast to the "real" use, which is directed toward knowledge of supersensible objects.[126]

Now, however, the center of gravity of the problem begins to shift: the division between objects, the dualism of the sensible and the intelligible world, is displaced by a division between cognitive functions which are the basis of any sort of objectivity or which claim objectivity for themselves. The boundary is no longer drawn between the *mundus intelligibilis* and the *mundus sensibilis*, but between sensibility and reason. And the latter is here taken in its broadest, most comprehensive sense. Just as we can ask what the essential form of objectivity belonging to space and time is, and just as we discover this form when we clarify the structure and the mode of knowledge of pure mathematics and pure mechanics, we can and must also inquire into the principle on which the necessity of pure knowledge of the understanding or the justness and validity of our basic ethical or

126. For the contrast between *usus logicus* and *usus realis* of the concepts of the understanding, see the Dissertation, §5 (II, 409 f.) (*Ak.* II, 393 f.).

aesthetic judgments rests. The first outline of a work that is to answer all these questions, that is to fix and define relative to one another the differing claims to validity within theoretical cognition, as well as in the realm of ethics and aesthetics, now stands before Kant's eyes; all that seems required to bring it to completion is the detailed execution of a design trenchantly conceived in all its fundamental features.

But after we have gotten to this point, the crucial question looms once more. Assuming that we had specified the boundaries between sensibility and understanding, and in addition the boundaries between theoretical, ethical, and aesthetic judgment, would we actually have then reached a "system" of reason, or perhaps nothing more than an "aggregate"? Is it enough to put this multiplicity and diversity simply on the same level and to handle it that way, or must we not look for a common point of view underlying all these diverse queries? Every dividing line we draw presupposes in the very division it creates an original unity of that which is divided; every analysis presupposes a synthesis. What does this connecting link consist in, if we are now going to search for it, according to the result we have now obtained, in the structure and lawfulness of "pure reason" and never in the world of things?

Kant's letter to Marcus Herz dated February 21, 1772, gives the answer to all these questions, an answer that at one stroke clarifies all the developments which precede and follow, and illuminates them from within, as it were. It has not unjustly been said of this letter that it marks the true hour of birth of the *Critique of Pure Reason*. "You do me no injustice if you become indignant at the total absence of my replies," Kant begins, and we must let his letter speak for itself in full, if all the delicate nuances of the course of his thinking are to be grasped, "but lest you draw any disagreeable conclusions from it, let me appeal to your understanding of the way I think. Instead of excuses, I shall give you a brief account of the kind of things that have occupied my thoughts and that cause me to put off letter-writing in my idle hours. After your departure from Königsberg I examined once more, in the intervals between my professional duties and my sorely needed relaxation, the project we have debated, in order to adapt it to the whole of philosophy and other knowledge and in order to understand its extent and limits. I had already previously made considerable progress in the effort to distinguish the sensible from the intellectual in the field of morals and the principles that spring therefrom. I had also long ago outlined, to my tolerable satisfaction, the principles of feeling, taste, and power of judgment, with their effects—the pleasant, the beautiful, and the good—and was then making plans for a work that might perhaps have the title, 'The Limits of Sense and Reason.' I planned to have it consist of two parts, a theoretical and a practical. The first part would have two sections, (1) general phenomenology and (2) metaphysics, but this only with regard to its nature and method. The second part likewise would have two sections, (1) the universal principles of feeling, taste, and desire and (2) the basic principles of morality. As I thought through the theoretical part, considering its whole scope and the reciprocal relations of all its parts, I noticed that I still lacked something essential, something that in my long metaphysical studies I, as well as others, had failed to pay attention to and that, in fact, constitutes the key to the whole secret of hitherto still obscure metaphysics. I asked myself: What is the ground of the relation of that in us which we call 'representation' to the object?"[127]

This relation, the exposition continues, is easily seen in two cases: when the object produces the representation, and conversely when the latter produces the former. We then understand where the conformity between the two arises, since we believe we see that every effect is proportional to its cause and must "copy" it in the precise sense of that term. Thus the problem seems solved, when we look at it from the standpoint of sensory perception as well as when we adopt the viewpoint of an understanding that itself produces the object that it apprehends. For in the first case, that of pure passivity, there arise no difference and tension, so to speak, between what is given externally and what is caused in us; the object impresses its whole state on us and leaves a sensory imprint which tells us about it. In the second case, however, that of the "divine understanding," the agreement between knowledge and object is again easy to see, for

127. [IX, 102 f. (*Ak.* X, 123).]

here one and the same original identity of the divine essence is exhibited and explained in knowing and forming, in contemplating and in
creating. Accordingly, the possibility of a pure creative understanding, an *intellectus archetypus*, is at least in general comprehensible, as
well as the possibility of a purely receptive understanding, an *intellectus ectypus*. But our understanding falls under neither the one nor
the other of these categories, since it neither of itself generates objects
connected with its cognition nor does it simply accept its effects as
they are immediately presented in sensory impressions. The Dissertation had already exhaustively ruled out the second alternative. "The
pure concepts of the understanding," Kant now goes on, "must not
be abstracted from sense perceptions, nor must they express the reception of representations through the senses; but though they must
have their origin in the nature of the soul, they are neither caused by
the object nor bring the object itself into being. In my dissertation I
was content to explain the nature of intellectual representations in a
merely negative way, namely, to state that they were not
modifications of the soul brought about by the object. However, I
silently passed over the further question of how a representation that
refers to an object without being in any way affected by it can be
possible. I had said: The sensuous representations present them as
they are. But by what means are these things given to us, if not by the
way in which they affect us? And if such intellectual representations
depend on our inner activity, whence comes the agreement that they
are supposed to have with objects. . . ?"[128]

In mathematics this may of course happen, since here the object in
fact arises in an intuitive and conceptual context. The Prize Essay of
1763 had already shown what a circle or a cone "is"; in those cases I
need only inquire as to the act of construction by which this figure is
produced. But what counsels us if we want to grant a similar "construction" for "metaphysical" concepts as well, and if we wish to
construct them in *this* sense "independently of experience"? Concepts of magnitudes may be spontaneous, because the magnitudes as
wholes are built up for us in the synthesis of the manifold "by taking

128. [IX, 103 f. (*Ak.* X, 123).]

numerical units a given number of times," and accordingly the principles of the pure theory of magnitude may hold a priori and with unconditional necessity. "But in the case of relationships involving qualities—as to how my understanding may form for itself concepts of things completely a priori, with which concepts the things must necessarily agree, and as to how my understanding may formulate *real* principles concerning the possibility of such concepts, with which principles experience must be in exact agreement and which nevertheless are independent of experience—this question, of how the faculty of the understanding achieves this conformity with the things themselves, is still left in a state of obscurity."[129] The whole of previous metaphysics leaves us in the lurch regarding this question. For what good is it if one thinks one has solved the riddle by pushing it back into the ultimate origin of things, into that mysterious unity where "being" and "thought" have not yet been separated? What advantage is it if Plato makes a prenatal intellectual intuition of what is divine the origin of the pure concepts of the understanding, if Malebranche postulates a continuing, present connection between the human and the divine mind that is verified and revealed in every cognition of a pure rational principle, if Leibniz or Crusius bases the agreement between the order of things and the order of the laws of the understanding in a "preestablished harmony"? In all these seeming "explanations," rather, is not something absolutely unknown used to explain something relatively unknown, something inconceivable and unintelligible in our concepts used as the explanation of something merely problematical? "But the *deus ex machina*," Kant protests against all attempts of this kind, "is the greatest absurdity one could hit upon in the determination of the origin and validity of our knowledge. It has—besides its deceptive circle in the conclusion concerning our cognitions—also this additional disadvantage: it encourages all sorts of wild notions and every pious and speculative brainstorm."[130] The fundamental question raised by knowledge, the question of what ensures its objective validity, its relation to the ob-

129. [IX, 104 (*Ak.* X, 123).]
130. [IX, 105 (*Ak.* X, 123).]

ject, must be answered in the clear light of reason and with the recognition of its essential conditions and limits.

The door to the *Critique of Pure Reason* was open, since this form of the question was now immutable. Kant himself says, later on in the letter to Herz, that he has projected an entire system of "transcendental philosophy," since he has reduced "all concepts of completely pure reason" to a certain number of categories—not like Aristotle who assembled his categories merely at random, but rather as they are divided into classes by a few basic laws of the understanding itself. "Without going into details here," he continues, "about the whole series of investigations that has continued right down to this last goal, I can say that, so far as my essential purpose is concerned, I have succeeded and that now I am in a position to bring out a 'Critique of Pure Reason' that will deal with the nature of theoretical as well as practical knowledge—insofar as the latter is purely intellectual. Of this, I will first work out the first part, which will deal with the sources of metaphysics, its methods and limits. After that I will work out the pure principles of morality. With respect to the first part, I should be in a position to publish it within three months."[131]

Strange as it may seem at first glance, Kant's illusion in believing himself able to finish in three months a book which was to occupy him exclusively for eight or nine years more is nonetheless understandable: having conceived this new task so positively and clearly, he might hope to have in that fact alone all the essential conditions of the solution. For all the fundamental insights from which the *Critique of Pure Reason* was wrought are actually achieved. What Kant later called his "revolution in thinking," the "Copernican" turn to the problem of knowledge,[132] is here complete. Reflection no longer begins with objects as things known and given, in order to show how an object migrates into our cognitive faculty and is pictured in it,[133] but it inquires about the meaning and stuff of the very concept of an object, about what the claim to objectivity universally means, whether in

---

131. [IX, 104 (*Ak.* X, 123).]
132. See the *Critique of Pure Reason,* preface to the 2d ed., B x ff. (III, 15 ff.).
133. Cf. *Prolegomena to Any Future Metaphysics,* §9 (IV, 31) (*Ak.* II, 282).

mathematics, natural science, metaphysics, or in morals and aesthetics. In this question is found the link that directly unifies all concepts
and problems of "pure reason" into a system. Whereas all previous
metaphysics had begun with the "what" of the object, Kant begins
with the "how" of judgment about objects. While the earlier
metaphysics knew how to give an account of the general quality of
things, Kant examines and analyzes simply the assertion of knowledge of objects, to establish what is posited and meant by it, by the
relation it expresses.

In this transformation of the question, "metaphysics" became
"transcendental philosophy" in the strict sense in which the *Critique
of Pure Reason* later defined the new term: "I call all knowledge transcendental which is in general concerned not with objects, but with
our mode of knowledge of objects, insofar as this is to be possible a
priori."[134] A whole not of things but of "modes of knowledge," to
which the essential features of our moral, teleological, and aesthetic
faculties of judgment belong, faces us and demands unification and
division, association in a common task and recognition of their specific work. And similarly, the idea, if not the expression, of the other
great question of the First Critique is arrived at: "How are synthetic
judgments a priori possible?" For this is precisely the problem posed
in Kant's letter to Herz: by what right can we speak of a priori knowledge which goes beyond all that is given in the passive elements of
perceptions and sensibility, just as it goes beyond any sheer conceptual analysis; knowledge which as a declaration concerning "real"
connection and real opposition is necessarily related to experience,
but which on the other hand, because it wants to be valid for "all
experience in general," is grounded in no *particular* experience? It is
the universally valid and necessary—what is found not only in
knowledge of quantities but also in that of qualities, that comes to
light not only in the unfolding of the relations of coexistence in space
or succession in time but also in "dynamic unity," in assertions about
things and properties, causes and effects—which has become the

134. *Critique of Pure Reason*, introduction, VII, A 11–12 = B 25 (III, 49).

problem, a problem which can be unlocked only with that same new view of the "concept of the object," in which in general "the key to the whole secret of hitherto still obscure metaphysics" is to be sought.

The closer Kant comes to mastery of the details, though, the more clearly the whole complexity of the task he has undertaken confronts him. Behind every solution new questions arise; behind every categorization of the concepts of reason into fixed classes and faculties arise further subdivisions, each of which leads to a fresh and subtle inquiry. The plan of his labor had already become known, and Herz in particular, with understandable impatience, presses him to finish the work. But Kant does not allow himself to be diverted from the clear requirements of the subject and from his progress by any expectation which he himself cherishes or which he had aroused in others. "Since I have come this far in my projected reworking of a science that has been so long cultivated in vain by half the philosophical world," he writes in his next letter to Herz, separated from the earlier one by almost two years, "since I see myself in possession of a principle that will completely solve what has hitherto been a riddle and that will bring the procedure of reason isolating itself under certain and easily applied rules, I therefore remain obstinate in my resolve not to let myself be seduced by any author's itch into seeking fame in easier, more popular fields, until I shall have freed my thorny and hard ground for general cultivation."[135] Still, Kant hopes to have the book ready to deliver "at Easter" of 1774, or to be able to promise it "almost certainly" shortly after Easter; but at the same time he emphasizes how much time and effort the "planning and complete execution of a whole new conceptual science" has cost him in the matters of method, divisions, and terminology that is exactly fitting. He intends to complete the transcendental philosophy first, then he wants to move on to metaphysics, which he will carry out in two parts: the "metaphysics of Nature" and the "metaphysics of morals." He adds that he contemplates publishing the latter first, and that he is already anticipating this with pleasure.

135. [IX, 114 (Ak. X, 136).]

It is of particular interest as regards his system that here ethical questions are treated on the same presuppositions and on the same plan as the questions of pure theoretical knowledge. The period in which Kant seemed to assimilate himself to the psychological method of ethics as practiced by the English, and in which he prized the procedure of a Shaftesbury, Hutcheson, and Hume as a "beautiful discovery of our age,"[136] now lies far behind him. The Inaugural Dissertation had ranged the problem of morality on the side of the "intelligible," and divested it of all sensuous determination on grounds of pleasure and pain, in express opposition to Shaftesbury.[137] Kant saw in his transformation of the foundations of ethics, as he wrote to Lambert when sending him the Dissertation, one of the most important goals of the now altered form of metaphysics.[138] Ethics, like the doctrine of space and time and like that of the pure concepts of reason, has become an a priori discipline; the characteristic objectivity of the ought on the one side is distinguished from the objectivity of being as on the other side it illuminates and is reciprocally illuminated by it.

This correspondence between Kant and Herz will not be gone into in further detail, however, since in it the same overall picture is repeated constantly. To an outside observer it might have seemed at times as if the plan Kant was contemplating were but a will-o'-the-wisp luring him blindly into unknown reaches of thought. Time and again he believes he is at the end, but the further he goes, the longer is the path he has yet to traverse. After he thinks, toward the end of 1773, that he can promise the termination of his work "almost certainly" at a time shortly after Easter of 1774, three more years pass in which, under the continuous influx of ever-new questions, he obviously has not even begun the systematic composition and writing. The expectations and queries directed at him from the literary and scholarly circles of Germany grow increasingly impatient and pressing. "Say something to me even in a couple of lines," Lavater writes

136. See the announcement of his course of lectures in 1765–66 (II, 326) (*Ak.* II, 312).
137. *De mundi sensibilis*, §9 (II, 412) (*Ak.* II, 396).
138. To Lambert, September 2, 1770 (IX, 73) (*Ak.* X, 92).

him in February, 1774; "are you dead? why do so many write who cannot—and you, who can write so exquisitely, write nothing? why are you silent—in this, this *modern* age—make not a sound? Asleep? Kant—no, I will not praise you—but tell me why you are silent? or rather: tell me that you will speak."[139] When Lavater wrote these words, he did not in the least suspect that it was precisely the advent of the "modern age" that this silence foretold.

"I am rebuked from all sides," Kant writes to Herz on November 24, 1776, "on account of the inactive state in which I seem to have been for so long, and yet I have never been more systematically and engrossingly busy than during the years you have not seen me. Topics which I might hope to earn fleeting acclaim by treating, pile up under my hands, as is usual when one has been seized by a fruitful principle. But they are all held in check by one main thing, as by a dam, a thing by which I hope to earn an enduring gain, which I actually think I now possess and which is less necessary to think through than to carry through. . . . It is the part of persistence, if I may say so, to follow a plan undistracted, and I am often tempted by difficulties to devote myself to different, pleasanter matters, an infidelity from which I have from time to time been restrained by overcoming some obstacles, partly by the importance of the business itself. You know that it must be possible to survey the field of judgment independent of all empirical principles, that is, of pure reason, because it lies in us a priori and needs await no revelations from experience. To specify the whole scope of it, the divisions, the boundaries, the entire substance of it by sure principles and to erect boundary stones so that in the future one can know confidently whether he finds himself on the terrain of reason or of sophistry, it takes: a critique, a discipline, a canon, and an architectonic of pure reason, hence a formal science, which can use nothing of what lies ready to hand and which requires for its foundation quite special technical expression."

Not only the systematic, but also the technical, outline of the First Critique is now clear to Kant's eyes, and above all the distinction

139. Lavater to Kant, February 8, 1774 (IX, 117) (*Ak.* X, 141).

between "analytic" and "dialectic," between the realm of reason and that of sophistry, has been vouchsafed him. But he still could not estimate the task of composition in its entirety, for there follows again the assurance, which is already rather dubious, that he hopes to be finished, to be sure not before Easter, but probably in the following summer. Nevertheless, he begs Herz not to have any expectations "which are wont occasionally to be troublesome and detrimental."[140] Three-quarters of a year later, in August, 1777, Kant informs him that the *Critique of Pure Reason* is still a "stumbling block" to all the other plans and labors he has in mind, nevertheless he is busy clearing it away; he now believes that he will have it done "this winter." What is holding him up now is nothing more than the labor of making his thoughts as clear as possible for others, because experience shows that what one is thoroughly familiar with, and which is clarified to the highest degree for oneself, is customarily misunderstood even by experts if it lies wholly off the beaten path.[141]

In April, 1778, however, he must once again counter the rumor that several pages from his "work in hand" are ready to be printed. But if one were to conclude from this expression that at least the first outline of the book and the literary form it was to take were firm for Kant, the following sentences, which speak explicitly of a writing "not very many pages of which have been ushered into the world," inform us otherwise.[142] In August of the same year we hear of the work as a "Handbook of Philosophy," which he is still working on tirelessly; and again a year later its completion is projected for Christmas of 1779.[143] The composition must in any case have begun by then, for in May, 1779, Hamann told Herder that Kant was working briskly away on his "Ethics of Pure Reason"; in June, 1780, it was further said that he prides himself on the delay, because that very thing will contribute to the perfection of his project.[144] The actual

140. To Herz, November 24, 1776 (IX, 151) (*Ak.* X, 184).
141. To Herz, August 20, 1777 (IX, 158) (*Ak.* X, 195).
142. To Herz, April 1778 (IX, 174) (*Ak.* X, 214).
143. To Engel, July 4, 1779 (IX, 191) (*Ak.* X, 238).
144. Hamann to Herder, May 17, 1779, and June 26, 1780, *Schriften* (ed. Roth), vol. 6, pp. 83, 146.

writing, aside from preparatory sketches and drafts, can have consumed only a very short time; Kant confirms this in telling Garve and Mendelssohn that he accomplished his exposition of the subjects which he had carefully pondered more than twelve years running "in some four or five months, on the wing, as it were." After a decade of the deepest meditation, after repeated postponement, the completion of the book is achieved only by a sudden resolution that energetically interrupts the spinning-out of his thoughts. Only the fear that death or the enfeeblement of old age might surprise him while still at work gave Kant the strength at last to put an outward conclusion to his thinking, one which he himself felt to be only preliminary and inadequate.[145] But in this as well the *Critique of Pure Reason* is a classic book, for the works of the great thinkers, unlike great works of literary art, appear in their truest form when the seal of perfection is not set on them, but when they still reflect the incessant movement and the inner restlessness of thought itself.

In the particular preparatory studies for the First Critique we still possess, this process comes to light with maximum clarity and vividness. The papers Rudolf Reicke has published under the title *Loose Papers from Kant's Literary Remains (Lose Blätter aus Kants Nachlass)* as well as the *Reflections (Reflexionen)* edited by Bruno Erdmann, contain notes that unmistakably belong to this stage of his preparations; one of the loose papers published by Reicke can be dated with fair precision, since Kant did his jotting in the empty space of a letter sheet bearing the date May 20, 1775. If one starts with this sheet and groups with it the other notes that are of a piece with its contents, the composite thus obtained sheds light from quite diverse angles on the point that Kant's thinking had reached at this period.[146] We cannot go further into the substance of these notes here; it is comprehensible only if we presuppose the way in which the problem is put in the *Critique of Pure Reason* and the basic concepts of the latter.

145. To Garve, August 7, 1783; to Mendelssohn, August 16, 1783 (IX, 223, 230) (*Ak.* X, 315, 322).

146. Further on this in Theodor Haering (who has edited and commented on the loose papers concerned), *Der Duisburgsche Nachlass und Kants Kritizismus um 1775* (Tübingen, 1910).

But almost as meaningful as the purely substantial content of these notes is the glimpse they afford us of Kant's manner of working. "Kant," Borowski tells us on this score, "first made general outlines in his head; then he worked these out in more detail; he wrote what was to be inserted here or there, or was to be explained more fully, on little scraps of paper which he then attached to that first, hastily jotted-down manuscript. After some time had elapsed, he worked the whole over again, and copied it out neatly and clearly, as he always wrote, for the printer."[147] The notes we have from 1775 still belong entirely to that first stage of preparation, in which Kant tries to get the ideas established purely for himself, without regard to the reader and the literary form of the book, and tries to vary his manner of expression in the most diverse ways. No definite, strictly maintained scheme of exposition reigns here, no attachment to a fixed arrangement or terminology. Greatly varying statements and ventures cut across and crowd each other out, without any of them achieving ultimate supremacy and a fixed and final form. Anyone who might picture Kant's thought as a steel-clad structure of definitions, scholastic distinctions, and analyses of concepts must be astonished by the freedom and flexibility found here. In particular, Kant maintains a truly sovereign neutrality toward all questions of terminology. He coins designations and distinctions according to the substantive demands of the problem in hand, only to drop them again as soon as a new turn his thought has taken demands it. Nowhere is his progress with the topic at hand hindered by a previously adopted stereotype, but the content always generates its appropriate form.

Thus there results, as though casually and by chance, a wealth of ideas, which even in comparison with the later, final expression of ideas in the *Critique of Pure Reason* have their own special and independent worth. In fact, for anyone who pursues Kant's statements with that pedantry which many seem to regard as the hallmark of genuine and "exact" Kant-Philologie, in order to show the variations and "contradictions" in the particular concepts and expressions he

147. Borowski, *Darstellung des Lebens und Charakters Immanuel Kants*, p. 191 f.

uses, these loose papers can only mean a chaos of heterogeneous instances. If, however, they are read, as they must be, as various attempts to pin down thought that is in motion and to give it a first, preliminary outline, one gains from them a picture of the peculiarity and style of Kant's thinking perhaps more vivid than from many a finished and eloquent book. Moreover, one understands what powerful internal and external difficulties had to be overcome before ideas of such a kind could take on the final form we encounter in the First Critique. So Kant was perhaps not in fact wrong when he made the difficulties of exposition ultimately responsible for the slow progress of the book.

The general outlines of the critical system were laid down as early as 1775, as nearly as we can tell from the notes dating from that time, but it seems that the printing of the *Critique of Pure Reason* began only in December, 1780, according to the allusions contained in Hamann's correspondence with Hartknoch. On the first of May, 1781, Kant is able to inform Herz in a letter of the imminent appearance of the book. "In the current Easter book fair there will appear a book of mine, entitled *Critique of Pure Reason.* . . . This book contains the result of all those varied investigations, which have their origin in the concepts we discussed under the heading 'The *mundus sensibilis* and *intelligibilis*,' and it is very important to me to deliver the summation of my efforts to the same perceptive man who deigned to cultivate my ideas, a man so discerning that he penetrated those ideas more deeply than anyone else."[148] Thus Kant retrospectively couples his book with his philosophical past. But while the man who was now fifty-seven years old may have looked on the book, born of twelve years' reflection, as the terminus of his life's work, he did himself an injustice by this judgment. For this book became, for Kant himself as well as for the history of philosophy, the beginning of a wholly new development.

148. [IX, 194 (*Ak.* X, 249).]

III THE CONSTRUCTION AND CENTRAL PROBLEMS OF THE *CRITIQUE OF PURE REASON*

1

If what is said about great thinkers is true, that the style is the man, this aspect of the *Critique of Pure Reason* poses a difficult problem for the biographer of Kant. For nowhere else in the history of literature and philosophy do we find so profound and involved an alteration of style as took place with Kant in the decade between 1770 and 1780— not even in Plato, the style of whose old age, in the *Philebus*, the *Sophist*, or the *Parmenides*, differs so markedly from the manner in which the early dialogues were written. Only with difficulty can one recognize in the author of the *Critique of Pure Reason* the man who wrote *Observations on the Feeling of the Beautiful and the Sublime* or the *Dreams of a Spirit-Seer*. Strictness in abstract analysis of concepts replaces the free play of humor and imagination; a kind of academic ponderousness supplants the reflective grace and cheerfulness of those other books. To be sure, anyone who knows how to read the *Critique of Pure Reason* rightly also finds in it, along with the acuteness and depth of thought, an extraordinary strength of intuition and an exceptional power of linguistic imagery. Goethe said that when he read a page in Kant, he always felt as though he were entering a lighted room. Alongside his skill at exhaustively analyzing the most difficult and knotty complexes of ideas stands Kant's gift for expressing and focusing the comprehensive result of a long deduction and conceptual analysis at one stroke, as it were, in striking images and

139

epigrammatic, unforgettable turns of phrase. On the whole, however, most readers have the overpowering impression that the expository form Kant chose fetters his thought and does not foster its adequate and limpid expression. In his concern for the stability and definiteness of terminology, for exactness in the definition and division of concepts, and for agreement and parallelism of schemata, Kant's natural, lively personal and intellectual form of expression seems struck dumb. He felt this himself, and said so. "The method of my discourse," he remarks in a diary note, "has a prejudicial countenance; it appears scholastic, hence pettifogging and arid, indeed crabbed and a far cry from the note of genius." But it is conscious intent that holds him back from every approximation, from every concession to the note of "genius." He says elsewhere: "I have adopted the scholastic method and preferred it to the free play of mind and wit, although I indeed found, since I wanted every thoughtful mind to share in this investigation, that the aridity of this method would frighten off readers of the kind who seek a direct connection with the practical. Even if I had the utmost command of wit and literary charm, I would want to exclude them from this, for it is very important to me not to leave the slightest suspicion that I wanted to beguile the reader and gain his assent that way, but rather I had to anticipate no concurrence whatsoever from him except through the sheer force of my insight. The method actually was the result of deliberation on my part."[1] His sole ideal now, in the face of which all other claims retreat, is to advance strict conceptual deduction and systematization.

But Kant did not renounce those claims lightheartedly. In the years immediately preceding the composition of the *Critique of Pure Reason,* he was continually occupied with weighing whether and how far it might be possible to give philosophical ideas a popular form, without loss of profundity. "For some time," he had written to Herz in January, 1779, "I have been thinking in certain idle moments about the principles of popularity in the sciences (such as are capable of it, of course, since mathematics is not), especially in philosophy, and I

---

1. *Reflexionen* on the *Critique of Pure Reason*, nos. 9 and 14.

think that I have been able to define from this aspect not just another alternative but an entirely different arrangement from that demanded by the scholastic method, which is still the foundation."[2] In point of fact, the early drafts of the First Critique were dominated by this outlook. Along with "discursive (logical) clarity through concepts," they strove for "intuitive (aesthetic) clarity through intuitions," and concrete examples. On this point we find in the preface to the finished book what it was that finally moved Kant to abandon this plan. "For the aids to clearness, though they may be of assistance in regard to details, often interfere with our grasp of the whole. The reader is not allowed to arrive sufficiently quickly at a conspectus of the whole; the bright coloring of the illustrative material intervenes to cover over and conceal the articulation and organization of the system, which, if we are to be able to judge of its unity and solidity, are what chiefly concern us."[3] In the place of the early attempts at an intuitive, generally comprehensible exposition, a deliberate renunciation has taken place: there is no more a royal road to transcendental philosophy, Kant sees, than there is to mathematics.

The deeper reason for this stylistic change, however, lies in the fact that Kant is presenting a completely novel *type of thinking,* one in opposition to his own past and to the philosophy of the Age of Enlightenment—to Hume and Mendelssohn, whom he envies for their way of writing, which is as elegant as it is profound. In the decades of withdrawn, lonely meditation in which Kant forged for himself his special method and questions, he had gradually moved away from the common presuppositions on which the philosophical and scientific thought of his age rested, as if by a silent consensus. He still often speaks the language of this age; he still uses the concepts it coined and the scholastic classifications it enforced in its textbooks on ontology, rational psychology, cosmology, and theology, but the whole bulk of these materials of expression and thought is now put into the service of a completely different goal. For Kant this goal is immutable, but he does not disdain terminological and expository

---

2. To Herz (IX, 188) (*Ak.* X, 230).
3. *Critique of Pure Reason,* preface to the 1st ed., A xix.

expedients, even though their precision is no longer strictly fitted to his own thinking. In fact, he often prefers to go back to these expedients, hoping to find in them the quickest route to a direct link with the reader's habitual conceptual realm. This very flexibility, however, becomes the source of a multitude of difficulties; precisely where Kant has descended to the standpoint of his age, he has failed to raise the age to his level.

Another factor has to be taken into consideration, one that made an entry into Kant's basic vision difficult for his contemporaries and which has continued to be a source of numerous errors and misunderstandings since then. If one considers only the external form Kant gave his writings, nothing seems to be clearer than that what unfolds before us is a finished, doctrinal system, complete as a whole and in every detail. The materials for its structure lie ready to hand in their totality; the basic outline is sketched out clearly and precisely in all particulars: all that needs be done is to put the pieces together according to the plan. But only when this endeavor is actually undertaken does the full magnitude of the task emerge. Fresh doubts and questions are encountered on every side; it is shown everywhere that the particular concepts we thought we could use as assumptions themselves need definition. The concepts become more and more altered, according to the place they occupy in the ongoing systematic composition of the whole. They are not a stable foundation for the movement of thought from its beginning to its end, but they evolve and are stabilized in the course of this very movement. Anyone who does not keep this tension in mind, anyone who believes that the meaning of a specific fundamental concept is exhausted with its initial definition and who tries to hold it to this meaning as something unchangeable, unaffected by the progress of thought, will go astray in his understanding of it.

Kant's distinctive style as a writer harmonizes with what was observed to be characteristic of him as a teacher. "His lecture," Jachmann says, "was always perfectly fitted to its material, yet it was not something memorized, but rather a freshly thought-out outpouring of his mind. . . . Even his course on metaphysics, with allowances for the difficulty of the material for the beginning thinker, was luminous and interesting. Kant displayed special artistry in expounding and defining metaphysical concepts, in that he experimented in front of his audience just as if he were starting to think about the subject, gradually adding on new defining concepts, trying out continually improved explanations, and finally passing on to a full conclusion with the concepts perfectly exhausted and illuminated from all sides; he thus not only acquainted the listener who paid strict attention with the matter under discussion but also introduced him to methodical thinking. Whoever failed to grasp this course of his lecture by observing him closely, and took his first explanation as the correct and completely exhaustive one, not making the effort to follow him further, gathered only half truths, as several reports from his auditors have convinced me."[4]

This fate of Kant's auditors has been the fate of many of his commentators as well. If one approaches the definitions of analytic and synthetic judgments, the concepts of experience and of the a priori, the concepts of the transcendental and of transcendental philosophy, as they appear in the beginning of the *Critique of Pure Reason*, with the idea that one is hitting upon ready-minted coins whose value is settled once and for all, then one must inevitably be perplexed by the further progress of the book. It repeatedly becomes obvious that an inquiry which was apparently concluded is taken up again, that an earlier explanation is supplemented, broadened, even entirely transformed, that problems which had just been treated separately abruptly enter into a totally new relationship in which their original meaning is altered. At bottom, however, the only natural and necessary situation is precisely this mutability, since it is a testimony to the fact that we stand here in the midst of a living process and a steady advance of thinking itself. Much that in isolation appears contradictory is illuminated only when it is reintegrated with this flow and interpreted in its whole context. Whereas Kant, on the strength of the synthetic method he uses in the First Critique, gradually proceeds step by step from the particular to the whole, the free reproduction of

4. Reinhold Bernhard Jachmann, *Immanuel Kant geschildert in Briefen an einen Freund* (Königsberg, 1804), Eighth Letter, pp. 28 ff.

his system must begin with the idea of the whole and specify the meaning of the particular relative to it, in a way analogous to the one he himself pointed out in the *Prolegomena*. As more and more threads are spun together in this process, at last the ingenious web of concepts stands before us; a retrospective analysis is the converse, disentangling only the major aspects from the numerous complexes of concepts and laying down the broadest principles that guide the idea in all its ramifications and developments. The totality of the particular questions comprised by the system of critical philosophy is never exhausted by this procedure; it must suffice if the general articulation seen by Kant himself as the essential moment and the decisive criterion for judging the unity and the solidity of his doctrine becomes visible and lucid.

2

The First Critique begins with a consideration of the idea of metaphysics and its shifting fortunes through the ages. Running through the entire history of metaphysics is the inner contradiction that, while metaphysics claims to be the highest court of appeal for the problem of "being" and "truth," it has not provided for itself any norm of certainty whatsoever. The succession of systems seems to mock any attempt to bring it into the "sure path of a science." But although metaphysics is impossible as a science, judging by its historical experiences, as a "natural disposition" it nevertheless remains necessary. For every attempt to renounce its fundamental questions is soon shown to be illusory. No voluntary resolve and no logical demonstration, however acute, can enable us to forgo the tasks that are set us. Dogmatism, which teaches us nothing, and scepticism, which promises us nothing, prove to be equally unsuccessful solutions to the problem of metaphysics. After centuries of intellectual effort, we have arrived at a point from which it seems we can move neither forward nor backward—a point at which it is as impossible to fulfill the demands implicit in the concept and the name of metaphysics as it is to give them up. "The mathematician, the sophisticated man, the natural philosopher: what do they accomplish when they make wanton mock of metaphysics? In their heart lies the call which bids them constantly to make trial in that selfsame field. If, as human beings, they do not seek their ultimate ends in the satisfaction of the goals of this life, they have no choice but to ask: From whence am I? What is the origin of all that is? The astronomer is even more compelled to these questions. He cannot avoid seeking something which will satisfy him on these matters. With the first judgment he makes on them, he is in the realm of metaphysics. Does he want simply to abandon himself, without any guidance, to the opinions which spring up in him if he has no map of the territory through which he wishes to roam? The critique of pure reason thrusts a torch into this gloom, but it illuminates the dark spaces of our own understanding, not the things unknown to us beyond the sense world."[5] Thus we see that it is not the *object* of metaphysics which is to undergo fresh consideration and clarification in the *Critique of Pure Reason*; it is the *question* of metaphysics itself which we are to understand more profoundly than before and gain insight into through examining its source in our understanding.

This expresses the first essential difference separating Kant's doctrine from the systems of the past. The old metaphysics was ontology: it began with definite general convictions about being as such, and attempted to press on from that basis to knowledge of the particular determinations of things. This is fundamentally just as true of those systems which call themselves "empirical" as it is of those which profess "rationalism." Empiricism and rationalism are distinguished by their intuitions about the specific cognitive means by which we assimilate being, but the fundamental view that there is such being, that there actually is a reality of things which the mind has to take into itself and copy, is common to both. Thus, although taken separately they may be thought in contrast to each other, their unity remains: both start with a specific assertion about reality—about the nature of things or of the soul—and derive as consequences from there all further propositions. Kant's initial reflection and his initial demand have their source at this point. The proud name of an ontology, which

5. *Reflexionen*, no. 128.

claims to give a systematic doctrine of universally valid and necessary cognitions of "things in general" must be replaced by the modest title of a mere analytic of pure understanding.[6] An ontology asks what being is, in order to show how it comes to be understood, that is, how it is presented and expressed in concepts and cognitions; here, in contrast, the first thing is to establish *what the question concerning being in general means.* While ontology takes being as the starting point, here being is taken as a problem or a postulate. Whereas heretofore some sort of definite structure of the world of objects was assumed as a secure beginning, and the task consisted simply in showing how this form of objectivity passes over into the form of subjectivity, as in cognition and representation, the demand here is for an explanation as to what in general the concept of reality and the claim to objectivity assert, before any theory of this transition is propounded. For objectivity, it is now recognized, is not a primordial, fixed state that is not further analyzable but a basic question of reason. It is a question which perhaps cannot be fully answered but concerning whose *meaning* a complete and exhaustive account must be given.

This might still seem obscure, but it is clarified if we go back to the first seed of the First Critique that is found in Kant's letter to Herz in 1772. In that letter Kant had stated that the "key to the whole secret of hitherto still obscure metaphysics" is the problem of what to call a representation in us that is founded on the object. He found no enlightenment in the theories of that relation up to his own time; they led either to a mere receptivity of the mind, which did not explain its capacity for universal and necessary cognitions, or else, since they did attribute this capacity to the mind, they traced it ultimately back to some kind of deus ex machina which had implanted them originally to agree with the "nature of things."[7] This mystical solution, however, is basically as unnecessary as it is unsatisfying, once we understand that the general question as to the object of knowledge is less a question of metaphysics than of logic. For in the contrast we make between representation and object it is not a matter of two fundamen-

---

6. *Critique of Pure Reason,* A 247 = B 303 (III, 217).
7. See above, pp. 129 ff.

tally different orders of absolute being, but of a definite quality and orientation of *judgment.* We attribute objectivity to a determinate connection of the contents of consciousness, we regard it as the expression of being, when we have grounds to assume that the form of this connection is not merely contingent and arbitrary but is something necessary and universally valid. For the moment, it is not yet certain what gives us the right to this assumption; nevertheless, this assumption is not only what our whole consciousness of truth and objective validity rests on, but is also what this consciousness essentially consists of. In other words, "things" are not given to us, of which certain and necessary knowledge can then be gained, but it is the certainty of these cognitions which is expressed otherwise in the assertions of "being," a "world," and "nature."

In the letter to Herz, the statement and solution of the problem had not yet progressed to this precision. In the *Critique of Pure Reason* it was reached only in the decisive chapters on the transcendental deduction of the categories. "At this point we must make clear to ourselves what we mean by the expression 'an object of representations,'" this passage states with especially impressive pregnancy. "What, then, is to be understood when we speak of an object corresponding to, and consequently also distinct from, our knowledge? It is easily seen that this object must be thought only as something in general = x, since outside our knowledge we have nothing which we could set over against this knowledge as corresponding to it. Now we find that our thought of the relation of all knowledge to its object carries with it an element of necessity; the object is viewed as that which prevents our modes of knowledge from being haphazard or arbitrary, and which determines them a priori in some definite fashion. For insofar as they are to relate to an object, they must necessarily agree with one another, that is, must possess that unity which constitutes the concept of an object.... It is only when we have thus produced synthetic unity in the manifold of intuition that we are in a position to say that we know the object.... Thus we think a triangle as an object, in that we are conscious of the combination of three straight lines according to a rule by which such an intuition can always be represented. This *unity of rule* determines

all the manifold, and limits it to conditions which make unity of
apperception possible. The concept of this unity is the representation
of the object = x, which I think through the predicates, above mentioned, of a triangle."[8] Thus the necessity of the judgment does not
stem from the unity of an object behind and beyond the cognition,
but this necessity is what constitutes for us the only conceivable sense
of the thought of an object. He who understands what this necessity
rests on and the constitutive conditions in which it is grounded will
have penetrated and solved the problem of being insofar as it is sol-
uble from the cognitive standpoint. For it is not because there is a
world of objects that there is for us, as their impression and image, a
world of cognitions and truths; rather, because there are unconditionally certain judgments—judgments whose validity is dependent
neither on the individual empirical subject from which they are
formed nor on the particular empirical and temporal conditions under
which they are formed—there is for us an order which is designated
not only as an order of impressions and representation, but also as an
order of objects.

The origin of the Kantian doctrine and of the disparity between it
and every earlier conception of the metaphysical problem is thus
defined once and for all. In order to express this contrast, Kant himself, in the preface to the second edition of the First Critique, coined
that famous image in which he compares his "intellectual revolution"
to what Copernicus did. "Hitherto it has been assumed that all our
knowledge must conform to objects. But all attempts to extend our
knowledge of objects by establishing something in regard to them a
priori, by means of concepts, have, on this assumption, ended in
failure. We must therefore make trial whether we may not have more
success in the tasks of metaphysics, if we suppose that objects must
conform to our knowledge. This would agree better with what is
desired, namely, that it should be possible to have knowledge of
objects a priori, determining something in regard to them prior to
their being given. We should then be proceeding precisely on the
lines of Copernicus's primary hypothesis. Failing of satisfactory pro-

8. *Critique of Pure Reason*, A 103 f (III, 615 ff.).

gress in explaining the movements of the heavenly bodies on the supposition that they all revolved around the spectator, he tried whether he might not have better success if he made the spectator to revolve and the stars to remain at rest."⁹ The analogy here to the "revolving of the spectator" consists in our reviewing all the cognitive functions at the disposal of reason in general, and examining each one individually, both as to its necessary mode of validity and as to its characteristically determinate and limited mode of validity.

Even in the cosmos of rational knowledge we are not allowed to stop, rigid and immobile, at any particular point, but we must successively traverse the whole range of positions that we can give to truth in relation to the object. There is a definite form of objectivity for us, which we call the *spatial order* of things: we must try to understand and determine it, not because we proceed from the existence of an absolute space but because we examine and analyze the laws of geometrical construction, those laws by which points, lines, planes, and bodies arise for us by way of continuous construction. There is for us a connection and a systematic interrelation between *numerical forms,* such that each individual number has its fixed place within the number system and its relation to all other members of this system. We must conceive this interconnection as necessary, since we can base it on no other datum than the universal procedure by which, beginning with the unit, we construct the whole domain of numbers out of its first elements, according to one constant principle. And finally, there is that whole of physical bodies and physical forces which we are accustomed to designate, in its narrower sense, as the world of nature. But here, too, in order to understand this whole we must take as our point of departure not the empirical existence of objects but the special mode of the cognitive functions, that "reason" embedded in our experience itself and in each of its judgments.

The path along which the critical revolution leads us is far from agreed upon. Metaphysics as a theory of being, as general ontology, recognizes but one mode of objectivity—only material and immaterial substances which in some form or other exist and endure. For the

9. Ibid., preface to the 2d ed., B xvi (III, 18).

system of reason, however, there are pure immanent necessities; thus there are claims to objective validity which as such are no longer expressible in the form of existence but belong to a new and totally different species. The necessity expressed in ethical or aesthetic judgment is of this kind. Both the realm of ends, the image of which is sketched by ethics, and the realm of pure shapes and forms disclosed to us in art "exist" in some sense, for they have a fixed status, divorced from any individual arbitrariness. But this status is neither the same as the empirical, spatiotemporal existence of things, nor basically comparable in any way, since it rests on special formative principles. From this essential difference in principles it follows that for us the world of duty and the world of artistic form must be other than that of concrete existence. It can be seen that it is the diversity found in reason itself, in its basic orientations and ways of questioning, that at bottom mediates and interprets the diversity of objects. Nonetheless, a universal and exhaustive systematic knowledge of it must be achieved, because the concept of reason consists in the fact that "we should be able to give an account of all our concepts, opinions, and assertions, either upon objective or, in the case of mere illusion, upon subjective grounds."[10] The revolution in thought consists in beginning with the reflection of reason on itself, on its presuppositions and principles, its problems and tasks; reflection on objects will follow if this starting point is made secure.

At the same time, this beginning indicates the peculiarity of two important basic concepts decisively significant for the question of the critique of reason. If we hold fast to what is essential in the "Copernican revolution," we have attained the full and exhaustive meaning of the Kantian concept of "subjectivity," and of the Kantian concept of the "transcendental" as well. From this we first fully understand that both are only determined jointly and by one another, because it is precisely the new *relation* they undergo toward each other that constitutes what is essential and special obtained by way of the First Critique. Let us start with the concept of the transcendental: Kant explains that he calls that knowledge "transcendental" which is con-

10. Ibid., A 614 = B 642 (III, 423).

cerned not so much with objects as with the mode of our knowledge of objects in general, insofar as this is possible a priori. "Neither space nor any a priori geometrical determination of it is a transcendental representation; what can alone be entitled transcendental is the knowledge that these representations are not of empirical origin, and the possibility that they can yet relate a priori to objects of experience."[11] If we trace this idea further, we see that the concepts of magnitude and number, of permanence or causality, can equally little be designated as transcendental concepts in the strict sense; this designation, on the contrary, properly belongs only to that theory showing us how the possibility of all knowledge of nature rests on these concepts as necessary conditions. Even the idea of freedom, taken in itself, cannot be called transcendental. This title must be reserved for the knowledge that the special quality of the consciousness of duty, and therefore the entire structure of the realm of the ought, is founded on the datum of freedom, and for the knowledge of how it is so founded.

In this way we understand only now in what sense, from the standpoint of strictly transcendental reflection, the factor of subjectivity can and must be ascribed to space and time, magnitude and number, substantiality and causality, etc. This "subjectivity" means nothing but what Kant's "Copernican revolution" implies: it signifies the result not of the object but of a specific lawfulness of cognition, to which a determinate form of objectivity (be it theoretical, ethical, or aesthetic in kind) is to be traced back. Once this is grasped, that secondary sense of "subjective," which infects it with the appearance of individuality and arbitrariness, immediately vanishes. In the relation we are establishing here, the concept of the subjective expresses a foundation in a necessary procedure and a universal law of reason. Thus, for instance, the subjective turn Kant gives to the theory of space does not imply that the essence of space is to be determined by an analysis of the spatial representation and by exhibiting the particular psychological moments which attach to it, but rather that insight into this essence follows from insight into the nature of geometrical

11. Ibid., A 56 = B 81; also A 11 = B 25 (III, 83 and 49).

knowledge and remains dependent on it. What must space be—the transcendental exposition asks—so that knowledge of it, hence cognition, may be possible such that, like the content of geometrical axioms, it is at once universal and concrete, unconditionally certain and purely intuitive. [12] To start with the special nature of the cognitive function so as to determine from it the special nature of the object of knowledge is thus the sole subjectivity in question here. Just as the ensemble of numbers is derived from the principle of numeration, so the order of objects in space and of events in time is derived from the principles and conditions of knowledge of experience, from the categories of causality and reciprocity. Thus also, in another realm of questions, the form of the ethical imperative, on which for us all obligation rests, is rendered comprehensible by the fundamental certainty disclosed to us in the idea of freedom. It is no longer possible to confuse this subjectivity of reason with the subjectivity of arbitrariness or of psychophysical organization, since the former must be assumed and implied even to dispose of the latter.

This relation emerges, even more clearly than in the First Critique itself, in several reflections and notes, in which the reconstruction of the new meaning and relation of the central concepts can be traced out in detail. Certain of these observations seem to belong to the period preceding the final completion of the *Critique of Pure Reason*, and they seem more to indicate the stage of thought in process than thought already finalized; but even where such a temporal relation is indemonstrable, the growth of the particular concepts is exhibited more keenly and vividly in these vacillating remarks and observations than in the presentation of the finished results. "Can something be discovered through metaphysics?" runs one of these reflections. "Yes; regarding the subject, but not the object." [13] But this assertion obviously only imperfectly describes the new turn, since if one took it in isolation, one would have to anticipate a metaphysics that promises us new insights concerning the "soul" but not about things, a

12. Ibid., B 40 f. (III, 59 f.).
13. *Reflexionen*, no. 102.

metaphysics fundamentally indistinguishable from earlier dogmatic systems of spiritualism.

Therefore, the concise and pregnant statement, made elsewhere, that metaphysics deals not with objects but with cognitions[14] is an essentially sharper formulation of the basic distinction. In this formulation the "subjectivity" relating to metaphysics is first rounded out and defined more exactly: it is not that of "human nature," as understood by Locke and Hume, but that which bears the stamp of the sciences, in the method of geometrical construction or arithmetic numbering procedure, in empirical observation and measurement or in the performance of physical experiments. "In all philosophy," another note explains, "that which is genuinely philosophical is the metaphysics of science. All sciences which employ reason have their metaphysic."[15] This definitely shows the sense in which the earlier, dogmatic, objective path of the old ontology is abandoned while the concept of metaphysics is held onto and deepened in the direction of the subjective.[16] What is objective in the sciences, it can now be said in Kant's sense, is their theorems; what is subjective is their principles. We view geometry objectively, for instance, when we look at it purely from the standpoint of its theoretical content as a sum of propositions concerning spatial forms and spatial relations. We view it subjectively when, instead of inquiring about its results, we ask about the principles of its construction, its basic axioms, which are valid not for this or that spatial figure but for every spatial construct as

14. *Reflexionen*, no. 91. That this *Reflexion* dates from the period which Benno Erdmann calls that of "critical empiricism," thus from the 1760s, is extremely improbable. The passage in the Prize Essay of 1763, which Erdmann invokes in support of his view, is no proof at all in this regard, since in that passage metaphysics (in the sense of πρώτη φιλοσοφία traditional since Aristotle) is described as a philosophy of the first grounds of our knowledge, but Kant could no more say here that it does not concern itself "with objects" than he could say this at any time prior to the decisive turn in his letter to Marcus Herz of 1772.

15. *Reflexionen*, no. 129.

16. Cf. *Reflexionen*, no. 215; "Progress in metaphysics has been fruitless up till now; no one has discovered anything by it. Equally, it cannot be given up. Subjective instead of objective?"

such. It is this thrust of the question which is henceforth unwaveringly adhered to. "Metaphysics is the science of the principles of all knowledge a priori and of all knowledge which follows from these principles. Mathematics contains such principles, but is not a science of the possibility of these principles."[17]

Herein, however, lies a new factor, peculiar to the Kantian definition of concepts. Even the transcendental philosophy intends to treat the various forms of objectivity, and must do so; but each objective form is conceivable by it and accessible to it only as mediated by a specific form of cognition. The material it is concerned with and relates to is hence always a material preformed in some manner. What transcendental analysis aims to discover and explain is how reality, seen through the medium of geometry or mathematical physics, is thought, or what it signifies in the light of artistic intuition or from the standpoint of ethical obligation. It has no answer to the question of what this reality may be in itself and apart from every relation to the mind's specific ways of understanding, because with that question philosophy would feel itself gone astray again in the empty space of abstraction; all firm footing would be lost. Metaphysics must be the metaphysic of the sciences, the theory of principles of mathematics and natural knowledge, or, if it claims specific content for itself, it must be the metaphysic of morality, of right, of religion, or of history. It integrates these multiple objective mental directions and activities as a single problem, not so as to make them vanish in this unity but so as to illuminate the essential individuality and proper limitation of each of them.

In this way philosophy is shown to be the necessary starting point of the entirety of intellectual and spiritual culture as it is given to us. Philosophy, however, no longer wishes to accept that culture as given, but rather to make its origin and the universally valid norms governing and guiding it comprehensible. Only now do we fully understand Kant's statement, that the torch of the critique of reason does not light up the objects unknown to us beyond the sense world, but rather the shadowy space of our own understanding. The

17. *Reflexionen*, no. 140.

"understanding" here is not to be taken in the empirical sense, as the psychological power of human thought, but rather in the purely transcendental sense, as the whole of intellectual and spiritual culture. It stands directly for that entity which we designate by the name "science" and for its axiomatic presuppositions, but further, in an extended sense, for all those orders of an intellectual, ethical, or aesthetic kind demonstrable in reason and perfectible by it. What appears in the experiential, historical life of mankind as detached and divided and laden with contingencies, is, by means of the transcendental critique, to be grasped as necessitated by its ultimate grounds, and conceived and exhibited as a system. Just as each individual figure in space is connected with the general law, which is itself grounded in the pure form of "coexistence," in the form of intuition, every "what" of the works of reason in the end goes back to a characteristic "how" of reason, to something fundamental and distinctive which all its products manifest and confirm. Philosophy now no longer has any special domain, no particular sphere of entities and objects that belongs solely and exclusively to it, distinct from the other sciences; rather, it conceives the relation of the basic functions of the mind only in their true universality and depth, a depth inaccessible to any one of them alone. The world is given over to the individual theoretical disciplines and to the particular productive powers of the mind, but the cosmos of these powers themselves, its multiplicity and its articulation, comprises the new "object" which philosophy has gained in its place.

If we begin with the structure of mathematics in order to make this clear in detail, it is less a matter of developing the stuff of mathematical principles in particular than of showing the universal procedure which is the sole means whereby there can be principles for us, that is, by means of which we can understand how every special spatial thing or every particular operation of numbering and measuring is tied to original universal conditions, from which it cannot be freed. Every geometrical proposition or proof is based on a concrete and to that extent individual intuition. But no such proof is about an individual; rather it passes from the individual to a judgment concerning an infinite totality of forms. A certain property is not asserted of this or that triangle, or of a specific circle, but of "the" triangle or "the" circle in general.

What justifies our passing in this case from the individual thing, which is all that can be given us in sensory representation, to the totality of possible cases, which as infinite is inconceivable in any empirical representation? How do we succeed in making limited, partial content the bearer of an assertion which as such is valid not of it but of an infinite content, which to us it "stands for"? To answer these questions it is sufficient, according to Kant, if we get clear in our minds the peculiar nature of the procedure of scientific geometry as it is actually practiced and as it has evolved historically. The elevation of geometry from its earliest, rudimentary state, in which it was nothing more than a practical art of measuring, to the rank of fundamental theoretical knowledge, is ascribable only to an intellectual revolution that is fully analogous to the one we previously contemplated in discussing the transcendental philosophy. "The history of this intellectual revolution—far more important than the discovery of the passage round the celebrated Cape of Good Hope—and of its fortunate author, has not been preserved. But the fact that Diogenes Laërtius, in handing down an account of these matters, names the reputed author of even the least important among the geometrical demonstrations, even of those which, for ordinary consciousness, stand in need of no such proof, does at least show that the memory of the revolution, brought about by the first glimpse of this new path, must have seemed to mathematicians of such outstanding importance as to cause it to survive the tide of oblivion. A new light flashed upon the mind of the first man (be he Thales or some other) who demonstrated the properties of the isosceles triangle. The true method, so he found, was not to inspect what he discerned either in the figure, or in the bare concept of it, and from this, as it were, to read off it properties; but to bring out what was necessarily implied in the concepts that he had himself formed a priori, and had put into the figure in the construction by which he presented it to himself."[18] If in order to carry out the geometrical proof we had to draw the figure, if it lay before us

18. *Critique of Pure Reason*, preface to the 2d ed., B xi f. (III, 15).

as something given, the specific properties of which we had to learn through observation, geometrical judgment could never go beyond the objective individual content of that particular shape. For what right would we have to infer from what is given to what is not given, from the special case as perceived to the whole sum of possible cases? In truth, however, such an inference is neither possible nor required here, for the totality of individual geometrical instances does not exist prior to and apart from construction but arises for us only in the act of construction itself. Since I not only think the parabola or the ellipse universally *in abstracto* but cause both to exist by construction, through a specific rule (as perhaps, by their definition as conic sections), I thus create the condition under which alone the particular parabola or ellipse can be thought. We now understand how the geometrical concept as constructive does not follow on the specific cases, but precedes them. Thus to that extent it is valid as a true a priori relative to them.

Seen in this connection, this designation obviously is in no way related to an empirical psychological subject and to temporal succession, to the before or after of its individual representations and cognitions, but it expresses purely and exclusively a relation within what is known, a relation of the thing itself. Geometrical construction is "prior" to the individual geometrical form, because the meaning of the individual form is established only via the construction, not the other way around—the meaning of the construction through the individual form. All the necessity belonging to geometrical judgments rests on this fact. In geometry the cases do not exist apart from the law, as things detached and independent; they basically issue from consciousness of the law. In geometry the particular does not constitute the presupposition of the universal; rather it is thought only by means of determining and specifying more exactly the universal in general. No particular shape and no particular number can contradict what is embodied in the general procedure of spatialization or of the synthesis of numeration, because only in this procedure does all that which participates in the concept of the spatial and the concept of number come into being. In this sense geometry and arithmetic furnish the immediate confirmation of a principle that Kant now puts forward as the universal norm and the touchstone of the "new method of thought," "namely, that we can know a priori of things only what we ourselves put into them."[19]

The third central and crucial concept of the First Critique, that of "synthesis a priori," emerged hand in hand with the concepts of the subjective and the transcendental. The significance of this synthesis becomes clear as soon as we contrast the procedure of geometry and arithmetic, as heretofore established, with that of ordinary empirical concept formation, as well as with the procedure of formal logic. In empirical concept formation (especially as practiced in the purely descriptive and classificatory sciences) we are content to add case to case, fact to fact, and inspect the resulting sum to see whether it exhibits any "common" characteristic unifying all the particulars. A decision as to whether there is a connection of this kind obviously can be made only after we have run through and examined the particulars that are relevant to our question, for since we know the determination here affirmed only as the observed property of a given thing, it is clear that before the thing as such is actually given, that is, established in experience, no more precise identifying characteristic can be assigned to it. Knowledge thus seems in this case to derive from a collection, a mere aggregate of elements that even outside of this connection and prior to it possess independent being and meaning.[20]

The situation seems to be totally different with those universal propositions an examination of formal logic supplies us with. In a genuine universal proposition of this logic, universality is not derived from the contemplation of particulars, but precedes and determines

19. Ibid., B xviii (III, 19).

20. It must, of course, be emphasized that in this exposition of empirical knowledge ("synthesis a posteriori"), it is less a matter of describing an actual state of affairs of cognition than of constructing a limiting case, which we use in order to show the special nature of a priori judgment more accurately, through contrast and opposition. Kant himself used this construction in his distinction between judgments of perception and judgments of experience, and in his emphasis on the purely subjective nature of the former; see the *Prolegomena*, §18 (IV, 48) (*Ak.* IV, 297 f.). In itself, though, there is for him no "particular judgment" which does not claim some kind of "universal" form; no "empirical" proposition which does not contain in itself some "a priori" assertion, since the form of judgment as such contains the requirement of "objective universal validity."

them. From the fact that all men are mortal, and from the certainty contained in this major premise, the mortality of Caius is proven as a necessary consequence. However, logic is satisfied to explicate the forms and the formulas of this proof, without reflecting on the content of cognition and its origin and justification. Hence it assumes as given the universal premise that is the starting point of a specific deduction, without further inquiry into the basis of its validity. It shows that if all A's are b's, this must also hold for a specific, particular A, while the question of whether and why the hypothetical major premise is valid lies outside its sphere of interest. Hence, general logic basically does nothing but analyze back into their parts specific complexes of concepts, which it has previously formed by composition. It defines a concept by asserting specific qualities as its content, and it then abstracts from the logical totality thus created an individual factor which it separates off from the others so as to predicate it of the whole. This predication does not create any new knowledge, but only reiterates separately what we already had before, in order to explicate and eludicate it; it serves as an "analysis of concepts which we already have of objects," in which there is no further inquiry into the cognitive source from which these concepts are derived.[21]

Now we recognize in the resulting twofold opposition the characteristic peculiarity that synthesis a priori displays. In mere judgment of experience, or a posteriori connection, the whole we are trying to achieve was composed of purely individual elements, which necessarily were given independently beforehand. In formal logical judgment, where a given logical whole was simply analyzed and divided into its parts, a priori synthesis reveals a completely different structure. Here we begin with a specific constructive connection, in and through which simultaneously a profusion of particular elements, which are conditioned by the universal form of the connection, arises for us. We think the diverse possibilities jointly in a single, comprehensive, and constructive rule: sections of a cone; and we have in that way simultaneously produced the totality of those geometric

---

21. Cf. *Critique of Pure Reason*, introduction, sect. III, A 5 = B 9 (III, 39). See also the *Prolegomena*, §2b (IV, 15) (*Ak.* IV, 267).

forms which we call second-order curves: circles, ellipses, parabolas, and hyperbolas. We think the construction of the system of natural numbers, according to one basic principle, and we have included in it from the first, under definite conditions, all the possible relations between the members of this set. Kant's Inaugural Dissertation had already introduced the essential expression "pure intuition" for this form of relation between part and whole. Thus the result is that all synthesis a priori is inseparably linked with the form of pure intuition, that it either is itself pure intuition, or else is mediately related to and rests on some such intuition.

When Eberhard later, in his polemic against Kant, deplored the absence in the *Critique of Pure Reason* of one clearly defined principle of synthetic judgments, Kant referred him to this relation. "All synthetic judgments of theoretical cognition," as Kant now formulates this principle, "are possible only through the relation of the given concept to an intuition."[22] Space and time hence remain the true models and archetypes, exhibiting purely and fully the characteristic relation holding between the infinite and the finite, between the universal and the particular and individual, in every a priori synthetic cognition. The infinity of space and of time assert nothing more than that all determinate individual spatial and temporal magnitudes are possible only through limitations of the one all-inclusive space or the unitary, unrestricted representation of time.[23] Space does not arise because we construct it out of points, nor time because we construct it out of instants, as though they were substantial elements; rather, points and instants (and hence indirectly all figures in space and time) can be posited only through a synthesis in which the form of coexistence or succession in general originates. Thus we do not locate these forms in space and time as given, but only produce them by means of "space" and "time," if both are understood as basic constructive acts of intuition. "Mathematics must first exhibit all its concepts in intuition, and pure mathematics in pure intuition, i.e., construct them, without which (because it cannot proceed analytically, namely

22. Cf. Kant's letter to Reinhold, dated May 12, 1789 (IX, 402) (*Ak.* XI, 33); see also the essay in reply to Eberhard (VI, 59 ff.) (*Ak.* VIII, 239 ff.).
    23. Cf. Transcendental Aesthetic, §4, A 31 f. = B 47 f. (III, 64).

through analysis of concepts, but only synthetically) it is impossible for it to take one step.... Geometry is founded on the pure intuition of space. Arithmetic achieves its number concepts by successive additions of units in time; in particular, however, pure mechanics can only achieve its concepts of motion by means of the representation of time."[24] Because the subject matters of geometry, arithmetic, and mechanics are arrived at in this fashion, because they are not physical *things* whose properties we must discover a posteriori, but rather limitations we place on the ideal wholes of extension and duration, all propositions implicit in these fundamental forms are necessarily and universally valid for them.

But if this consideration seems to explain to us the employment and the validity of a priori synthesis in mathematics, it seems at the same time to close off every path to the claim of a similar validity for the realm of the actual, for the domain of empirical science. In fact, it was precisely this touchstone that Kant pointed out to us: "that we know a priori only what we ourselves put into things." Such a "putting into" was understandable in ideal mathematical constructions, but what would tell us if we may do it in some fashion with empirical objects as well? Is not the decisive trait which basically marks the objects as real, as "actual," precisely that they exist in all their particularity prior to all mental developments and positings, that they thus fundamentally determine our representation and thinking, not that they are determined by the latter? And would not the ground necessarily cave in under our feet the moment we try to reverse this relationship? Space and time may be conceivable for us in universal principles, because they can be construed by these principles; it is the actuality of things in space and time, the existence of bodies and their motions, that seems to constitute the insuperable limit to all constructions of that sort. Here, it seems, there is no other course than to await the influence of things and to observe them in sensory perception. We call objects "actual" to the extent that they are made known to us in this form of actuality, and by this we are thus made acquainted with their individual qualities. Hence a general assertion

24. [*Prolegomena*, §10 (IV, 32) (*Ak.* IV, 283)]

about physical existences may be possible; in no case is its possibility understandable save through amassing particular instances, through the collection and comparison of the many impressions of the things which we have experienced.

And in fact Kant's transcendental idealism does not aim to eliminate the special nature of empirical knowledge; indeed, its essential merit is to be sought in its affirmation of this nature. Kant's saying that his field is the "fertile lowland of experience" is well known. But his general counsel holds also for the new critical determination of the concept of experience itself: that here as well we have to begin not with the observation of objects, but with the analysis of knowledge. The question of what an empirical object, an individual natural thing, may be, and whether it is accessible to us in any way other than through direct perception of its particular properties, must thus be left open for the moment. For before it can be meaningfully decided as a general matter, we must have succeeded in being completely clear as to what the cognitive mode of the natural sciences means, what the structure and systematic of physics is. Here we quickly see a fundamental difficulty in the traditional way of looking at the matter. Let us pursue this approach to the point where we assume that the object of mathematics rests in fact on the pure proposition of thought and has to that extent ideal validity, while the physical object is given to us and is conceivable by us exclusively by means of the various types of sensory perception. The possibility of a pure mathematical theory on the one side and a pure empiricism on the other is then understandable, that is, how on the one hand there can be a complex of propositions which, independently of all experience, treat only of such matters as we can produce by free construction, and how on the other hand a descriptive science can be built up which consists of sheer individual, factual observations of given things. What remains completely inexplicable under this assumption is the essential mutual involvement of both moments which we encounter in the actual structure of mathematical natural science. For in this latter measurement does not simply go hand in hand with observation, nor are experiment and theory simply opposed to each other or interchangeable, but they mutually condition each other. Theory leads to experiment and decides the character of the experiment, just as experiment determines the content of theory.

Once again the preface to the second edition of the *Critique of Pure Reason* has, in its broad survey of the whole realm of knowledge, displayed this relationship with masterful, unsurpassable clarity. "When Galileo caused balls, the weights of which he had himself previously determined, to roll down an inclined plane; when Torricelli made the air carry a weight which he had calculated beforehand to be equal to that of a definite column of water; or in more recent times, when Stahl changed metal into calx, and calx back into metal, by withdrawing something and then restoring it, a light broke upon all students of nature. They learned that reason has insight only into that which it produces after a plan of its own, and that it must not allow itself to be kept, as it were, in nature's leading strings, but must itself show the way with principles of judgment based upon fixed laws, constraining nature to give answer to questions of reason's own determining. Accidental observations, made in obedience to no previously thought-out plan, can never be made to yield a necessary law, which alone reason is concerned to discover. Reason, holding in one hand its principles, according to which alone concordant appearances can be admitted as equivalent to laws, and in the other hand the experiment which it has devised in conformity with these principles, must approach nature in order to be taught by it. It must not, however, do so in the character of a pupil who listens to everything that the teacher chooses to say, but of an appointed judge who compels the witnesses to answer questions which he has himself formulated. Even physics, therefore, owes the beneficent revolution in its point of view entirely to the happy thought, that while reason must seek in nature, not fictitiously ascribe to it, whatever as not being knowable through reason's own resources has to be learned, if learned at all, only from nature, in so seeking it must adopt as its guide that which it has itself put into nature. It is thus that the study of nature has entered on the secure path of a science, after having for so many centuries been nothing but a process of merely random groping."[25]

25. *Critique of Pure Reason,* preface to the 2d ed., B xii f. (III, 16 f.).

Thus while a lone sensory perception or a mere collection of such perceptions may be able to get along without the guidance of a plan of reason, it is still the latter that first makes experiment precise and possible, "experience" in the sense of physical knowledge. By use of that rational method, isolated sense impressions can become physical observations and facts; for that to occur it is of primary importance to transform the originally purely qualitative manifold and diversity of perceptions into a quantitative manifold; the aggregate of sensations must be changed into a system of measurable magnitudes. The idea of such a system is basic to every single experiment. Before Galileo could measure the magnitude of acceleration in free fall, the conception of acceleration itself, as well as measuring apparatus, had to exist, and it was this mathematical conception which once and for all differentiated his unadorned way of putting the question from that of the medieval scholastic physics. The outcome of the experiment determined not only what magnitudes are true of free fall, but also that in general such magnitudes must be sought for and insisted upon. What Galileo laid down in advance, according to that plan of reason, is what initially made it possible for the experiment to be conceived and directed.

From this point on, the structure of mathematical physics becomes truly transparent. The scientific theory of nature is not a logical hybrid; it does not spring from the eclectic combination of epistemologically heterogeneous elements but forms a self-contained and integral method. To understand this unity and to explain it by a universal principle, analogously to the unity of pure mathematics, is the task the transcendental critique sets itself. In its conception of this task, it has overcome the onesidedness of rationalism and of empiricism alike. Neither an appeal to concepts nor an appeal to perception and experience, as is now plain to see, has anything to do with the essence of natural scientific theory, for both single out but one moment, in isolation, instead of defining the peculiar relation between the moments, on which this whole question depends.

However, this does not solve the problem, but only states it in its most comprehensive form. For what synthesis a priori in pure mathematics explained and made comprehensible was this: the "whole" of the form of intuition—pure space and pure time as a whole—was prior to and underlay all particular spatial and temporal forms. Can the same relation or one of a similar kind be asserted of the realm of nature as well? Can a statement be made about nature as a whole that does not just follow on collection of individual observations, but is rather one that first makes observation of the individual itself possible? Is there here too something particular which can be arrived at and established in no way except by the limitation of an original totality? As long as we think of nature in the usual sense, as the assemblage of material physical things, we will have to answer all these questions in the negative, since how can anything be said about a totality of things without our having run through them and examined them one by one? But the concept of nature already contains a determination that points our reflection in another direction. For we do not call every complex of things "nature," but understand by that term a whole of elements and events ordered and determined by universal laws. "Nature," as Kant defines it, "is the existence of things so far as it is determined according to universal laws." Thus although in the material sense it signifies the set of all objects of experience, in the formal sense it signifies the conformity to law of all these objects.

The general task is thus reformulated: instead of asking what the conformity to law of things as objects of experience rests on, we ask how it is possible to recognize the necessary conformity to law of experience itself in respect to its objects in general. "Accordingly," it is said in the *Prolegomena to Any Future Metaphysics*, "we shall here be concerned with experience only and the universal conditions of its possibility, which are given a priori. Thence we shall define Nature as the whole object of all possible experience. I think it will be understood that I here do not mean the rules of the observation of a Nature that is already given . . . but how the a priori conditions of the possibility of experience are at the same time the sources from which all universal laws of nature must be derived."[26] Thus the question is redirected from the contents of experience, from empirical objects, to

26. *Prolegomena*, §14, §17 (IV, 44, 46 ff.) (*Ak.* IV, 294, 296 f.).

the function of experience. This function has a basic definiteness comparable to that disclosed to us in the pure form of space and time. It cannot be fulfilled without specific concepts coming into play, just as when every scientific experiment is performed, there is contained in the question which, in that act, we put to nature itself the presupposition that nature is determinately quantified, the presupposition that specific elements in it are unchanging and conserved, and the presupposition that events follow one another according to a rule. Without the idea of an equality which determines the relation of distance and time of fall, without the idea of the conservation of the quantity of motion, without the universal concept and the universal procedure of measurement and quantification, not a single experiment of Galileo's would have been possible, because without these preconditions Galileo's whole problem remains incomprehensible.

Accordingly, experience itself is a "mode of cognitions which requires understanding," that is, a process of inference and judgment which rests on specific logical preconditions.[27] And, in fact, with this we are again shown a whole which is not put together from separate parts but which is the basis for the possibility of first asserting parts and specific content. Nature, too, must be thought as a system before its details can be observed. Just as a particular spatial form previously appeared as a limitation of the one space and as a specific span of time appeared as a limitation of infinite duration, now all particular laws of nature, looked at in this connection, appear as "specifications" of universal principles of the understanding. For there are many laws which we can know only by means of experience, "but conformity to law in the connection of appearances, that is, in Nature in general, we cannot discover by any experience, because experience itself requires laws which are a priori at the basis of its possibility."[28] Extravagant and paradoxical as it sounds to say that the understanding itself is the source of the laws of nature and hence of the formal unity of nature, such an assertion is nonetheless correct and conforms with its object, namely experience. "Certainly, empirical laws as such can never de-

---

27. See the *Critique of Pure Reason*, preface to the 2d ed., B xviii (III, 18).
28. *Prolegomena*, §36 (IV, 71) (*Ak.* IV, 318–19).

rive their origin from pure understanding. That is as little possible as to understand completely the inexhaustible multiplicity of appearances merely by reference to the pure form of sensible intuition. But all empirical laws are only special determinations of the pure laws of understanding, under which, and according to the norm of which, they first become possible. Through them appearances take on an orderly character, just as these same appearances, despite the differences of their empirical form, must nonetheless always be in harmony with the pure form of sensibility."[29] We can establish the specific numerical constants that are characteristic of a particular realm of nature only through empirical measurement, and discover individual causal connections only by observation, but that we universally search for such constants, that we demand and presuppose universal causal lawfulness in the succession of events, issues from that plan of reason which we do not derive from nature but which we put into it. What is comprised in this plan is what alone yields a priori knowledge.

The second basic line of synthesis a priori, the synthesis of the pure concepts of the understanding, or the categories, is thus established, and it is justified by the same principle as that of pure intuition. For the pure concept does not display its true and essential action in a mere description of what is given in experience, but in construction of the pure form of experience; not where it collects and classifies the contents of experience, but where it is the foundation of the systematic unity of our way of cognition. It is in no way sufficient, as is commonly imagined, for experience to compare perceptions and to unite them by means of judgment in one consciousness, for by this alone we would never get beyond the specific validity of the perceptual consciousness, and would never reach the universal validity and necessity of a scientific principle. "Quite another judgment therefore is required before perception can become experience. The given intuition must be subsumed under a concept which determines the form of judging in general relatively to the intuition, connects empirical consciousness of intuition in consciousness in general, and thereby

29. *Critique of Pure Reason,* A 127 ff. (III, 627 ff.).

procures universal validity for empirical judgments. A concept of this nature is a pure a priori concept of the understanding, which does nothing but determine for an intuition the general way in which it can be used for judgments."

Even the judgments of pure mathematics are not exempted from this condition: the proposition, for instance, that a straight line is the shortest distance between two points presupposes as a general matter that the line is conceived from the standpoint and under the concept of magnitude, a concept "which certainly is no mere intuition, but has its seat in the understanding alone and serves to determine the intuition (of the line) with regard to the judgments which may be made about it, in respect to their quantity, that is, plurality.... For under them it is understood that in a given intuition there is contained a plurality of homogeneous parts."[30] This connection emerges still more clearly where it is not a matter of a simple mathematical determination of the object, but of a dynamic one, that is, where not only is an individual spatiotemporal form produced as a quantity by successive synthesis of similar parts,[31] but in addition its relation to another object is to be established. For it will be shown that every such relational determination—the order we give to individual bodies in space and individual events in time—is founded on a form of the actual assumed to hold between them; the idea of actuality, however, presupposes functional dependence, and hence a pure concept of the understanding.

If, however, the cooperation and the reciprocal relation of the two basic forms of a priori synthesis shed light on these simple examples, at the moment we still lack any further principle by which to develop the systematic of the second form completely. We can indeed point out and give names to individual applications of the pure concepts of the understanding, but at this point we have no criterion whatsoever

---

30. *Prolegomena,* §20 (IV, 51 f.) (*Ak.* IV, 301–02).

31. Cf. *Critique of Pure Reason,* Transcendental Doctrine of Method, chap. 1, sect. 1, "The Discipline of Pure Reason in its Dogmatic Employment": "[Thus] we can determine our concepts in a priori intuition, inasmuch as we create for ourselves, in space and time, through a homogeneous synthesis, the objects themselves—these objects being viewed simply as *quanta.*" A 723 = B 751 (III, 491).

to assure us of the formal unity and completeness of our knowledge. Kant was led to precisely this latter requirement, as we recall, by the train of thought he entered upon immediately after the Inaugural Dissertation. In the letter to Marcus Herz of 1772 he posed as the task of the newly discovered science of "transcendental philosophy," "to reduce all concepts of completely pure reason to a certain number of categories, but not like Aristotle, who, in his ten predicaments, placed them side by side as he found them, in a purely chance disposition, but as they are of themselves divided into classes according to a few basic laws of the understanding."[32]

A new *fundamentum divisionis* for this long-standing demand is now reached. "The *possibility of experience*," as the basis for this division is called in the section "The Highest Principle of All Synthetic Judgments," "is, then, what gives objective reality to all our a priori modes of knowledge. Experience, however, rests on the synthetic unity of appearances, that is, on a synthesis according to concepts of an object of appearances in general. Apart from such synthesis it would not be knowledge, but a rhapsody of perceptions that would not fit into any context according to rules of a completely interconnected (possible) consciousness, and so would not conform to the transcendental and necessary unity of apperception. Experience depends, therefore, upon a priori principles of its form, that is, upon universal rules of unity in the synthesis of appearances. Their objective reality, as necessary conditions of experience, and indeed of its very possibility, can always be shown in experience. Apart from this relation synthetic a priori principles are completely impossible. For they have then no third something, that is, no object, in which the synthetic unity can exhibit the objective reality of its concepts. . . . Accordingly, since experience, as empirical synthesis, is, insofar as such experience is possible, the one species of knowledge which is capable of imparting reality to any nonempirical synthesis, this latter [type of synthesis], as knowledge a priori, can possess truth, that is, agreement with the object, only insofar as it contains nothing save what is necessary to synthetic unity of experience in general. . . . Synthetic a

32. See above, p. 130.

priori judgments are thus possible when we . . . assert that the conditions of the *possibility of experience* in general are likewise conditions of the *possibility of the objects of experience,* and that for this reason they have objective validity in a synthetic a priori judgment."[33]

In these sentences the entire internal structure of the *Critique of Pure Reason* is revealed to us. Experience is the starting point—but not as a sum of ready-made things with determinate, equally ready-made properties, nor as a mere rhapsody of perceptions; the concept of experience is, rather, characterized and determined by the necessity of interconnection, the rule of objective laws. Up to this point, the transcendental method has only established what had been valid in mathematical physics for a long time and was recognized in it, whether consciously or unconsciously. Kant's assertion that every genuine experiential judgment must contain necessity in the synthesis of perceptions in fact only brings the demand already stated by Galileo to its most concise and striking expression. In it, the sensualist concept of experience is simply replaced by that of mathematical empiricism.[34]

At this point, however, the essential intellectual revolution begins. While until now necessity was held to be founded in objects and only indirectly carried over from them into knowledge, now it is understood that the reverse is true, that every idea of the object arises from an original necessity in knowledge itself: "for this object is no more than that something, the concept of which expresses such a necessity of synthesis."[35] In the flow of our sensations and representations it is not arbitrariness that rules, but a strict lawfulness which excludes every subjective whim; for that reason and that reason alone phenomena are for us objectively coherent. That which characterizes and constitutes experience as a mode of knowledge conditions and thus renders possible the assertion of empirical objects. Whether any other objects might be given to us apart from this

33. *Critique of Pure Reason,* A 156 ff. = B 195 ff. (III, 152 ff.).

34. *Prolegomena,* §22 (IV, 32) (*Ak.* IV, 304–05). Cf. *Critique of Pure Reason,* B 218 (III, 166): "Experience is possible only through the representation of a necessary connection of perceptions."

35. *Critique of Pure Reason,* A 106 (III, 616).

relation is a question that is completely superfluous for us, and so it must be, according to the transcendental principles, as long as no other mode of knowledge whose structure is essentially distinguished from that of experience is demonstrated for this presumed different type of object. Here, however, where the demand for such a mode of knowledge is incomprehensible, or where at the very least its fulfillment remains completely problematical, no conclusion is possible other than the one which the highest principle draws. The conditions on which experience as a function rests are at the same time the conditions of everything it yields us, for every determination of an object rests on the interpenetration of the pure forms of intuition and the pure concepts of the understanding, through which the manifold of mere sensations is first woven into a system of rules, and thereby constituted as an object.

3

We have expressed in the foregoing reflections the great classical principles of the *Critique of Pure Reason.* Now the question of the classification and systematic division of the pure concepts of the understanding introduces us for the first time into its detailed workings. Immediately it seems as though we stand on different ground, as though here it is no longer the objective necessity of things that purely and exclusively holds sway, but instead a manner of explication and exposition that ultimately is only fully understood and evaluated by tracing it back to certain personal peculiarities of Kant's mind. Delight in comprehensive architectonic structure, in the parallelism of the art form of systematization, in the monolithic schematism of concepts seems to play a greater part in the detailed working out of the doctrine of the categories than is proper. In fact, one of the essential objections that has always been leveled against the overall form of the First Critique is that the table of the pure concepts of the understanding it draws up copies the logical table of judgments with great analytical artistry but with equal artificiality. Since judgments, according to the view of traditional logic as Kant found it, are divided into the four classes of quantity, quality, relation, and modality, the concepts of the understanding should exhibit the same structure; just as in every main class of logical judgments a triad of particular forms is assumed, where the third is the result of synthesizing the first and second, so in the structure of the concepts of the understanding this standpoint is adhered to and rigorously carried out. Under quantity, the subcategories of unity, plurality, and totality are the result; in the domain of quality, the concepts of reality, negation, and limitation; while relation is analyzed into substance, causality, and community, and modality into possibility, existence, and necessity.

Whatever complaints may be raised against this form of the deduction, however, in general all the polemics directed against the systematic relation between category and judgment fall short. For they ignore the true sense of the central and fundamental transcendental question; they overlook the fact that the significant and preeminent place that Kant allots to judgment is of necessity already rooted in the initial presuppositions of his way of putting the problem. Judgment is the natural, factually demanded correlate of the object, since it expresses in the most general sense the consummation of and demand for that combination to which the concept of the object has been reduced for us. "Consequently, we say that we recognize the object when we have effected synthetic unity in the manifold of intuition"; however, when expressed in exact logical notation, the types and forms of synthetic unity are precisely what yield the forms of judgment. Only one objection could still be validly made here, namely, that if one grants this connection, the system of formal logic might not be the court before which the forms of objective interconnection have to be defended, for is not the essence of this logic, and its basic operation, analysis rather than synthesis? Doesn't it abstract from that relation, from that content of knowledge that must be decisive and essential for us? In reply, it is important to keep clearly in mind that for Kant there is indeed such an abstraction, but that it is always to be understood only in a relative, not in an absolute sense. An analysis that is nothing but analysis, that does not in any way relate indirectly to and rest on an underlying synthesis is impossible, "for where the understanding has not previously combined, it cannot dissolve, since only as having been combined *by the under-standing* can anything that allows of analysis be given to the faculty of representation."[36] Thus general logic is concerned with "analysis of the concepts which we already have of objects,"[37] and explicates the judgments which result from presupposing such objects as a ready-made substrate, so to speak, of a proposition.

But as soon as we reflect on the origin of this substrate itself, and inquire as to the possibility of the state assumed by logic—which of course lies outside its province—we are entering the sphere of a different consideration, which demands a deeper explanation and a fundamental deduction of judgment itself. Now it appears that the function which unites diverse representations in one judgment is one and the same as that which also combines the manifold of sensory elements so that they achieve objective validity. "The same understanding, through the same operations by which in concepts, by means of analytical unity, it produced the logical form of a judgment, also introduces a transcendental content into its representations, by means of the synthetic unity of the manifold in intuition in general. On this account we are entitled to call these representations pure concepts of the understanding, and to regard them as applying a priori to objects—a conclusion general logic is not in a position to establish."[38] While general logic can similarly be employed as the "clue to the discovery of all the pure concepts of the understanding," this is not done with the aim of basing the transcendental concepts on the formal ones, but, conversely, with the aim of basing the latter on the former, and in that way yielding a more profound understanding of the ultimate ground of their validity.

"Aristotle," as Kant himself summarizes this whole development in the *Prolegomena*, "collected ten pure elementary concepts under the name of categories. To these, which are also called 'predicaments,' he found himself obliged afterwards to add five post-predicaments, some of which however (*prius, simul,* and *motus*) are contained in the former; but this rhapsody must be considered (and commended) as a

---

36. Ibid., B 130 (III, 113).
37. Ibid., A 5 = B 9 (III, 39).
38. Ibid., A 79 = B 105 (III, 98).

mere hint for future inquirers, not as an idea developed according to
rule.... After long reflection on the pure elements of human knowledge (those which contain nothing empirical), I at last succeeded in
distinguishing with certainty and in separating the pure elementary
notions of the sensibility (space and time) from those of the understanding. Thus the seventh, eighth, and ninth categories had to be
excluded from the old list. And the others were of no service to me
because there was no principle on which the understanding could be
exhaustively investigated, and all the functions, whence its pure concepts arise, determined exhaustively and precisely. But in order to
discover such a principle, I looked about for an act of the understanding which comprises all the rest and is distinguished only by various
modifications or phases, in reducing the multiplicity of representation
to the unity of thinking in general. I found this act of the understanding to consist in judging. Here, then, the labors of the logicians were
ready at hand, though not yet quite free from defects; and with this
help I was enabled to exhibit a complete table of the pure functions of
the understanding, which are however undetermined with respect to
any object. I finally referred these functions of judging to objects in
general, or rather to the condition of determining judgments as objectively valid; and so there arose the pure concepts of the understanding, concerning which I could make certain that these, and this exact
number only, constitute our whole knowledge of things by pure
understanding."[39] The course of the deduction Kant describes in this
passage fully conforms with his general basic tendency. Aristotle had
determined the elements of knowledge, while Kant wishes to discover the principle of these elements; Aristotle's starting point was
the fundamental properties of being, while Kant's was judgment as
the unity of the logical act,[40] in which we achieve permanence and
necessity of the content of representation, and thus objective validity.

The essential meaning of each individual category cannot, of
course, be fully gauged if we simply relate it back in this way to the
form of logical judgment corresponding to it; we must also look for-

39. *Prolegomena*, §39 (IV, 75 f.) (*Ak.* IV, 323-24).
40. Cf. in particular the *Critique of Pure Reason*, A 68 f. = B 93 f. (III, 90 f.) and B 140
ff. (III, 120 ff.).

ward to the work it is responsible for in the structure of objective experience. This work, though, does not belong to the abstract categories as such, but appears only in that concrete form which is given to the concepts of pure understanding, thus transforming them into principles of pure understanding. One of the fundamental merits of Cohen's books on Kant is that they fully and clearly defined this relationship for the first time. It is urged again and again in these books[41] that the system of synthetic principles forms the true touchstone for the validity and the truth of the system of the categories. For a synthetic principle arises because the function that characterizes a specific category relates to the form of pure intuition and permeates it in a systematic unity. Empirical objects—this is settled from the first sentences of the "Transcendental Aesthetic"—can be given to us in no way except through the mediation of intuition, by the mediation of the forms of space and time. This necessary condition is not, however, sufficient. Intuition as such contains only the pure manifold of coexistence and succession; for definite forms defined relative to one another to stand out in this manifold, its elements have to be run through and combined from a definite point of view and in accordance with a fixed rule, and thus composed into relatively substantial unities. This is precisely the work of the understanding, which therefore does not discover the connection of the manifold as already existing in some way in space and time, but which itself produces it originally, since it affects both.[42]

While a synthesis of that kind is needed to produce concrete geometrical figures,[43] it proves to be completely indispensable in matters of specifying physical objects. For to determine a physical object I must indicate its "where" and "when," I must assign it a definite place in the whole of space and duration. This is, in turn, only possible if I produce a definite rule, or rather a total structure and system of rules, by which this particular thing to be established is seen as thoroughly interconnected with and functionally dependent on other

41. See esp. Hermann Cohen, *Kants Theorie der Erfahrung,* 2d ed. (Berlin, 1885), pp. 242 ff.

42. *Critique of Pure Reason,* B 155 (III, 128 f.); cf. esp. B 160, note (III, 132).

43. Cf. esp. *Prolegomena,* §38 (IV, 73) (*Ak.* IV, 320 ff.).

things. Places in space, moments in time are, in the physical sense, determinable only on the basis of forces and relations of forces; the order of coexistence and succession can be established in a lawful way only if we assume certain universally valid dynamic relationships between the individual elements of experience. To lay down the form of these presuppositions and thus to indicate the conditions of the universal possibility of a mutual interconnection of objects in space and in time is the general task the system of synthetic principles sets for itself. If one holds fast to this aim, the principle that orders this system and by which it advances from the simple to the composite immediately becomes evident.

The first step will doubtless have to be that the object, insofar as it is to be intuited in space and time, participates in the fundamental character of both orders, that is, that it is determined as an *extensive* magnitude. But if the concrete physical thing, in the customary way of looking at it, "has" magnitude, here, in conformity with the critical, transcendental view, this proposition is reversed. The predicate of magnitude does not attach to things as their most general and essential property; rather, the synthesis in which the concept of quantity arises for us is the same one by which the manifold of mere perceptions becomes a manifold organized and governed by rules through which it first becomes an order of objects. Magnitude is not a basic ontological property, which we passively receive from objects and can isolate by comparison and abstraction; nor is it some simple sensation given to us, like that of color or sound. It is, rather, an instrument of thinking itself, a pure means of knowledge, with which we originally construct for ourselves "nature" as a universal, lawful order of appearances. For "appearances cannot be apprehended, that is, taken up into empirical consciousness, except through that synthesis of the manifold whereby the representations of a determinate space or time are generated, that is, through combination of the homogeneous manifold and consciousness of its synthetic unity." The concept of the quantum in general is, however, just this consciousness of the homogeneous manifold, insofar as the representation of an object only becomes possible through it. "Thus even the perception of an object, as appearance, is only possible through the same synthetic unity of the manifold of the given sensible intuition as that whereby the unity of the combination of the manifold [and] homogeneous is thought in the concept of a *magnitude*. In other words, appearances are all without exception magnitudes, indeed *extensive magnitudes*. As intuitions in space or time, they must be represented through the same synthesis whereby space and time in general are determined."[44]

The question of the possibility of applying exact mathematical concepts to the appearances of nature—a question that had continuously engrossed not only all prior philosophy, but also Kant himself in his precritical period—is answered at one stroke. For it is now plain that the question is falsely put: it is a matter not of the application of given concepts to a world equally given, to things heterogeneous with the concepts and contrasting with them, but of a special way of ordering to which we subject the "simple" sensations and by which we transform them into objective intuitions. "It will always remain a remarkable phenomenon in the history of philosophy," Kant remarks in the *Prolegomena*, "that there was a time when even mathematicians who at the same time were philosophers began to doubt, not of the accuracy of their geometrical propositions so far as they concerned space, but of their objective validity and the applicability of this concept itself, and of all its corollaries, to nature. They showed much concern whether a line in Nature might not consist of physical points, and consequently that true space in the object might consist of simple parts, while the space which the geometer has in his mind cannot be such."[45] They failed to see that it is precisely this mental space which makes physical space possible, that is to say, that makes the extension of matter itself possible, that this is the same procedure by which we sketch out the image of ideal space in pure geometry to posit a quantitative connection and relation between the sensory empirical elements. All objections to this are but "the chicanery of a falsely instructed reason" which is unable to discover the true ground of its own cognitions because it erroneously searches for it in a world of transcendent things, instead of among its own principles. As long as we regard pure mathematical

44. [*Critique of Pure Reason*, A 162 = B 202 f. (III, 157).]
45. *Prolegomena*, §13, Remark I (IV, 37) (*Ak*. IV, 287–88).

determinations as *data* of experience, we cannot achieve complete certainty as to the precision of these determinations, since all empirical measurement is necessarily inexact; this becomes irrelevant, however, the moment we learn to understand magnitude as a principle instead of as a property. The only thing that joins the representation of the possibility of such a *thing* with this *concept* is that space is a formal a priori condition of external experiences, that the productive synthesis by which we construct a triangle in imagination is completely identical with the synthesis we employ when apprehending an appearance so as to make a concept of experience out of it.[46]

The deduction of the second synthetic principle, which Kant calls the principle of the "Anticipations of Perception," seems more difficult, for here it is a matter of how this designation is to indicate in advance, in a general proposition, not merely the form of perception but its content as well. Since, however, perception is simply "empirical consciousness," any such requirement must seem paradoxical; how can something be anticipated in what can only be given to us a posteriori? Quantity may be susceptible to universally valid propositions, but how such propositions are possible regarding quality, which is given us by the agency of sensation, is at first impossible to see at all. And yet there is a definite moment which we assert of all qualities in nature and which, taken strictly, cannot be sensed in any way. We differentiate extensive magnitudes according to their extent in space and in time when we ascribe to them differing extension and duration, but this means of measurement and comparison deserts us in regard to qualities. For if we think a certain quality (as, say, the speed of a body or its temperature, its electrical or magnetic potential, etc.), it is not bound up with the form of externality that is essential to space and time. We can think the speed of a body in nonuniform motion as changing from place to place, from moment to moment, without stopping to conceive it as a magnitude at each indivisible point of space and time and attributing a definite value to it with respect to other velocities. And similarly, what we call the tempera-

---

46. See the *Critique of Pure Reason*, A 162–66 = B 202–07 (III, 157–59), A 224 = B 271 (III, 198).

ture or the electrical energy of a body can be regarded as determinate at one particular point and as different from point to point. This qualitative magnitude specified at a point thus is not composed, like extensive magnitudes, of individual, separate parts, but rather is present in the point wholly and indivisibly all at once, so that it displays a definite "more" or "less" in relation to other magnitudes of the same sort, and hence permits an exact comparison. Extensive magnitude here contrasts with intensive magnitude; extensional or durational magnitude is opposed to magnitude of degree, which also has a definite, assignable value for the spatiotemporal differential when differentiated with respect to space and time. That this value, that the particular qualities of particular bodies cannot be determined except through empirical measurement, is of course immediately evident.

And yet it appears, if we analyze the whole of our knowledge of nature, that it is not the determinateness of individual qualities and degrees, but what is demonstrable in them that is a universal basic relation, a universal requirement which they collectively satisfy. We presuppose that the transition from one degree to another proceeds continuously, not by leaps; that a specific value a is not replaced directly by another one, larger or smaller, but that in a change of that kind all intermediate values thinkable between a and b are traversed and in fact passed through and actually assumed one after the other. This proposition also rests on empirical observation; can it be proved or disproved by sensation? Obviously not, since however one may determine the relation of a sensation to an objective quality, one thing is clear in every case: that the evidence of sensation is always related to the immediately given individual case, and therefore, however many data we collect about it, it never goes beyond a specific, finite circle of conditions. The principle of the continuity of all physical changes, however, is an assertion which does not concern a sum of finite elements, although it is essential to infinitely many elements. Between any two points in time which we think of as the starting point and the end point of a certain process, however close they may be to one another, infinitely many instants can be interpolated, on the basis of the unlimited divisibility of time, and there corresponds to each of these moments, as the assertion of continuity of change says, a definite, unambiguous quantitative value of the variable quality, a value which is actually assumed once in the course of the whole process.

Regardless of how many of these values may be empirically demonstrated or demonstrable, there always remains an infinity of values for which this demonstration is not made. Nonetheless we may assert that they fall under the same universal rule. For if we thought that the continuity of change was interrupted at any point, we would have no further way of connecting the change with a unitary, identical subject. Assume that a body exhibits a state x at moment a and at moment b a state x', without having run through the values intermediate between the two: we would conclude from this that it was no longer a question of the "same" body; we would assert that at moment a a body in state x disappeared and at moment b a *different* body in state x' appeared. From this it is seen that the assumption of continuity in physical changes is not a matter of a particular result of observation, but of a presupposition of natural knowledge in general, that it is a question not of a *theorem* but of a *principle*. As the first synthetic principle, that of the "Axioms of Intuition," subjects the physical object to the conditions of geometric and arithmetic magnitude, the second principle subjects the object in nature to conditions expressed and scientifically worked out in the analysis of the infinite. This analysis is the true *mathesis intensorum*, the mathematics of intensive magnitudes.[47] While previously appearances were determined as quanta in space and time, now their quality, which has its subjective, psychological expression in sensation, is grasped by a pure concept and thus the "real" in appearance achieves its first scientific designation and objectification.

"In all appearance," as Kant formulates the principle of the "Anticipations of Perception," "the real that is an object of sensation has intensive magnitude, that is, a degree." Empty regions of space and time would be completely identical with one another because of the thoroughgoing homogeneity of pure space and pure time, and hence

47. See esp. Cohen, *Kants Theorie der Erfahrung*, 2d ed., p. 422; *Das Prinzip der Infinitesimalmethode und seine Geschichte* (Berlin, 1883), pp. 105 ff.

indistinguishable. A way of distinguishing between them is obtained only when we put a definite content into them and conceive a difference of "greater" and "lesser," of "more" or "less" in this content. A purely sensory apprehension, though, strictly speaking, occupies only an instant; to an indivisible "now" there corresponds an indivisible sensory content, which one can think as varying from moment to moment. "As sensation is that element in the [field of] appearance the apprehension of which does not involve a successive synthesis proceeding from parts to the whole representation, it has no extensive magnitude. The absence of sensation at that instant would involve the representation of the instant as empty, therefore as = 0. Now what corresponds in empirical intuition to sensation is reality (*realitas phaenomenon*); what corresponds to its absence is negation = 0. Every sensation, however, is capable of diminution, so that it can decrease and gradually vanish. Between reality in the [field of] appearance and negation there is therefore a continuum of many possible intermediate sensations, the difference between any two of which is always smaller than the difference between the given sensation and zero or complete negation. In other words, the real in the [field of] appearance has always a magnitude ... but not extensive magnitude."[48] All sensations as such are therefore given a posteriori, but their property of having a degree, and further that this degree, so far as it undergoes change, must change continuously, can be understood a priori as necessary. In this sense the quality of the empirical, the essential determinateness of perceptions themselves, can be anticipated. "It is remarkable that of magnitudes in general we can know a priori only a single *quality*, namely, that of continuity, and that in all quality (the real in appearances) we can know a priori nothing save [in regard to] their intensive *quantity*, namely that they have degree. Everything else has to be left to experience."[49] What was true earlier of the concept of spatial and temporal magnitudes now holds for the concept of degree: it too affords less the recognition of a universal property of the thing as it is than a constitutive condition which first makes

48. [*Critique of Pure Reason*, A 167 f. = B 209 f. (III, 160 f.).]
49. Ibid., A 176 = B 218 (III, 166).

it possible to establish and differentiate empirical objects themselves.

But if the individual object is taken only in its particularity, the essential concept of "nature" is not yet fulfilled, for the system of nature claims to be a system of laws and therefore is not concerned with the isolated object as such, but instead with the thoroughgoing interconnection of appearances and the way in which they are related to one another by a form of mutual dependence. This idea leads us to a new set of principles, intended to express the principal presupposition less for the purpose of establishing individual things than for establishing relations. When Kant calls these principles the "Analogies of Experience," he is following the way of speaking of the mathematics of his time, in which the term "analogy" was used as the universal expression for any kind of proportion. The fundamental proportion to be established here, however, is the reciprocal place occupied by the particular appearances in space and time, thus the objective relation of their community and succession. In order that such a relation can be expressed, it seems necessary first of all to introduce the individual things, each separately, into space and time alike, that is, to assign them a definite point in the given manifold of space and time in general that marks their individual "here" and "now."

In this, however, we run directly into a peculiar difficulty. In order to use space and especially time in this way as the basis of determination, we would initially have to possess both as absolute and established orders. A fixed structure of space and a fixed succession of time would have to be given us, to which we could relate all motion in space and all qualitative change, just as to a permanent basic scale. But even if it is assumed that such a scale exists, is it recognizable by us in any way? Newton speaks of "absolute, true, and mathematical time," which flows in itself and by reason of its nature uniformly and without relation to any sort of external object. But if we grant him the right to this explanation, can the instants of this uniform time be differentiated independently of every relation to physical objects? Do we know temporal instants and their series directly, or is not rather all knowledge of them which we think we have mediated by our knowledge of the contents of space and time and by the dynamic interconnection which we assume between them? It is not from the absolute "where" and "when" of things that we can draw a conclusion about how they act; on the contrary, what allows us to assign to them a definite order in space and in time is the form of the action that we assume between them, on the basis of experience or inference. On the basis of the law of gravitation, thus on the basis of an assertion about the distribution and relation of forces, we mentally sketch out the picture of the cosmos as it exists in space and as it has unfolded in time. In this theoretical structure much of what is encountered in initial sensory perception, in the sheer coexistence and in the succession of impressions, is spatially and temporally separated (as, for example, we mentally relate the light of extinct fixed stars, the perception of which reaches us simultaneously with the perception of some sort of nearby body, to an object that is centuries or millennia distant in time). On the other hand, many things that are distinct from one another in sensation are combined and transformed into a unity by objective scientific judgment.

But although the *particular* order which we ascribe to the contents of space and time seems always to rest on certain particular laws of action that we assume to hold between them, it is now important, from the transcendental point of view, to convert this knowledge into something universal. There are three different basic determinations, three modes which we distinguish in time and in which the idea of time itself is fulfilled: duration, succession, and simultaneity. We must understand that these three determinations themselves are not immediately given, that they are not simply to be read off impressions, but for each of them to be comprehensible by us, a definite synthesis of the understanding is needed, which for its part is a universal presupposition of the form of experience itself. "There will, therefore, be three rules of all relations of appearances in time, and these rules will be prior to all experience, and indeed make it possible. By means of these rules the existence of every appearance can be determined in respect of the unity of all time."[50] It is these three fundamental rules which Kant formulates in his three "Analogies of

---

50. Ibid., B 219 (III, 167).

Experience." They are the presupposition for our success in determining objective temporal relations in general, that is, that we are not simply abandoned to the chance sequence of impressions in ourselves according to the mere play of association, which is different for each individual and indeed governed by his private circumstances, but rather that we can pronounce universally valid judgments about temporal relations. For instance, to establish in an objective sense the occurrence of change, it is not enough that we posit diverse substances and attribute them directly to different instants of time—for time and instant are not, as such, objects of possible experience; we must point to something enduring and unchanging in the appearances themselves, relative to which the change can be ascertained by certain other determinations. This idea of something relatively constant and something relatively changeable in phenomena, this category of substance and accident, is thus the necessary condition for the emergence of the concept of the unity of time, of duration in change, out of the totality of our representations in general. The permanent is the "substratum of the empirical representation of time itself; in it alone is any determination of time possible."[51] *What* quantum in nature we have to regard as constant always remains a question, the answer to which we must leave to factual observation, but the assumption of *some* quantum in general that remains constant in this fashion is a fundamental presupposition without which the concept of "nature" and of natural knowledge itself would be invalid for us.

The same consideration holds for the relation of causality and reciprocity, which are defined in the second and third analogies of experience. Hume's sensualist critique of the causal concept began by attacking the objective and necessary validity of this concept, since the criticism tries to reduce its whole content to a statement about the more or less regular succession of representations. The coupling of phenomena which we believe we understand in the idea of causality signifies, according to this view, actually nothing other than that they frequently follow one another and hence are joined by our imagination into a relatively firm psychological association of representations.

51. [Ibid., A 183 = B 226 (III, 171).]

If this view is to be refuted in principle and at its root, it can once again happen only through that reversal of the question characteristic of the basic transcendental interpretation: it has to be shown that regularity in the succession of our sensations and perceptions does not produce the concept of causality, but that, conversely, this concept, the idea of and demand for a rule which we bring to perceptions, is what first makes it possible for us to extract determinate forms and definite factually necessary connections from the uniform, flowing series of perceptions, and hence to give our representations an object.

For in fact, when we inquire as to what new property the relation to an object adds to our representations, and what the dignity, the special logical validity, may be that is bestowed on it thereby, we find "that it does nothing more than make the connection of representations necessary in a certain manner and subject them to a rule; that conversely, only a secure order of temporal relations is needed for our perceptions, to impart objective meaning to them."⁵² But the causal relation does precisely this, for if I put two phenomena *a* and *b* in the relation of cause and effect, this means nothing but the assertion that the passage from one to the other cannot be performed at will (as perhaps in a dream or in fantasizing subjectively we can arbitrarily shift the individual elements around at will, like the colored bits of glass in a kaleidoscope, and combine them this way or that way), but that it obeys a fixed law by which *b* must always and necessarily follow *a*, but not also precede *a*. In thus subjecting a given empirical relation to the concept of causality, we have thereby first truly fixed and unambiguously determined the temporal order in the succession of its members. "Let us suppose that there is nothing antecedent to an event, upon which it must follow according to rule. All succession of perception would then be only in the apprehension, that is, would be merely subjective, and would never enable us to determine objectively which perceptions are those that really precede and which are those that follow. We should then have only a play of representations, relating to no object; that is to say, it would not be

52. [Ibid., A 197 = B 242 f. (III, 181).]

possible through our perception to distinguish one appearance from
another as regards relations of time.... I could not then assert that
two states follow upon one another in the [field of] appearance, but
only that one apprehension follows upon the other. That is something subjective, determining no object; and may not, therefore, be
regarded as knowledge of any object.... We have, then, to
show ... that we never, even in experience, ascribe succession ... to
the object, and so distinguish it from subjective sequence in our apprehension, except when there is an underlying rule which compels
us to observe this order of perceptions rather than any other; nay,
*that this compulsion is really what first makes possible the representation of a
succession in the object.*"[53]

And in this way Hume's problem is solved—indeed, very much
"contrary to the expectation of its author." In his entire psychological
analysis, Hume made one uncritical presupposition: that in general
certain impressions are given in an objective and regular succession.
For were this not the case, it would be purely at our option that the
thing *a* might now precede the thing *b*, now be altogether dissociated
from it but included in a different sequence—thus it would be impossible to establish a customary association between *a* and *b*, which is
the condition for repeated encounter with the same items of experience connected in the same way.[54] In this one assumption of an
objective sequence of elements of experience, however—as Kant
charges—what is essential to the causal concept under attack is already granted, so that all subsequent sceptical criticism which is attempted is defective. Only from the perspective of cause and effect,
only by the idea of a rule whereby the appearances are understood for
themselves independently of the subjective consciousness of the individual observer, can one speak of a sequence in "nature" or of
"things" in contrast to the sheer mosaic of representations "in us."
"It is with these," Kant notes, "as with other pure a priori
representations—for instance, space and time. We can extract clear
concepts of them from experience only because we have put them

53. [Ibid., A 194-97 = B 239-42, italics added (III, 179 f.).]
54. Cf. esp. *Critique of Pure Reason*, A 100 ff. (III, 613 ff.).

into experience, and because experience is thus itself brought about only by their means."[55]

For dogmatic metaphysics, causality is valid as an objective power, a sort of fate, rooted in things themselves or in the ultimate ground of things. Sceptical psychological criticism demolishes this view, but, considered more closely, it posits in place of the compulsion of things only the compulsion lying in the mechanism of representations and their connection. In contrast, the critical method bases the necessity that we think in the cause-and-effect relation on nothing other than a necessary synthesis of the understanding, which shapes disparate and isolated impressions into experience. The method cannot yield any more secure and fixed objectivity, but neither is that necessary, since its highest principle says that objects are given us in experience by means of its conditions. The causal concept is not obtained through perception and comparison of similar sequences from experience, that is, from sensory impression; rather, the fundamental principle of causality reveals "how in regard to that which happens we are in a position to obtain in experience any concept whatsoever that is really determinate."[56]

The third "Analogy of Experience" rests on the same idea, in principle; Kant expresses it as the "principle of coexistence, in accordance with the law of *reciprocity* or *community*." "All substances, insofar as they can be perceived to coexist in space, are in thoroughgoing reciprocity." For as it was only possible to objectify succession by linking the elements by a causal rule, in a sequence regarded as necessary, so the objectivity of coexistence can only be assured when the two factors we say are so related stand in a dynamic relation, by means of which each seems to be as much the cause of the other as its effect. As long as we abandon ourselves simply to the stream of sensations and impressions, there is for us no simultaneity in the strict sense, because what we apprehend is just something flowing and successive, within which a single item can only exist by displacing and excluding its predecessor. "The synthesis of imagination in

55. [*Critique of Pure Reason*, A 196 = B 241 (III, 180).]
56. Ibid., A 301 = B 357 (III, 249); for the whole discussion, see A 189 ff. = B 232 ff. (III, 175 ff.).

apprehension would only reveal that the one perception is in the subject when the other is not there, and vice versa, but not that the objects are coexistent, that is, that if the one exists the other exists at the same time. . . . Consequently, in the case of things which coexist externally to one another, a pure concept of the reciprocal sequence of their determinations is required, if we are to be able to say that the reciprocal sequence of the perceptions is grounded in the object and so to represent the coexistence as objective."[57] The general nature of this concept of the understanding is established through the preceding principle: the form of action or functional dependence is that which affords us the ground for assuming a definite temporal connection in the object itself. Here, however, the elements do not, as in the case of causality, stand in a unilateral dependence, so that one element, *a*, presupposes the other, *b*, in the temporal as well as the concrete sense; rather, inasmuch as they are to be simultaneous, it must be possible to make the transition between the two equally well from *a* to *b* as from *b* to *a*. Thus we arrive at a causal system which involves both members in such a way that there can be passage from one to the other just as readily as from the other to the one. A system of this kind is presented in the set of mathematico-physical equations derived from Newton's law of gravitation. Through it, the spatial position and motion of every member of the cosmos is explained as a function of all the rest, and these in turn as a function of it, and this total reciprocity, which is perfect from mass to mass, constitutes for us the objective whole of physical space itself and the ordering and structuring of its individual parts.[58]

This last great example, however, which from early on always signified for Kant himself the essential archetype of all natural knowledge, is at the same time an indication that, with the principle we have before us here, the task of determining what an object in nature is has reached its conclusion. The principles that now follow, and that are assembled by Kant under the name of the "Postulates of Empirical Thought," add no further novelty to this determination. For, as their

57. [Ibid., B 257 (III, 189 f.).]
58. Ibid., A 211 ff. = B 256 ff. (III, 189 ff.).

name indicates, they concern the content of objective appearance itself less than the place which we ourselves give it in empirical thinking. Whether we regard a substance simply as possible, whether we regard it as empirically actual or even as necessary, changes nothing in its nature as such, and does not add a single new characteristic to its concept; but it comprises a different status in the whole of our knowledge, which we give it. Thus the categories of modality, which express this threefold status, have the peculiarity "that, in determining an object, they do not in the least enlarge the concept to which they are attached as predicates. They only express the relation of the concept to the faculty of knowledge. Even when the concept of a thing is quite complete, I can still inquire whether this object is merely possible or is also actual, or if actual, whether it is not also necessary. No additional determinations are thereby thought in the object itself; the question is only how the object, together with all its determinations, is related to understanding and its empirical employment, to empirical judgment, and to reason in its application to experience."[59] This relation to the understanding signifies, accordingly, when considered more closely and designated more precisely, the relation to the system of experience, in which alone objects can be known as given, and hence also as "actual," "possible," or "necessary." What agrees with the formal conditions of experience (intuition and concepts)—according to the three modal postulates—is *possible*; what is bound up with the material conditions of experience (sensation) is *actual*; that which in its connection with the actual is determined according to universal conditions of experience is (or exists) *necessarily*. We see that here it is not a matter of defining the purely formal logical concepts of the possible, actual, and necessary; the distinction between the three stages is, rather, the result of a completely specific epistemological concern. Something would be called possible, in the sense of general logic, which included no contradictory characteristics and hence no internal contradiction, but by the criterion we are examining here, the assurance that this is not the case is far from sufficient. For even without bothering about a formal ab-

59. Ibid., A 219 = B 266 (III, 195).

sence of contradiction, a definite concept can nevertheless be so completely empty for us that it does not unambiguously determine any
object of knowledge at all. Thus there is nothing contradictory in the
concept of a figure enclosed by two straight lines, since the concepts
of two straight lines and their intersection do not include the negation
of a figure, and yet this concept can refer to no particular spatial form
that is essentially distinguishable from other forms. To get such a
form, we would have to pass from the analytic rules of logic to the
synthetic conditions of construction in pure intuition. But even the
addition of these latter conditions is not enough to yield the full,
concrete sense of the possible, which is what is to be defined here. We
accomplish this only when we come to know that the pure synthesis
of space as such is necessarily ingredient in every empirical synthesis
of perceptions, through which alone there arises the idea of a physical, sensory "thing." Thus, for example, the act of construction by
which we trace in our imagination the form of a triangle would be
entirely homogeneous with that act we perform in apprehending an
appearance so as to make it into a concept of experience.[60] It is not the
fulfillment of this or that particular condition, but the fulfillment of all
conditions essential for the object of experience which thus comprises
the true conception of the "possible."

The first modal principle, however, only asserts the validity of the
formal conditions of experience—pure intuition and the pure concepts of the understanding. If, on the other hand, we progress from
claiming possibility to claiming actuality, we see we are directed to a
totally different cognitive factor. Something real *in concreto*, a definite
individual thing, is given to us neither through a pure concept nor
through pure intuition. For in the bare concept of a thing absolutely
no mark of its concrete existence can be formed; and as to the constructive synthesis by which geometric forms arise for us, this also
never goes as far as the individual determinations that are what we
mean when we speak of the existence of a particular object. We construct "the" triangle or "the" circle as a schema and general model
which can be actualized in infinitely many separate examples that are

60. Ibid., A 223 f. = B 271 f. (III, 198); cf. above, p. 177.

individualized and different one from the other; but as soon as we wish to extract one actual specimen from this ensemble of possible examples, as soon as we conceive a form as particularized in every part, as in, say, the length of its sides and the size of its angles, or in the specificity of its "here," its position in absolute space, then we have gone beyond the mathematical way of stating the problem and the foundations of mathematical knowledge in general. Only sensation includes reference to such details of the individual thing. "The postulate bearing on the knowledge of things as *actual* does not, indeed, demand immediate *perception* (and, therefore, sensation of which we are conscious) of the object whose existence is to be known. What we do, however, require is the connection of the objects with some actual perception, in accordance with the analogies of experience, which define all real connection in an experience in general."[61] Thus a specific substance need not in any way be capable of being sensed in order to be designated as actual, as existing, but it must at least exhibit that link with some sort of given perceptions that we call the system and the order of empirical causality (in the broadest sense). The existence of a magnetic material which penetrates all bodies, for instance, cannot be shown through immediate sense perception, but it is enough if it can be disclosed on the basis of observable data (as, say, the attraction of iron filings) through causal laws.

Thus, the relation of perceptions to laws of this sort, and conversely, the relation of the laws to perception, is what constitutes for us the essential nature of empirical actuality. "That there may be inhabitants in the moon, although no one has ever perceived them, must certainly be admitted. This, however, only means that in the possible advance of experience we may encounter them. For everything is real which stands in connection with a perception in accordance with the laws of empirical advance."[62] Neither do we have any criterion for the difference between dreaming and waking that is other than and better than the one laid down by this proposition. For this distinction can never be shown in the bare character of the con-

61. Ibid., A 225 ff. = B 272 ff. (III, 198 ff.).
62. Ibid., A 493 = B 521 (III, 350).

tents of consciousness as such, in the peculiar nature of the individual representations which are given to us in the one and in the other state, since these data are alike in both cases. The only thing that makes the decisive difference is that in one case we are able to integrate the totality of these data into one whole, which agrees with itself and is governed by laws, while in the other case they remain for us merely a disjointed conglomerate of individual impressions which displace one another.[63]

In this definition, the postulate of actuality at the same time makes direct contact with the postulate of necessity. For the meaning of necessity, as here understood, is not the formal and logical necessity of conceptual connections, but refers rather to a cognitive value that has its roots in empirical thinking, hence in physics. In this way of thought we call a determinate fact necessary not by claiming it to be a fact on the basis of observation, but by regarding and demonstrating this factuality to be the consequence of a universal law. In this sense, for example, the rules of planetary motion as stated by Kepler signify a merely factual determination, but they were raised to the rank of empirical necessity when Newton succeeded in finding a universal formulation of the law of gravitation, in which those rules are contained as special cases and are deducible from it mathematically. It is obvious that this necessity is nothing absolute, but merely hypothetical. It holds only under the presupposition that the major premise of the deduction—in our case the Newtonian law of attraction as in direct proportion to the masses and in inverse proportion to the square of the distance—is regarded as established and valid. Thus the existence of sensory objects can never be known completely a priori, "but only comparatively a priori, relatively to some other previously given existence. . . ."[64] The relation of perceptions to laws is therefore treated in the postulate of necessity just as it was in the postulate of actuality, but the orientation of this relation is different in the two cases. The one instance moves from the particular to the universal, while the other leads from the universal to the particular; the former

63. Cf. *Prolegomena*, §13, Remark III (IV, 40) (*Ak.* IV, 290).
64. *Critique of Pure Reason*, A 226 = B 279 (III, 203).

is tied to the individual instance that appears in sensation and perception, whereas in the latter the movement of thought is from the law to the individual case. The principle of actuality thus refers to the form of physical induction, that of necessity to the form of physical deduction. In this way it is shown that neither is an independent mode of procedure, but that they are reciprocally related and that only as thus correlated do they determine the overall form of experience in general. In this context we recognize once again the special place the modal postulates occupy within the system of synthetic principles: they no longer directly relate to the interconnection of empirical objects, but rather to the coherence of empirical methods; they are aimed at determining the relative justification of each method, and defining its significance in the whole of experiential knowledge.

4

The "subjectivity" that was the starting point of transcendental reflection has until now been presented in a precisely defined, terminologically restricted sense. It meant going in no way beyond the bounds of the individual knower, nor beyond the psychological processes through which the world of sensations, of ideas and their connection, is generated for an individual. Rather, it held fast only to this: that determination of the pure *form* of knowledge must precede determination of the object of knowledge. In conceiving space as a unitary synthetic procedure, the lawfulness of geometric and physical geometric forms is revealed to us. When we analyze the method of experiment, and point out the pure concepts of magnitude and mass, and the universal presuppositions of permanence and causal dependence in it, we have thereby accounted for the universality and the objective validity of experiential judgments through their true origin. The "subject" spoken of here is hence none other than reason itself, in its universal and its particular functions. In this sense alone could we style Kant's system "idealism"; the ideality to which it is related and on which it rests is that of the highest rational principles, in which all special and derivative results are prefigured in some sense and by which they are necessarily "determined a priori."

But is there not a completely different sense of subjectivity, which, although it is not the starting point for the *Critique of Pure Reason*, still at least merits its consideration? And are there not other forms of idealism well recognized in the history of philosophy, in contradistinction to which this new doctrine must be sharply and surely delimited if it is not to foster continual misunderstandings? No problem of exposition occupied Kant's thoughts so deeply and lastingly as this one. Again and again he sought to distinguish the special nature of his "critical" idealism from Descartes's "sceptical" or "problematic" idealism; against the "dogmatic" idealism of Berkeley he tried to guard his own fundamental ideas, which concern simply the determination of the form of experience, from confusion with common and material psychological idealism. But although Kant could explain all confusion of this sort simply as due to an "almost deliberate misapprehension," it appears in a different light to purely historical judgment. For an essential basic element of the First Critique is precisely that it contains as much a novel doctrine of consciousness as it does a new theory of the object. If his contemporaries singled out the former component above all from the whole of the critical system and tried to interpret the entire *Critique* by it, the primary reason for this was their discovery of a language of philosophical concepts that seemed to afford the quickest link with accepted modes of thought. For while in the objective deduction of the categories, in the proof that the conditions of the possibility of experience are at the same time conditions of the possibility of the objects of experience, Kant had to create singlehandedly not only the concepts themselves but also their logical expression, in the subjective deduction he concurred throughout with the common psychological nomenclature of his time. Hamann says in a letter to Herder that Tetens's major work, the *Philosophische Versuche über die menschliche Natur*, lay open on Kant's table during the writing of the First Critique.[65] Thus the impression might arise that what was created here is a novel transcendental substructure for empirical psychology, that concrete psychological facts were translated into a different, metaphysical language.

65. See *Hamanns Schriften*, ed. F. Roth (Augsburg, 1821–43), vol. 6, p. 83.

In truth, however, the First Critique is aimed against psychological "idealism" as much as it is against dogmatic "realism," since it is intended no less as a critique of the concept of ego than as a critique of the concept of the object. Psychological metaphysics, which found its typical expression in Berkeley's system, is characterized through and through by its assertion of the certainty of the ego as an original datum, and the certainty of external things as merely inferred datum. In the existence of the ego we possess an immediate and indubitable concrete existent, while everything else that we designate by the name of "reality," as in particular the being of things in space, is dependent on the fundamental fact of the ego. Thus "souls" (and the infinite spirit of God which stands over them) comprise the sole truly "substantial" actuality. The totality of what we call "existence" can be expressed and understood, then, as nothing but psychic substance, as "perceiver" or "perceived." Kant divorced himself from this view chiefly in that for him the ego, the psychological unity of self-consciousness, formed a terminus, not a starting point, of the deduction. If one does not judge from the standpoint of an absolute metaphysics but from the standpoint of experience and its possibilities, it is obvious that the fact of the ego has no preeminence and no prerogative over and above other facts attested to by perception and empirical thought. For even the self is not given to us originally as a simple substance: the idea of it only arises in us on the basis of the same synthesis, the identical functions of unification of the manifold by which sense-content becomes the content of experience, impression becomes object. Empirical self-consciousness does not precede the empirical consciousness of objects temporally and concretely; rather, in one and the same process of objectification and determination the whole of experience is divided for us into the field of the inner and of the outer, the self and the world.[66]

In the "Transcendental Aesthetic" time had already been called the "form of inner sense, that is, of the intuition of ourselves and of our inner state."[67] In this first condition immediately all others are

---

66. See the Refutation of Idealism, *Critique of Pure Reason*, B 274 ff. (III, 200 ff.).
67. Transcendental Aesthetic, §6 (III, 65).

ultimately contained, for now it is only a matter of analyzing the consciousness of time itself, so as to elicit in detail all the determining factors that make it up. The presence of a problem here appears most clearly if we ask what is the basis for the possibility of comprehending a temporal *whole* in thought and showing that it is a definite unity. This possibility may be understandable in the case of space, for since by its essential concept its parts are taken to be simultaneous, nothing further seems to be needed than to pull together that which exists simultaneously also in thought, so as to arrive at the intuition of a definite spatial extension. A single instant of time is, on the other hand, characterized by its being given as the fleeting, pointlike boundary between past and future, by its thus basically existing only as something singular, excluding all other moments. Only the indivisible, present "now" actually exists, while every other point in time must be regarded as something which is not yet or which is no longer. Thus it is obvious that no aggregate, no sum of the individual elements in the ordinary sense, is possible in this case, for how can a sum be formed when the first member vanishes as I move on to the second one? But if a whole, the totality of an entire series, is to be posited in time—and this is precisely what constitutes the necessary presupposition for that unity we call the unity of self-consciousness—it must be at least indirectly possible to hold on to the moment without losing thereby the general nature of time as a continuous progress and transition. Temporal moments may not be simply posited and apprehended, but they must be created anew repeatedly; the "synthesis of apprehension" must operate simultaneously and within one and the same indivisible fundamental act as a "synthesis of reproduction."[68] In this way the present can be added to the past, the past preserved in the present, and both thought jointly. Basically, however, the temporal process would not yet be grasped as a unity even so if reproduction, when complete, were not at the same time also known to be reproduction: that is, if what is posited severally and at diverse points in time were not nonetheless determined by thought to be one, as identical. To all the diversities in

68. See the *Critique of Pure Reason*, A 100 ff. (III, 613).

the qualitative contents of sensation and all the multiplicity of temporal locations, however essential they are to pure intuition, the unity
of the synthesis of the understanding must be superadded. "If we
were not conscious that what we think is the same as what we
thought a moment before, all reproduction in the series of representations would be useless. For it would in its present state be a new
representation which would not in any way belong to the act whereby
it was to be gradually generated. The manifold of the representation
would never, therefore, form a whole, since it would lack that unity
which only consciousness can impart to it. If, in counting, I forget that
the units, which now hover before me, have been added to one
another in succession, I should never know that a total is being produced through this successive addition of unit to unit, and so would remain ignorant of the number. For the concept of the number is nothing
but the consciousness of this unity of synthesis. The word 'concept'
might of itself suggest this remark. For this unitary consciousness is
what combines the manifold, successively intuited, and thereupon
also reproduced, into one representation. This consciousness may
often be only faint, so that we do not connect it with the act itself, that
is, not in any direct manner with the *generation* of the representation,
but only with the outcome [that which is thereby represented]. But
notwithstanding these variations, such consciousness, however in-
distinct, must always be present; without it, concepts, and therewith
knowledge of objects, are altogether impossible."[69]

Only in this last stage of the synthesis, this "recognition in a
concept," does that substance arise for us which we oppose to sheer
flux and alteration of sensory impressions and representations as the
"abiding and unchanging 'I'." Although it appeared that sensualism
had provided an adequate explanation of the concept of the self by
calling the self a loose structure of separate psychic entities, a mere
"bundle of perceptions," that explanation rested on an extremely
crude and incomplete analysis, as is now demonstrated. For aside
from the fact that even the loosest and most superficial form of that
connection would already involve a critical epistemological problem,

69. *Critique of Pure Reason*, A 103 f. (III, 614 f.).

the transcendental inversion holds here also. The self, so far from being the product of individual perceptions, actually constitutes the fundamental presupposition for something that can in general be called "perception." The "self" as identical reference point imparts to what is particular and diverse its qualitative meaning as content of consciousness. In this sense the ego of pure apperception is the "correlate of all our representations," with regard to the pure possibility of our becoming conscious of them, and "all consciousness as truly belongs to an all-comprehensive pure apperception, as all sensible intuition, as representation, does to a pure inner intuition, namely, to time."[70] The unity of time, in and through which alone there is for us a unity of empirical consciousness, is thus here traced back to universal conditions, and on closer analysis these conditions, together with the principles flowing from them, are demonstrated to be the same ones on which all assertion of objectively valid interconnections, and hence all knowledge of the object, rest.

Only now is the relation between inner and outer experience, between self-consciousness and consciousness of the object, clarified. These two do not comprise "halves" of experience as a whole, which subsist independently of each other, but they are conjoined in the same ensemble of universally valid and necessary logical presuppositions, and inseparably related to each other through this ensemble. We now no longer ask how the "I" makes contact with things in themselves, nor how things in themselves begin to participate in the "I." Now the expression for both "self" and "object" is one and the same: the lawfulness of "experience in general" signified in the concept of transcendental apperception. This is the sole mediator and agency for us of any entities whatsoever, be they of inner or of outer sense.

The moment we fail to grant this meaning and source of the concept of the ego, we are straightway entangled in all the insoluble problems that crop up in every metaphysical psychology. If we cease to think the "transcendental unity of apperception" in the form of a pure condition, if we try to intuit it as something given and existing

70. Ibid., A 123 f. (III, 625).

and to make it imaginable, we blunder onto the path of a dialectic which, step by step, consequence by consequence, becomes more and more difficult and complicated. This dialectic arises whenever we try to convert a definite relation, which is valid within experience and for the purpose of uniting its separate members, into an independent substance prior to all experience. In this conversion of a pure relation into an absolute substantiality there lurks no mere chance or personal deception for which the individual empirical subject would be responsible: we have to do here rather with a sophistry of reason itself, which is unavoidable before it is fully revealed by the transcendental critique and the reasons for it completely fathomed. A new field of questions and tasks is thus presented to the First Critique. The "Transcendental Aesthetic" and the "Transcendental Analytic" were aimed at showing the conditions of *genuine* objectification, which takes place in experience and by means of its principles, whereas the "Transcendental Dialectic" is oriented negatively, toward guarding against the false objects generated for us by transgression of these conditions; the "logic of truth" was occupied with the former, the "logic of appearance"[71] with the latter.

If we first apply this conceptual distinction simply to the psychological problem, it will be a matter of rendering comprehensible the illusion that results from the hypostatization of the universal unifying function of consciousness into a particular simple soul substance. All the paralogisms of rational psychology, all the fallacies of the pure metaphysical theory of the soul, are rooted in this hypostatization. For the whole previous conception of the soul rests on the fact that we abstract a unity that can be shown in the series of phenomena of consciousness itself and whose necessity is demonstrable within this realm from the totality of this very series, and ascribe this unity to an original, self-subsistent substrate, of which the particular phenomena of consciousness are supposed to be but an indirect consequence. Thus instead of simply thinking the phenomena themselves as interconnected, we now superadd to them in thought a nonempirical ground, from which we attempt to explain and derive

71. See ibid., A 60 f. = B 85 f., A 293 ff. = B 349 ff. (III, 86, 244 ff.).

the multiplicity of phenomena. A simple, indivisible, and unchangeable something is now posited, and, although its general form as a
thing is analogous to things in space and comparable with them,
nevertheless it is essentially distinguished from them by its specific
structure, and hence it supposedly never enters into any relation with
them except a purely contingent and dissoluble one. But this assertion, and hence all assertions about immaterial nature and about the
permanence of the soul, is the basis of the same unresolved contradiction. The sole text of rational psychology is the proposition "I think,"
which must be able to accompany all our representations in that they
are to be explained only by its means as belonging to one and the
same self-consciousness, whether it be expressly attached to them or
only latent in them.

But this reference of all psychic contents to one common central
point neither says anything whatsoever about any sort of enduring
concrete existent to which it points, nor does it determine a single
actual predicate belonging to this concrete existent. It is indubitably
certain that the concept of the "I" as a constant unity, identical with
itself in all particular representing and thinking, is met with again and
again, but that in no way gets us to the intuition of a self-existent
object corresponding to this concept. Every inference from the logical
unity of intellectual functioning to the real and metaphysical unity of
the substantial soul means, instead, a μετάβασις εἰς ἄλλο γένος,
an illicit transition to a completely different field of problems. "It
follows, therefore, that the first syllogism of transcendental psychology, when it puts forward the constant logical subject of thought as
being knowledge of the real subject in which the thought inheres, is
palming off upon us what is a mere pretence of new insight. We do
not have, and cannot have, any knowledge whatsoever of any such
subject. Consciousness is, indeed, that which alone makes all representations to be thoughts, and in it, therefore, as the transcendental
subject, all our perceptions must be found; but beyond this logical
meaning of the 'I,' we have no knowledge of the subject in itself,
which as substratum underlies this 'I,' as it does all thoughts. The
proposition, *'The soul is substance,'* may, however, quite well be
allowed to stand, if only it be recognized that this concept [of the soul

as substance] does not carry us a single step further, and so cannot yield us any of the usual deductions of the pseudo-rational doctrine of the soul, as, for instance, the everlasting duration of the human soul in all changes and even in death—if, that is to say, we recognize that this concept signifies *a substance only in idea,* not in reality."[72] And it is precisely in this that the intellectual labor the transcendental dialectic has to perform at this point consists: to completely transform the earlier metaphysical definitions of the soul as substance into epistemological definitions of the soul as Idea. The "I," the "transcendental apperception," is permanent and unchangeable, but it is only an invariable relation *between* the contents of consciousness, not the unvarying substratum *from* which they arise. It is simple and undivided, but this is only so relative to the synthetic act of unification of the manifold, which as such can either be thought only totally and completely or else not thought at all. No bridge leads from the indivisibility of this act to the assertion of an indivisible thing that stands behind it and as its foundation. Hence my own simplicity (as soul) is not deduced from the proposition "I think," but is already involved in that very idea. "The proposition '*I am simple,*' must be regarded as an immediate expression of apperception, just as what is referred to as the Cartesian inference, *cogito, ergo sum,* is really a tautology, since the *cogito* (*sum cogitans*) asserts my existence immediately. '*I am simple*' means nothing more than that this representation, 'I,' does not contain in itself the least manifoldness and that it is absolute (although merely logical) unity."[73]

The terms in which the problem is put in the "Transcendental Dialectic" and its basic tendency are even more sharply evident in the critique of the concept of the cosmos than in that of the concept of the soul. First of all, it seems as though the "Transcendental Analytic" had arrived at a finally valid answer to the question, for what does the concept of the cosmos assert except the concept of "nature," and what is nature, according to the highest principle of all synthetic judgments, except the whole of possible experience, whose structure

72. Ibid., A 350 f. (III, 637).
73. Ibid., A 354 f. (III, 639).

and limits have been precisely established by the system of the pure principles of the understanding? But in speaking of the whole of experience we have already suggested the new problem that goes beyond the limitations of the Analytic. The experience, the possibility of which we inquired into, is not a particular sort of thing, but a specific "mode of knowledge." It signifies an ensemble of modes of understanding, which science employs less to construct a given actuality than to accomplish the universal and necessary connection of phenomena, which we call their "reality." Still, seen from this perspective, it is not a finished product but instead a process that progressively shapes itself. We are able to determine the conditions of this process, but not its outcome. In that way, to be sure, an unambiguous direction is prescribed to our cognition of experience, since its progress is furthered by universal and constant fundamental methods; however, in so doing its sum and its outcome are not equivalently indicated and fixed. What is available to us here is an ensemble of various ways of determining objects, but the goal to which these ways all point is in fact never reached by any of them.

Thus we are in command of the fundamental forms of pure space and pure time, by which we combine appearances into the orders of coexistence and succession; thus with the help of the causal concept we abstract from the manifold of events specific causal series and sets of causal series. The process of determination, however, never reaches an ultimate terminus this way, for not only does an individual member in every particular series always point to another that precedes it, without our ever succeeding to a last member, but also, when we grasp each series as a unity, the moment we wish to indicate how it coordinates with other series and depends on them, the result is a nexus of ever-new functional connections, which, when we try to follow it out and express it, leads us straight into the indefinite distance. What we call "experience" consists in such a set of progressive relations, not in a whole of absolute data. The demands posed at this point not only by dogmatic metaphysics but also by naive realism are in no way satisfied by this. For the mark of this view is not only that it wishes to think the object as progressively determined through experiential knowledge, but that it assumes the world, as a totality, prior to the process of this determination. Though we may *conceive* the world in our empirical knowledge only piecemeal and fragmentarily, it is nonetheless present as a whole, finished and perfect in every respect. But now the transcendental critique asks what this "being present" means. It is clear that it cannot be demonstrability in immediate sensation and perception that is meant, since what must be stressed here is precisely that the portion of being given us from time to time in actual perception constitutes but a vanishingly small fragment of the whole. Hence it is once again a definite hallmark of the *judgment* of objectivity that we have before us in this assertion of a present, closed world. At the very least, it is important to understand this judgment and evaluate its peculiar logic—even if we have to deny the absolute existence of the object to which it refers.

So from the standpoint of transcendental reflection, we must first of all begin by admitting that the comparison between experience and the object, as it has been maintained and understood up until now, does not contain any ultimate and unambiguous solution to our question. For the necessity for thought to reach out beyond what is empirically known and given is undeniable. If, in the critical sense, we regard experience as a product of intuition and understanding, if we distinguish within it the individual conditions of space, time, magnitude, substantiality and causality, etc., it appears that, when we single out any one of these functions, it is never exhausted in any specific result. As, for instance, according to a proposition of the "Transcendental Aesthetic," the infinity of time signifies nothing more than that all definite temporal magnitudes are possible only through limitations of one single fundamental time, an analogous infinity is attributable to each particular form of pure synthesis. Every determinate quantum is thinkable only on the basis of the universal procedure of assigning quantity and defining it; every individual case of causal connection is thinkable only as the specification of the causal principle in general. By means of this infinity, which is already incorporated in its pure logical form, each of the constitutive factors in experiential cognition insists on its exhaustive application, which exceeds every actually attained limit. Each cause that we can point to in experience has only a limited and relative being, since we can always posit it as something individual by relating it to another, more remote cause. But the principle and the idea of causality is unrestrictedly valid. To carry out this principle in a systematically complete way throughout the whole field of phenomena, so that no one phenomenon as ostensibly "ultimate," and hence not ever traceable back to something further, stands in our path and attempts to block our progress—that is a demand raised by reason itself and founded in reason. "Reason" in the specific sense this concept has, through the "Transcendental Dialectic," means nothing but this very demand.

"Understanding may be regarded as a faculty which secures the unity of appearances by means of rules, and reason as being the faculty which secures the unity of the rules of understanding under principles. Accordingly, reason never applies itself directly to experience or to any object, but to understanding, in order to give to the manifold knowledge of the latter an a priori unity by means of concepts, a unity which may be called the unity of reason, and which is quite different in kind from any unity that can be accomplished by the understanding."[74] The categories of the understanding, taken together, are only means of leading us from one conditioned thing to another, while the transcendental concept of reason invariably proceeds to the absolute totality in the synthesis of conditions, and hence never terminates in what is absolutely (i.e., in every relation) unconditioned. "Reason accordingly occupies itself solely with the employment of understanding, not indeed insofar as the latter contains the ground of possible experience (for the concept of the absolute totality of conditions is not applicable in any experience, since no experience is unconditioned), but solely in order to prescribe to the understanding its direction toward a certain unity of which it has itself no concept, and in such manner as to unite all the acts of the understanding, in respect of every object, into an *absolute whole*."[75] But the justified transcendental claim contained herein immediately becomes transcendent if one attempts to exhibit it under the image of an absolute thing; if one makes the totality of beings into an existing,

74. Ibid., A 302 = B 359 (III, 250).
75. Ibid., A 326 = B 383 (III, 264).

given object—which constitutes the endless task of experiential knowledge. That which was not only permissible but necessary, which was regarded as a maxim and as a guide for empirical inquiry, now appears as a substance that on closer analysis disintegrates into obviously contradictory factors and individual attributes. Thus, concerning the world as a given whole, we can successively demonstrate, with equal logical justification, that it has a beginning in time and a limit in space, as well as that in respect of time as well as space, it is infinite; thus with the same validity it can be shown that the world is composed of absolutely simple substances, as well as that division, in the physical realm and also in pure space, is never complete and hence that absolute simplicity is an unrealized idea.

The real basis of all these antinomies in the concept of the world, the content and systematic significance of which had already emerged in the historical evolution of Kant's thinking,[76] can now be indicated in its full import and simplicity from the general presuppositions of the critical system. That two diametrically opposite determinations and conclusions can be deduced from a single concept is possible only if the latter itself already contains an internal contradiction in its construction and in the original systhesis on which it rests. In our case, though, this contradiction, inspected more closely, lies in the fact that the content of the world concept is bound up with the definite article, that "the" world is used as a substantive. For experience as a whole is never given to us as such, as a rigid, closed entity; it is not a result lying behind us, but a goal lying before us. The state we ascribe to it is therefore ultimately grounded in nothing other than the rule of progress itself, in which, starting from what is particular, we ascend to the concept of the world as the total nexus of empirical being. This rule, for its part, has its definite objective validity also, but it cannot be thought in the form of a "thinglike" whole, which would be given together with all its parts. It cannot determine what the object may be, only how the empirical regress is to be carried on so as to arrive at the complete concept of the object.[77] "It [the rule] cannot be regarded

76. See above, pp. 110 ff.
77. *Critique of Pure Reason,* A 510 = B 438 (III, 360 f.).

as maintaining that the series of conditions for a given conditioned is in
itself either finite or infinite. That would be to treat a mere idea of absolute totality, which is only produced in the idea, as equivalent to thinking an object that cannot be given in any experience. For in terms of it we
should be ascribing to a series of appearances an objective reality that
is independent of empirical synthesis. This idea of reason can therefore do no more than prescribe a rule to the regressive synthesis in the
series of conditions; and in accordance with this rule the synthesis
must proceed from the conditioned, through all subordinate conditions, up to the unconditioned. Yet it can never reach this goal, for the
absolutely unconditioned is not to be met with in experience."[78]

In this sense, the idea of totality is "regulative," not "constitutive," because it contains only a prescription as to what we are to do
in the regress, but does not determine and anticipate what is given in
the object prior to any regress. The distinction set up herein concerns
only transcendental reflection on the source of the principle, but not
its actual empirical employment. In regard to this latter, it is "a matter
of indifference whether I say that in the empirical advance in space I
can meet with stars a hundred times farther removed than the outer-
most now perceptible to me, or whether I say that they are perhaps to
be met with in cosmical space even though no human being has ever
perceived or ever will perceive them."[79] For the presence of an empirical object, viewed more exactly, means and can mean nothing more
than its determinability, direct or indirect, by way of the empirical
method: by sensation or pure intuition, by the "analogies of experience" or the "postulates of empirical thought," by the synthetic principles or the regulative Ideas of reason. Accordingly, if I think to
myself all existing objects of sense in the whole of time and space, I do
not place them in both prior to experience; rather, this thought is
nothing but the idea of a possible experience in its absolute perfection.[80] This idea is as such unavoidable, but it is entangled in contradictions the moment we elect to isolate and hypostatize its content,
which is to say, the moment we fabricate a thing unrelated to it,

78. [Ibid.]
79. [Ibid., A 496 = B 524 (III, 352).]
80. Ibid., A 495 = B 523 f. (III, 352).

intended to correspond to it, instead of using it and holding fast to it as a guideline within empirical inquiry.

This insight yields the principal solution to those problems covered by the *Critique of Pure Reason* in its third and final part. The critique of rational psychology and cosmology moves on to the critique of rational theology: the analysis of the Idea of the soul and that of the cosmos terminates in the analysis of the Idea of God. Here, too, consistent with the general methodological tendency, the point is to show that in the Idea of God it is not so much that a definite absolute entity is thought, as rather that a special principle of possible experience is posited and hence a mediate relation to the general tasks of empirical inquiry is set up. But this turn contains a paradox. For does not the whole meaning of the concept of God lie in His "transcendence"? Does it not lie precisely in the fact that we assert the certainty of an ultimate Being, which exists apart from all contingency and conditions of finite empirical being? This is the sense in which the concept seems to have been assumed by all previous metaphysics from the time of Aristotle. From time immemorial it had been concluded that if there is no entity which is purely "in itself" and "through itself"—then neither is the being of any secondary and dependent thing thinkable; thus all actuality as a whole dissolves into insubstantial illusion. Even Kant's own precritical essay, "The Only Possible Basis of Proof for a Demonstration of God's Existence," stood by and large within this basic outlook; indeed, it strengthened and confirmed it, by seeking to demonstrate the absolutely necessary Being as the ground, not only of everything actual, but also of all possible being, or of all truth of conceptual and ideal relations.[81] From the critical viewpoint, however, this reflection too must be reversed. Instead of moving from a universal concept of the logically possible to the special concept of the possibility of experience, now it is instead "possible experience" which is viewed as the foundation that can confer on all concepts, as cognitive, their value and their objective validity.

And with that, the whole ontological way of reasoning, the foun-

81. Cf. above pp. 62 ff.

dation of all previous rational theology, has become untenable. For the core of all ontology is that inference can be made from the concept of the most perfect Being to its existence, because existence itself is a perfection which thus cannot be excluded from the predicates of this concept without contradiction. From the transcendental standpoint, though, it is finally realized that existence in general is not a specific conceptual predicate, standing on an equal footing with others, but that it is a problem of knowledge, which must be progressively defined and mastered with every epistemological means. Only the sum total of these techniques can define for us what it means in general to exist empirically. Here neither the mere analytical logical concept nor the pure intuition of space and time, nor even sensation and sense perception suffices; it is only the mutual relation of all these factors on which experience, and in and through that the object, is founded for us. Within the system of synthetic principles, it was above all the "Postulates of Empirical Thought," and of them especially the "Postulate of Actuality," that established this connection. In these we learned how sensation, intuition, and concept must cooperate to result in any valid statement about a "concrete existent." Ontology, however, not only arbitrarily and onesidedly abstracts the function of thinking from this whole complex, but it takes thinking itself to be the merely analytic dissection of a given conceptual content, instead of the synthetic function of combining in relation with the manifold of intuition.

But regarded thus, thinking is blocked from any access to being and from any foothold therein. It can now only infer, by a *petitio principii*, from the possible to the actual; for the simple reason that, purely from its own resources, it neither knows nor understands the full difference between possibility and actuality. A hundred actual dollars contain, if I simply reflect on the concept and on the predicates that can be abstracted analytically from it, not the least bit more than a hundred possible dollars. "By whatever and by however many predicates we may think a thing ... we do not make the least addition to the thing when we further declare that this thing *is*. Otherwise, it would not be exactly the same thing that exists, but something more than we had thought in the concept; and we could not, therefore, say that the exact object of my concept exists. . . . When, therefore, I think a being as the supreme reality, without any defect, the question still remains whether it exists or not. For though, in my concept, nothing may be lacking of the possible real content of a thing in general, something is still lacking in its relation to my whole state of thought, namely, [insofar as I am unable to assert] that knowledge of this object is also possible a posteriori. . . . For through the concept the object is thought only as conforming to the *universal conditions* of possible empirical knowledge in general, whereas through its existence it is thought as belonging to the context of experience as a whole. In being thus connected with the *content* of experience as a whole, the concept of the object is not, however, in the least enlarged; all that has happened is that our thought has thereby obtained an additional possible perception."[82]

Hence only connection with the content of experience and the context of its assertions and judgments has the power to justify every statement about actuality. If the existence of God is to be shown demonstratively at all, we seem to be guided from the a priori proof of ontology to the a posteriori forms of proof, to the cosmological and the physico-theological proofs. The former follows from the circumstance that, within the series of causes in the world, we always pass from one conditioned and dependent existence to another, so that by this route the absolute ground of the whole series is never evident; thus, it must be sought outside the series in the existence of a being which exists as *causa sui,* not through some other being but through itself. The second proof concludes from the rational and purposive order that is visible in individual parts of the cosmos and in its overall structure to a highest intelligence from which it has its origin and by which it is conserved in its continuing state. But aside from the internal logical flaws in these proofs, which Kant had already recognized and revealed early on,[83] they are invalid because they are only seemingly independent and self-sufficient. They are proposed in previous metaphysics as a support and supplement to the ontological

82. *Critique of Pure Reason,* A 600 f. = B 628 f. (III, 414 f.).
83. See above, pp. 58 f.

proof, but in truth they completely presuppose it in its entirety. For even if it were assumed that the path of the cosmological proof could be followed to a supreme cause of the world, or that inference can be made from purposiveness internal to appearances to a rational ground of the world, it would not be thereby demonstrated that this cause and this ground are identical with what we are accustomed to designate by the concept and the name of God. In order to make this identification, involving not only the existence of an ultimate ground but also its more precise description and its specific predicates, we are forced back into the use of the ontological proof. We must try to show that the absolutely substantial and necessary Being is at the same time the most real Being, that all reality and perfection is included in it and derivable from it. The circularity of the proof therefore becomes blatant, for what is produced here to confirm the ontological proof is devoid of any precise and unambiguous definition, so long as it itself is not presumed to be valid by presupposition.[84]

In general, the critique of the proofs of God again uncovers the basic flaw for which Kant reproaches all previous metaphysics: that in it the true relation between experience and thought is not recognized accurately and surely, and expressed with clear consciousness. The kind of thought that shuts its eyes to everything else in order to spin actuality out of itself is shown to be compelled at last to submit to this very actuality, because it smuggles into its presuppositions certain fundamental empirical determinations. When it does so, however, it muddies the character of pure thinking on the one hand, and equally, on the other, it falls short of the pure concept of experience.

In place of this, the "Transcendental Dialectic" now seeks, here as elsewhere, to transform the negative outcome of the critique of the proofs for God into a positive insight, by bringing into relief a factor in the earlier understanding of the concept of God which, when translated from the language of metaphysics into that of transcendental philosophy, has essential significance for the nature of experience itself and its ongoing process. In metaphysics, God is thought as the

---

84. *Critique of Pure Reason*, A 606 f. = B 634 f. (III, 418 f.). For the whole discussion, see A 603–30 = B 631–59 (III, 416–33).

most real Being, that is to say, as that which unites in itself all pure affirmations and perfections, while excluding all negations and defects. In this, nothing but absolute being, devoid of all nonbeing, is asserted, for that a thing is something and not something else, that a definite predicate *a* belongs to it while other predicates *b, c, d, . . .* are denied of it, is simply the expression for the fact that something is thought as limited and finite. The proposition *omnis determinatio est negatio* accurately designates the nature and method of that definition which is the only one possible here, in the realm of empirical, finite existence, since in positing such an existent, we have at the same time severed it from the totality of reality and assigned to it only a limited sphere of reality. In God, on the contrary, we do not think a determinate individual as distinguished from others; we think the perfect Ideal of total determination. Here we conceive the idea of a "sum of reality," which is not only "a concept which, as regards its transcendental content, comprehends all predicates *under itself*; it also contains them *within itself*; and the complete determination of any and every thing rests on the limitation of this *total* reality, inasmuch as part of it is ascribed to the thing, and the rest is excluded. . . ."[85]

For its own purpose, however, reason does not need the existence of such a being in accord with the ideal, but only the *Idea* of it. "The ideal is, therefore, the archetype (*prototypon*) of all things, which one and all, as imperfect copies (*ectypa*), derive from it the material of their possibility, and while approximating to it in varying degrees, yet always fall very far short of actually attaining it. All possibility of things . . . must therefore be regarded as derivative, with only one exception, namely, the possibility of that which includes in itself all reality. This latter possibility must be regarded as original. . . . All manifoldness of things is only a correspondingly varied mode of limiting the concept of the highest reality which forms their common substratum, just as all figures are only possible as so many different modes of limiting infinite space. The object of the ideal of reason, an object which is present to us only in and through reason, is therefore entitled the *primordial being (ens originarium)*. As it has nothing above

85. [Ibid., A 577 = B 605 (III, 401).]

it, it is also entitled the *highest being (ens summum)*; and as everything
that is conditioned is subject to it, the *being of all beings (ens entium)*."[86]
But just as space, which underlies all particular shapes, is not to be
thought as a separate, absolute thing, this "thing of all things" that is
asserted in the concept of God is still to be understood, in the transcendental sense, as "form," although as form belonging to a realm of
validity completely separate from that of the forms of sensibility and
the concepts of pure understanding. Its essential value lies in its
regulative significance, as with all the Ideas of reason. Experience as
one and all-encompassing, and its coherence under laws, is that
wherein alone everything that is real for us in all particular appearances can be given. That this "whole" of experience precedes all
individual empirical experiences was, in point of fact, the insight on
which the *Critique of Pure Reason*'s solution to the riddle of synthetic a
priori judgments rested. This whole was to be thought primarily as an
ensemble of principles and fundamental propositions, but it is determined in and through these principles as an ensemble of objects as
well. We cannot fix a particular empirical object in any way except by
assigning it a place within this system relative to all other elements of
this ensemble, actual or even only possible.

Hence we have arrived at the transcendental analogue to the
metaphysical concept of God as the "most real being." But at the
same time we see that the totality we find ourselves referred to here is
not the totality of absolute existence but is only the expression of a
definite epistemological postulate. For the qualitative whole of the
objects of possible experience is like the quantitative whole, to which
we are accustomed to give the name "world"; it is never a whole that
is given, but always one set us as a task. The dialectial illusion of
transcendental theology is generated as soon as we hypostatize this
Idea of the ensemble of all reality. We are betrayed into doing this by
a natural illusion of the understanding, since we "substitute dialecti-
cally for the *distributive* unity of the empirical employment of the
understanding, the *collective* unity of experience as a whole; and then
think this whole [realm] of appearance as one single thing that con-

86. Ibid., A 578 = B 606 (III, 401 f.).

tains all empirical reality in itself; and then... substitute for it the concept of a thing which stands at the source of the possibility of all things, and supplies the real conditions for their complete determination."[87] Three stages of this false dialectical reification can be distinguished: the ideal of the most real being is first *realized*, that is, combined generally into the concept of an object; next it is *hypostatized*; and last of all *personified*, in that we bestow intelligence and self-consciousness on it. But from the standpoint of pure theoretical reflection, the whole idea of the divine essence and self-sufficiency formed in this way is resolved into a mere "transcendental subreption," into an intellectual fraud by which we attribute objective reality to an Idea that functions solely as a rule.[88]

With this insight we come to the end of the "Transcendental Dialectic," and hence of the entire structure of the critique of pure theoretical reason. This critique has discovered the universal and necessary conditions of all objective judgments, and therefore of all objective assertions possible within experience. Since it refers the empirical object back to these conditions and confines it within them, it has thus defined the empirical object as the object of appearance. For "appearance," understood in the purely transcendental sense, signifies nothing other than the object of a possible experience; thus it does not denote the object thought "in itself" and apart from all cognitive functions, but the object which is mediated precisely through these functions, through the forms of pure intuition and of pure thinking, and is "given through their efficacy alone." If we now wanted to inquire what the object might be if we abstract from all these constitutive moments of it, if we no longer think it in space and time, no longer as extensive or intensive magnitude, no longer in the relations of substantiality, causality, reciprocity, etc., we must acknowledge this question as such not to be self-contradictory. A contradiction arises only where I combine two positive predicates that are antithetical into a single concept and hence posit them jointly. Here, though, I have not posited anything in general; I have merely can-

87. Ibid., A 582 f. = B 610 f. (III, 404).
88. Ibid., A 509 = B 537 (III, 360).

celed out the conditions known to me under which I can posit something. The result is thus not a contradiction but pure nothing, insofar as not the slightest further basis can be shown for the idea of such an object existing in itself, apart from any relation to laws of the form of cognition. The idea is, of course, possible in an analytic sense, under the rule of formal logic, but not valid in a synthetic sense as any real content of knowledge. And even when we do not abstract from the conditions of knowledge to such a degree, as is conceptually possible, if we think an absolute object not in the sense that it abstracts from all formal principles of cognition, but only in that we assume between these principles a different relation from that holding in any given experiential knowledge, the same objection obtains. For what we know as experience rests on the essential cooperation of those two basic factors which the *Critique* has called sensibility and understanding, pure intuition and pure thinking.

On the other hand, we have no sort of positive concept of what form an experience might have, in which one of these factors were to be eliminated, or if a radically different relation to the other were defined; indeed, we have no idea whether under this assumption any form whatsoever, any definite, lawful structure of experience, would remain. For we truly know only the relation between understanding and intuition, not either separately as absolute element and substratum. If we detach pure thinking from its connection with pure and empirical sensibility, its objective reference falls away for us; thus it forfeits its specific "sense," as language characteristically expresses it.[89] The functional unity resident in the categories is what basically yields us positive cognitive content, so that it is schematized in the form of space and time.

Thus the concept of magnitude cannot be explained except by including in this explanation the "how many times" a basic unity is iterated, but what this "how many times" means is comprehensible only if one goes back to successive repetition, hence to time and the synthesis of similar elements. In just the same way, if in the idea of substance I omit the factor of permanence in time, the logical repre-

89. Ibid., A 240 = B 299 (III, 214 f.).

sentation of a subject would remain, which can never be the predicate of anything. The merely formal account has no way of determining, however, whether such a thing could be given as an object, be it of outer or inner experience. The same is true of the concepts of causality and community, which we also only deduced, that is, their validity could be shown for every determination of the empirical object, in that we recognized them as related to spatiotemporal intuition and as presuppositions of the order therein. "In a word, if all sensible intuition, the only kind of intuition which we possess, is removed, not one of these concepts can in any fashion *verify* itself, so as to show its *real* possibility. Only *logical* possibility then remains, that is, that the concept or thought is possible. That, however, is not what we are discussing, but whether the concept relates to an object and so signifies something."[90]

Thus the pure categories, shorn of the formal conditions of sensibility, have merely transcendental significance, but they have no transcendental (that is, exceeding the possibility of experience and its objects) use. Although their origin is a priori, still the application that we can make of them is invariably empirical, in the sense that they are limited to the bounds of experience "and that the principles of pure understanding can apply only to objects of the senses under the universal conditions of a possible experience, never to things in general without regard to the mode in which we are able to intuit them."[91] The concept of a "noumenon," that is, of a thing which is to be thought in no way as an object of sense, but as a thing in itself, simply through pure understanding, hence remains in every case a purely problematical concept, even if we concede the logical possibility. The object thus conceived is hence not a particular intelligible object of our understanding, but "the [sort of] understanding to which it might belong is itself a problem";[92] it is a mode of knowledge as to the possibility of which we can form not the slightest representation. Such a concept can serve as a limiting concept, to constrain sensibility (since it impresses on us that the field of sensible objects does not

90. [Ibid., B 302, note (III, 216 f.).]
91. [Ibid., A 246 = B 303 (III, 217).]
92. [Ibid., A 256 = B 311 (III, 222).]

coincide completely with that of thinkable objects in general), but it can never establish anything positive beyond the perimeter of its domain.[93]

The *Critique of Pure Reason,* taken strictly, is incapable of taking us beyond this insight into the doctrine of the noumenon "in the negative sense"; its structure stops at this point, and there is a fundamental sense in which we have to forgo a clear view into the problem thus defined, namely, giving a new positive meaning to the problematic concept. Kant himself did not shy away from this prospect, and he proclaimed ever more decisively and powerfully the new direction the question was taking, despite all the obstacles and fetters imposed by the threefold division of his system into the realms of theoretical reason, practical reason, and judgment. This new direction is no longer related to being but to obligation, as that which is essentially and truly "unconditioned." An essential defect of Kant's exposition in the First Critique was that it was unable to illuminate this relation fully, and only hinted at it through a number of vague suggestions. Thus from the beginning Kant's doctrine of the "noumenon" and of the "thing in itself," in the form in which it initially appeared in the *Critique of Pure Reason,* continued to labor under an obscurity which was to prove fateful for its reception and its historical development. We do not need here, however, to make the effort to foresee the new form and the new solution of the problem of the thing in itself, which is achieved in Kant's doctrine of freedom, for it does not affect the theory of appearance as such, the systematic analysis of pure experiential knowledge. It comprises a self-contained whole, resting on independent presuppositions, which can and must be understood by purely immanent reflection. Whether outside of this sphere of concrete, empirical existence, which has thus far been shown us as all that is determinable, there is yet another sphere that yields not so much objects as, rather, objective value judgments, and whether our whole transcendental concept of objectivity itself thereby undergoes an enrichment and deepening of its content, is a question

93. Ibid., A 248 ff. = B 305 ff. (III, 218 ff.). For the whole discussion, cf. esp. the chapter "The Ground of the Distinction of All Objects into Phenomena and Noumena," A 235 ff. = B 294 ff. (III, 212 ff.).

to which only critical ethics and aesthetics can give the final answer. It is only there that we will discover the true, positive meaning of the noumenon, the underlying, ultimate "datum" on which the separation of the sensible and the intelligible, the appearance and the thing in itself, in the last analysis rests.

IV FIRST FRUITS OF THE CRITICAL PHILOSOPHY. THE *PROLEGOMENA*. HERDER'S *IDEAS* AND THE FOUNDATION OF THE PHILOSOPHY OF HISTORY

Strengthened by the firmness of his will, shortly before the end of his fifty-seventh year Kant was deep in the continuously revised and perpetually expanding intellectual tasks implied in the Inaugural Dissertation of 1770. The *Critique of Pure Reason* was finished within the span of a few months, an accomplishment that is scarcely rivaled, even as a purely literary feat, in the entire history of thought. During the period of its execution, in supreme concentration of mind and will on the goal of completing the book, Kant had to keep in the background every question as to the consequences it might entail. As he had in the years of solitary meditation, he abandoned himself to the prosecution of the matter in hand, not asking how the book might gain the readiest reception from contemporary readers and the schools of philosophy. Indeed, the motto from Bacon that Kant later made the epigraph to the second edition of the *Critique of Pure Reason* accurately expressed his thought in this regard: "Of ourselves, we say nothing; but as concerns the matter here treated, we ask that men regard it not as opinion, but as a necessary work, and be assured that we do not here undertake to found a sect or any arbitrarily spun-out system, but to uphold the greatness and utility of mankind."

Yet Kant was immediately wrenched out of this mood, in which he had carried out the labor on the First Critique, by the initial critical evaluations the *Critique* received. Whatever these judgments might be, they were unanimous on one point: where Kant had believed he was posing an absolutely necessary and universally valid problem, they saw only the expression of a personal view and dogma. Whether someone was attracted to or repelled by the First Critique depended on whether this view seemed consistent with or opposed to his own; but nowhere was there the slightest recognition of the fact that Kant's whole way of putting the question was not in any way a graft onto the traditionally prescribed branches of the schools of philosophy. The interpreters' only concern for a long time was whether the system should be called or thought of as "idealism" or "realism," "empiricism" or "rationalism." Mendelssohn leveled the strongest criticism against it when, in a well-known expression, he called Kant the "all-destroyer," at least demonstrating a correct sense of the gap between it and traditional philosophy.

To Kant himself, this type of outlook and evaluation was made crystal clear in the penetrating review that appeared in the *Göttingische Gelehrte Anzeigen* of January 19, 1782. The story of the genesis of this review is famous.[1] On a trip that took him to Göttingen, Christian Garve—a writer of popular philosophy universally esteemed in the eighteenth century—had undertaken to do a major critical piece for the *Gelehrte Anzeigen* of Göttingen, as thanks for the "many demonstrations of courtesy and friendship" he had received. He requested for this purpose the *Critique of Pure Reason*, which he had not read until then, yet which, he wrote in his letter to Kant dated July 13, 1783, "promised a very great pleasure" to him because he had "already gotten so much from Kant's previous little writings." The first few pages he read in the book must have convinced him of his error. A wealth of difficulties confronted him from the start; it was a sort of reading for which he was totally unprepared by his previous studies, which had been mainly in the areas of aesthetics and moral psychology; he was in addition suffering from the after-effects of a severe

1. It receives the best treatment from Emil Arnoldt: "Vergleichung der Garveschen und der Federschen Rezension über die Kritik der reinen Vernunft" (Arnoldt, *Gesammelte Schriften*, ed. Otto Schöndörffer, vol. 4, p. 1 ff.); see also Albert Stern, *Über die Beziehungen Chr. Garves zu Kant* (Leipzig, 1884).

illness. Only his respect for his given word motivated him to carry through his labors and compose an exceptional review, which, after he had more than once rewritten and shortened it, he finally sent to the editor of the journal.

The office of editor was held by a man who felt none of the scruples and doubts that Garve had experienced during his reading of the First Critique. Johann Georg Feder belonged to that circle of Göttingen professors who allowed themselves complete certainty in their judgment about Kant. When Christian Jacob Kraus, shortly before the First Critique appeared, asserted in this circle that there was a work lying on Kant's desk which would certainly put philosophers into yet another cold sweat of anxiety, they laughingly replied that it would be hard to expect anything of that sort from a "dilettante in philosophy."[2] Feder added to this unshatterable complacency of the members of a learned profession the facileness of the editor, who having few concrete ideas of his own, knows how to tailor the scope and content of each contribution adroitly to the momentary needs of his journal. Powerful strokes of his pen reduced Garve's review of the *Critique* to almost one-third of its original length, altering it in many stylistic respects. Further, there were many long insertions by Feder himself intended to lay out for the reader a specific standpoint for studying and understanding Kant's book. The systematic devices he added for this purpose were the most petty imaginable: they consisted of nothing but the application of the familiar rubrics of the history of philosophy laid down in every manual and hallowed by custom. "This work," Feder's version of the Göttingen review began, "which continuously exercises the reader's understanding though not always informing it, often taxes one's attention to the point of exhaustion, occasionally coming to its aid with felicitous images or rewarding it with unforeseen, widely useful consequences, is a system of the higher, or as the author puts it, of transcendental idealism. This idealism extends impartially to mind and matter, translating the world and ourselves into representations and thus making all objects

---

2. See Johannes Voigt, *Das Leben des Professors Christian Jacob Kraus* (Königsberg, 1819), p. 87.

arise from appearances, so that the understanding connects them into a *single* experiential series and so that reason tries inevitably, yet fruitlessly, to expand and unify them into *one* whole and complete world-system."

In these opening sentences we can imagine the impression Kant must have gotten from this review. Nothing he said about it—and he expressed himself very harshly—is excessive, taken simply at face value; his one mistake was to see a personal intent to distort and misrepresent where in fact there was only the naive and open expression of pettiness and conceit. But, provoked by the criticism from Göttingen, he proceeded to develop the basic ideas of his theory all over again, with trenchant brevity, and this book that seemed accidentally extorted from his pen quickly took on under his hands a universal and systematic significance. Out of a mere rejoinder to the Garve-Feder review there grew the *Prolegomena to Any Future Metaphysics Which Can Come Forth as Science* (*Prolegomena zu einer jeden künftigen Metaphysik, die als Wissenschaft auftreten können*).

From the standpoint of literary history, we are present here at the decisive crisis of the philosophy of the German Enlightenment. The old kind of popular philosophy, as upheld by Garve in an honorable and straightforward way, is annihilated at a stroke by the *Prolegomena*. "Hammer and chisel," says the preface, "serve quite adequately to work a piece of timber, but for engraving on copper, one needs to use the etching needle." Kant himself never practiced this subtle art of rendering visible the most delicate distinctions and nuances in the basic concepts of cognition, together with their universal interrelations, more superbly than here. Now it was he who was in the position of being reader and critic of the completed book; now he could once again fully expound the complex web, picking out the main threads with a sure hand, and showing how it held together as a whole. Though Kant had been thinking for a long time, as he writes in a letter to Marcus Herz dated January, 1779, "about the basic premises of popularity in the sciences in general, especially in philosophy," the problem he had set himself now received both a theoretical and a practical solution. For the *Prolegomena* inaugurates a new form of truly philosophical popularity, unrivaled for clarity and keenness.

We shall not explicate the detailed content of this work again here; we have already included it in the exposition of the basic ideas of the First Critique, since it contains the most certain and authentic interpretation of that book. But along with this detailed content, the *Prolegomena* has a personal meaning in Kant's development. Through his free survey of what he had achieved so far, he now felt himself spurred on to new, comprehensive productivity. The work on the *Critique* was not yet over, but he already began to lay the foundation for the future systematic working-out which was to encompass all three *Critiques*.

In 1786 the *Metaphysical Foundations of Natural Science* brought the new sketch of the Kantian natural philosophy. It gives a definition of the concept of matter, which is taken in the transcendental spirit, in that the reality of matter appears here not as something posited as ultimate, but as derived, since the existence of matter is seen only as another expression for the reality and lawfulness of forces. A defined dynamic relation, a balance between attraction and repulsion, is what our pure experiential conception of matter rests on. Our analysis does not normally go beyond this, and it cannot penetrate any deeper into the fact. For the so-called metaphysical essence of matter, the "absolutely intrinsic," which is perhaps still taken for granted in it, is an empty notion; it is "a mere something, which we could in no wise understand, even if somebody should be able to tell us what it is." In actual fact, what we can empirically grasp of it is a mathematically determinable proportion in the effect itself, thus something only relatively intrinsic which itself in turn consists of external relations.[3] How these relations are governed, how they are subordinated and fitted to universal conceptual laws, had already been shown by the *Critique of Pure Reason* in the chapter on the analogies of experience. The *Metaphysical Foundations of Natural Science* is the concrete execution of the basic ideas elaborated there. It puts forward the three *Leges motus* from which Newton had worked: the law of inertia, the law of proportionality of cause and effect, and the law of the equality of action

---

3. See *Critique of Pure Reason*, A 277 = B 333; for further material on Kant's dynamic construction of matter, see August Stadler, *Kants Theorie der Materie* (Leipzig, 1883).

and reaction, as specific expressions of the universal synthetic principles of relation.

As a companion to this work on the metaphysics of natural science stands Kant's novel outlook on the metaphysics of history. The two treatises "Idea for a Universal History from a Cosmopolitan Standpoint" ("Idee zu einer allgemeinen Geschichte im weltbürgerliche Absicht") and "What Is Enlightenment?" (Beantwortung der Frage: Was ist Aufklarung?") appeared in the issues of the *Berlinische Monatsschrift* for November and December, 1784; these were augmented by his review in 1785 of the first and second parts of Herder's *Ideas for a Philosophy of the History of Mankind,* in the *Allgemeine Literaturzeitung* of Jena. We seem to have before us in these essays only brief, casual works, tossed off quickly, and yet they present the whole foundation of the new conception of the essence of the state and of history that Kant had developed. These writings were hardly less momentous for the internal development of German idealism than the *Critique of Pure Reason* was within its own field. The first-mentioned essay especially, the "Idea for a Universal History from a Cosmopolitan Standpoint," reminds us of something that was significant in universal intellectual history: it was the first of Kant's writings that Schiller read, and the one that awakened in him the decision to study Kant's philosophy more deeply.[4]

But in yet another sense this document constitutes a potent watershed in the movement of intellectual development. On the one hand it is still of a piece with the political and historical ideas of the earlier eighteenth century, while on the other it clearly foreshadows the new insights of the nineteenth century. Kant still uses the language of Rousseau here, but he has gone beyond Rousseau in the systematic and methodological foundations of his ideas. While Rousseau sees all of man's history as a fall from the condition of innocence and happiness in which man lived before he entered into society and before he banded into social groups, to Kant the idea of such an original state appears utopian if taken as a fact, and ambiguous and unclear if regarded as a moral ideal. His ethics orients him toward the

4. See Schiller's letter to Körner, August 29, 1787.

individual and toward the basic concept of the moral personality and its autonomy; but his view of history and its philosophy leads to the conviction that it is only through the medium of society that the ideal task of moral self-consciousness can find its actual empirical fulfillment. The value of society may seem negative when measured by the happiness of the individual, but this shows only that this point of view for evaluating and the standard of evaluation itself have been falsely chosen. The true criterion of this value lies not in what the social and political community accomplishes for the needs of the individual, for the security of his empirical existence, but in what it signifies as an instrument in his education into freedom.

In this regard the fundamental antithesis that is the substance of Kant's whole view of history now arises. Theodicy, the inherent ethical justification of history, is the result here if one thinks that the way to true, ideal unity of mankind leads only through struggle and opposition, that the only route to autonomy is through compulsion. Because nature, because providence, has decreed that man must produce everything beyond the routine ordering of his animal existence entirely out of himself, and that he participate in no happiness or perfection other than what he himself has created through his own reason, unaided by instinct—he therefore had to be put in a position in which, physically speaking, he was inferior to all other creatures. He was made more needy and defenseless than other beings, so that this very insufficiency would be a stimulus for him to escape from his natural limitations and his natural isolation. It was not a drive toward society originally implanted in man but rather need that founded the first societal groupings, and need further formed one of the essential conditions for erecting and consolidating a social structure.

What the *Metaphysical Foundations of Natural Science* asserts in regard to physical bodies is also valid, if rightly understood, for social bodies. Society is not simply held together through an original intrinsic harmony of individual wills, on which the optimism of Shaftesbury and Rousseau had relied; but its existence, like that of matter, is rooted in attraction and repulsion, in an antagonism of forces. This opposition forms the heart and the presupposition of any social order. "Thus are taken the first true steps from barbarism to culture, which consists in the social worth of man; thence gradually develop all talents, and taste is refined; through continued enlightenment the foundations are laid for a way of thought which can in time convert the coarse, natural disposition for moral discrimination into definite practical principles, and thereby change a society of men driven together by their natural feelings into a moral whole. Without those in themselves unamiable characteristics of unsociability from whence opposition springs—characteristics each man must find in his own selfish pretensions—all talents would remain hidden, unborn in an Arcadian shepherd's life, with all its concord, contentment, and mutual affection. Men, good-natured as the sheep they herd, would hardly reach a higher worth than their beasts; they would not fill the empty place in creation by achieving their end, which is rational nature. Thanks be to Nature, then, for the incompatibility, for the heartless competitive vanity, for the insatiable desire to possess and to rule! Without them, all the excellent natural capacities of humanity would forever sleep, undeveloped."[5] Thus evil itself becomes the source of good in the course and progress of history; thus out of discord alone can true, self-confident moral harmony emerge.

The essential idea of social order consists not in bringing individual wills to a common level by force, but in preserving their individuality and hence their opposition, at the same time, however, defining the freedom of the individual in such a way that it discovers its own limits in other people. To assimilate this determination, initially enforceable only by external power, into the will itself and to acknowledge it as the realization of the will's own form and fundamental demand is the ethical goal proposed for all historical development. Herein resides the most difficult problem mankind has to master, and the end to which all external politico-social institutions, the very order of the state itself in all forms of its historical existence, are but means. A philosophical attempt to survey universal world history from this standpoint and to see in it the progressive actualization of a plan of nature, which aims at the complete unification of the

5. "Idea for a Universal History from a Cosmopolitan Standpoint," Fourth Thesis (IV, 151–166) (*Ak.* VIII, 2–31).

human race in society, is hence not only possible but must itself be
regarded as conducing to this intent of nature. "Such a justification of
Nature—or, better, of providence—" as Kant concludes this discussion, "is no unimportant reason for choosing a standpoint toward
world history. For what is the good of esteeming the majesty and
wisdom of Creation in the realm of brute nature and of recommend-
ing that we contemplate it, if that part of the great stage of supreme
wisdom which contains the purpose of all the others—the history of
mankind—must remain an unceasing reproach to it? If we are forced
to turn our eyes from it in disgust, doubting that we can ever find a
perfectly rational purpose in it and hoping for that only in another
world?"[6]

Again, adopting the standpoint of the transcendental inquiry, it is
the essential method of this view of history, not its content, that has a
primary claim on our interest. A new perspective for contemplating
the world, an alteration in the stance our historical knowledge takes
relative to the flux of empirical historical existence, is the basic object
of this search. Kant explicitly stresses at the end of his treatise that
this stance is in no way intended to harm or displace the customary
historical outlook, which tries to grasp phenomena in their pure factuality and to give a narrative account of them.[7] But hand in hand
with this manner of proceeding there must be another, through
which their significance is revealed totally differently from the way it
is in the empirical, sequential arranging of facts. At this point, however, the basic character of this new procedure cannot be fully surveyed and defined with the exactitude of principles, for Kant's philosophy of history constitutes only one component of his universal
system of teleology. Not until this system has been completely explicated in his fundamental ethical works and in the *Critique of Judgment*
(*Kritik der Urteilskraft*) will the final critical verdict on the questions
of historical teleology be rendered.

But in these first stirrings of the Kantian philosophy of history, we
encounter a decisive turn that is completely clear. In the opening

6. Ibid., Ninth Thesis (IV, 165) (*Ak.* VIII, 30).
7. [Ibid. (IV, 165 ff.) (*Ak.* VIII, 29 ff.).]

sentences of the Kantian doctrine we are transported from the realm of being, where the critical task has been pursued until now, to the realm of obligation. According to Kant, the concept of "history" in the strict sense exists for us only where we contemplate a certain series of events in such a way that we do not look at the temporal sequence of its individual moments or its causal connectedness but relate the series to the ideal unity of an immanent end. Only when we apply this idea, this novel way of judging, and persevere, is historical process in its unique character and independence made manifest in the homogeneous stream of becoming, the complex of sheer natural causes and effects. In this connection, it is immediately evident that the question of the goal of history has quite a different ring for Kant, with his transcendental point of view, than it does for those who contemplate the world in the usual way and for traditional metaphysicians. Just as full insight into the validity of the laws of nature was only attained when we saw that nature as given does not "have" laws, but that the concept of a law is what creates and constitutes nature—so history as a well-established set of facts and events equally little has a "meaning" and a special *telos*. Rather, its own "possibility," its special significance, originates in the assumption of a meaning of this sort. "History" first truly exists where we as contemplators no longer stand in the series of sheer events, but in the series of actions; the idea of an action, however, includes the idea of freedom. Thus the principle of Kant's philosophy of history foreshadows the principle of Kantian ethics, where it will find its resting place and its full explication.

Since this correlation comprises the original *form* of Kant's conception of history—and therefore cannot be eliminated in the methodological sense—it is also decisive for its substance. The evolution of mankind's spiritual history coincides with the progress, the ever keener comprehension, and the progressive deepening of the idea of freedom. The philosophy of the Enlightenment has here reached its supreme goal, and in Kant's "An Answer to the Question: 'What Is Enlightenment?'" it now finds its lucid, programmatic conclusion. "Enlightenment is man's release from his self-incurred tutelage. Tutelage is man's inability to make use of his understanding without direction from another. Self-incurred is this tutelage when its cause lies not in lack of reason but in lack of resolution and courage to use it without direction from another. *Sapere aude!* Have the courage to use your own reason!—that is the motto of enlightenment."[8] But this is at the same time the motto of all human history, for the process of self-liberation, the progress from natural bondage toward the spirit's autonomous consciousness of itself and of its task, constitutes the only thing that can be called genuine "becoming" in the spiritual sense.

In this mood and with this conviction Kant comes to Herder's *Ideas for a Philosophy of the History of Mankind,* and the inevitable opening up of antagonism between him and Herder is understandable from now on. In the conception of this, his basic work, Herder remained the pupil of Kant, who in Herder's student years in Königsberg had first shown him the way to that "humanistic" philosophy which henceforth hovered before him as an enduring ideal. But Hamann's world view affected the whole of Herder's view of history more profoundly than Kant's did; with Hamann he felt himself truly and essentially congenial. What Herder sought in history was a vision of the infinitely manifold, infinitely diverse expressions of the life of mankind, a vision that unveils and reveals itself in them all as one and the same. The deeper he plunges into this whole, not to reduce it to concepts and rules but rather to feel it and to adapt to it, the more clearly it is impressed on him that no single abstract standard of measure, no uniform ethical norm and ideal could create its content. Every age and every period, every epoch and every nation contains the measure of its fulfillment and its perfection in itself. Here there is no valid comparison between what they are and what they want to be, no selection of common traits in which the essence binding the particular into a living unity is effaced and destroyed. The stuff of the child's life is incommensurable with that of the middle-aged or elderly man, but possesses within itself the focus of its own being and worth, and the same is true for the historical life of peoples. The idea of the perpetually ongoing intellectual and moral perfectibility of the

8. [IV, 169 (*Ak.* VIII, 35).]

human race is nothing but an audacious fiction, on the strength of which every age thinks itself superior to all its predecessors, as evolutionary stages that have been abandoned and surpassed. We only grasp the true image of history when we let it work on us with all its brilliance, all its color, and hence with all the irreducible multiplicity of its individual elements.

To this extent Herder's work makes no pretension to be history but rather philosophy of history; to this extent it lays down specific teleological guidelines through the endless manifold of becoming. A plan of providence is unveiled in the ongoing progress of history, but this plan signifies no external ultimate purpose set for becoming and no universal goal into which all particular goals are absorbed. It is rather the thoroughly individual thing itself in which the form of totality is finally achieved, in which the idea of man finds its concrete fulfillment. In the play of events and scenes, of ethnic individualities and destinies, of the rise and fall of specific historical forms of existence there ultimately stands before us a whole which is to be conceived not as the detached product of all these moments, but only as their living totality. Herder inquires no deeper into the vision of this totality. To him who has it, history has revealed its meaning; he requires no further norm to elucidate and explain it to him. While Kant needs the abstract unity of an ethical postulate to comprehend the meaning of history, while he sees in it the ever more complete solution of an endless task, Herder lingers in its pure givenness. If to Kant the stream of occurrences must be projected against an intelligible "ought" to make it intrinsically comprehensible, Herder remains equally immovable on the plane of pure becoming. Ethical insight into the world, resting on the dualism of being and obligation, of nature and freedom, is in sharp contrast to organic and dynamic insight into nature, which tries to conceive both as aspects of one and the same development.

Only when one reflects on them from the perspective of this basic contradiction over the history of the spirit can one do justice to the two reviews of Herder's *Ideas* that Kant wrote. It was Herder's tragic fate that, unable to follow the evolution of Kant and the critical philosophy since the sixties, he failed to rise to this perspective, and that consequently his polemic with Kant slipped more and more into the petty and personal. For his part, insofar as one can talk of guilt and innocence in this sort of intellectual combat, Kant cannot be said to be completely free of blame, since in the superiority afforded him by his critical analysis of the basic concepts he shut his eyes to the grand vision of the whole that was vivid everywhere in Herder, despite all the conceptual defects of his historico-philosophical deductions. He who fixed his eye above all on strictness of proofs, precise inference to principles, and sharp distinction of spheres of validity, could see in Herder's methodology nothing but "an adroitness in unearthing analogies, in wielding which he shows a bold imagination. This is combined with cleverness in soliciting sympathy for his subject—kept in increasingly hazy remoteness—by means of sentiment and sensation. Further suspicion is aroused as to whether these emotions are effects of a prodigious system of thought or only equivocal hints which cool, critical examination would uncover in them."[9] The philosophical critic and analyst here inexorably forces the renunciation of every form of methodological syncretism[10]—a renunciation which would have also meant dispensing with the most characteristic personal merits of Herder's way of looking at things.[11] For this style of contemplation consists precisely in its incessant direct passage from intuition to conception and from conception to intuition; Herder as a poet is a philosopher, and as a philosopher, a poet. The irritation with which he now took up the cudgels against Kant, and the growing bitterness with which he waged the battle, is thus explicable: he sensed and knew that it was not just an isolated question that was at issue here, but that his essence, his most intimate gift, was jeopardized by Kant's fundamental theoretical demands.

In Kant's two reviews of Herder's *Ideas*, the conflict has not yet come to a head. For as long as Kant had not completed the foun-

9. ["Review of Herder's *Ideas for a Philosophy of the History of Mankind*," Sect. I (IV, 179) (*Ak.* VIII, 45).]

10. Cf. Kant's letter to Friedrich Heinrich Jacobi, August 30, 1789 (IX, 433) (*Ak.* XI, 72).

11. For further details on Herder's battle against Kant, see Eugen Kühnemann's exceptional account: *Herder*, 2d ed. (Munich, 1912), pp. 383 ff.

dations of ethics, as long as his conception of freedom had not yet reached its ultimate clarity, one of the essential presuppositions of this conflict was missing. To be sure, as early as the *Critique of Pure Reason* the concept of freedom had been put forward and the antinomy between freedom and causality discussed, but the matter stopped at that, with what was on the whole a purely negative definition of the idea of freedom. Only with the *Foundations of the Metaphysics of Morals (Grundlegung zur Metaphysik der Sitten)* in 1785 does his progress take a new, positive turn, one destined to shake to its foundations the whole previous contrast between determinism and indeterminism, which the First Critique seemed still attached to. Only from this point on does the significance of the essays on the philosophy of history belonging to the years 1784 and 1785 emerge within the whole context of Kant's activity as a philosophical writer. They are the link with a whole new circle of problems, on which his systematic interest is ever more strongly concentrated. The Kantian conception of history only poses a single concrete example of a complex of questions, focused as a whole in the concept of "practical reason"; Kant now moves on to the more precise definition of that concept.

V THE GROWTH AND STRUCTURE OF CRITICAL ETHICS

Upon the completion of the First Critique, Kant did not tack the *Critique of Practical Reason* (*Kritik der praktischen Vernunft*) onto the theoretical portion as a second component of his system. He had conceived his philosophy from the very first as a self-contained whole, and ethical problems formed an essential, integrating constituent of it. We grasp the special and most profound concept of "reason" itself, as Kant understands it, only through this relation. When, in the Prize Essay of 1763, Kant examined the universal method of metaphysics and put it on a new foundation, he was above all concerned to include in his scrutiny, in accordance with the Berlin Academy's formulation of the question that was set, the basic concepts of morals as well. Their value and utility being beyond question, it is their distinctness that is inquired into here, and they too are to be conceived on the grounds of their universal validity. Although even an empiricist like Locke had put the type of relation dominant in moral truths on the same plane with the interconnection of geometric judgments and theorems, and had attributed to morality the selfsame demonstrative certainty as in metaphysics, Kant finds the first principles of morality in their contemporary state entirely insusceptible of the degree of evidence required. For the basic concept of obligation itself (which was the cornerstone of the deduction of natural rights and duties in Wolff's philosophy of natural law) is infected with obscurity. "One ought to do this or that and leave something else undone; this is the formula under which every obligation is enunciated. Now that 'ought' expresses a necessity of action and is capable of two meanings. That is, either I ought to do something (as a means) if I wish something else (as an end), or I ought directly to do something else and make it real (as an end). The former we can call the necessity of means (*necessitas problematica*), and the latter the necessity of ends (*necessitas legalis*). No obligation is present in necessity of the first kind; it only prescribes the solution of a problem, saying what are the means I must use if I wish to reach a particular end. When anyone prescribes to another the actions which he should do or refrain from doing if he wishes to promote his happiness, perhaps all the teachings of morals could be brought under the precepts; but they are then no longer obligations but only like what might be called an obligation to make two arcs if I wish to bisect a line. That is, they are not obligations at all but only counsels to suitable actions if one wishes to attain a particular end. Since the use of means has no other necessity than that which pertains to the end, it follows that all actions which morals prescribes under the condition of particular ends are contingent and cannot be called obligations so long as they are not subordinated to an end necessary in itself. I ought, for example, to promote the greatest possible total perfection, or I ought to act according to the will of God; to whichever of these propositions all practical philosophy were subordinated, that proposition, if it is said to be a rule and principle of obligation, must command the action as directly necessary, not commanding it merely under the condition of some particular end. And here we find that such an immediate supreme rule of all obligation would have to be absolutely indemonstrable. For from no consideration of a thing or concept, whatever it is, is it possible to know and infer what we should do, unless what is presupposed is an end and the action a means. But this it must not be, because it would then be a formula not of obligation but only of problematic skill."[1]

When Kant wrote these words, none of his contemporary readers and critics could have foreseen that in these few and simple sentences every moral system produced by the eighteenth century was essen-

1. *Inquiry into the Distinctness of the Principles of Natural Theology and Morals*, Fourth Observation, §2 (II, 199 f.) (*Ak.* II, 298–99).

tially felled. In fact, this passage contains the fundamental concept of his ethics yet to come: the strict distinction between the categorical imperative of the moral law and the hypothetical imperatives of merely mediate ends is discussed here with full precision and clarity. Nothing further can be deduced or established concerning the content of the unconditional moral law, as Kant emphasizes, for every deduction of this sort, having made the validity of the command dependent on something else—be it the existence of a thing or the presumed necessity of a concept—would locate the moral law once again in the sphere of the conditioned, from which it had just had to be liberated. Thus the formal nature of the first basic ethical certainty already immediately includes the moment of its indemonstrability. That it must bestow absolute moral worth, a good in itself not given through something else, cannot be deduced and understood by way of mere concepts; we can presuppose this assertion for the purpose of constructing a pure ethics only in the same sense as we must posit materially certain but indemonstrable propositions in the construction of logic and mathematics, together with the purely formal principles of identity and contradiction. For this special mode of knowledge and certainty will here, as regards ethical problems, trace back to the psychological faculty of feeling. "In these times we have first begun to realize that the faculty of conceiving truth is intellection, while that of sensing the good is feeling, and that they must not be interchanged. Just as there are unanalyzable concepts of the true, that is, what is met with in the objects of intellection considered by themselves, there is also an unanalyzable feeling for the good. . . . It is a task of the understanding to resolve the compounded and confused concept of the good and to make it distinct by showing how it arises from simpler sensations of the good. But if the sensation of the good is simple, the judgment, 'This is good,' is completely indemonstrable and a direct effect of the consciousness of the feeling of pleasure associated with the conception of the object. And since many simple sensations of the good are certainly in us, there are many simple unanalyzable conceptions of the good."[2]

2. Ibid. (II, 201) (*Ak.* II, 299).

This link with the psychological language of the eighteenth century, which refers back in particular to the theory of "moral sentiment" developed by Adam Smith and his school, carries the danger for Kant that through it the distinctiveness of the novel direction he had won for the foundation of ethics is already once more being gradually effaced. In fact, in his subsequent writings the analysis of the pure concept of "obligation," which Kant had made the locus of the special task of moral philosophy, retreats more and more into the background. His interest seems ever more energetically concentrated on being and becoming, on the viewpoint of genetic development instead of the ought; the ethical way of putting questions is crowded out by that of psychology and anthropology.

In the information on his course of lectures for the winter term, 1765–66, Kant says explicitly that he proposes to make use of the method of moral inquiry which Shaftesbury, Hutcheson, and Hume had founded, as a "beautiful discovery of our age": that method which, before pointing out what ought to happen, always examines historically and philosophically what does happen, and hence proceeds not from abstract premises but from the actual nature of man.[3] When we take a closer look at these propositions and consider the connection between them, we recognize that Kant is not tempted to subscribe to the technique of English moral psychology with no critical reservations. That human nature on which he wishes to take his stand is, as he instantly adds, to be understood not as a variable but as a constant magnitude. Man is not to be comprehended and presented in the shifting form his momentary contingent state impresses on him, but rather his eternal essence is to be sought out and revealed as the foundation for moral laws. What Kant here understands by nature and by human nature is drawn less from the influence of English psychology than from that of Rousseau. It is he who essentially determines the substance of Kant's ethics during this period. Rousseau is the one who "set him right," who freed him from an intellectual overvaluation of pure thinking and reoriented his philosophy toward the act. The delusory superiority, the false luster of pure

3. (II, 326) (*Ak.* II, 311).

knowing vanishes: "I learn to honor men, and would find myself more useless than the humblest laborer if I did not believe that this perspective could bestow worth on all others, and restore the rights of man."[4] But this opens the way, in the purely methodological sense, to yet another path of reflection, for Rousseau's concept of nature is an existential concept only in its expression, while in its pure content it is unmistakably an ideal and normative concept. In Rousseau's work both meanings indeed exist side by side yet completely intertwined: nature is that original state from which man emerged, as it is the goal and end to which he is to return. But this mixture could not long withstand Kant's analytical mind. He distinguished between the is and the ought even where he seemed to be basing the latter on the former. The more keenly and clearly this distinction took shape for him, the more progress he made in his critical analysis of the pure concept of knowledge and the more definitively he separated the question of the parentage and birth of cognitions from that of their value and their objective validity.

Since this separation receives its first full systematic expression in Kant's dissertation *On the Form and Principles of the Sensible and the Intelligible World*, the problem of ethics is hence also given a completely new foundation. Just as there is a pure cognitive a priori, there is now a moral a priori as well. In the same way as the former is not deducible from mere sensory perceptions, but has its roots in an original spontaneity of the understanding, an *actus animi*, the latter also, conceived with respect to its content and its validity, is loosed from any dependence on the sensory feelings of pleasure and pain, and cleansed of any contamination by them. Thus it was as early as this that Kant broke with all morality based on eudaemonism. He turns away so brusquely that from now on among those who make happiness the principle of ethics he even numbers Shaftesbury, who uses pleasure as a moral criterion not at all in the sense of an immediate sensory feeling but in its maximum aesthetic refinement and sublimation. Such an equation could not help evoking astonishment

---

4. *Fragmente aus Kants Nachlass;* concerning the relation between Kant and Rousseau, see above, pp. 86 ff.

in his contemporaries, and Mendelssohn was unable to contain his surprise at seeing Shaftesbury ranked beside Epicurus.[5]

But Kant now saw that between himself and the whole of previous ethics there was a difference not merely of content but of significance and basic outlook. From this point on he must have felt increasingly pressed to go beyond the meager hints about his ethical system contained in the Dissertation. But every time he resolved on a closer exposition and crystallization of his new standpoint—and his correspondence from 1772 to 1781 contains indubitable evidence that he put his hand to this at various times during this period—this labor was "blocked as though by a dam"[6] by the "chief subject" occupying his thoughts at this time. Repeatedly, Kant seemed on the verge of overcoming this hesitation by a precipitate decision to lay aside the *Critique of Pure Reason* for a while, its completion being postponed again and again, and to apply himself to working out his ethics as a desirable rest from the difficulties of his epistemological inquiry. "I have made up my mind," he writes in September, 1770, on sending the Dissertation to Lambert, "to rid myself of a long indisposition which seized on me this summer, and so as not to be without occupation in my spare time this winter, to set in order and to ready my researches into pure moral wisdom, in which no empirical principles are to be found, and also the metaphysics of morals. In various ways it will smooth the pathway for the most important points of the altered form of metaphysics, and it seems to me in addition to be equally necessary for the principles of the practical sciences which are still so ill-judged at present."[7] But however frequently this inquiry might entice him in the course of the next decade, which was filled with the most abstract speculation, nevertheless his systematic mind always stood in opposition. He demanded of himself, as the unavoidable methodological foundation, that the pure transcendental philosophy be outlined and carried out, so as to apply himself to the "metaphysics of Nature and of morals" only when both were com-

5. See *De mundi sensibilis,* §9 (II, 412) (*Ak.* II, 396); cf. Mendelssohn's letter to Kant, December 25, 1770 (IX, 90) (*Ak.* X, 108).

6. See his letter to Marcus Herz, November 24, 1776 (IX, 151) (*Ak.* X, 184).

7. To Lambert, September 2, 1770 (IX, 73) (*Ak.* X, 92).

plete. Regarding the latter, his intention was to bring it out first, and a letter to Herz in 1773 reports that he was already "rejoicing in advance" about it.[8]

Thus the *Foundations of the Metaphysics of Morals*, on its appearance in 1785, was, like the *Critique of Pure Reason*, the product of more than a dozen years' reflection. The vivacity, the suppleness, and the drive of his exposition did not suffer in the slightest from this, however. In none of his major critical works is Kant's personality so immediately evident as here; in none is the rigor of the deduction united in the same perfect way with such a free movement of thought, ethical power and stature with the sense of psychological detail, and acuteness of conceptual discrimination with the noble concreteness of a popular way of speaking rich in felicitous images and examples. Here for the first time, the subjective ethos that forms the inmost core of Kant's nature could unfold and express itself in its purity. This ethos is not something which "comes into being"; it appears already fullblown in his youthful writings, in the *Universal Natural History and Theory of the Heavens* and in the *Dreams of a Spirit-Seer*. Only here, though, does it achieve full self-consciousness and forge its adequate philosophical expression in deliberate contrast to the philosophy of the Enlightenment.

If we try to say what the most universal content of critical ethics is—here we are looking ahead to the *Critique of Practical Reason* that appeared three years later, so as not to separate what in fact belongs together—we must not be confused and led astray by the handy catchwords that have played so large a role in characterizing Kant's doctrines. Again and again people have talked about the "formalistic" character of Kantian ethics; they have charged that the principle from which it proceeds yields but one universal and hence empty formula for moral conduct, inadequate for deciding concrete individual cases and choices. Kant himself, since he granted this reproach and in a certain sense recognized it, had a counter to objections of this kind. "A critic who wished to say something against that work," he remarks, "really did better than he intended when he said that there

8. To Herz, the end of 1773 (IX, 114) (*Ak.* X, 136).

was no new principle of morality in it but only a new formula. Who would want to introduce a new principle of morality and, as it were, be its inventor, as if the world had hitherto been ignorant of what duty is or had been thoroughly wrong about it? Those who know what a formula means to a mathematician, in determining what is to be done in solving a problem without letting him go astray, will not regard a formula which will do this for all duties as something insignificant and unnecessary."[9]

The special foundation for Kant's "formalism" is to be sought in a still deeper vein of his thought, for it lies in that universal transcendental concept of form that precedes and underlies mathematics as well. The *Critique of Pure Reason* has established that the objectivity of knowledge cannot be founded on material, sensory data nor on the "what" of individual sensations. Sensation is just the expression of the individual subject's state, varying from moment to moment; it constitutes that which is wholly contingent, different from case to case, from subject to subject, and hence is not determinable by any unambiguous rule. If judgments with universally valid truth content are to be constructed from such infinitely variable circumstances, if the appearances that originally are totally unclear are to be legible as experiences, it is necessary that there be definite basic types of relations, which as such are invariant and which produce the objective unity of cognition and only thus make possible its object and are its foundation. It was these fundamental syntheses that the critical theory discovered and raised into prominence as the "forms" of pure intuition, the "forms" of pure understanding, and so on. There is for Kant the most intimate analogy between introduction into the problem of ethics and this basic idea. As was the case earlier for mere "representation," now it is necessary to discover the factor that leads to the quality of objective validity for the realm of practice, of desire and act. Only if such a factor is demonstrable can we use it to pass from the sphere of the arbitrary into that of the voluntary. Will and cognition are alike in this respect: they exist only insofar as a permanent and stable rule constituting their unity and identity is estab-

9. *Critique of Practical Reason,* preface (V, 8) (*Ak.* V, 8).

lished. Just as this cognitive rule was not abstracted from the object, but posited through the analytic of the understanding; just as it was shown that the conditions of the possibility of experience, as an ensemble of cognitive functions, are at the same time the conditions under which definite individual objects can alone be said to be for us, so we now try to translate this way of posing the problem into the realm of the ethical. Is there here also a lawfulness that is rooted not in the concrete substance and the concrete differentia of what is willed, but in the peculiar basic orientation of willing itself and that, on the strength of this origin, has the power to form the basis of ethical objectivity in the transcendental sense of that term, that is to say, the necessity and the universal validity of moral worth?

Starting from this form of the question, it is immediately comprehensible on what grounds pleasure and pain, of whatever form and coloration, are for Kant untenable as ethical principles. For pleasure, however it may be conceived, stands on the same plane of validity as sensory perception insofar as it signifies the sheer passivity of impression. It changes in accordance with the state of the individual subject and the external attraction that influences him, and is as infinitely variable as the diversity of these two factors. To be sure, naturalistic metaphysics, accustomed to founding ethics on the pleasure principle, tries to conceal this situation, since it appeals to the psychological universality of this principle. But although it may be true that it is innate in all subjects to strive for pleasure, this biological fact is totally worthless for setting up an identical standard in which individual wills might find unity and harmony. For since everyone strives not so much for pleasure as for *his* pleasure or what he thinks is his, the sum of these strivings disintegrates into a chaotic mass, a confusion of the most diverse intertwined and entangled tendencies, each of which is qualitatively completely opposed to the others even where they are seemingly directed toward the same goal. "It is therefore astonishing," Kant remarks, "how intelligent men have thought of proclaiming as a universal practical law the desire for happiness, and therewith to make this desire the determining ground of the will merely because this desire is universal. Though elsewhere natural laws make everything harmonious, if one here attributed the universality of law to this maxim, there would be the extreme opposite of harmony, the most arrant conflict, and the complete annihilation of the maxim itself and its purpose. For the wills of all do not have one and the same object, but each person has his own (his own welfare), which, to be sure, can accidentally agree with the purposes of others who are pursuing their own, though this agreement is far from suffic- ing for a law because the occasional exceptions which one is permit- ted to make are endless and cannot be definitely comprehended in a universal rule. In this way a harmony may result resembling that depicted in a certain satirical poem as existing between a married couple bent on going to ruin, 'Oh, marvelous harmony, what he wants is what she wants'; or like the pledge which is said to have been given by Francis I to the Emperor Charles V, 'What my brother wants (Milan), that I want too.' "[10] The harmonizing of different indi- vidual acts of will thus cannot be attained by directing them toward the same concrete object, toward one and the same material goal of the will, for that would instead result in their total conflict; it is at- tained only through the subjecting of each to the guidance of a uni- versal and overriding ground of determination. In the unity of such a ground that which is ethically objective, a truly self-sufficient and unconditional moral value, could be founded, just as it was the unity and indestructible necessity of the basic logical principles of cognition that enabled us to posit an object of our representations.

Hence it is not any particular *state* of pleasure, but rather its essen- tial nature, that unfits it as the foundation of ethics. In the analysis of the problem of knowledge, the particular nature of individual sense perceptions could remain outside Kant's consideration, since for him the proposition that the "coarseness or subtlety of sensation has noth- ing to do with the form of possible experience" was valid; the same is true for the analysis of will. Whether one takes pleasure in its "coarse" meaning, or whether one is concerned to purify and subli- mate it through all the stages of refinement on up to the most elevated intellectual pleasure, may perhaps make a difference in the content of ethical principles, but not in how they are deduced and justified.

10. Ibid., §4, Theorem III (V, 31 f.) (*Ak.* V, 27 f.).

Similarly, as every sensation, regardless of its clarity and distinctness, has a certain cognitive character that sets it off from pure intuition and from the pure concept of the understanding, in the realm of practice as well the character of subjective desire must be distinguished from that of pure will. As long as the individual in his striving is not oriented and committed to any goal other than the satisfaction of his subjective drive, he remains enclosed and fettered within his particularity, whatever the particular form of this impulse may be. In this respect, all material practical principles—all those which seat the value of willing in what is willed—are "of one and the same kind and belong under the general principle of self-love or one's own happiness." "It is astonishing," Kant says in support of this proposition, "how otherwise acute men believe they can find a difference between the lower and the higher faculty of desire by noting whether the conceptions which are associated with pleasure have their origin in the senses or in the understanding. When one inquires into the determining grounds of desire and finds them in an expected agreeableness resulting from something or other, it is not a question of where the conception of this enjoyable object comes from, but merely of how much it can be enjoyed. If a conception, even though it has its origin and status in the understanding, can determine choice only by presupposing a feeling of pleasure in the subject, then its becoming a determining ground of choice is wholly dependent on the nature of the inner sense, that is, it depends on whether the latter can be agreeably affected by that conception. However dissimilar the conceptions of the objects, be they proper to the understanding or even to the reason instead of to the senses, the feeling of pleasure, by virtue of which they constitute the determining ground of the will (since it is the agreeableness and enjoyment which one expects from the object which impels the activity toward producing it) is always the same. This sameness lies not merely in the fact that all feelings of pleasure can be known only empirically, but even more in the fact that the feeling of pleasure always affects one and the same life-force which is manifested in the faculty of desire, and in this respect one determining ground can differ from any other only in degree.... As the man who wants money to spend does not care whether the gold in it was mined in the mountains or washed from the sand, provided it is accepted everywhere as having the same value, so also no man asks, when he is concerned only with the agreeableness of life, whether the ideas are from the sense or understanding; he asks only how much and how great is the pleasure which they will afford him over the longest time."[11]

The common character of all types and qualities of pleasure is thus thrown into sharp relief: it consists in consciousness keeping itself purely passive with regard to all material attractions, so that it is affected and determined by their influence. But such an "affect" is not enough to serve as a basis for the concept of truth and the objective validity of knowledge; equally little can an objective norm of what is moral be gotten from it. What is needed is the selfsame complement we have already encountered in its full significance in the theoretical structure of the First Critique. To affection there must be opposed function, to the receptivity of impressions, the spontaneity of the concepts of reason. It is necessary to exhibit a relation between the will and its object in which the object, the particular "matter" of desire, determines the will less than will determines this object. If we keep in mind the critical result of the analytic of the understanding, no longer can any paradox be discovered in this demand, for even the matter of sensation acquired its objective cognitive worth only in that transcendental apperception demonstrated the fundamental lawfulness on which all synthesis of the manifold and hence all its objective significance rests.

Now we need only transfer this result from the theoretical into the practical sphere to arrive at the basic concept of Kantian ethics: the concept of autonomy. Autonomy signifies that binding together of theoretical and practical reason alike, in which the latter is conscious of itself as the bonding agent. In it, the will submits to no other rule than that which it has itself set up as a universal norm and proposed to itself. Wherever this form is achieved, wherever individual desire and wish know themselves to be participants in and subject to a law valid for all ethical subjects without exception, and where on the

11. Ibid., §3, Theorem II, Remark I (V, 25 f.) (*Ak.* V, 22 f.).

other hand they understand and affirm that this law is their own, then and only then are we in the realm of ethical questions. Popular moral consciousness, with the analysis of which the *Foundations of the Metaphysics of Morals* begins, already leads to this insight. For the conception of duty, by which it is ruled and guided, includes in itself all the essential determinations we have met so far. An action is said to be in accordance with duty only when every thought of advantage to be expected from it, every calculation of present or future pleasure likely to result from it, indeed every material aim of any other kind, is eliminated and only adherence to the universality of the law, which reins in all contingent and particular impulses, remains as the sole ground of determination. "An action done from duty does not have its moral worth in the purpose which is to be achieved through it, but in the maxim by which it is determined. Its moral value, therefore, does not depend on the reality of the object of the action but merely on the principle of volition by which the action is done without any regard to the objects of the faculty of desire.... It is clear that the purposes we may have for our actions and their effects as ends and incentives of the will cannot give the actions any unconditional moral worth. Wherein, then, can this worth lie, if it is not in the will in relation to its hoped-for effect? It can lie nowhere else than in the principle of the will irrespective of the ends which can be realized by such action. For the will stands, as it were, at the crossroads halfway between its a priori principle which is formal and its a posteriori incentive which is material. Since it must be determined by some-thing, if it is done from duty, it must be determined by the formal principle of volition as such, since every material principle has been withdrawn from it."[12]

In the same fashion, the truth of a representation, according to Kant, does not consist in its likeness to an external transcendent thing, as an image to its original, but in the fact that the content of the representation is wholly and necessarily connected with other similar elements that we designate by the name of experiential knowledge; thus the predicate of good belongs to that act of will that is directed

---

12. *Foundations of the Metaphysics of Morals*, first sect. (IV, 256) (*Ak.* IV, 399–400).

not by a contingent and private impulse but rather by regard for the entirety of possible determinations of will and for their inner harmony. The "good" will is the will to law, and hence to agreement—an accord that concerns the relation between diverse individuals as well as the inner consequence of the manifold volitions and actions of one and the same subject, insofar as they display, above and beyond any fluctuations of particular motives and impulses, that essential self-containedness that we are accustomed to call by the name of "character." In this sense—and only in this sense—it is "form" that is the foundation of the value of truth as well as of the value of good, since it renders possible and consists in, in the one case, the interconnection of empirical perceptions into a system of necessary and a priori knowledge, in the other the unification of particular ends into the unity of a single goal and an enveloping purposiveness.

Thus we are standing directly in the presence of the ultimate statement of the basic principle of critical ethics: the formula of the "categorical imperative." An imperative is called hypothetical when it indicates which means must be willed or employed in order that something further, which is presupposed as the end, may be realized. It is called categorical when it manifests itself as an unconditional demand that has no need to borrow its validity from some further end, but instead possesses its own validity in that it presents an ultimate, self-evident value. But since this fundamental value is not to be sought in any particular content of willing, but only in its universal lawfulness, both the content and the object of the only possible categorical imperative are fully articulated herein. "Act only according to that maxim," states the fundamental rule, "by which you can at the same time will that it should become a universal law."[13] The methodical advance to the achievement of this proposition, by the power of pure analysis of the concept of duty, constitutes the clearest and most definitive exposition of its substance as well. Were any particular determinations whatsoever assimilated into this substance, were one single concrete good asserted by it to be the supreme good, we could not dismiss the question of the ground for the privilege of

13. See *Foundations*, second sect. (IV, 279 ff.) (*Ak.* IV, 421).

this value, unless we wanted merely to accept this assertion as a dogma. Every attempt to answer that question, however, would lead us straight on to discover, in this ground itself, another and higher value from which the value first posited would be derived. The categorical imperative would thus have been converted into a hypothetical one, and the unconditional value into a conditioned one.

Only by the idea of universal lawfulness in general as the substance of the supreme principle of value are we delivered from this dilemma. For here we have reached a point at which every question as to a further "why?" must fall silent, where indeed it loses its meaning and its significance. In the theoretical realm we progress synthetically from bare perceptions to judgments and complexes of judgments, from individual appearances to increasingly comprehensive associations, until we have at last discovered in the a priori principles of pure understanding the archetype and model of all theoretical lawfulness, on which we must take our stand as the ultimate justification of experience, without being able to deduce this lawfulness itself in turn from something deeper, from some concrete transcendent entity. The same relation obtains here also. We measure the singular against unity, a particular concrete psychological motive against the totality of possible determinations of the will, and we evaluate it by its relation to this totality, but we have no confirmation of this measure as such save that which is inherent in it. Critical ethics affords us no answer as to why order takes precedence over chaos, free subordination to the universality of a self-given law over arbitrariness of individual desires. [14] In the critique of reason, theoretical as well as practical, the idea of reason, the idea of a final and supreme union of knowledge and will is taken for granted. Whoever fails to acknowledge this idea thus excludes himself from the orbit of its manner of posing problems, and from its conceptions of "true" and "false," "good" and "evil," which it alone can substantiate, empowered by its method. [15]

<hr />

14. Cf. in particular the opening part of the section "Of the Interest Attaching to the Ideas of Morality" (IV, 308 ff.) (*Ak.* IV, 448 ff.).

15. Cf. the preface to the *Critique of Practical Reason:* "Nothing worse could happen to all these labors, however, than that someone should make the unexpected discovery

Thus it is only here that a premise underlying all the developments hitherto finds its true substantial consummation. It is only in self-determination of the will that reason knows and comprehends itself, and it is this knowledge that comprises its peculiar, most profound essence. We encountered the pure "spontaneity" of thought also in the realm of theoretical cognition, but this spontaneity was knowable only through its image and reflection. What the unity of apperception and the individual concepts and principles founded thereon are, only becomes apparent in the growth of the objective world, which these concepts served to complete. A world of things, ordered in space and time, determined in accordance with the analogies of experience, the relations of substantiality, causality, and reciprocity, was the outcome in which the composition of the understanding and its special structure first became clearly visible to us. Consciousness of the ego, pure transcendental apperception, is given us only in and with consciousness of the object as an objective appearance. Now, however, we confront a problem in which even this last limitation vanishes. For we are constrained to think the pure will as something bound by law and hence "objective," but this objectivity belongs to a sphere totally distinct from that which is expressed in the spatiotemporal phenomenon. It is not a world of things we are assured of here, but one of free personalities; not a set of causally related objects, but a republic of self-sufficient subjects purposively united.

From this perspective, what was indicated earlier by the general theoretical expression of the appearance of the object of experience now dwindles to the value of a mere fact in comparison with the person as its own self-assured unity. Only in a person is the idea of the end in itself and the ultimate end fulfilled. Only with respect to a natural thing, embedded in a determinate web of causes and effects, can we inquire as to its "whence" and "whither." By contrast, this question becomes superfluous regarding the person who by virtue of

---

that there is and can be no a priori knowledge at all. But there is no danger of this. It would be like proving by reason that there is no such thing as reason" (V, 12) (*Ak.* V, 12).

his original legislation gives to himself the unified maxims of his volition, and hence his "intelligible character." The relativity, the reciprocal conditioning of the mean, has here uncovered its limit in an absolute value. "The ends which a rational being arbitrarily proposes to himself as consequences of his action are material ends and are without exception only relative, for only their relation to a particularly constituted faculty of desire in the subject gives them their worth. And this worth cannot, therefore, afford any universal principles for all rational beings or valid and necessary principles for every volition. That is, it cannot give rise to any practical laws. All these relative ends, therefore, are grounds for hypothetical imperatives only.... Therefore the worth of any objects to be obtained by our actions is at all times conditional. Beings whose existence does not depend on our will but on Nature, if they are not rational beings, have only a relative worth as means and are therefore called 'things'; on the other hand, rational beings are designated 'persons,' because their nature indicates that they are ends in themselves, i.e., things which may not be used merely as means. Such a being is thus an object of respect and, so far, restricts all [arbitrary] choice....Thus if there is to be a supreme practical principle and a categorical imperative for the human will, it must be one that forms an objective principle of the will from the conception of that which is necessarily an end for everyone because it is an end in itself. Hence this objective principle can serve as a universal practical law. The ground of this principle is: rational nature exists as an end in itself. . . .The practical imperative, therefore, is the following: Act so that you treat humanity, whether in your own person or in that of another, always as an end and never as a means only."[16]

Thus the order of means coincides with the order of natural things, while the order of ends is equated with that of pure, self-determined intelligences. The concept of such a rational being, which must be regarded as legislating universally by all maxims of its will so as to judge itself and its actions from this perspective, leads directly to the correlative conception of a community of rational beings in a

16. *Foundations*, second sect. (IV, 286–87) (*Ak.* IV, 427–29).

"realm of ends." If all rational beings stand under the law so that, in constituting their personhood, they are in relation with the moral individuality of all others, and so that they also demand the fundamental worth which they thus grant themselves from every other subject and acknowledge it in all other subjects, from this there springs "a systematic union of rational beings through common objective laws. This is a realm which may be called a realm of ends (certainly only as an ideal), because what these laws have in view is just the relation of these beings to each other as ends and means."[17] In this realm there is no longer any price for things that serve as means to the attainment of a further end, but there is a worth, which each subject bestows on himself in conceiving himself—as the source of his voluntary decision—as simultaneously individual and universal.[18]

With this we certainly seem, since we are oriented toward an order totally different from that of empirical phenomenal things, to be standing once more in the precincts of metaphysics, but this metaphysics is not rooted in a new conception of things that contrasts and competes with the concept of the object of experience, but purely and exclusively in that basic certainty that we receive in our consciousness of the ethical law as the consciousness of freedom. Every other access to the world of the intelligible and to the unconditioned is closed off to us. The new standpoint, which we give to ourselves in the ought, is our sole guarantee of a sphere of validity superordinate to the purely phenomenal flux. Indeed, the antinomy between freedom and causality is once again posed for us in all its poignancy. For in the selfsame event and the selfsame action in which the idea of causality claims necessity and the impossibility of being otherwise, the idea of the pure will and the ethical law says that they might have occurred otherwise than they did. The whole sequence of causes interconnected and dependent on one another is here annulled as though by a decree; the very fundamental principle of the logic of pure natural knowledge is dissolved.

17. [Ibid. (IV, 285 f.) (Ak. IV, 426 ff.).]
18. [Cf. ibid.]

But putting the question in this fashion, it is then valid to consider whether here it may be a matter of opposition between two types of determinism, but not in any way of opposition between determinism and indeterminism. It is in this sense that freedom is introduced by Kant himself—to be sure, expressed imprecisely and ambiguously—as a "special mode of causality." "Since the concept of a causality entails that of laws according to which something, i.e., the effect, must be established through something else which we call cause, it follows that freedom is by no means lawless even though it is not a property of the will according to laws of Nature. Rather, it must be a causality according to immutable laws, but of a peculiar kind. Otherwise a free will would be an absurdity. Natural necessity is, as we have seen, a heteronomy of efficient causes, for every effect is possible only according to the law that something else determines the efficient cause as to its causality. What else, then, can the freedom of the will be but autonomy, i.e., the property of the will to be a law to itself? The proposition that the will is a law to itself in all its actions, however, only expresses the principle that we should not act according to any other maxim than that which can also have itself as a universal law for its object. And this is just the formula of the categorical imperative and the principle of morality. Therefore a free will and a will under moral laws are identical."[19] The will and its act are thus unfree when they are determined by an individual, given object of desire, by a particular material incentive. They are free when we allow them to be determined by the idea of the totality of determining ends and the requirement of their unity. For in the first case the essential character of a merely mechanical occurrence, as we ascribe it to the physical world of things, is not yet overcome. In the same way that the properties of and changes in a corporeal substance succeed one another and proceed from one another, and as the later state is already fully latent in the preceding one and is derivable from it by a quantitative conservation rule, there unfolds here the procession of inner stirrings and strivings. A given objective incentive releases a corresponding urge, and the latter sets off a specific action with the

19. *Foundations*, third sect. (IV, 305 f.) (*Ak.* IV, 446–47).

same necessity we see in the impact of bodies. But where the action comes under the idea of autonomy, under the requirement of obligation, limits are placed on this sort of analogy. For here the series of temporal moments and the particular empirical content located in them does not simply unroll; in this instance what was present in an earlier instant is not carried over into the succeeding instant, but instead we take our stand in a nontemporal contemplation, in which we bind past and present into one even as we anticipate the future.

According to Kant, we encounter this basic feature in every elemental moral judgment. In every one, "pure reason is practical of itself alone"; that is, it judges what has happened and thus what had to happen in accordance with the empirical causal order as something which, viewed from the standpoint of the certainty of its norms, reason has the freedom either to accept or to reject.[20] This relation to a supreme, self-evident criterion of value adds a new dimension to any contemplation of the factual order. In place of the flux of events, ever-similar to itself, the succession of which we are able to trace simply as it is and which we can shape into an objective temporal order through the understanding's basic principle of causality, in which each component is unambiguously determined in its before and after, here there is introduced the conception and the anticipation of a teleological system in which one element exists "for" another, and in which all particular material ends are ultimately comprehended under the form of one lawfulness, one unconditional value. That will which can grasp this value and subordinate itself to it is the truly free will, for it no longer submits to accidental, shifting, and momentary determinations, but instead opposes them in its pure spontaneity. And hence the order of "experience," which we were firmly restricted to in the Critique of Pure Reason and especially in the deduction of the categories, is transcended, although it is still the case that the transcendence does not result from any theoretical datum, and hence does not furnish us with any new theoretical datum to construct and enlarge this new "intelligible" world. Liberation from experience, from empirical objects in space and time, is not the work

20. Critique of Practical Reason, §7 (V, 36) (Ak. V, 31).

of the understanding, as if the latter had discovered another realm of knowledge divorced from the conditions of sensuous intuition, but instead comes about through the will, which beholds opportunity for its application independently of all incentives of sense and empirical, material motivations. It is the will that vaults over concrete actuality and the mere existence of things in each of its truly authentic acts, for it is not bound by the given but is purely and exclusively committed to the moral task, which lifts it above and impels it beyond all that is given. It pursues this task with all its might and in all its purity, unhampered by the opposition seemingly offered to it by the whole actual state of existing being and the entire previous empirical course of things. Anyone who tries to confine this impulse of the will and of the moral idea by pointing to the limits of experience and of feasibility, is answered by the basic conception of idealism and by the new link it sets up between idea and actuality. It is no accident that Kant invokes Plato in precisely this connection, here feeling and speaking as a complete Platonist.

"Plato," it has already been said in the *Critique of Pure Reason,* "very well realized that our faculty of knowledge feels a much higher need than merely to spell out appearances according to a synthetic unity, in order to be able to read them as experience. He knew that our reason naturally exalts itself to modes of knowledge which so far transcend the bounds of experience that no given empirical object can ever coincide with them, but which must nonetheless be recognized as having their own reality, and which are by no means mere fictions of the brain.

"Plato found the chief instances of his ideas in the field of the practical, that is, in what rests on freedom, which in its turn rests upon modes of knowledge that are a peculiar product of reason. Whoever would derive the concepts of virtue from experience and make (as many have actually done) what at best can only serve as an example in an imperfect kind of exposition, into a pattern from which to derive knowledge, would make of virtue something which changes according to time and circumstances, an ambiguous monstrosity not admitting of the formation of any rule. . . .That no one of us will ever act in a way which is adequate to what is contained in the pure idea of virtue is far from proving this thought to be in any respect chimerical. For it is only by means of this data that any judgment as to moral worth or its opposite is possible; and it therefore serves as an indispensable foundation for every approach to moral perfection—however the obstacles in human nature, to the degree of which there are no assignable limits, may keep us far removed from its complete achievement.

"The *Republic* of Plato has become proverbial as a striking example of a supposedly visionary perfection, such as can exist only in the brain of the idle thinker; and Brucker has ridiculed the philosopher for asserting that a prince can rule well only insofar as he participates in the ideas. We should, however, be better advised to follow up this thought, and, where the great philosopher leaves us without help, to place it, through fresh efforts, in a proper light, rather than to set it aside as useless on the very sorry and harmful pretext of impracticability.... Nothing, indeed, can be more injurious, or more unworthy of a philosophy, than the vulgar appeal to so-called adverse experience. Such experience would never have existed at all, if at the proper time these institutions had been established in accordance with ideas, and if ideas had not been displaced by crude conceptions which, just because they have been derived from experience, have nullified all good intention.... If we set aside the exaggerations in Plato's methods of expression, the philosopher's spiritual flight from the ectypal mode of reflecting upon the physical world-order to the architectonic ordering of it according to ends, that is, according to ideas is an enterprise which calls for respect and imitation. It is, however, in regard to the principles of morality, legislation, and religion, where the experience, in this case of the good, is itself made possible only by the ideas—incomplete as their empirical expression must always remain—that Plato's teaching exhibits its quite peculiar merits. When it fails to obtain recognition, this is due to its having been judged in accordance with precisely these empirical rules, the invalidity of which, regarded as principles, it has itself demonstrated. For whereas, so far as nature is concerned, experience supplies the rules and is the source of truth, in respect of the moral laws it is, alas, the mother of illusion! Nothing is more reprehensible than to derive the laws prescribing what *ought to be done* from what *is done,* or to impose upon them the limits by which the latter is circumscribed."[21]

The basic difference between the causality of being and the causality of obligation, on which the idea of freedom rests, is thus stated as pointedly as it can be. The causality of obligation is not confined to the actual, but is oriented toward what is not actual, indeed to what is empirically impossible. The pure content and the pure validity of the categorical imperative thus hold, even when experience affords us no proof that any actual subject has ever acted in accordance with it; in fact, no such proof may ever be provided, strictly speaking, since it is not given to us to see into the heart of the agent and determine what sort of guiding maxim he has. Nonetheless, the moral law stands as given, "as an apodictically certain fact, as it were, of pure reason, a fact of which we are a priori conscious, even if it be granted that no example could be found in which it has been followed exactly."[22] Here nothing can protect us against totally discarding our ideas of duty save the clear conviction that, even if there never have been acts which sprang from such pure sources, yet the question here is not at all whether this or that did happen, "but that reason of itself and independently of all appearances commands what ought to be done. Our concern is with actions of which perhaps the world has never had an example, with actions whose feasibility might be seriously doubted by those who base everything on experience, and yet with actions inexorably commanded by reason."[23] The essential and specific reality of the idea of freedom is precisely that, uncowed by the demand for what seems impossible, it only thus discloses the true realm of the possible, which the empiricist thought to be limited to what is already actual. Thus the concept of freedom, as the preface to the *Critique of Practical Reason* puts it, becomes "the stumbling block of all empiricists but the key to the most sublime practical principles to all critical moralists, who see, through it, that they must necessarily proceed rationally."[24] This sublimity stands out the more purely

---

21. *Critique of Pure Reason,* A 314 ff. = B 370 ff. (III, 257 ff.).

22. *Critique of Practical Reason,* "Of the Deduction of the Principles of Pure Practical Reason" (V, 53) (*Ak.* V, 47).

23. *Foundations,* second sect. (IV, 264 f.) (*Ak.* IV, 408).

24. [*Critique of Practical Reason,* preface (V, 8) (*Ak.* V, 7–8).]

where the law to which the willing subject submits himself negates and cancels the empirical existence of this subject himself; where life, regarded as physical existence, is sacrificed to the idea. It is only in a determination of this kind, by motives of action which are above and beyond the sensory, that we truly are in contact with being that is supersensory: the world of the "intelligible" in the critical sense. This being cannot be laid hold of otherwise than through the medium of the pure will. If we set that aside, the world of the intelligible is lost to our view, just as there is no longer any world of empirical forms for us if we abstract from the pure intuition of space, as there is no "nature" made up of physical things except through the understanding's fundamental principle of causality.

Even at this point, where we stand in contemplation of the sole "Absolute" to which the critical viewpoint can lead us, the characteristic nature of the basic transcendental stance is preserved. It consists in the correlation of every assertion about something objective with a basic form of consciousness, the necessity to search for the basis and justification of each assertion about an existent in a fundamental function of reason. This relation is completely preserved here. The concept of a rational world, as Kant explains clearly and definitively, is but a standpoint outside appearances which reason sees itself forced to adopt in order to think itself as practical: "If the influences of sensibility were determining for man, this would not be possible; but it is necessary unless he is to be denied the consciousness of himself as an intelligence, and thus as a rational and rationally active cause, that is, a cause acting in freedom."[25] The possibility of such a supersensuous nature thus does not call for an a priori intuition of an intelligible world, which in this case, as supersensuous must needs be impossible for us; rather, in the end it becomes a matter of the will's determining ground in its own maxims: "Is the determining ground empirical, or is it a concept of pure reason (a concept of its lawfulness in general)? And how can it be the latter?"[26]

The explanation of the Kantian proposition so well known and so widely misunderstood, that we are to take the intelligible as justified

25. *Foundations*, third sect. (IV, 318) (*Ak*. IV, 458).

26. *Critique of Practical Reason*, "Of the Deduction of the Principles of Pure Practical Reason" (V, 52) (*Ak*. V, 45).

only "in the practical respect," is thus given in full. The *causa noumenon* continues to be an empty concept in respect to the theoretical employment of reason, though possible and thinkable. In now using this concept as the foundation of ethics, however, we do not obtain any theoretical knowledge of the constitution of a being that has a pure will; it is enough for us merely to designate it thereby as such a being, hence simply to connect the concept of causality with that of freedom (and with what is inseparable therefrom, with the moral law as its determining ground).[27] Anyone who goes beyond this, or even tries to, who attempts to depict the intelligible world instead of thinking of it as the norm and the task of his activity, who sees in it a state of objects instead of an order of ends and a purposive communion of free intelligences as moral persons—that man has abandoned the solid ground of critical philosophy. A sphere of the "in itself" is indeed pointed to and defined by freedom in contrast to the world of appearances, the objective reality of which is manifested in the moral law "just as through a fact," but we can approach it only in action, not in intuition and thought; we grasp it only in the form of a goal and a task, not in the form of a "thing."

Many a difficulty and finespun speculation about Kant's doctrine of the thing in itself—which is admittedly paradoxical and ambiguous as he expresses it—would have been obviated if scholars had always kept this connection in mind with complete clarity. The "in itself," construed practically, does not in the slightest define the transcendental cause of the world of appearances, but it leads adequately to the intelligible ground thereof, since we only become fully cognizant of its meaning and import thereby, and also are shown the ultimate end of all empirical willing and acting. Thus what is accomplished here is not an extension of our knowledge of given supersensuous objects, but a broadening of theoretical reason and its knowledge regarding the supersensuous in general. The Ideas lose their character of transcendence here; they become "immanent and constitutive, since they are the grounds of the possibility of realizing the necessary object of pure practical reason (the highest good)."[28]

27. *Critique of Practical Reason*, Analytic of Pure Practical Reason, chap. I, §8, II (V, 63) (*Ak.* V, 56).

28. Ibid., Dialectic, chap. II, sect. VII (V, 146 f.) (*Ak.* V, 135 f.). Cf. introduction,

Kant's doctrine of the opposition between our empirical and our intelligible nature takes on its full significance only within this all-embracing complex of problems. If we think our intelligible nature, as Schopenhauer did, in such a way that the willing subject has given to itself its determinate essence once for all in a primitive act underlying its empirical existence, so that it now remains inexorably bound to this essence in the experiential world, we are precipitated into an absolutely insoluble labyrinth of metaphysical questions. For we have not a single category that might enable us to clarify and explain that sort of relation between the "in itself" and appearance, between what is absolutely atemporal and extratemporal and the field of the temporal. But all these hesitations vanish immediately if at this point we transplant Kant's theory once more from the soil of metaphysics and mysticism to that of pure ethics, if we take it in the sense in which Schiller and Fichte understood it. Only then does it become apparent that the significance of the intelligible essence does not orient us backward, into a mythical past, but forward into the ethical future. The givenness which our intelligible nature leads us to and which its concept truly certifies to us is nothing more than the givenness of our endless practical task. One and the same act stands on the one hand under the compulsion of causes that are past and gone, while on the other hand it is seen from the point of view of future ends and their systematic unity. It receives its empirical, concrete significance from the first consideration, its nature as value from the second; in the former sense it belongs to the series of events, in the latter to the intelligible order of obligation and free, ideal determination.

Here Kant can once again refer to the way the ordinary popular mind expresses this dual form of judging. Common human reason's legal claim to freedom of the will, he explains, is founded on consciousness and the admitted presupposition of the independence of reason from sensuous causes and motives that determine merely subjectively. The man who believes himself endowed with an autonomous will thus places himself in another order of things and relates himself to determining grounds of an entirely different sort from

"Of the Idea of a Critique of Practical Reason" (V, 17) (*Ak.* V, 15), and also the Deduction (V, 54) (*Ak.* V, 43).

when he perceives himself as a phenomenon in the sense-world and subordinates his causality to external determination under natural laws. The fact that he has to represent and think everything in this twofold way is not at all contradictory, for it rests in the first place on his consciousness of himself as an object affected by the senses, in the second on the consciousness of himself as intelligence, that is, as an active subject who, in using reason, is freed from any passive attachment to sensory impressions.[29] Thus, in line with the basic orientation of the transcendental method, here too determination of the object is the result of the mediation of the analysis of judgment. If I judge that I ought not to have done this or that act which I did do, such an assertion would be meaningless if the "I" in it were taken in a simple sense. For the self as a sensory, empirical phenomenon, as this determinate will amid these determinate conditions, had to carry out the act; if the empirical nature of a man were fully known to us, we could predict everything he does and all his behavior as precisely as we can calculate in advance an eclipse of the sun or moon. But the truth is that in this judgment quite another connection is postulated and intended. The act is reprehensible insofar as it is determined only by particular and contingent motives, corresponding to the passing moment, which overrode respect for teleological grounds of determination in their entirety. The self has denied its true, its intelligible "essence" when it permits this momentary contingency of a particular situation and a particular impulse to become its master; it strengthens its essence whenever it examines and sits in judgment on the particular mode of action out of the postulated integrity of its character. Thus the intelligible, the unity in thought of normative determinations, appears as the continuing standard of measure to which we submit everything empirical. The phenomenon is related to the noumenon as to its own ground, not in the sense that it is known as a given supersensory substrate, but in the sense that its own worth, its place in the realm of ends, is assured in that way.

The fact that the idea of the *mundus intelligibilis*, in the form it has had ever since the Dissertation, nonetheless retains its power, that

29. Cf. *Foundations*, third sect. (IV, 317) (*Ak.* IV, 452).

the idea of obligation in a general sense crystallizes in the shape of a "world," has its profound methodological basis. For wherever critical analysis reveals and makes known to us a specifically characteristic mode of judgment, a particular form of object is coordinated with this form of judgment as well. This objectification is a basic function of pure theoretical reason itself, which we cannot divorce ourselves from, but it is important to distinguish in each particular case precisely which sphere of validity the cognition and the judgment belong to, and what the corresponding mode of being grounded in it is. For the domain of practical reason, Kant carried out this investigation in that important section he titles "The Typic of Pure Practical Judgment." Here the contrast between sensuous and supersensuous objectification is made comprehensible through the contrast between "type" and "schema." The world of experience, that of physics and natural science in general, arises for us by the understanding relating its universal principles to the pure intuitions of space and time, inscribing them in these fundamental pure Forms. Empirical concepts of the "thing" and its physical qualities and changes come about in that we flesh out the pure categories of substance and accident, of cause and effect, with concrete intuitive content, and think of substance as not simply the bearer and the purely logical subject of individual qualities but also in terms of conservation and duration, of causality as not just the relation of the ground to the grounded and dependent but also as the determination of objective temporal relation in an empirical series of appearances. When it comes to the nature of the intelligible, all such forms of asserting things are denied us. There is indeed here an *analogon* of the law of nature: one of the best-known formulations of the categorical imperative bids the will so to act as if the maxim of its action were through it to become a "universal law of Nature."[30] But the "nature" meant here is not the sensuous existence of objects, but the systematic interrelation of individual ends and their harmonious composition in a "final end." It is a model, a type, against which we measure every particular determination of the will, not an objectively existing archetype that permits

30. Ibid., second sect. (IV, 279) (*Ak.* IV, 421).

itself to be intuited apart from this relationship. What it has in common with the sensuous physical world is the factor of stability, of an immovable order, which we think equally in both. But in the one case it is a matter of an order that we intuit immediately as external to ourselves; in the other, one that we actively produce by the power of the autonomy of the moral law.

So it is permissible to use the nature of the sense world as the type of an intelligible nature, "so long as we do not carry over to the latter intuitions and what depends on them but only apply to it the form of lawfulness in general. . . ."[31] Should this carrying-over occur, however, we let the boundaries of the sensuous and the supersensuous blur together inadvertently; the inevitable upshot is once again that species of mysticism which Kant has been combating tirelessly ever since the *Dreams of a Spirit-Seer*. Since obligation is transformed into an image, it loses its productive, regulative force. This path leads us to a "mysticism of practical reason," which converts into a schema what served only as a symbol, that is, it bases the application of moral concepts on real and yet nonsensuous intuitions (an invisible kingdom of God) and meanders off into balderdash. And it is importantly and methodologically significant in all this that it is not the doctrine of the pure a priori that betrays us most readily into such mystical ecstasies, but, on the contrary, the purely empirical foundation of ethics, the view of morality as a doctrine of happiness. Because this point of view recognizes nothing but sensuous motives, it can never get truly clear of sensuous descriptions in all its illusory transcendence of experience and in all its depiction of what is "beyond" sense. To the degree that practical reason is pathologically determined, that is, with the interest of the inclinations in sole command, under the sensuous principle of happiness, "Mohammed's paradise or the fusion with the deity of the theosophists and mystics, according to the taste of each, would press their monstrosities on reason, and it would be as well to have no reason at all as to surrender it in such a manner to all sorts of dreams."[32] And we should not be afraid

31. *Critique of Practical Reason*, "Of the Typic of Pure Practical Judgment" (V, 78) (*Ak*. V, 70).

32. Ibid., "On the Primacy of the Pure Practical Reason" (V, 131) (*Ak*. V, 120–21).

that, if we renounce such sensuous props and aids, the pure ethical imperative would remain abstract and formal, and hence ineffective. "The fear that, if we divest this representation of everything that can commend itself to the sense," the *Critique of Judgment* emphasizes— and in words like these we are in touch with Kant whole and entire—"it will thereupon be attended only with a cold and lifeless approbation and not with any moving force or emotion, is wholly unwarranted. The very reverse is the truth. For when nothing any longer meets the eye of sense, and the unmistakable and ineffaceable idea of morality is left in possession of the field, there would be need rather of tempering the ardor of an unbounded imagination to prevent it rising to enthusiasm, than of seeking to lend these ideas the aid of images and childish devices for fear of their being wanting in potency.... This pure, elevating, merely negative presentation of morality involves . . . no fear of *fanaticism*, which is a delusion that would *will some vision beyond all the bounds of sensibility*; i.e., would dream according to principles (rational raving). The safeguard is the purely negative character of the presentation. For *the inscrutability of the idea of freedom* precludes all positive presentation. The moral law, however, is a sufficient and original source of determination within us; so it does not for a moment permit us to cast about for a ground of determination external to itself."[33]

Thus here too Kant's doctrine terminates in something inscrutable, yet it is a completely different relation from the one we met in his critique of mere theoretical reason. When we speak of the "thing in itself," when we claim it has a form of being but on the other hand challenge its knowability, seemingly insoluble difficulties lurk therein. For even to assert its mere presence, aside from any closer determination of it, is impossible save by those forms of cognition any transcendent employment of which the *Critique of Pure Reason* wants to excise. In the domain of the Kantian doctrine of freedom, however, we are absolved of this conflict. Freedom and the moral—which are put forward in the categorical imperative—indeed do have to be rec-

---

33. *Critique of Aesthetic Judgment.* "Analytic of the Sublime," §29, General Remark (V, 347) (*Ak.* V, 274–75).

ognized as inscrutable in Kant's sense. They signify for us the ulti-mate "Why" of all being and becoming, since they relate becoming to its ultimate end and anchor it in one supreme value, but no further "why" can be demanded of them themselves.

Thus, in the purely logical sense, it is true that we are trapped in a sort of circle, from which it seems there is no escape. We take our-selves to be free in the order of active causes, so as to think ourselves under moral laws in the order of ends, and then we think ourselves in submission to these laws because we have attributed freedom of the will to ourselves. "Freedom and self-legislation of the will are both autonomy and thus are reciprocal concepts, and for that reason one of them cannot be used to explain the other and to furnish a ground for it. At most they can be used for the logical purpose of bringing appar-ently different conceptions of the same object under a single concept (as we reduce different fractions of the same value to the lowest common terms)."[34] But this logical dilemma cannot and should not confuse us in our willing and acting. We need no further explanation here for the fact of freedom, because what is indescribable is done for us. The limits of knowledge are no limitation on certainty, since there can be no higher certainty for us than that which assures us of our moral self, or our own autonomous personality. Reason would be utterly out of bounds if it ventured to explain how pure reason could be practical, which would be identical with the task of explaining how freedom is possible. For how a law might be, immediately and of itself, the basis of determination of the will, how we have to represent this sort of causality theoretically and positively to ourselves, cannot be known by any further sort of datum that theory can show us; we can and must simply assume that there is such a causality by the moral law and for its service.[35] But nevertheless we are now face to face with the inscrutable, no longer as something abstract, not as an unknown substantial being; rather, it has unveiled itself to us in the ultimate law of our intelligence as free personality, and therefore has become inwardly comprehensible to us, even though it is not further

34. *Foundations,* third sect. (IV, 310) (*Ak.* IV, 450).

35. Ibid. (IV, 319 ff.) (*Ak.* IV, 459 f.); *Critique of Practical Reason* (V, 80, 145) (*Ak.* V, 72, 134).

explicable. Thus we have no grasp of the practical unconditional necessity of the moral imperative, "yet we do comprehend its incomprehensibility, which is all that can be fairly demanded of a philosophy which in its principles strives to reach the limit of human reason."[36] But it is imperative to press on to this point, so that reason does not, on the one hand, stumble about in the sense world, in a fashion that is ethically shameful, seeking the supreme ground of action and a conceptual, though empirical interest, "and so that it will not, on the other hand, impotently flap its wings in the space (for it, an empty space) of transcendent concepts which we call the intelligible world, without being able to move from its starting point and losing itself amid phantoms."[37] The shadow that lies over theoretical knowledge as to this point is illuminated for us in acting, but this light is imparted to us only so long as we actually continue in the midst of action and do not try to analyze and interpret it by mere abstract speculations.

Thus, where knowledge ends, "rational moral faith" enters, proceeding from freedom as a basic fact, not to infer the certainty of God and immortality, but to demand it. The nature of this postulate with which Kant brings to a close the development of his ethics indeed seems in the first instance not to be defined without some purely methodological question. For, strictly speaking, it offers the idea of freedom as little further supplementation as it does additional substantiation. By it, as supreme principle, the realm of obligation is delimited and fully exhausted, but it is applicable to the realm of being only by a complete μετάβασις εἰς ἄλλο γένος. Of course, there was not the slightest doubt remaining in Kant's mind that the concept of God did not afford any newer and firmer basis for the idea of freedom than was already contained in the consciousness and the validity of the moral law itself. This concept was not intended for the deduction of the validity of the idea of self-legislation from a supreme metaphysical reality; rather, it was intended only to express and guarantee the application of this idea to empirical, phenomenal actu-

36. [*Foundations*, third sect. (IV, 324) (*Ak.* IV, 463).]
37. Ibid. (IV, 322 f.) (*Ak.* IV, 462).

ality. The decisions of pure will are determined neither by considerations of feasibility nor by foresight as to the empirical consequences of action; what characterizes pure will is precisely that it receives its worth not through what it effects or accomplishes, not through its utility in achieving any sort of predetermined end, but solely from the form of willing itself, from its disposition and the maxims from which it flows. Its fruitfulness or fruitlessness can neither add to nor subtract from this worth.[38] However, little as the will in its decisions depends on consideration of results, on the other hand, in our practical thought and action we are just as unable to determine whether in general the given empirical actuality of things lends itself to the progressive actualization of the goal of the pure will. If the is and the ought are totally disparate spheres, it is at the very least not logically contradictory to think that the two might be forever mutually exclusive, that there might be in the realm of existence insuperable obstacles to carrying out the command of the ought, the unconditional validity of which cannot be watered down. The ultimate convergence of both series, the claim that the order of nature in its empirical course will and in fact must lead to a state of the world that conforms to the order of ends, is not demonstrated thereby but only postulated. And it is the content of this demand that, according to Kant, constitutes the practical meaning of the concept of God. God is thought here not as Creator, not as the explanation of the genesis of the world, but as the guarantee of its moral goal and end. The highest good in the world, the final harmony between happiness and being worthy of happiness, is possible only insofar as we assume a supreme cause of nature, which has a causality that accords with the moral disposition. Consequently, the postulate of the possibility of the highest derivative good (the best possible world) is at the same time the postulate of the actuality of a highest original good, namely the existence of God.[39] This assumption is in no way necessary *for* morality, but rather is necessitated *by* it. We must assume a moral cause of the world in order to set before ourselves a final purpose in accordance

38. Ibid., first sect. (IV, 250) (*Ak.* IV, 394).

39. *Critique of Practical Reason*, "The Existence of God as a Postulate of Pure Practical Reason" (V, 136) (*Ak.* V, 124).

with the moral law, and insofar as the purpose is necessary, to that extent (that is, in the same degree and on the same basis) it is necessary to assume the existence of God.[40] Thus here as elsewhere, the aim is definitely not to comprehend God in the metaphysical sense as the infinite substance with attributes and properties, but to try to determine ourselves and our wills appropriately.[41] The concept of God is the concrete form under which we think our intelligible moral task and its progressive empirical fulfillment.

The idea of immortality takes on an analogous significance, according to Kant, since this idea too arises in us when we clothe the thought of the infinitude of our vocation, of the unending task set for rational beings, in the temporal form of duration and eternity. Total conformity of the will to the moral law is a perfection of which a rational being is never capable while he exists in the world of sense, "but since it is required as practically necessary, it can be found only in an endless progress to that complete fitness; on principles of pure practical reason, it is necessary to assume such a practical progress as the real object of our will."[42] Here more than at any other place in his philosophy, Kant is in continuity with the philosophical world view of the eighteenth century. Like Lessing in his *Education of Mankind*, in the idea of immortality Kant maintains the requirement of an endless potentiality for development in the ethical subject, and, like Lessing, he disdains to make this idea into the determining ground of the ethical will, which must rather pursue the immanent, self-given ground unhampered by hope of the future.[43] The power of ethical action must itself be sufficient witness on this score. Every foreign and external impulse joined to it would necessarily enfeeble it and introduce confusion into it and its peculiar energy. Even if it were assumed that there were some way to demonstrate the personal continuance of the individual, by the most compelling of arguments, so

40. *Critique of Teleological Judgment*, §87 (V, 531 f.) (*Ak.* V, 447 f.); see especially, V, 553, note (*Ak.* V, 471).

41. *Critique of Teleological Judgment*, §88 (V, 538) (*Ak.* V, 457).

42. *Critique of Practical Reason*, "The Immortality of the Soul as a Postulate of Pure Practical Reason" (V, 132) (*Ak.* V, 122).

43. Cf. above, pp. 82 f.

that we might have it before our very eyes as an indubitably settled fact, from the standpoint of behavior more would be lost than gained. Transgression of the moral law would then be avoided, in the certainty of a future punishment, and that which is commanded be done, "but because the disposition from which actions should be done cannot be instilled by any command . . . most actions conforming to the law would be done from fear, few would be done from hope, none from duty. The moral worth of actions, on which alone the worth of the person and even of the world depends in the eyes of supreme wisdom, would not exist at all. The conduct of man, so long as his nature remained as it now is, would be changed into mere mechanism, where, as in a puppet show, everything would gesticulate well but no life would be found in the figures."[44] Thus the factor of uncertainty, which attaches to the idea of immortality taken in the purely abstract sense, liberates our life from the rigidity of merely abstract knowledge, and gives it the dye of decision and deed. "Rational practical faith" conducts us to this point more surely than any logical deduction could because, proceeding directly from the focal point of action, it straightway reenters the domain of action and determines its course.

The critical ethical system culminates in the doctrine of the postulates, and at this point we can make a retrospective survey of the major phases in the evolution of Kant's ethical life-view. The problem of immortality can serve as our guide in this connection, for it runs through all the periods of Kant's speculation. It is evident from the very first, the period essentially oriented toward natural science and the philosophy of nature; the world-picture of modern astronomy and Newtonian cosmology and cosmophysics serves as a backdrop for metaphysical reflections on the duration of the individual soul and its capacity for development. There is no gulf here between the world of the is and the world of the ought, but rather the eye roves directly from one to the other. The conflicts between the two are resolved in

---

44. *Critique of Practical Reason*, "Of the Wise Man's Adaptation of Man's Cognitive Faculties to his Practical Vocation" (V, 159) (*Ak.* V, 147).

the unity of the aesthetic disposition underlying this world view. "Should the immortal soul," Kant concludes the *Universal Natural History and Theory of the Heavens*, "in the whole infinity of its future duration... remain fixed forever at the point of the universe, our earth?... Who can say that it is not its destiny to come some day to know close at hand those distant globes of the cosmos and the perfection of their economies, which from afar already entrance its curiosity? Possibly some orbs of the planetary system are being formed to prepare new dwelling places for us under other skies, on completion of the temporal course prescribed for our sojourn here. Who knows if those satellites of Jupiter do not make their rounds so as to light us perpetually?... In fact, if one has filled his mind... with such meditations, the sight of a starry heaven on a serene night yields a sort of pleasure felt by none but noble souls. In the universal stillness of Nature and the calm of the senses, the hidden cognitive faculties of the immortal spirit speak a nameless tongue, and yield muffled concepts, which can be felt but not described."[45]

Thus this passage already sets forth that penetrating analogy the *Critique of Practical Reason* later expressed and elaborated on in its familiar and famous concluding sentences. The "starry heavens above me and the moral law within me" reciprocally point to each other and interpret each other. "I do not merely conjecture them and seek them as though obscured in darkness or in the transcendent region beyond my horizon: I see them before me, and I associate them directly with the consciousness of my own existence. The former begins from the place I occupy in the external world of sense, and it broadens the connection in which I stand into an unbounded magnitude of worlds beyond worlds and systems of systems and into the limitless times of their periodic motion, their beginning and continuance. The latter begins from my invisible self, my personality, and exhibits me in a world which has true infinity but which is comprehensible only to the understanding—a world with which I recognize myself as existing in a universal and necessary (and not only, as

45. [*Universal Natural History*, part three, conclusion (I, 368 f.) (*Ak.* I, 366 f.).]

in the first case, contingent) connection, and thereby also in connection with all those visible worlds."⁴⁶ If we put these words side by side with the final remarks of the *Universal Natural History and Theory of the Heavens*, the decisive advance made by the *Critique of Pure Reason* will be plain, for all the profound affinity of basic intellectual outlook. Consideration of nature and consideration of purpose are now as much united as they are separated, as much interrelated as in opposition. We must hold fast to this twofold distinction if, on the one hand, science is to be protected in its own preserve from all foreign encroachments and if, on the other, morality is to be upheld as regards the power of its pure and characteristic motive. We are just as little entitled to seek out the absolutely unconditioned, spiritual "inner being of nature," which is rather a mere phantom and will remain so,⁴⁷ as we are permitted to seek the realm of freedom and of the ought on any other basis than that resident in the content of the highest moral law itself. In the course of the empirical history of culture, both demands have been violated. "The observation of the world began from the noblest spectacle that was ever placed before the human sense and that our understanding can bear to follow in its vast expanse, and it ended in—astrology. Morals began with the noblest attribute of human nature, the development and cultivation of which promised infinite utility, and it ended in—fanaticism or superstition."⁴⁸ Only the critique of theoretical and practical reason alike can safeguard against both of these false paths, can prevent us from explaining the orbits of the heavenly bodies by spiritual powers and guiding intelligences instead of mathematically and mechanically, and, conversely, keep us from trying to describe in terms of sensuous images the pure laws of obligation and the intelligible order it opens to us. To inculcate this distinction, this "dualism" between idea and experience, between the is and the ought, and to assert the unity of reason in and through this distinction: this can now be described as the most comprehensive task set by the critical system for itself.

Coordinate with this objective unity of his philosophy, there now

46. [*Critique of Practical Reason*, conclusion (V, 174) (*Ak.* V, 161–62).]
47. See the *Critique of Pure Reason*, A 277 = B 333 (III, 235).
48. [*Critique of Practical Reason*, conclusion (V, 175) (*Ak.* V, 162).]

stands before us in full clarity the integrity of Kant's personality, the nature of the man himself, with his incorruptible critical sense of truth and his unshakable moral conviction, immune to the confusions of doubt, with the sober strength of his thought and the fire and enthusiasm of his will. This dual pattern of his nature has been minted with growing explicitness in the course of Kant's evolution as thinker and writer. In his youthful works, in which the full power of synthesizing phantasy still rules by the side of acuteness and clarity of analytical thinking, Kant's thought is often carried away with an almost lyrical and enthusiastic excess, and many a trait of the *Universal Natural History and Theory of the Heavens* shows us that we are here in the age of sensibility. But the further Kant goes, the more he rids himself in this respect of the prevailing sentimentality. In the struggle against the moral and aesthetic ideals of the Age of Sensibility, he now stands shoulder to shoulder with Lessing. It is especially characteristic how, in his lectures on anthropology, he takes up and endorses the well-known judgment that Lessing passed on Klopstock in his *Literaturbriefe*. For Kant, Klopstock is "no real poet at all," because the essential creative power is denied him; he moves only "per sympathy," since he is himself speaking as one who is moved. Kant's literary and ethical judgment is aimed even more sharply and inexorably against the whole tribe of "novel writers," who, like Richardson, depict in their characters a chimerical idealistic perfection, hoping thereby to spur the will into emulation. All these "masters of the feeling-and-affect-laden style of writing" are for him merely "mystics of taste and sentiment."[49] Feelings naturally evoke tears, but nothing in the world dries sooner than tears; basic principles of action, in contrast, must be built on concepts. "On any other foundation only passing moods can be achieved which give the person no moral worth and not even confidence in himself, without which the consciousness of his moral disposition and character, the highest good in man, cannot arise."[50] Only in this context does full light fall on the

---

49. On Kant's opinions about Klopstock and Richardson, see O. Schlapp, *Kants Lehre vom Genie und die Entstehung der Kritik der Urteilskraft* (Göttingen, 1901), pp. 170, 175, and 299.

50. *Critique of Practical Reason*, Methodology (V, 166 ff.) (*Ak.* V, 157).

much-hailed and much-deplored rigorism of Kantian ethics. It is the reaction of Kant's completely virile way of thinking to the effeminacy and over-softness that he saw in control all around him. It is in this sense, in fact, that he came to be understood by those who had experienced in themselves the value and power of the Kantian act of liberation. Not only Schiller, who explicitly lamented in a letter to Kant that he had momentarily taken on the "aspect of an opponent,"[51] but Wilhelm von Humboldt, Goethe, and Hölderlin also concur in this judgment. Goethe extols as Kant's "immortal service" that he released morality from the feeble and servile estate into which it had fallen, through the crude calculus of happiness, and thus "brought us all back from that effeminacy in which we were wallowing."[52] Thus it was exactly the formalistic nature of Kantian ethics that proved historically to be the peculiarly fruitful and effective moment; by the very fact that it conceived the moral law in its maximum purity and abstraction, Kantian ethics immediately and tangibly invaded the life of Kant's nation and his age, imparting to them a new direction.

51. Schiller to Kant, June 13, 1794 (X, 242) (Ak. XI, 487).
52. Goethe to Chancellor von Müller, April 29, 1818.

VI THE *CRITIQUE OF JUDGMENT*

1

In a letter to Schütz dated June 25, 1787, informing him that the manuscript of the *Critique of Pure Reason* was finished, Kant declined to review the second part of Herder's *Ideas for a Philosophy of the History of Mankind* in the Jena *Literaturzeitung*, on the grounds that he must shun any collateral work in order to make progress on the "Foundations of the Critique of Taste." One can thus see that momentous literary and philosophical tasks were crowding in on him in this period, the most productive and fruitful of his life. No relaxation or response was afforded by tasks accomplished; instead the implications of his unfolding thought pressed on relentlessly toward fresh problems. During the decade of his life from sixty to seventy, Kant experienced, in the fullest and deepest sense, that continuous surpassing of self ordinarily granted to even the greatest men only in the happy time of youth or in the period of their maturity. His works from this time show the creative power of youth united with the ripeness and consummation of age. They build upward and outward at the same time; they extend simultaneously to the disclosure of novel realms of questions and to the more and more precise architectonic ordering of the intellectual material already assimilated. In the *Critique of Judgment*, at first glance the latter tendency seems to have overpowered the former. The conception of the work seems decided more by an external, systematic analysis of the most important basic concepts of the *Critique* than by the discovery of an essential, specifically new lawfulness of consciousness. The power of judgment itself is presented, in its initial conceptual definition, as a mediating element, an insertion between theoretical and practical reason, with the object of welding the two into a new unity. According to the fundamental ideas of the critical theory, nature and freedom, the is and the ought, are permanently separated. Nonetheless the search is for a standpoint from which we may survey them both, less for their differences than in their mutual relation, less in their conceptual separation than in their harmonious interconnection. Even in the preface, the *Critique of Judgment* is treated as a "means of uniting the two parts of philosophy into a whole." "The concepts of Nature, which contain the basis of all theoretical knowledge, rest on the legislation of the understanding. The concept of Freedom, which contains a priori the basis of all practical precepts unconditioned by sense experience, rests on the legislation of the reason. . . .But in the family of the higher faculties of knowledge there is in addition a middle term between the understanding and the reason. This is the power of *judgment*, of which one, by analogy, has reason to suspect that it, too, may contain if not a special power of legislating, still a principle peculiar to it of operating under laws, although in any case a purely subjective a priori. If no field of objects corresponds to it as its domain, still it can have some sort of grounds with a certain character for which this principle alone can be valid."[1]

It has become a standing and generally accepted opinion in the literature that the analogy Kant refers to here was precisely what guided him to the discovery of the problem of the *Critique of Judgment*. It was not out of an immediate interest in the problems of art and artistic creation—so it is said—that Kant's aesthetic grew, nor does it have an integral connection with the problem of natural purposiveness that is by a necessity rooted in the subject matter itself. In both instances, Kant's predilection for the subtle and artistic architectonic of his systems, for divisions and subdivisions of concepts, and for the coordination of the faculties of knowledge into particular families is

---

1. *Critique of Judgment*, introduction, III (V, 245) (*Ak.* V, 176–77).

impressively evinced. To the adherent of this opinion about the historical origin of the *Critique of Judgment*, its historical effect must appear almost miraculous. For a strange thing came to pass, that with this work, which seems to have grown out of the special demands of his system and to be designed only to fill a gap in it, Kant touched the nerve of the entire spiritual and intellectual culture of his time more than with any other of his works. Both Goethe and Schiller—each by his own route—discovered and confirmed his own essential relation to Kant through the *Critique of Judgment;* and it, more than any other work of Kant's, launched a whole new movement of thought, which determined the direction of the entire post-Kantian philosophy. That "happy dispensation," by which what was only a consequence of the elaboration of the transcendental schematism could grow into the expression of what were in fact the deepest intellectual and cultural problems in the eighteenth and the early nineteenth centuries, is often a source of wonder, but it has hardly been explained with complete satisfaction. It remains a most noteworthy paradox that upon simply completing the scholastic framework of his theory and working it out in detail, Kant was led to a point that can be called the crucial one of all living intellectual interests in his epoch, and that in particular he succeeded "in constructing the concept of Goethe's poetry."[2]

Something more is added to this, heightening the paradox. It was not actually the content of the *Critique of Judgment* that captivated Goethe but rather its detailed arrangement and the way it was constructed. By the special mode of composition he recognized that the work could be attributed to "one of the happiest periods of his life." "Here I saw my most diverse thoughts brought together, artistic and natural production handled the same way; the powers of aesthetic and teleological judgment mutually illuminating each other.... I rejoiced that poetic art and comparative natural knowledge are so closely related, since both are subjected to the power of judgment." It was precisely this fundamental tendency of the work, which had

2. Cf. Wilhelm Windelband, *Die Geschichte der neueren Philosophie,* 3d. ed. (Leipzig, 1904), vol. 2, p. 173.

attracted Goethe, that constituted a stumbling block for the technical philosophical critics who evaluated this Critique. What unlocked the gates of understanding for Goethe was regarded on the whole, and particularly for the contemporary way of thinking, as one of the oddest manifestations of Kant's views and mode of presentation. Even Stadler, although he followed the development of the *Critique of Teleological Judgment* with acute understanding, expressed his astonishment at it. He found the linking of the aesthetic problem with the problem of natural teleology almost pointless, because it leads to the imputation of entirely too much value to a moment of purely formal significance and hence results in error as to the deeper worth of the book.[3] So we face a peculiar dilemma; precisely what seems, by analysis of only the philosophical content of the *Critique of Judgment*, to be a relatively accidental and dispensable element appears to have been the essential ingredient of the immediate impression it made in its own time and in its far-reaching effect. Must we acquiesce in this conclusion—or is there perhaps a deeper connection between the formal division of the *Critique of Judgment* and its actual problem, a connection that has gradually become obscured for us, although it was still immediate for and accessible to the intellectual culture of the eighteenth century?

When the question is put this way, it points to a general difficulty standing in the way of a historical and systematic comprehension of the *Critique of Judgment*. It is fundamental to Kant's transcendental method that it is always related to a specific "fact" on which philosophical criticism is performed. Difficult and involved as the progress of this criticism itself may be, nevertheless the object to which it is directed is unmistakably clear from the outset. In the *Critique of Pure Reason* this is found in the form and structure of mathematics and mathematical physics; in the *Critique of Practical Reason* the conduct of "common human reason" and the criterion it employs in all moral judgments constitute the requisite starting point. But for the questions Kant grouped under the single concept of "judgment"

3. August Stadler, *Kants Teleologie und ihre erkenntnistheoretische Bedeutung* (Leipzig, 1874), p. 25.

any foundation like this for the inquiry seems to be lacking. Every special scientific discipline that might be named, and every specific psychologically characterizable aspect of consciousness sought in support, proves on closer inspection to be insufficient. No path leads straight from the problems of descriptive and classificatory natural science to the problems of aesthetic form, and, conversely, no bridge can be found from aesthetic consciousness to the concept of teleology as a particular method of observing nature. Thus the parts indeed seem susceptible of being transcendentally anchored in a unitary "datum," but not the *whole*, which, however, ought to present the intellectual connection between them. On this point we must assume an actual unity to which the philosophical question can be related and on which it is founded, if the *Critique of Judgment* is to be seen not as a leap into the void but rather as a development and deduction with methodical continuity and power from previous problems. We shall try, before taking another step and before launching into the analysis of the individual questions of the *Critique of Judgment*, to specify this underlying unity more precisely—an attempt which compels us to leave the discussion of the critical system for a moment and to go back to the concrete historical origins of metaphysics.

2

The wording of Kant's first definition of judgment, as a faculty of giving laws a priori, points more to a problem of general formal logic than to a basic question belonging to the sphere of transcendental philosophy. "Judgment in general," Kant explains, "is the faculty of thinking the particular as subsumed under the universal. If the universal (the rule, the principle, the law) is given, the judgment which subsumes the particular under it (even if it prescribes as transcendental judgment) *a priori* the conditions under which alone it can be subsumed under that universal) is *determinative*. But if only the particular is given, for which the universal is to be found, the judgment is merely reflective."[4] According to this explanation, the prob-

4. *Critique of Judgment*, introduction, IV (V, 248) (*Ak*. V, 179).

lem of judgment would be joined with the problem of concept formation, for it is precisely the concept that groups particular cases into a
higher genus, thinking them as contained under its generality. But
even cursory historical consideration quickly shows a wealth of problems lying hidden in this seemingly narrow logical question, problems relating to the theory of being that are decisive for this theory.
Aristotle called Socrates the discoverer of the concept, because he first
recognized the relation between the particular and the general—
which is expressed through the concept—as worthy of examination.
In the question of the τί ἔστι, which he addressed to the concept, he
saw the germ of a new meaning of the general question concerning
being. This meaning emerged in its full purity when the Socratic *eidos*
went on to unfold into the Platonic "Idea." In this latter conception
the problem of the relation between the general and the particular
was raised to a new stage of contemplation. For now the universal no
longer appears, as was still possible in the Socratic meaning, as mere
grouping, which the particulars undergo in and through the genus,
but it is considered the archetype of all individual form. Particular
things "are" by imitation of the universal and through participation in
it, insofar as any sort of being is to be attributed to them.

A new development for the whole history of philosophy begins
with this fundamental idea. It would doubtless be entirely too simple
a formula to label this development as transposing the question of the
connection of the universal and the particular from the sphere of logic
into that of metaphysics. For such a label would presuppose logic and
metaphysics as previously known elements, while the special interest
of the intellectual development before us lies rather in the knowledge
of how both fields are gradually shaped and have their boundaries
defined under their reciprocal influence. Aristotle's achievement of
such a sharp delimitation was only apparent. Also, Aristotle is, of
course, no empiricist; even for him what is central to his consideration
is not the individual and its basis but the understanding of essence.
But where Socrates and Plato had raised the question of the concept,
Aristotle sees a concrete ontological question confronting him. The
Socratic τί ἔστι is displaced by the τὸ τί ἦν εἶναι: the problem of
the concept is transformed into the problem of teleology. The end

itself, however, does not remain confined, as with Socrates, to the technical goals and functions of men: Aristotle tries to demonstrate it as the ultimate ground of all events in nature. The universality of the end contains the key to knowledge of the universality of being (essence). Amid all the multiplicity and particularization of empirical becoming, there emerges something universal and typical, which gives this becoming its direction. The world of "Forms" does not stand beyond phenomena as something prior to and separate from them, but it is immanent in phenomena themselves as a whole of teleological forces, which rule and guide the consummation of purely material events. Hence within the Aristotelian system it is the concept of development that is designed to reconcile the opposition of matter and form, of the particular and the universal. The individual "is" not the universal; but it strives to become the universal as it runs the course of its possible forms. In this transition from the possible to the actual, from potency to act, resides what Aristotle designates in the most general sense by the concept of motion. Natural motion thus is organic motion, according to its pure concept. The Aristotelian entelechy thus signifies the fulfillment sought earlier in the Socratic *eidos* and the Platonic Idea. The question of how the particular stands in relation to the universal, how it differs from it and how it is identical, is answered for Aristotle in the idea of the end; for by this idea we immediately grasp how every individual event is joined to the whole and is conditioned and brought forth by a comprehensive whole. Being and becoming, form and matter, the intelligible world and the sensible world appear as united in the end; the truly concrete actuality seems given, comprising in itself all these oppositions as individual determinations.

The Neoplatonic system, which in general is intended to be a union of fundamental Aristotelian and Platonic ideas, assumes this definition, but in it the concept of development receives a different stamp than it did in Aristotle. Although in Neoplatonism development is connected above all with the phenomenon of organic life, Plotinus tries to restore it to its broadest and most abstract meaning, since he understands by it not so much natural becoming itself, but rather that transition from the absolutely One and First to mediated and derivative being which constitutes the fundamental conception of his system. Development here appears in the metaphysical guise of emanation; it is that primordial process through which the descent from the intelligible ground to the sense world is accomplished by determinate stages and phases. In this conception of the question, however, there emerges distinctly for the first time in the history of philosophy the relation and intellectual parallelism between biological and aesthetic problems, between the idea of organism and the idea of the beautiful. Both, according to Plotinus, are rooted in the problem of form and express, although in differing senses, the relation of the pure world of forms to the world of appearances. As in the case of animals we see that not just material and mechanical causes are at work, but that the formative *logos* is active inwardly as the special motive force, transmitting the generic structure to the newborn individual; the creative process in the artist, as well, shows the same relation seen from another perspective. For here too the Idea, which originally is encountered only as something mental and thus as an indivisible unity, is extended into the material world; the mental archetype carried by the artist within himself commands matter and molds it into a reflection of the unity of the Form. The more perfectly this is carried out, the more purely the appearance of the Beautiful is actualized. The essential outcome of the idealistic aesthetic, insofar as it had received a strictly systematic form prior to Kant, was basically contained in this one idea. The speculative aesthetics that grew out of the circle of the Florentine Academy, thence to have its effects from Michelangelo and Giordano Bruno down to Shaftesbury and Winckelmann, is an extension and development of the fundamental motif sounded by Plotinus and Neoplatonism. In this view, the work of art is only one particularly notable specimen of that "inner Form" on which the cohesiveness of the universe as a whole rests. Its composition and articulation are the immediately intuitive isolated expressions of what the world *as a whole* is. It displays, as in a specimen of being, the all-pervasive law; it demonstrates that thoroughgoing interrelation of all individual moments, whose highest and most perfect example we behold before ourselves in the starry heavens. Where empirical observation perceives but things separated by space and time, where for it the world fragments into a manifold of unrelated parts, aesthetic intuition discerns that interpenetration of formative forces on which the possibility of the beautiful and the possibility of life equally rest; for the phenomenon of beauty and that of life both are comprised and enfolded in the single underlying phenomenon of creation.

From this point, however, speculative metaphysics presses on to a further result, which seems necessitated and adumbrated by its very way of putting the question. From the standpoint of this metaphysics, the structuralization which actuality displays as a whole as well as in its individual parts, in general and in particular, is only comprehensible if its cause can be shown to lie in a supreme absolute understanding. The abstract doctrine of the *logos* in this way receives its specific theological stamp. The actual is form and has form, because behind it stand a formative Intelligence and a supreme Will-to-form. The *logos* is the principle of explanation of the world because, and insofar as, it is the principle of the creation of the world. This thought henceforward determines not only the ontology, but along with it the entire epistemology as well. For now it is valid to distinguish two fundamentally opposed modes of knowledge, one of which corresponds to the standpoint of the finite and dependent intellect and the other to the standpoint of the unconditioned and creative intellect. For the empirical mode of observation, which proceeds from particular things and remains the prisoner of comparison and collection of particulars, there is no other way to progress to the laws of the actual than to note the likenesses and differences of particulars and to unite them in this way in classes and types, in empirical "concepts." But how would this empirical form of concept, as a union of particulars in space and time into logical species, be possible, if the actual were not in fact so ordered that it is adapted and fitted to the form of a conceptual system? Everywhere that we seem merely to array particular with particular, to pass from the special case to the genus and to divide this once more into species, a prior, implicit, deeper assumption holds sway. Without the assumption that the world as a totality possesses a pervasive, all-embracing logical structure, so that one can find no element in it which is totally unconnected with all else, sheer empirical classification and comparison would lose all force. But once this is recognized, at that moment the right is granted to reverse the whole former viewpoint. Truth in its essential and full sense will only be disclosed to us when we no longer begin with the particular, as the given and actual, but end with it, when we return to the primordial principles of formation itself instead of stationing ourselves in the midst of being already possessed of form. For these principles are what is first by nature, by which the individual form of everything particular is determinate and controlled.

For this way of thinking, which in the universality of a supreme principle of being includes and possesses the fullness of all derivative elements of existence, Plotinus coined the concept and term "intuitive understanding." The infinite, divine intellect, which does not take up into itself something lying outside it but itself produces the object of its knowledge, consists not in the mere intuition of a particular thing, out of which it derives, by the rules of empirical connection or according to logical rules of deduction, another individual—and so forth in an endless sequence—but in the totality of the actual and the possible which is enclosed in and given to it in a single glance. It has no need to link any concept to other concepts, proposition to proposition, achieving in this way an apparent whole of knowledge which still must remain but an aggregate and fragment; for this intellect, the individual is the same as the All, the nearest the same as the farthest, premises and consequences are comprised in one and the same mental act. Under this notion of the divine and archetypal understanding, temporal distinctions become as accidental as the distinction in the gradations of the Universal, with which logical classification and logical rules of validity are concerned. This understanding sees the total form of the actual, because it actively produces it each moment and because it is immanent in the formative law which underlies all existence.[5]

This basic conception runs through the whole philosophy of the Middle Ages, and even modern philosophy from Descartes on contains it almost unaltered, although it impresses on it the characteristic

---

5. On the concept of the *intellectus archetypus,* cf. the statements by Kant in his letter to Marcus Herz, above pp. 126 ff.

stamp of its own problems. Thus one finds, for example, in Spinoza's work *De intellectus emendatione* and in the form of the ontological proof of God's existence it supports, the notion of the archetypal and creative intellect still in its full force; but the entire philosophical point of view into which this idea has been woven and the consequences it leads to have changed. The world-picture within which Spinoza stands is not the organic, teleological one of Aristotle and Neoplatonism; it·is the mechanical cosmos of Descartes and modern science. But this newly won content, too, now shows itself capable of adaptation to the old metaphysical form of concept, remarkable as this seems at first glance. For it is precisely mathematical thinking, which ordinarily had been construed as an illustration of a syllogistic and therefore discursive procedure, which for Spinoza becomes the token and offspring of the possibility of a different, purely intuitive sort of knowledge. All true mathematical knowledge proceeds genetically; it determines the properties and characteristics of the object, since it produces this object itself. From the adequate idea of the sphere, understood not as a mute, inert image on a blackboard but as the constructive law out of which the sphere arises, all its specific determinations can be deduced with irrefragable certainty and completeness. If one transfers the requirement contained in this geometric ideal of knowledge to the whole of the world and its contents, here too it will be a question of grasping an idea of the whole in which all its particular properties and modes are included. The thought of the one substance with infinitely many attributes presents the solution that Spinoza's system gives to this task; he attributes, as it were, the realistic copy to the thought of the archetypal and creative intellect. A universal concept of being is here conceived, in which, according to the claim of the Spinozistic system, all particular manifestations and laws of being are contained as necessary, just as it is essential to the nature of the triangle that the sum of its angles should be equal to two right angles. The true order and connection of things thus reveals itself as identical with the order and connection of ideas. But in contrast to the connection of ideas stands the merely accidental sequence of our subjective perceptions; opposed to insight into the structure of the cosmos stands bare knowledge of the empirical, temporal course of events and the empirical, spatial togetherness of bodies within a limited portion of being. If, with Spinoza, we designate the knowledge of these spatiotemporal connections of appearances as the epistemological form of imagination, then the form of pure intuition, which constitutes the only truly adequate stage of knowledge, is thus once more differentiated from it in strict, thorough opposition.

And as it becomes clear here, so it becomes clear in the history of philosophy generally that the idea of the "intuitive understanding" in its most universal sense, which has been constant since Plotinus and Neoplatonism, at the same time has a variable meaning through which it serves the expression of the concrete world view of a period, to which it adapts itself. Hence the whole development of the modern speculative systems in general can be traced in the progressive transformation this idea undergoes in modern thought. Kepler's conception of the notion of the "creative understanding," for example, contains, together with the basic mathematical motif, the basic aesthetic motif of this theory: since the Creator of the universe, the "Demiurge," bore within himself aesthetic proportions and "harmonies," besides mathematical numbers and forms, we encounter their reflected glow and splendor everywhere, even within conditioned empirical existence. Next, with Shaftesbury, this idealism directly rejoins its ancient origins, when it unites with the problem of life and the Aristotelian-Neoplatonic conception of the concept of organism. The concept of "inner form" again occupies the center of interest, to be demonstrated to be as meaningful and fruitful for the progress of speculation as for the artistic view of the world and of life. All living things owe the individuality of their particular being to the specific form actual in them; the unity of the universe, however, rests on the ultimate inclusion of all particular forms in a "Form of forms" and hence the cohesiveness of nature appears as the expression of one and the same life-bestowing and purpose-giving "Genius" of the All. The eighteenth century, especially in Germany, still holds to this fundamental view,[6] and it comprises one of the latent presuppositions at which the *Critique of Judgment* hints.

6. More detailed information on this can be found in my book *Freiheit und Form: Studien zur deutschen Geistesgeschichte*, 2d ed. (Berlin, 1918), esp. pp. 206 ff.

It is necessary to bring ourselves up to date on this general historical background of the Kantian statement of the problem, even to
come to a full understanding of merely the external structure of the
Critique of Judgment. The individual underlying concepts we have met
in the metaphysical and speculative unfolding of the problem of form
as the principal phases of a historical line of development simultaneously constitute, within the working out of the *Critique of Judgment,*
the specific milestones of the systematic thought process. The relation
of the universal and the particular is forced into the center of the
inquiry by the definition of judgment itself. The relation and inner
connection to be assumed between the aesthetic and the teleological
problem, between the idea of the beautiful and the idea of organism,
is expressed in the arrangement by which the main parts of the work,
both correlative to each other and mutually supplementary, are juxtaposed. The train of thought proceeds from this point; the connection between the problem of empirical concepts and the problem of
ends emerges, the meaning of the unfolding thoughts is determined
more precisely, until at last the whole Kantian question is involved in
that profound discussion of the possibility of an archetypal understanding, in which Fichte and Schelling deemed that philosophic reason had attained its supreme height, beyond which no further step
could be made. For the time being we shall not inquire into the precise content of all these special problems but shall next fix our eye
simply on the general disposition of the work, the joining of the
partial questions into an overall question. Modern *Kant-Philologie* and
Kant-Kritik have overlooked this overall question primarily because it
restricted itself, in systematically judging Kant's thought, too onesidedly to that narrow concept of development that had become important in the scientific biology of the second half of the nineteenth
century. Even Stadler's outstanding inquiry into Kant's teleology is
limited exclusively to a comparison between Kant and Darwin. If
some thought to honor Goethe's view of nature most highly by
stamping him as "a Darwinian before Darwin," the attempt was
made to establish the same claim for Kant too—his well-known saying, that it is "preposterous for mankind" to conceive the plan of a
mechanical explanation of organic existence and to hope for a "New-

ton of the grass blade" ought to have been an especial admonition to prudence here. In truth, however, the historical place of the *Critique of Judgment* can be made fully clear only if one resists the attempt to project the work onto the standpoint of modern biology and regards it always within its proper context. Metaphysical teleology, as it evolved in the most varied transformations and ramifications from antiquity to the eighteenth century, constitutes the matter for Kant's critical question. This does not mean that he takes the decisive directions of his thought from it, but only that it delimits the totality of objects of inquiry to which his solution intends to do justice. Actually, perhaps nowhere else does the opposition of this solution to the traditional categories of metaphysical thought emerge so sharply and clearly as at this point; nowhere is the critical revolution in thinking revealed as so decisive as it is here, where metaphysics is tracked down in a realm that for ages has been its exclusive domain and its especial dominion.

Here too, Kant once again begins with that inversion of the question which represents his universal methodological scheme. It is not the special characteristics of the concrete things which arrest his attention; for him the question is not the conditions for the existence of purposive structures in nature and art. What he wants to establish is the peculiar orientation of our knowledge when it judges some existing thing as purposive, as the coinage of an inner form. The justification and the objective validity of such judgment is all that is in question. The assignment of the teleological and the aesthetic problem to a unitary critique of judgment finds its deeper explanation and foundation only here. The term "faculty of judgment," which had been first introduced by Baumgarten's pupil Meier, was in common use before Kant; but it is only through the whole of the basic transcendental point of view that the new and special meaning it now receives attaches to it. If one takes the point of view of naive or metaphysical realism, the treatment of the question, whose starting point is the analysis of the judgment, must always and in every way appear subjective; to proceed from the judgment seems the opposite of proceeding from the object. A completely different picture of the matter is seen, however, when one reflects that under the general conviction the *Critique of Pure Reason* had established, judgment and object are strictly correlative concepts, so that in the critical sense, the truth of the object is always to be grasped and substantiated only through the truth of the judgment. When we inquire what is meant by the relation of a representation to its object, and, accordingly, what it means to assume "things" as contents of experience in general, we find that the datum which is our ultimate support is the distinction of validity existing between those different forms of judgment which the *Prolegomena* contrasts as judgments of perception and judgments of experience. The necessity and universal validity we ascribe to the latter originally constitute the object of empirical knowledge; the a priori synthesis underlying the form and the unity of the object is also the ground of the unity of the object, insofar as it is thought as an object of possible experience. Thus theoretically considered, what we call being and empirical actuality is revealed to be founded in the specific validity and the particular nature of determinate judgments. We were presented with an analogous form of inquiry in the construction of ethics. Since one and the same action was brought sometimes under the viewpoint of empirical causality and sometimes under that of moral obligation, the realm of nature and the realm of freedom were in opposition as sharply differentiated areas.

From the presuppositions one can further see that, if the aesthetic sphere is to be put forward as self-sufficient and independent, and if, moreover, in addition to the causal and mechanical explanation of natural events the teleological view of things as natural ends is to be justified, these two results can be attained only by discovery of a new realm of judgments, to be distinguished in their structure and in their objective validity from theoretical as well as practical judgments. Only in this way do the realms of art and of organic natural forms present a different world from that of mechanical causality and ethical norms, because the connection between the individual forms that we assume in both is governed by a characteristic form of law, which is expressible neither through the theoretical analogies of experience, through the relations of substance, causality, and reciprocity, nor through the ethical imperative. What is this form of law, and on what is the necessity we attribute to it founded? Is it a subjective or an objective necessity? Does it rest on a connection residing only in our human thinking and falsely transferred to objects, or is it grounded in the essence of these objects? Is the idea of an end, as Spinoza wishes to maintain, always an *asylum ignorantiae* or, as Aristotle and Leibniz assert, does it form the objective foundation of all profounder explanations of nature? Or, if we transfer all these questions from the realm of nature to that of art, is art a sign of natural truth or a sign of illusion; is it the imitation of something existing or a free creation of fantasy, which rules the given according to its own pleasure and free choice? These problems can be traced through the entire history of the theory of organic nature just as through that of aesthetics; but now it is necessary to assign them to a firmly systematic place, so that they are already half solved.

This task does not add any wholly novel moments to the development of the critical philosophy, for, since the classic letter from Kant to Marcus Herz, in which a new foundation for judgments of taste is demanded and promised, the general transcendental question is so conceived that it subsumes under it all the various modes, by means of which in general any sort of objective validity can be grounded.[7] This objectivity may arise from the necessity of thinking or of intuition, from the necessity of being or of obligation; thus it always constitutes a determinate, unified problem. The *Critique of Judgment* brings a new differentiation of this problem; it uncovers a new type of general claim to validity, but even here it remains completely within the framework established by the first comprehensive draft of the critical philosophy. The true mediation between the world of freedom and that of nature cannot consist in our inserting between the realms of being and of willing any sort of middle realm of essence, but consists instead in our discovery of a type of contemplation that participates equally in the principle of empirical explanation of nature and in the principle of ethical judgment. The question is whether nature cannot be so thought of "that the conformity to law of its form may at least agree with the possibility in it of ends acting in accordance with laws of freedom."[8] If this question is posed, an entirely

---

7. See above, pp. 130 ff.
8. *Critique of Judgment*, introduction, II (V, 244) (*Ak.* V, 176).

fresh perspective is immediately opened to us—thus it comprises nothing less than a change in the mutual systematic arrangement of all the basic critical concepts previously acquired and established. The task arises of seeing in detail how far this transformation confirms the earlier foundations and how far it extends and adjusts them.

3

The problem of the individual structuring of the actual existent, which is central to the *Critique of Judgment,* has its intellectual and terminological focus in the concept of purposiveness, which is Kant's starting point. According to the modern outlook on language, this initial expression of the basic question is not entirely adequate to its true content, for we are used to attaching to the purposiveness of a specific structure the idea of conscious adaptation to an end, of deliberate creation, which we must completely lay aside here if we want to grasp the true universality of the question. The linguistic usage of the eighteenth century construes "purposiveness" in a wider sense: it sees in the term the general expression for every harmonious unification of the parts of a manifold, regardless of the grounds on which this agreement may rest and the sources from which it may stem. In this sense the word represents merely the transcription and German rendering of that concept which Leibniz, in his system, signified by the expression "harmony." A totality is called "purposive" when in it there exists a structure such that every part not only stands adjacent to the next but its special import is dependent on the other. Only in a relationship of this kind is the totality converted from a mere aggregate into a closed system, in which each member possesses its characteristic function; but all these functions accord with one another so that altogether they have a unified, concerted action and a single overall significance. For Leibniz, the exemplar of such a cohesiveness was the universe itself, in which each monad is self-existent, and, cut off from all external physical influence, follows solely its own law, yet all these individual laws are so regulated that the most precise correspondence holds between them, and their results accordingly are in complete mutual agreement.

In comparison with the metaphysical concept of a whole, the critical standpoint seems to pose what is essentially a less pretentious and simpler task. Following its fundamental tendency, it works not so much toward the form of actuality itself but toward the form of our concepts of the actual; the system of these concepts, not the system of the world, constitutes its starting point. For wherever we have before us a whole, not of things but of knowledge and truths, the same question is posed. Every such logical whole is at the same time a logical construction, in which each member conditions the community of all the rest, just as it is simultaneously conditioned by them. The elements are not arranged adjacent to one another but exist only because of one another; within the complex the relation in which they stand necessarily and essentially belongs to their own logical existence. This mode of interconnection emerges clearly in the system of pure mathematical knowledge. If one considers such a system, if one surveys, for example, the content of the theorems we ordinarily combine in the concept of Euclidean geometry, it is seen as a progressive sequence from relatively simple beginnings, according to a fixed form of intuitive connection and deductive inference, to ever-richer and more advanced results. The manner of this progression guarantees that no member can be obtained that is not perfectly definable in terms of what precedes, although on the other hand each fresh step expands the previous content of knowledge and adds synthetically to it a specific new modification. Thus there reigns here a unity of principle that maintains itself continuously and enduringly in a manifold of consequences, a simple, intuitive seed that is unfolded conceptually for us and divides itself into a series of new forms, which is in itself unlimited but fully controllable and surveyable. This yields precisely that cohesiveness and correlation of parts which constitutes the essential factor in Kant's concept of purposiveness. Purposiveness thus can be found not only in the accidental formations of nature but also in the strictly necessary formation of pure intuition and pure concept.

Before we seek it out in the realm of natural forms, it is worthwhile to discover and grasp it in the realm of geometric forms. "In such a simple figure as the circle lies the key to the solution of a host of problems every one of which would separately require elaborate materials, and this solution follows, we might say, directly as one of the infinite number of excellent properties of that figure. . . . All conic sections, taken separately or compared with one another, are, however simple their definition, fruitful in principles for solving a host of possible problems.—It is a real joy to see the ardour with which the older geometricians investigated these properties of such lines, without allowing themselves to be troubled by the question which shallow minds raise, as to the supposed use of such knowledge. Thus they investigated the properties of the parabola in ignorance of the law of terrestrial gravitation which would have shown them its application to the trajectory of heavy bodies. . . .While in all these labors they were working unwittingly for those who were to come after them, they delighted themselves with a finality which, although belonging to the nature of the things, they were able to present completely a priori as necessary. Plato, himself a master of this science, was fired with the idea of an original constitution of things, for the discovery of which we could dispense with all experience, and of a power of the mind enabling it to derive the harmony of real things from their supersensible principle. . . .Thus inspired he transcended the conceptions of experience and rose to ideas that seemed only explicable to him on the assumption of a community of intellect with the original source of all things real. No wonder that he banished from his school the man that was ignorant of geometry, since he thought that from the pure intuition residing in the depths of the human soul he could derive all that Anaxagoras inferred from the objects of experience and their purposive combination. For it is the necessity of that which, while appearing to be an original attribute belonging to the essential nature of things regardless of service to us, is yet final, and formed as if purposely designed for our use, that is the source of our great admiration of nature—a source not so much external to ourselves as seated in our reason. Surely we may pardon this admiration if, as the result of a misapprehension, it is inclined to rise by degrees to fanatical heights."[9]

If one has fully digested the fundamental results of the "Tran-

---

9. *Critique of Teleological Judgment,* §62 (V, 440 f.) (*Ak.* V, 362–64).

scendental Aesthetic," however, one sees that this enthusiastic flight
of the spirit, born of wonderment at the internally harmonized structure of geometric forms, weakens the calm critical transcendental insight. For here it is shown that the order and regularity that we think
we perceive in spatial forms lies rather in ourselves. The unity of the
manifold in the field of geometry becomes comprehensible as soon as
one is convinced that the geometric manifold is not something given,
but something constructed. The law governing every element by its
original formation is shown to be the a priori ground of that unity and
flawless consistency we admire in the deduced consequences. A
completely different state of affairs, and hence a totally new problem,
is presented as soon as we deal with an empirical manifold instead of
a mathematical manifold (such as pure space). This is precisely the
assumption that we make in any empirical inquiry: that not only the
whole domain of pure intuitions but also the domain of sensations
and perceptions itself can be unified into a system analogous and
comparable to that of geometry. Kepler not only speculates on the
interconnection of conic sections as arbitrarily produced geometrical
forms, but he maintains that in these forms he possesses the model of
and key to the understanding and exposition of the movements of
astronomical bodies. Whence comes this confidence that not only the
purely artificially constructed but the given itself must be conceivable
in this sense, that is to say, that we can regard its elements as if they
were not completely alien to one another, but as if they stood in a
fundamental intellectual affinity which needs only to be discovered
and specified more exactly?

It might seem as though this question—insofar as it may be posed
in general—is already answered by the principal results of the *Critique
of Pure Reason*. For the *Critique of Pure Reason* is the critique of experience; its intent is to demonstrate that the lawful order which the
understanding only appears to discover in experience is something
grounded in the categories and rules of this understanding itself, and
to this extent necessary. That appearances are joined to the synthetic
unities of thinking, that not chaos but the solidity and determinateness of a causal order reigns amid them, that out of the flux of "accidents" a permanent and constant something is raised: we com-

prehend all this once we have seen that the ideas of causality and substantiality belong to that class of concepts with which we "spell out appearances so as to be able to read them as experiences." The lawfulness of appearances *in general* thereby ceases to be a riddle, for it is presented merely as another expression for the lawfulness of the understanding. The concrete structure of empirical science, however, confronts us at the same time with another task, which has not been solved and overcome along with the first one. For here we find not only a lawfulness of events as such, but a connection and interpenetration of particular laws of such a type that the whole of a determinate complex of appearances is progressively combined and dissected for our thought in a fixed sequence, in a progression from the simple to the complex, from the easier to the more difficult.

If we consider the classical example of modern mechanics, it is shown in the *Critique of Pure Reason* and in the *Metaphysical Foundations of Natural Science,* which is an appendix to the former, that three general laws of the understanding correspond to and underlie the three basic laws laid down by Newton: the law of inertia, the law of the proportionality of cause and effect, and the law of equality of action and reaction. But the structure and the historical development of mechanics is not thereby adequately circumscribed and comprehended. If we trace its progress from Galileo to Descartes and Kepler, from these men to Huyghens and Newton, yet another connection than the one stipulated by the three analogies of experience is revealed. Galileo begins with observations of the free fall of bodies and motion on an inclined plane, as well as the determination of the parabolic trajectory of a projectile; Kepler adds empirical determinations of the orbit of Mars, Huyghens the laws of centrifugal motion and the oscillations of a pendulum; finally all these particular moments are combined by Newton and are demonstrated to be capable, as thus integrated, of encompassing the whole system of the universe. Thus in a steady advance from minor, relatively simple primary elements and primary phenomena the entire picture of the actual is sketched, as we encounter it in cosmic mechanics. We reach in this way not just any old order of events, but an order that our understanding can survey and comprehend. Such comprehensibility cannot be demonstrated and seen as a priori necessary through the pure laws of the understanding alone, however. According to these laws, it could be thought that empirical reality indeed obeyed the general premise of causality, but that the various causal sequences which interpenetrate to form it ultimately determine in it a complexity such that it would be impossible for us to isolate and trace out individually the individual threads in the whole sprawling tangle of the actual.

In this case, too, it would be impossible for us to grasp the given in that characteristic order which is the foundation of the essential nature of our empirical science. For this order is required more as a sheer opposition between the empirical and particular and the abstract and universal, more as a mere stuff underlying the pure forms of thought as given by transcendental logic in some fashion not subject to further determination in detail. The empirical concept must determine the given by progressively mediating between it and the universal, since it relates the data to the universal through a continuous series of intermediate conceptual stages. The highest laws themselves, since they are mutually interrelated, must be specified to the particularities of the individual laws and cases—just as conversely the latter, purely because they are juxtaposed and illuminate one another, must permit the exposition of the universal connections holding between them. Only then do we possess that concrete unification and presentation of the factual our thinking seeks and insists on.

How this task is carried out in the growth of physics was already patent in its history, but it emerges still more clearly and definitely in biology and in all descriptive natural sciences. Here we seem to confront a totally unassessable mass of individual facts, which we first of all must take one by one and simply record. The idea that this material can be analyzed according to definite points of view and that it can be divided into species and subspecies signifies only a requirement laid on experience, but fulfillment of which the latter seems in no wise to guarantee. Nonetheless, scientific thinking, undisturbed by any consideration of a philosophical and epistemological nature, does not hesitate in the slightest to pose this requirement and to carry it right through into the realm of the given. In things which are absolutely individual it seeks similarities, common qualities, and properties and no apparent lack of success is allowed to divert it from this original line. If a certain class concept has not proved correct, if it is overthrown by fresh observations, it is replaced by another one; collection into genera and division into species as such, however, remain undisturbed by these fatalities among the individual concepts. Thus there is here revealed an inviolable function of our concepts, which to be sure prescribes a priori no particular content for them, but which is decisive for the total form of the descriptive and classificatory sciences.

And in this way we have also achieved a new transcendental insight of essential significance, for the term "transcendental" must be applicable to any characteristic which does not directly concern objects themselves but which concerns the mode of our knowledge of objects. We *discover* in nature what we call the affinity of species and of natural forms only because we are constrained by a principle of our power of judgment to *seek* it in nature. This shows, of course, that the relation between principle of knowledge and object has altered if we compare this example with that established by the analytic of pure understanding. Whereas the pure understanding was revealed to be "legislator for nature" because of the demonstration that it contains the conditions of the possibility of its object, here reason approaches empirical material not as if commanding but as if questioning and inquiring; thus the relation is not constitutive, but regulative, not determinative but reflective. For in this case the particular is not deduced from the universal so as to specify its nature, but the attempt is to discover in the particular itself, by successive considerations of the relations it bears within itself, and the similarities and differences which its individual parts show with respect to one another, a connection that can be expressed in ever more comprehensive concepts and rules. However, the fact that an empirical science does exist and progressively unfolds ensures that this attempt is not undertaken in vain. The manifold of facts seems, as it were, to accommodate itself to our knowledge, to meet it halfway and to prove tractable to it. Precisely because such a harmony of the content, on which our empirical knowledge rests, with the will to form by which it is guided, is not self-evident, because it is not deduced as being necessary from universally logical premises but can only be considered as something accidental, we have no choice but to see herein a certain purposiveness: namely, an appropriateness of appearances to the conditions of our judgment. This purposiveness is "formal," since it does not relate directly to things and their inner nature, but rather to concepts and their connections in one mind; but at the same time it is thoroughly objective in the sense that it undergirds nothing less than the status of empirical science and the orientation of empirical research.

Until now we have tried to develop the problem strictly according to its purely objective content, without going into detail on the particular formulation in which we encounter it in Kant. Only this way of contemplating the problem can show clearly that it is the immanent development of the actual tasks of the critique of reason, and not merely the extension and the elaboration of the Kantian architectonic of concepts, which leads to the critique of judgment as a particular portion of the system. Once these tasks are clearly understood, the expression of them Kant chose and the synthesis to which he attaches them by content and by terminology no longer offers any essential difficulty. In the first draft of the introduction to the *Critique of Judgment*, Kant gave that exposition of the fundamental question which is both the most profound and the most comprehensive; because of its great length, however, he replaced it with a shorter version in the final process of editing the work. Only much later did he recall this first draft, when Johann Sigismund Beck asked him for contributions for the commentary to the critical works he planned; yet Beck, to whom Kant gave the draft to be used as he pleased, published it with severe and arbitrary cuts and under a misleading title. To make the full content of Kant's presentation lucid, one must go to the original manuscript of the introduction.[10] Kant here sets out to reconcile the opposition of the theoretical and the practical—which is an apparent result of this whole theory—by introducing a new concept. As a step toward the systematic reconciliation he seeks, however, he deems it advisable first to reject a different, popular reconciliation, which at first glance seems to present itself. It is sometimes thought that a

10. The first appearance in print of this manuscript is in the present edition of Kant's works: see V, 177–231. For further information on its composition and its subsequent fate, see the notes (V, 581 ff.).

unification of the practical and the theoretical sphere has been produced when a given theoretical proposition is considered not only with regard to its purely conceptual grounds and its conceptual consequences, but also when the applications it permits are taken into consideration. Insofar as we think to reckon, say, statecraft and political economy as practical science, we think it possible to call hygiene and dietetics practical medicine, pedagogy practical psychology, because in all these disciplines the problem is not so much the achievement of theoretical propositions as it is the use of certain cognitions which have their foundations elsewhere. But practical propositions of this kind are not truly and in principle differentiable from theoretical ones; this separation, in its true precision, is only present where it is a question of the opposition between motivation by natural causality and by freedom. All the rest of the so-called practical propositions are nothing but the theory of the nature of things, merely applied to the manner in which we can produce them according to a principle. Thus the solution of any problem in practical mechanics (e.g., the solution of the task of finding for a given force which is to be in equilibrium with a given weight, the ratio of the respective lever arms) in fact contains nothing else and requires no other assumptions than those which are already expressed simply in the formula for the law of the lever; and it merely indicates a different bent of temporary, subjective interest, not a difference in the content of the problem itself, whether I clothe it on one occasion in the form of a pure judgment of knowledge or on another in that of a precept for the production of a particular set of conditions. Such propositions ought to be called technical rather than practical, where technic means less something opposed to theory than its execution with respect to a given particular case. Its rules belong to the art of bringing about the realization of one's desires, "which is always merely an extension of a complete theory, and never an independent part of any species of precepts."

But now Kant's treatment of the question presses on beyond technic, the middle term thus established, and achieves a new broadening and deepening of the theoretical field. For besides technic as a particular artistic human institution which perpetually clings to the illusion of free choice, there is also, as Kant notes, a technic of nature itself, namely, so far as we regard the nature of things as if their possibility rested on art, or in other words as if they were the expression of a creative will. To be sure, such a mode of conception is not given us by the object itself—for regarded as an object of experience, "nature" is nothing but the totality of appearances, insofar as it is governed by universal and therefore mathematico-physical laws; it is a standpoint which we adopt in reflection. It therefore arises neither from the mere awareness of the given, nor from its arrangement in causal connections, but the interpretation which we attach to it is a special and independent one. It can in a certain sense, of course, be quite generally asserted, from the standpoint of the critical view of the world, that it is the form of knowledge which determines the form of objectivity. Here, however, this proportion is valid in a more restricted and specific sense, for it is a second-stage creative process, as it were, that we have before us here. A whole, which as such is contained directly under the pure concepts of the understanding and experiences its objectification through them, now embodies a new meaning, in that the interrelations and mutual dependence of its parts are subjected to a new principle of contemplation. The idea of a technic of nature, in contrast to that of the purely mechanical and causal succession of appearances, is one which "determines neither the nature of objects nor the manner of producing them; rather, nature is judged by means of them, but only by analogy with an art and, more particularly, in a subjective relation to our faculty of knowledge and not in an objective relation to the objects." Only one question can and must now be asked: whether this judgment is possible—that is, whether it is compatible with the prior judgment by which the manifold is grasped under the unifying form of the pure understanding. We cannot as yet anticipate the answer which Kant gives to this question; nevertheless, it may be expected that such consistency between the principle of knowledge via the understanding and that via reflective judgment will be able to be effected only if the new principle does not trespass upon the domain of the old one, but advances an entirely separate claim to validity, which needs to be clarified and delimited with respect to the earlier one.

The idea of a technic of nature, and what sets it off from the idea of a deliberate contrivance for attaining some external goal, emerges most clearly if one first abstracts from all relation to the will at this point and holds firmly to the relation with the understanding, thus expressing the form with which nature invests it strictly in analogy with the logical interconnection of forms. That such an analogy exists is clear the moment one reflects that nature in the critical sense means for us nothing more than the totality of the objects of possible experience; and that moreover experience consists as little of a mere sum of separate observations patched together as it does of a sheer abstract set of universal rules and principles. It is only the conjunction of the moments of individuality and universality in the concept of "experience as a system of empirical laws" that constitutes the concrete whole of the connectedness of experience. "For although experience forms a system under *transcendental* laws, which comprise the condition of the possibility of experience in general, there might still occur such an *infinite multiplicity of empirical laws* and so *great a heterogeneity of natural forms* in particular experience that the concept of a system in accordance with these empirical laws would necessarily be alien to the understanding, and neither the possibility nor still less the necessity of such a unified whole is conceivable. Yet particular experience, which is thoroughly coherent under invariable principles, demands this systematic connection of empirical laws as well, whereby it becomes possible for judgment to subsume the particular under the universal, remaining always within the empirical sphere, proceeding to the highest empirical laws and their appropriate natural forms. Hence the *aggregate* of particular experiences has to be regarded as a *system*, for without this assumption total coherence under laws, that is, the empirical unity of them, cannot come about."[11] Were the multiplicity and dissimilarity of the empirical laws so great that it would be possible to organize individual ones under a general class concept but never to comprehend the totality of them in a unitary series ordered by degrees of generality, we would have in nature, even if we thought of it as subjected to the law of causality, just a "crude chaotic

---

11. [*Critique of Judgment*, first introduction, II (V, 185 f.) (*Ak.* XX, 202 f.). Cf. *Critique of Judgment*, introduction, V.]

aggregate." But now the judgment confronts the idea of such formlessness, not with an absolute logical decree but with the maxim that acts as its incentive and guidepost in all its inquiries. It posits a progressive lawfulness of nature, which is contingent by the concepts of the understanding alone, but which it "assumes for its own benefit." Of course, in the midst of all this it has to remain aware that in this formal purposiveness of nature, that is to say, in its quality of comprising for us a permanently interconnected whole of particular laws and particular forms, it does not posit and establish either theoretical knowledge or a practical principle of freedom, but rather provides a firm rule for our judging and inquiry. This does not contribute any new division to philosophy as the doctrinal system of the knowledge of nature and freedom; on the contrary, our concept of a technic of nature belongs to the critique of our faculty of knowledge, as a heuristic principle for judging nature. The "aphorisms of metaphysical wisdom" with which descriptive natural science in particular is accustomed to work, and which the *Critique of Pure Reason* had censured in the section on the regulative principles of reason, are only here seen in their true light. All those maxims—that nature always chooses the shortest path, that she does nothing in vain, that she suffers no leap in the manifold of forms, and though rich in varieties is poor in species—now appear less as absolute determinations of the essence of nature than as "transcendental utterances of judgment."

"All comparisons of empirical representations, so as to perceive in natural things empirical laws and the corresponding *specific* forms, and yet through comparison of these with others to detect *generically harmonious* forms, presupposes that Nature has observed in its empirical laws a certain economy, proportional to our judgment, and a similarity among forms which we can comprehend, and this presupposition must precede all comparison, being an a priori principle of the judgment."[12] For here, too, it is a matter of an a priori principle, since this hierarchy and this formal simplicity of natural laws cannot be deduced from individual experiences, but are the presuppositions

---

12. [First introduction, V (V, 194). Cf. *Critique of Judgment,* introduction, V.]

that are the only basis on which we are able to systematize experiences.[13]

Here at last one can see fully the evolution through which the critical philosophy and metaphysics come to diverge at this point. Whenever the problem of individual forms of actual things had been debated in pre-Kantian metaphysics, it was united with the idea of an absolute teleological understanding, which had inserted a primordial formative act into the heart of being, of which the purposiveness confirmed by our empirical concepts is but a reflection and image. We have seen how the doctrine of the *logos* held fast to this idea from its origins with Plotinus, and how it was expressed in the most diverse ways. Here too Kant carries through the characteristic transformation that is the hallmark of the whole course of his idealism: the Idea changes from an objective and active power in things into the principle and basic premise of the knowability of things as objects of experience. To be sure, to relate the order of appearances in general, which is teleological for our understanding and conforms to its requirements, to a higher level of purposiveness and to a creative and "archetypal" Intelligence, seems to him to be a step necessarily demanded by reason itself, but deception enters in as soon as we change the idea of a relation of this kind into the idea of an actually existing primal Being. We thereupon transmute, by the power of the selfsame innate sophistry of reason which the "Transcendental Dialectic" had disclosed, a goal which experiential knowledge looks forward to and from which it cannot divorce itself, into a transcendent Being which lies behind us; we conceive as a finished and factual condition an order which is posited for us in the process of knowledge itself and is grounded more deeply and solidly with each new step. It is a sufficient critique of this position to recall the transcendental point of view that the "Absolute" is not so much given as proposed to us. Even the thoroughgoing unity of the particular forms of actuality and the particular laws of experience may thus be regarded as if an understanding (though not our own) had produced them for the benefit of our

13. On the whole of this, see *Critique of Judgment*, first introduction, I, II, IV, V (V, 179 ff.) (*Ak.* XX, 195 ff.); cf. *Critique of Judgment*, introduction, I, IV, V (V, 239 ff., 248 ff.) (*Ak.* V, 171 ff., 179 ff.).

faculties of cognition, so as to render possible a system of experience under particular laws of nature. But we do not thereby assert that this forces us really to postulate such an understanding; rather, the judgment in this case legislates only for itself, not for nature, since it is mapping a course for its own reflections. One cannot ascribe to the products of nature themselves anything like the relation to ends (even to the ends of thoroughly systematic understandability); this concept is only useful in reflecting on that relation in respect to the interconnection of appearances given under empirical laws. The judgment thus has in itself an a priori principle for the possibility of nature, but only in a subjective respect, whereby it does not legislate for nature as autonomous but for itself as heautonomous. "So when it is said that Nature specifies its universal laws on a principle of finality for our cognitive faculties, i.e., of suitability for the human understanding and its necessary function of finding the universal for the particular presented to it by perception, and again for varieties . . . connexion in the unity of principle, we do not thereby either prescribe a law to Nature, or learn one from it by observation—although the principle in question may be confirmed by this means. For it is not a principle of the determinant but merely of the reflective judgment. All that is intended is that, no matter what is the order and disposition of Nature in respect of its universal laws, we must investigate its empirical laws throughout on that principle and the maxims founded thereon, because only so far as that principle applies can we make any headway in the employment of our understanding in experience, or gain knowledge."[14]

The contrast in the two methods is now sharply and unmistakably indicated. Speculative metaphysics tries to account for the individual formation of nature as arising from something universal that progressively specifies itself; the critical perspective is unable to say anything about any such self-unfolding of the Absolute as a real process, but rather, where metaphysics discovers a final solution, it sees only a question that we must needs put to nature, with the ongoing reply necessarily left to experience. There can be whole ranges of experi-

---

14. *Critique of Judgment*, introduction, V (V, 250–55) (*Ak.* V, 181–86).

ence (and there undoubtedly are such in each of its incompleted phases) within which this requirement is not yet fulfilled, thus where the given particular is not yet truly fused with the conceptual universal but the two confront each other as still relatively disparate. In a case like this, the judgment cannot simply impress its principle on experience, it cannot force order on the empirical material and interpret it at its own whim. It can and will assert just one thing: that simply because the problem is unsolved, it should not be taken as insoluble. Its effort at the continuous reconciliation of individual things with the particular and the universal is never-ending and is not dependent on occasional success, because this is not an effort undertaken arbitrarily but one undeniably based on an essential function of reason itself.

And here the logical technic of nature which we have discovered now points to the deeper and more comprehensive question that completes the overall orientation of the *Critique of Judgment.* If we regard nature in reflective judgment as if it specified its general basic laws so that they combine in a thoroughly comprehensible hierarchy of empirical concepts, it is regarded as *art.* The idea of the "nomothetic by transcendental laws of the understanding" that constitutes the special key for the deduction of the categories no longer suffices here, because the new standpoint that now emerges validates its right not as law but only as presupposition.[15] But now, how is the state of affairs which hereby appears from the substantive, objective side to be presented subjectively; how is the grasp of that specific "artistic" peculiarity of the laws of nature to be consciously expressed and mirrored forth? We must needs pose this question, for by the basic methodical ideas of the critical doctrine it is firmly established that each of its problems is susceptible of such a double aspect and indeed cries out for it. As the unity of space and time can equally well be called unity of pure intuition, and as the unity of the object of experience is simultaneously that of transcendental apperception, here too we may expect that for the new substantive determination the idea of the technic of nature has simultaneously revealed a corresponding

15. See *Critique of Judgment,* first introduction, V (V, 196) (*Ak.* XX, 215).

new function of consciousness. But the answer Kant gives to this question is very surprising and striking. For the psychological content to which he now points is precisely that which in all the preceding consideration—in the *Critique of Pure Reason* and even more sharply and energetically in the *Critique of Practical Reason*—had been designated as the sole example of a content not determinable according to laws and hence in no way objectifiable. The subjective expression of every purposiveness that we encounter in the order of appearance is the feeling of pleasure that is connected with it. Wherever we detect an agreement for which no sufficient reason can be found in the general laws of the understanding, but which proves to be necessary for the whole of our cognitive powers and their coordinated use, there we accompany this demand, which falls to our lot equally as a free benefit, with a sensation of pleasure. We feel ourselves—just as if in this sort of structural consonance of the substance of experience it were a matter of a lucky accident which was favorable to our way of looking at things—rejoicing in it and "relieved of a want." The universal laws of nature, of which the basic laws of mechanics can serve as a model, do not carry such an agreement with themselves. For the same is true of them as of purely mathematical relationships: wonder over them ceases the moment we have grasped their exceptionless, strictly deducible necessity.

"But it is contingent, so far as we can see, that the order of Nature in its particular laws, with their wealth of at least possible variety and heterogeneity transcending all our powers of comprehension, should still in actual fact be commensurate with these powers. To find out this order is an undertaking on the part of our understanding, which pursues it with a regard to a necessary end of its own, that, namely, of introducing into Nature unity of principle. . . .The attainment of every aim is coupled with a feeling of pleasure. Now where such attainment has for its condition a representation a priori—as here a principle for the reflective judgment in general—the feeling of pleasure also is determined by a ground which is a priori and valid for all men. . . .As a matter of fact, we do not, and cannot, find in ourselves the slightest effect on the feeling of pleasure from the coincidence of perceptions with the laws in accordance with the universal concepts of Nature (the Categories), since in their case understanding necessarily follows the bent of its own nature without ulterior aim. But while this is so, the discovery, on the other hand, that two or more empirical heterogeneous laws of Nature are allied under one principle that embraces them both, is the ground of a very appreciable pleasure. . . . It is true that we no longer notice any decided pleasure in the comprehensibility of Nature, or in the unity of its divisions into genera and species, without which the empirical concepts, that afford us our knowledge of Nature in its particular laws, would not be possible. Still it is certain that the pleasure appeared in due course, and only by reason of the most ordinary experience being impossible without it, has it become gradually fused with simple cognition, and no longer arrests particular attention. . . . As against this a representation of Nature would be altogether displeasing to us, were we to be forewarned by it that, on the least investigation carried beyond the commonest experience, we should come into contact with such a heterogeneity of its laws as would make the union of its particular laws under universal empirical laws impossible for our understanding. For this would conflict with the principle of the subjectively final specification of Nature in its genera and with our own reflective judgment in respect thereof."[16]

In these Kantian sentences we hew first and foremost to that path which makes them meaningful and striking in the methodical sense. Pleasure, which heretofore had been reckoned as totally empirical, is now included in the domain of that which can be determined and known a priori; previously regarded as completely private and arbitrary, something wherein each subject differs from the other, it now contains—at least in one of its fundamental moments—a universal significance for everyone. The principle of transcendental critique is in this way applied to a realm which up to now it seemed to exclude. The first edition of the *Critique of Pure Reason* had stigmatized the hope of the "admirable analyst Baumgarten" to achieve a scientifically based "critique of taste" as abortive, because the elements of aesthetic liking and disliking consist in pleasure and pain; these stem

16. *Critique of Judgment*, introduction, V and VI (V, 253–57) (*Ak.* V, 184–88).

from purely empirical sources, however, and hence could never furnish a priori laws.[17] This outlook is now revised: the peculiar thing
about this revision, however, is that it is not the direct consideration
of the phenomenon of art and artistic creation that leads to it, but a
step forward in the critique of theoretical knowledge. An extension
and deepening of the concept of the a priori in theory first makes
possible the a priori in aesthetics and paves the way for its determination and perfection. Because it has been shown that the condition of
the universal laws of the understanding is necessary but not sufficient
for the complete form of experience; because a singular form and a
singular teleological connection of the particular was discovered,
which in its turn first completed the systematic concept of experience,
a moment of consciousness is sought on which the lawfulness of the
particular and contingent is stamped. If this moment is found, however, the limits of the inquiry thus far have been pushed back. It no
longer stops short at the question of the individual, since it treats the
individual as that which changes from case to case and hence is determinable by nothing except immediate particular experience and by
the material factor of sensation—but it seeks to discover even in this
formerly blocked-off realm the basic moments of a priori creation.

By this route Kant transcends the purely logical theory of empirical concept formation and the question of the critical conditions of a
system and classification of natural forms, and arrives at the
threshold of critical aesthetics.[18] Here the concept of a technic of

17. *Critique of Pure Reason,* Transcendental Aesthetic, §1, A 21 = B 35 (III, 56 f.).
18. Kant's well-known letter to Reinhold is to be taken in this sense, which sheds
light on the origin of the *Critique of Judgment.* Here Kant writes, on December 28, 1787:
"I may without being guilty of conceit, assert that the longer I persevere on my road the
less concerned I become that a contradiction or even an alliance (which is nothing out of
the ordinary nowadays) might be capable of doing my system some grave injury. This
is an inward conviction which grows on me since in my progress to other endeavors I
not only find myself always consistent, but also, when I occasionally do not know just
how to apply my method of investigation to something, I need only look back over that
general list of the elements of knowledge and the mental powers belonging to them, to
arrive at conclusions I had not foreseen. I am now busy with the critique of taste, which
has been the opportunity to discover another sort of a priori principles from the previous ones. For there are three capacities of the mind: the faculty of knowledge, the
feeling of pleasure and pain, and the faculty of desire. For the first, I found the a priori

nature is mediated from the objective side, the transcendental psychological analysis of the feeling of pleasure and pain from the subjective side. We saw already that nature, insofar as it is thought as specified in its types and varieties according to a principle that can be grasped by our judgment, is here regarded as art, but this ingenious analysis, taken by itself, at the same time appears "artistic."[19] This is true so far as it does not disclose itself immediately to the ordinary consciousness and has to be elicited by a special application of the epistemological consideration. The average human understanding takes the stability and the systematic subordination and superordination of the laws of nature as given facts that call for no explanation. But precisely for that reason, because it sees no problem here, it overlooks the solution of the problem and the specific feeling of pleasure that is connected with it. Thus if nature revealed nothing but this logical purposiveness, this would be grounds for amazement, "but hardly anyone but a transcendental philosopher would be capable of this astonishment, and even he could cite no determinate case where

principles in the critique of pure (theoretical) reason, for the third in the critique of practical reason. I sought also for those of the second, and although I used to think it impossible to find them, the *systematization* which permitted me to discover the analysis of the above faculties and which yields me enough material to marvel at and, if possible, to investigate for the rest of my life, set me on this road, so that I now recognize three parts of philosophy, each of which has its a priori principles, which can be enumerated and the range of knowledge possible in each mode determined: theoretical philosophy, teleology, and practical philosophy. Of these, the middle one is found to be the poorest in a priori grounds of determination" (IX, 343) (*Ak*. IV, 487). If these declarations by Kant are taken not only in a superficial, literal sense, but also if one combines them with what the *Critique of Judgment* itself tells us about the actual connection of the problems in Kant's mind, no doubt can remain as to which role "systematization" played in the discovery of critical aesthetics. Kant has not contrived a third thing in addition to the two already existing a priori principles for the sake of symmetry; it was an extension and a keener comprehension of the concept of apriority itself that came to him on what were basically theoretical grounds—in the idea of the logical "adequation" of Nature to our cognitive faculties. But in this the consideration of ends in general—or, to put it from the transcendental psychological point of view, the realm of pleasure and pain—had been shown to him to be a possible object of a priori determination, and the trail led on further from this point, ultimately to the winning of the a priori foundation of *aesthetics* as a part of a system of universal teleology.

19. Cf. *Critique of Judgment*, first introduction, V (V, 196) (*Ak*. XX, 215).

this purposiveness is manifested *in concreto*, but would have to think it only in the universal."[20] In this limitation of the previous results there is also clearly indicated the direction wherein their systematic development and growth must be looked for. Is there, we must ask, a purposive form of appearances which is not disclosed to us only through the mediation of the concept and of transcendental reflection, but instead speaks directly to us in the feeling of pleasure and pain? Is there an individual configuration of being, a union of phenomena, which presents to the world of pure and empirical thinking an unknowable singularity and hence is in no way to be grasped by the methods of classification and systematization in scientific laws—and yet which displays an independent and fundamental lawfulness of its own? When we pose these two questions we are led directly to the point at which the metaphorical sense of art, as we encounter it in the concept of a technic of nature, goes beyond the special sense, and at which the system of universal teleology assimilates into itself the critique of aesthetic judgment as its most important member.

4

As the question of individual formation brought about the transition from the universe of the pure laws of the understanding to the world of particular laws, so the same question can also serve as an intimate and direct introduction into the basic problems of critical aesthetics. For the realm of art is a realm of pure forms, each of which is complete in itself and possesses its own individual center, while it simultaneously belongs together with other things in a peculiar unity of natures and effects. How can this interconnection of essences be shown, and how can it be expressed and characterized so as not to lose the independent individual quality and the life of the particular form? In the domain of pure theory and in that of practical, moral reason we have no truly appropriate and distinctive model for such a fundamental relation. The "individual" of theory is always but the special case of a

20. Ibid., V (V, 197).

general law, from which it derives its meaning and its truth value, just as the individual as a moral subject, from the basic viewpoint of Kantian ethics, is regarded only as the bearer of the universally valid precepts of practical reason. The free personality becomes what it is only in the full sacrifice of its contingent impulses and inclinations and in unconditional subordination to the universally governing and universally binding rules of obligation. In both cases the individual seems to find its true basis and justification only by being taken up into the universal. Only in artistic intuition does a completely new relationship in this matter emerge. The work of art is something singular and apart, which is its own basis and has its goal purely within itself, and yet at the same time in it we are presented with a new whole, and a new image of reality and of the mental cosmos itself. Here the individual does not point to an abstract universal that stands behind it, but it is this universal itself, because it comprises its substance symbolically in itself.

We saw how, in the theoretical scientific consideration of the concept of a whole of experience, the further critical insight progresses the more clearly it manifests itself as an unfulfillable demand. Insistence on comprehending the entire universe in thought led us into the midst of the dialectical antinomies of the concept of infinity. We are to conceive this whole not as given but only as proposed; it is not put before us as an object having a fixed form and delimitation, but dissolves into an unlimited process, of which we can determine the direction but not the goal. In this sense every theoretical judgment of experience necessarily remains a fragment; it recognizes its fragmentary nature as soon as it has achieved critical clarity about itself. Each member of the experiential series, in order to be scientifically conceived, requires yet another, which as its "cause" determines its fixed spatiotemporal location; but this other one in its turn succumbs to the same dependence, so that it has to seek its ground once more outside of itself. As element is joined to element, series to series, in this way, the object of experience which itself is nothing but a nexus of relations, is built up for us. A totally different sort of connection of the individual to the whole, of the manifold to unity is presented to us, however, when we proceed from the datum of art and artistic creation. The datum itself we presuppose in this case—as everywhere in the transcendental inquiry. We do not ask whether it is, but how it may be; we do not move toward its historical or psychological origin, but seek to understand its pure existence and the conditions of this existence. In so doing we necessarily see ourselves guided to a new form of judgment; for every connection between contents of consciousness, objectively grasped, expresses itself as a judgment. But the judgment itself has here outgrown the confines of its heretofore purely logical definition. It is no longer a matter of the subordination of the particular to the universal or the mere application of a universal cognition to the particular, as was taught in the *Critique of Pure Reason* (principally in the chapter on the schematism of the concepts of the understanding) as the feature of the determining judgment; instead a completely different type of relation is presented. This type must be positively described and differentiated from all other syntheses of consciousness if the special character of this new range of problems is to emerge distinctly.

But before this differentiation is carried out in detail, it is worthwhile keeping vividly in mind that we are not erasing the unity of the function of judgment and the essential critical insights we have achieved concerning it. Every judgment is for Kant an act not of receptivity but of pure spontaneity; insofar as it possesses true a priori validity it does not present a mere relation to given objects, but it is the positing of objects themselves. In this sense there exists then an essential opposition between Kant's "aesthetic judgment" and what German aesthetics of the eighteenth century called "critical power" and had tried to analyze. This critical power begins with given works of "taste" and intends to show how to move from them, by analysis and comparison, to general rules and criteria of taste. Kant's viewpoint, on the contrary, achieves its end in the opposite movement: it does not wish to abstract the rules from any sort of given objects—in this case from given examples and models—but it inquires about the basic lawfulness of consciousness, on which every aesthetic perception and every designation of an item of nature or art as beautiful or ugly rests. Thus for this view that which is already formed is only the standpoint from which it strives to reach the conditions of the possibility of creation itself. These conditions can in the main be designated only negatively, since in that way we determine less what they are than what they are not. The fact that the unity of aesthetic harmony and aesthetic form rests on a principle different from the one authorizing us to combine particular elements in common and scientific experience into complex wholes and under integrated rules has already been shown. This latter unification is in the last analysis always a matter of a relation of causal superordination and subordination, of the exposition of an unbroken coherence of conditions, which can be conceived as the analogue of a connection between premises and conclusions. One experience is joined to another in a kind of dependency relation, in which both relate to each other as ground and consequent. The aesthetic grasp of a whole and its individual partial moments, on the other hand, excludes this kind of view. Here the appearance is not dissolved into its conditions, but it is affirmed as it is immediately given to us; here we do not become swamped in conceptual grounds or consequences, but we stay with the thing itself, surrendering ourselves to the impression that pure contemplation of it arouses. Instead of analysis into parts, and their superordination and subordination for the purpose of a conceptual classification, here it is proper to grasp them all together and unify them in an overall perspective for our imagination; in place of the effects, through which they link into the causal chain of appearances and are prolonged therein, we focus on the value of their sheer presence as it is disclosed to intuition itself.

This indicates the difference dividing aesthetic consciousness from practical consciousness, the world of pure form from that of will and act. As the theoretical point of view dissolves the existent into a nexus of causes and effects, of conditions and limitations, so the practical point of view dissolves it into a web of ends and means. The given manifold of content is thereby determined and structured so that in the first case an element is there through the other, in the second for the sake of the other. In pure aesthetic contemplation, on the other hand, all this kind of decomposition of the content into correlative parts and contrasts falls away. The content here appears in that qualitative perfection which requires no external completion, no ground or goal lying outside itself, and it brooks no such addition. The aesthetic consciousness possesses in itself that form of concrete realization through which, wholly abandoned to its temporary passivity, it grasps in this very fleeting passivity a factor of purely timeless meaning. The "before" and "after" that we objectify conceptually in the idea of the causal relation and shape into the empirical time sequence and time order, are here blotted out and brought to a standstill equally with that foresight and aiming at a goal which characterizes our desire and willing. And thus we have in hand the essential and decisive moments that are fused in Kant's definition of the beautiful. If we style as "pleasant" what is attractive and pleasing to the senses in the act of sensation, if we call "good" what pleases on the basis of a rule of obligation, thus by means of reason through the concept alone, so we designate as beautiful what pleases in "mere contemplation." In this expression, "mere contemplation," is indirectly included everything making up the special nature of the aesthetic perception in general, and from it all further determinations which the aesthetic judgment may reveal are deducible.

Here we have thrust upon us a question which, with regard to method, is the counterpart and the necessary completion of the previous result. If up to this point the task was to designate the special quality of the aesthetic perception, now it is, conversely, a matter of establishing unambiguously the mode of objectivity of the aesthetic object. For each function of consciousness, however it may be constituted in detail, reveals an orientation toward the object belonging to it alone and giving it a special stamp. Once again in this connection there emerges a negative determination: the objectivity of the aesthetic content is totally divorced from actuality, as the latter is posited in empirical judgment or pursued in empirical desiring. The satisfaction that determines the judgment of taste is devoid of all interest, interest being understood as interest in the existence of the thing, in the production or existence of the object contemplated.

"If anyone asks me whether I consider that the palace I see before me is beautiful, I may, perhaps, reply that I do not care for things of that sort that are merely made to be gaped at. Or I may reply in the same strain as that Iroquois sachem who said that nothing in Paris pleased him better than the eating-houses. I may even go a step further and inveigh with the vigor of a Rousseau against the vanity of the great who spend the sweat of the people on such superfluous things. Or, in fine, I may quite easily persuade myself that if I found myself on an uninhabited island, without hope of ever again coming among men, and could conjure such a palace into existence by a mere wish, I should still not trouble to do so, so long as I had a hut there that was comfortable enough for me. All this may be admitted and approved; only it is not the point now at issue. All one wants to know is whether the mere representation of the object is to my liking, no matter how indifferent I may be to the real existence of the object of this representation. It is quite plain that in order to say that the object *is beautiful*, and to show that I have taste, everything turns on the meaning which I can give to this representation, and not on any factor which makes me dependent on the real existence of the object. Everyone must allow that a judgment on the beautiful which is tinged with the slightest interest, is very partial and not a pure judgment of taste. One must not be in the least prepossessed in favor of the real existence of the thing, but must preserve complete indifference in this respect, in order to play the part of judge in matters of taste."[21] The peculiarity of aesthetic self-activity, and hence the special nature of aesthetic subjectivity, come forward clearly at this point. The logical spontaneity of the understanding concerns the determination of the object of appearance through universal laws; ethical autonomy issues from the spring of the free personality, but it wants nonetheless to introduce the demands thus grounded into the empirically given things and states of affairs and to actualize them therein. The aesthetic function alone does not ask what the object may be and do, but rather what I make of its representation in me. The actual retreats to its real status, and into its place steps ideal determination and ideal unity of the pure image.

In this sense—but only in this sense—the aesthetic world is a world of appearance. The concept of appearance is intended only to ward off the false notion of an actuality which would precipitate us

21. *Critique of Aesthetic Judgment*, §2 (V, 273) (*Ak*. V, 204–05).

once again into the machinations of the theoretical concept of nature or the practical concept of reason. It elevates the beautiful above the sphere of causality—for freedom is also a special kind of causality for Kant—so as to place it purely under the rule of inner creation. The latter also legislates for appearance—because appearance receives from it the essential connection of its separate moments. As in every situation where we apply the contrast of subjective and objective, here too it is valid to specify this opposition sharply and carefully, so as to avoid the dialectic concealed in it. Leaving out of account the existence of the thing is precisely the characteristic and essential reality of the aesthetic representation. For it is just this way that it becomes the intuition of pure form, in leaving out of consideration all the associated conditions and consequences which unavoidably cling to the "thing." Where both are still mingled, where the interest in the structure of the form and its analysis still intersects with and is elbowed aside by interest in the actuality of it which is the image, the essential viewpoint which constitutes and is the hallmark of the aesthetic as such has not yet been attained.

The idea of purposiveness without purpose, by which Kant designates and circumscribes the whole ambit of the aesthetic, is now divested of the final paradox that clung to it. For purposiveness means, as has been shown, nothing other than individual creation, which displays a unified form in itself and in its structure, while purpose means the external determination which is allotted to it. A purposive creation has its center of gravity in itself; one that is goal-oriented has its center external to itself; the worth of the one resides in its being, that of the other in its results. The sole function of the concept of "disinterested pleasure" is to bring this state of affairs, considered subjectively, into thought. Hence the essential sense of this central concept is missed when—as has happened—Kant's aesthetic ideal is designated as "indolent repose" and therefore Herder's and Schiller's dynamic ideal of beauty, which takes beauty to be a "living form," is thought to be opposed to it.[22] The Kantian insis-

22. See Robert Sommer, *Grundzüge einer Geschichte der deutschen Psychologie und Aesthetik* (Würzburg, 1892), pp. 296, 337 ff., 349.

tence on disregarding all interest leaves full and unhampered room for the activity of the imagination; only the activity of the will and the activity of sensory desire are routed from the threshold of the aesthetic on methodological grounds. Adherence to immediate attraction and immediate need is precisely rejected thereby, because it hems in and stifles that immediate life of the representation, that free figuration of the formative imagination which constitutes for Kant the special characteristic of the artistic. To this extent Kant in no way contradicts the "energetic" aesthetic of the eighteenth century, but as the focus of aesthetic interest has been shifted from the actuality of the thing to the actuality of the image, so the passive stimulation of the emotions is translated into the excitement of their pure play. In the freedom of this play the whole passionate inner excitement of emotion is conserved; but in it the play is separated from its purely material foundations. Hence in the last analysis it is not emotion itself, as an isolated psychological state, that is drawn into this arousal, but the elements of the play compose the universal basic functions of consciousness, from which each individual psychic content issues and to which it refers back. This universality explains the universal communicability of the aesthetic state, which we presuppose, since we ascribe to the judgment of taste a "validity for everyone," although we are incapable of conceptualizing the grounds of the validity thus asserted and of deducing it from concepts. The mental state of the aesthetic representation is that of "a feeling of the free play of the powers of representation on a given representation for a cognition in general."

"Now a representation, whereby an object is given, involves, in order that it may become a source of cognition at all, *imagination* for bringing together the manifold of intuition, and *understanding* for the unity of the concept uniting the representations. This state of *free play* of the cognitive faculties attending a representation by which an object is given must admit of universal communication: because cognition, as a definition of the Object with which given representations (in any Subject whatever) are to accord, is the one and only representation which is valid for everyone.

"As the subjective universal communicability of the mode of rep-

resentation in a judgment of taste is to subsist apart from the presupposition of any definite concept, it can be nothing else than the mental state present in the free play of imagination and understanding (so
far as these are in mutual accord, as is requisite for *cognition in general*): for we are conscious that this subjective relation suitable for a
cognition in general must be just as valid for every one, and consequently as universally communicable, as is any determinate cognition, which always rests upon that relation as its subjective condition."[23]

It seems indeed as though, with this explanation of the universal
communicability of the aesthetic state, we are again diverted from its
proper domain, for its separation from the sensory, private feeling of
pleasure and pain seems at bottom attainable only by once again
reentering the path of the logically objectifying way of thinking.
When the imagination and the understanding thus are unified, as is
requisite for a "cognition in general," it is the empirical use of the
productive imagination, as developed by the *Critique of Pure Reason*,
rather than its specifically aesthetic use that is thus explained. In fact,
according to a basic insight of that *Critique*, which is enlarged on in
particular in the chapter on the schematism of the pure concepts of
the understanding, even the spatiotemporal connection of the perceptions of the senses and their unification into objects of experience
rests precisely on cooperation between the understanding and the
imagination. The mutual determination of these two functions seems
to constitute no truly new relationship, such as we would expect and
demand as an explanatory ground for the new problem that appears
here. Yet we must take into consideration at this point the fact that
the earlier insight does receive a new emphasis. A specific unity of
knowledge is achieved for theoretical as well as for aesthetic representation; but if in the former the tone and emphasis lie on the factor
of knowledge, so in the latter they lie on the factor of unity. The
aesthetic relation is "purposive for the cognition of objects *in general*,"
but exactly thereby it renounces the sorting of objects into particular
classes, designating and defining them by particular differentiating

23. *Critique of Aesthetic Judgment,* §9 (V, 286 f.) (*Ak.* V, 217 f.).

characters as they are expressed in empirical concepts. The intuitive
unity of the form has no need of this ongoing discursive sorting. The
free process of imaging itself is not here tied down and confined by
reference to the objective existence of things, as we fix it through
scientific concepts and laws. On the other hand, of course, the role of
the understanding is recognizable in this creative activity of the imagination if the concept of the understanding itself is taken in a sense
above and beyond the exclusively logico-theoretical one. The understanding, in its most universal meaning, is the capacity of setting
limits; it is what arrests the steady activity of representation itself, and
facilitates its circumscription into a definite image. When this synthesis occurs, when we succeed in fixing the movement of the imagination this way, without making a detour via the conceptual abstractions of empirical thinking, so that the imagination does not get lost in
vagueness but crystallizes into solid forms and configurations, then
that harmonious interpenetration of both functions is achieved which
Kant calls for as a basic moment of the genuine aesthetic attitude.

For now understanding and intuition are no longer in opposition
as things totally dissimilar, so that they have to be brought together
through the agency of a foreign mediator and conjoined through a
cunning schematism, but they are truly blended and absorbed in each
other. The capacity for specification acts directly in the actual course
of imaging and beholding, since it articulates and vivifies the flowing,
ever-constant series of images. In the empirical judgment of subsumption a determinate individual intuition is related to a determinate concept and subordinated to it, as, for instance, the curvature of
the table that we see before us is related to the geometric concept of a
circle and cognized through the latter.[24] Nothing like this is found in
aesthetic consciousness. For here the individual concept and the individual intuition do not stand in contrast to each other; it is rather a
question of harmonizing the *function* of the understanding and that of
beholding. The free play that is required concerns not representation
but the powers of representation; not the results in which intuition
and understanding are made concrete and in which they both come to

24. See *Critique of Pure Reason*, A 137 = B 176 (III, 141).

rest, but rather the living excitation that occupies them. In this way every utterance of this sort, wherein a particular image is not compared with a particular concept but rather the totality of the powers of the mind first is disclosed in its true completeness, lays hold immediately of the "life-feeling" of the very subject. "To apprehend a regular and appropriate building," it is remarked in the opening of the *Critique of Aesthetic Judgment*, "with one's cognitive faculties, be the mode of representation clear or confused, is quite a different thing from being conscious of this representation with an accompanying sensation of delight. Here the representation is referred wholly to the Subject, and what is more to its feeling of life—under the name of the feeling of pleasure or displeasure—and this forms the basis of a quite separate faculty of discriminating and estimating, that contributes nothing to knowledge. All it does is to compare the given representation in the Subject with the entire faculty of representations of which the mind is conscious in the feeling of its state."[25] In empirical theoretical judgment the individual experience that is present to me is held up to the system of experiences (actual or possible) and its objective truth value is only determined through this comparison; in the aesthetic situation the present individual intuition or the present impression brings the whole of the perceiving and representing powers into direct resonance. If, then, the unity of experience and its object must be built up by the labor of concept formation, line by line, and element by element, the perfected work of art in one stroke presents that unity of mood which is for us the unmediated expression of the unity of our ego, of our concrete feeling of life and self.

This new relation set up between the singular and the universal holds the exact key to the solution of the problem of what form of universality is to be ascribed to aesthetic judgment. That it must contain some sort of universality has been already settled, so far as Kant is concerned, through the connection in which he approaches the basic question of aesthetics, for it is in consolidating and deepening his concept of the a priori that he first encounters the problem of aesthetic judgment. At the same time, however, the behavior of ordinary con-

25. *Critique of Aesthetic Judgment*, §1 (V, 272) (Ak. V, 204).

sciousness affords direct confirmation of the claim to universal validity made by the judgment of taste. In what concerns judgment about
the pleasant in sensation, everyone is reconciled to the fact that,
because it is founded on a private feeling, it is confined to himself.
The situation is the reverse with the beautiful. "It would... be
ridiculous if any one who plumed himself on his taste were to think of
justifying himself by saying: This object (the building we see, the
dress that person has on, the concert we hear, the poem submitted to
our criticism) is beautiful *for me*. For if it merely pleases *him*, he must
not call it *beautiful*. Many things may for him possess charm and
agreeableness—no one cares about that; but when he puts a thing on
a pedestal and calls it beautiful, he demands the same delight from
others. He judges not merely for himself, but for all men, and then
speaks of beauty as if it were a property of things. Thus he says the
thing is beautiful; and it is not as if he counted on others agreeing in
his judgment of liking owing to his having found them in such
agreement on a number of occasions, but he *demands* this agreement
of them. He blames them if they judge differently, and denies them
taste, which he still requires of them as something they ought to have;
and to this extent it is not open to men to say: Every one has his own
taste. This would be equivalent to saying that there is no such thing at
all as taste, i.e., no aesthetic judgment capable of making a rightful
claim upon the assent of all men."[26]

And yet this pure value claim of the aesthetic is not interchangeable with its demonstrability from concepts alone, as was virtually
universally assumed in the German aesthetics of the Enlightenment
(Gottsched and the Swiss, for example, agree on this point). At this
juncture the critical task consists rather in the insight as to the possibility of universality, which nonetheless spurns mediation by means
of logical concepts. Now it was shown above that in and through
aesthetic harmony an immediate relation of the contingently given
individual content of consciousness to the totality of the powers of the
mind is established. The aesthetic state concerns the subject and his
life-feeling exclusively, but it takes this feeling not in an isolated and

26. Ibid., §7 (V, 281 ff.) (*Ak.* V, 212 ff.).

to that extent contingent moment, but rather in the ensemble of its moments. Only where this resonance of the whole in the particular and singular is present are we immersed in the freedom of play and experience this freedom. But only with this experience do we attain the full estate of subjectivity itself. In the case of sensory perception the individual ego has no way to communicate it to another ego other than by transposing it into the sphere of the objective and defining it therein. The color that I see, the tone that I hear is presented as the joint possession of the knowing subjects, since by applying the basic principles of extensive and intensive magnitude and the categories of substance and causality, which are exactly knowable and measurable, both are translated into vibrations. But with this translation into the spheres of number and measure that is a condition of scientific objectification, color and tone as such have ceased to exist; their being in the theoretical sense is absorbed into the reality and the lawfulness of motion. If this is done, however, the method of universal communication, as practiced in the theoretical concept, has really made the content to be communicated vanish, to be replaced by a mere abstract symbol. The fact that color and tone, besides what they mean as physical elements, are also experiences in a perceiving and feeling subject is completely eliminated from this way of determining them. Here the problem of aesthetic consciousness comes in. This consciousness asserts that there is a universal communicability from subject to subject, which thus does not need to detour through the conceptually objective and be swallowed up in it. In the phenomenon of the beautiful the inconceivable thing happens, that in contemplating beauty every subject remains in itself and is immersed purely in its own inner state, while at the same time it is absolved of all contingent particularity and knows itself to be the bearer of a total feeling which no longer belongs to "this" or "that."

Only now do we understand the expression "subjective universality" that Kant coins as the mark of the aesthetic judgment. "Subjective universality" is the assertion and requirement of a universality of subjectivity itself. The designation "subjective" does not act to restrict the claim to validity made by the aesthetic, but just the opposite: it designates an enlargement of the realm of validity, which is here perfected. Universality is not prevented by the individuality of the subject, for as it is true that the subjects have their life not only in passive sensory perceptions or in pathological desires, but can stimulate themselves to the free play of the representational powers, it is equally true that in such activity they employ one and the same essential basic function. In this functioning, which first properly makes the self into a self, every ego is akin to every other, and hence the function may be assumed in each other. The artistic feeling remains a feeling of self, but precisely as such it is at the same time a universal feeling of the world and life. The "self" detaches itself from its individuality when it objectifies itself in a construction of aesthetic fantasy; its individual unique stimulation is nevertheless not destroyed in this construction, but rather dwells powerfully in it and is communicated to all those who are capable of grasping it. Thus the subject is placed in a universal medium, one which however is something completely different from the medium of reification into which the natural scientific way of contemplation plunges us. What differentiates the most complete description of a landscape resulting from concepts of descriptive natural science from its artistic presentation in a painting or a lyric poem? Only that in the latter all the features of the object, the sharper and more clearly they stand out, prove even more intensely to be features of a psychic excitation, communicated to the beholder through the graphic or lyrical construction. Here the inner passion flows out into the object only to be received back from it in a stronger and purer form. As the self in a state of aesthetic contemplation does not just remain attached to its contingent representation, but in Kant's expression "holds it up against the whole faculty of representation," a new cosmos is revealed to it, which is not the system of objectivity but the whole of subjectivity. In this whole it finds itself also to be an individuality closed to all others. In this way aesthetic consciousness solves the paradoxical task of presenting a universal which is not contrary to the individual but which is its pure correlate, because it finds its fulfillment and embodiment in it alone.

And in this way the question of universal communicability—which is not universal demonstrability—is also answered. Since in the aesthetic attitude the judge feels himself to be fully free in respect to the pleasure he centers on the object, he can discover, as grounds of this pleasure, no private conditions on which its subject might depend and must therefore regard it as grounded in what can be presupposed of everyone else; consequently, he must believe that he can justifiably attribute to everyone a similar pleasure. "Accordingly he will speak of the beautiful as if beauty were a quality of the object and the judgment logical (forming a cognition of the Object by concepts of it); although it is only aesthetic, and contains merely a reference of the representation of the object to the Subject;—because it still bears this resemblance to the logical judgment, that it may be presupposed to be valid for all men. But this universality cannot spring from concepts. . . . Here, now, we may perceive that nothing is postulated in the judgment of taste but such a *universal voice* in respect of delight that is not mediated by concepts; consequently, only the *possibility* of an aesthetic judgment capable of being at the same time deemed valid for every one. The judgment of taste itself does not *postulate* the agreement of every one (for it is only competent for a logically universal judgment to do this, in that it is able to bring forward reasons); it only *imputes* this agreement to every one, as an instance of the rule in respect of which it looks for confirmation, not from concepts, but from the concurrence of others."[27]

Hence Kant has arrived at the principal question standing at the crossroads of all aesthetic discussions in the eighteenth century by a new route and in a completely different systematic connection. Is a rule to be abstracted from given works of art, from classical prototypes and models, which prescribes specific objective limits to creation—or does the freedom of the imagination, which is bound to no external norm, reign here? Is there a conceptually determinable law of artistic creation, from which one cannot depart if its goal is not to be aborted—or is everything ceded to the creative will of the gifted subject, which moves from an unknown beginning to an unknown end? These questions, which recur in the aesthetic doctrines of the eighteenth century in the most diverse forms, were brought to a

27. Ibid., §§6, 8 (V, 280, 285) (*Ak.* V, 211, 216).

sharp and clear dialectical formulation in the area of literary criticism by Lessing. The struggle between genius and rule, between imagination and reason—so run the decisive discussions of the *Hamburg Dramaturgy*—is pointless, for the creation of genius receives no rule from outside, but it is this rule itself. In it is shrouded an inner lawfulness and purposiveness, which, however, appears and leaves its imprint nowhere else than in the concrete and individual art form itself. Kant unhesitatingly adheres to this conclusion of Lessing's, but it now guides him back into the whole depth and universality of the questions that for him are comprised in the idea of the self-legislation of the spirit. "Genius"—thus he even defines it—"is the talent (natural gift) which gives the rule to art. . . .For every art presupposes rules which are laid down as the foundation which first enables a product, if it is to be called one of art, to be represented as possible. The concept of fine art, however, does not permit of the judgment upon the beauty of its product being derived from any rule that has a *concept* for its determining ground. . . .Consequently fine art cannot of its own self excogitate the rule according to which it is to effectuate its product. But since, for all that, a product can never be called art unless there is a preceding rule, it follows that nature in the individual (and by virtue of the harmony of his faculties) must give the rule to art, i.e., fine art is only possible as a product of genius."[28]

Thus the unity of the harmony precedes the objective unity of the form. Genius and its act stand at the point where supreme individuality and supreme universality, freedom and necessity, pure creation and pure lawfulness indissolubly coalesce. In every line of its activity it is thoroughly original but nonetheless thoroughly exemplary. For just where we stand in the true focus of personality, where the latter gives itself purely without any external consideration and expresses itself in the individually necessary law of its creating, all the accidental limitations clinging to the individual in his particular empirical existence and his particular empirical interests fall away. In its immersion in this unadornedly personal sphere genius finds the secret and the power of universal communicability, and each great work of art

---

28. Ibid., §46 (V, 382) (*Ak.* V, 307).

presents nothing but the objectification of this basic power. As a temporally unique psychic event, never recurring in the same way, the work of genius testifies straightforwardly and unambiguously how the most intimate subjective feeling at the same time reaches down into the deepest sphere of pure validity and timeless necessity. And this highest form of communication is also the only one which is at the disposal of genius. Were genius to try to speak to us elsewhere than in the immediate creation of its work, it would have precisely in that act cut itself off from the soil in which it is rooted. Hence what it is and what it signifies, as a "natural gift," cannot be expressed in a general formula and thus put forward as a prescription; the rule must, so far as it does exist, be abstracted from the act, that is, from the product, which serves as an example not for imitation but for comparable creation. Herein Lessing's saying that a genius can only be kindled by a genius is also taken up by Kant. "The artist's ideas arouse like ideas on the part of his pupil, presuming nature to have visited him with a like proportion of mental powers." It is this "proportion" which is the characteristic generative motive in the creation of genius.

And from this aspect artistic productivity can also be differentiated from scientific productivity. Kant's assertion that there can be no genius in the sciences[29] can only be rightly evaluated if one keeps in mind that in this discussion it is for him always a matter of the systematic difference of meaning of these two cultural realms, not of the psychological difference of individuals. Whether the scientific discoverer may not also make "one case stand for a thousand," whether along with the discursive comparison of individual things an intuitive anticipation of the whole may not also be possible and actual: these are questions about which nothing can be decided at this point. The decisive difference lies solely in that everything which pretends to be scientific insight, as soon as it is to be communicated and established, possesses no form for this save that of the objective concept and objective deduction. The personality of the creator must be expunged if the accuracy of the result is to be protected. Only in the great artist

29. See ibid., §47 (V, 383 f.) (*Ak.* V, 308 f.).

is this division nonexistent, for everything he gives is endowed with its peculiar and supreme value only through what he is. He does not alienate himself in any work which then continues to exist as an isolated thing of value in itself, but in each particular work he creates a new symbolic expression of that univocal basic relation given in his "nature," in the "proportion of his mental powers."

Considered historically, this Kantian doctrine of genius signifies the achievement of a reconciliation between two diverse spiritual worlds, for it shares a crucial motive with the fundamental outlook of the Enlightenment, while on the other hand it shatters the conceptual schema of the philosophy of the Enlightenment from within. Kant's theory of genius became the historical point of departure for all those romantic, speculative developments of the concept of genius that attributed significance to the productive aesthetic imagination as begetter of the world and reality. Schelling's theory of intellectual intuition as the basic transcendental faculty, Friedrich Schlegel's theory of the ego and of "irony" were developed along this line. However, what distinguishes Kant's own view once and for all from these attempts is the form and the direction of his concept of the a priori. That his a priorism is a critical one is further manifested in that the a priori is not traced back to one single basic metaphysical power of consciousness but is firmly kept within the strict particularity of its specific applications. Thus the concept of "reason," as it was evolved by the eighteenth century, is for Kant expanded into the deeper concept of "spontaneity" of consciousness, but he does not regard the latter as exhausted in any finished work and activity of consciousness. It is impossible for the aesthetic spontaneity of fantasy here to become, as it did in romanticism, the final founding and unifying principle, since the essential intention aims at differentiating it strictly and decisively from the logical spontaneity of judgment and from the ethical spontaneity of will. The whole scale of degrees of subjectivity and objectivity which Kant sets forth, and which receives its most important completion and its essential conclusion only in the *Critique of Judgment*, subserves this task above all. The being of the laws of nature, the ought of the moral law, should not be abandoned in favor of the

play of the imagination, but on the other hand this play is in possession of its own autonomous realm into which no conceptual demand
and no moral imperative may intrude.

The essential meaning of the restriction of the concept of genius to
art lies in assisting this thought to its clear expression. The concept of
the "sciences of the beautiful" had won a dangerous importance and
degree of dissemination in the second half of the eighteenth century.
Sterner, more profound minds, like Lambert—who expressed himself
on the topic in a letter to Kant in 1765[30]—never tired of opposing
this by demanding exact conceptual definition as the foundation
of all scientific knowledge, but the muddling together of the realms
nonetheless remains the characteristic mark of popular philosophy.
Lessing as a young man once remarked, in opposition to the fashionable current of the time, that the true *beaux esprits* were generally the
really shallow minds. At this Kant's theory of genius draws a sharp
line. Whatever the great scientific mind may discover, still he is not to
be called a genius for that reason: "For what is accomplished in this
way is something that *could* have been learned. Hence it all lies in the
natural path of investigation and reflection according to rules, and so
is not specifically distinguishable from what may be acquired as the
result of industry backed up by imitation. So all that *Newton* has set
forth in his immortal work on the Principles of Natural Philosophy
may well be learned, however great a mind it took to find it all out,
but we cannot learn to write in a true poetic vein, no matter how
complete all the precepts of the poetic art may be, or however excellent its models. The reason is that all the steps that Newton had to
take from the first elements of geometry to his greatest and most
profound discoveries were such as he could make intuitively evident
and plain to follow, not only for himself but for every one else. On the
other hand no *Homer* or *Wieland* can show how his ideas, so rich at
once in fancy and in thought, enter and assemble themselves in his
brain, for the good reason that he does not himself know, and so
cannot teach others. In matters of science, therefore, the greatest
inventor differs only in degree from the most laborious imitator and

30. See Lambert's letter to Kant, dated November 13, 1765 (IX, 42) (*Ak.* X, 48).

apprentice, whereas he differs specifically from one endowed by nature for fine art."[31] This insight as to the "unconscious" creativity of artistic genius becomes yet more meaningful where it comprises less the opposite to theoretical grounding than the opposite to the intent of desire and action. In this direction, too, Kant's theory transcends philosophical systematic and joins with the essential cultural problems of the age. In Baumgarten's doctrine, which contains the first elevation of aesthetics to the rank of an independent science, the concept of the beautiful is subordinated to that of perfection. All beauty is perfection, however of a kind such that it is not known in pure concept but can be grasped only mediately in a sensory, intuitive image. The whole of German academic philosophy is dominated by this view, which is further developed by Mendelssohn and put on a universal metaphysical foundation, and from this vantage point it works itself out into the circle of artistic creativity. Even Schiller's "artists" present little more than a poetic circumscription and spinning out of Baumgarten's idea.

Kant's critique constituted on this point also a clear historical boundary line. "Purposiveness without purpose," which he finds actualized in the work of art, excludes equally the mundane concept of need and the idealistic concept of perfection. For any concept of perfection presupposes an objective measure, to which the art work can be related and with which it can be compared; and to propose a formal objective purposiveness without purpose, that is, the mere form of a perfection (without content and concept of what is harmonized in it) would be a genuine contradiction.[32] Thus it was Kant the ethical rigorist who in his foundation of aesthetics was the first to break with the ruling moral rationalism. This constitutes no paradox, but is rather the necessary completion and the exact confirmation of his basic ethical view. As he founded obligation on the pure concept of reason and tried to repel all appeals to "moral feeling," to subjective perception and inclination, so on the other side the aesthetic aspect of feeling is to be held onto firmly and is not to be abandoned

---

31. *Critique of Aesthetic Judgment,* §47 (V, 383 f.) (*Ak.* V, 308–09).
32. Ibid., §15 (V, 296 f.) (*Ak.* V, 226–28).

in favor of the logical and moral concept. The exclusion of pleasure and pain from the basis of ethics does not mean, as now appears, an unconditional rejection, but it opens the way to a new objectification and makes possible another specific form of universality of which they are susceptible. Thus only the overcoming of ethical utilitarianism and hedonism paves the way for the idea of the autonomy and self-purpose of art. The concept of disinterested delight in the beauty of nature and art, regarded purely substantively, presents no radically new tendency in the evolution of aesthetics. It was already laid down by Plotinus, and was independently carried further in the modern era by Shaftesbury, by Mendelssohn, and Karl Philipp Moritz in his work "On the Creative Imitation of the Beautiful."[33] But only through the systematic exposition that it received in Kant's theory could it unfold its essential meaning, could it, in opposition to the philosophy and poetics of the Enlightenment, lay down nothing less than a new concept of the nature and the origin of the spiritual itself.

Kant, however, reached the highest synthesis between his ethical and his aesthetic basic principles only in the second part of the *Critique of Aesthetic Judgment,* in the "Analytic of the Sublime." In the concept of the sublime itself aesthetic and ethical interest undergo a new fusion, and here the critical separation of the two points of view is even more compellingly demonstrated. In the discussions he directs to this point, Kant moves once again on terrain that is personally and genuinely his. In the "Analytic of the Beautiful" one still detects, behind all the precision and acuity of the conceptual development, a certain foreign quality as soon as the inquiry leaves the region of pure principles and turns to concrete applications, for the fullness of individual artistic intuition is denied to Kant. The "Analytic of the Sublime," on the contrary, displays all the moments of the Kantian spirit and all those properties indicative of the man as well as of the writer in genuine fulfillment and in the most felicitous mutual interpenetration. Here the trenchancy of the analysis of pure concepts is found united with the moral sensitivity that forms the core of Kant's person-

33. [*Über die bildende Nachahmung des Schönen* (Braunschweig, 1788).]

ality; here the eye for psychological detail that Kant had already evidenced in the precritical *Observations on the Feeling of the Beautiful and the Sublime* is allied with the encompassing transcendental perspectives, which he had achieved since that time over the whole domain of consciousness.

The place occupied by the problem of the sublime within the total system of critical aesthetics can be seen most clearly if one looks back to the peculiar relation between the basic faculties of consciousness presented in the phenomenon of the beautiful. This phenomenon ought to emerge from a free play of the power of imagination and the understanding; in this case, however, "understanding" does not mean the capacity for logically conceiving and judging, but the capacity for simply delimiting. It is this that invades the movement of the imagination and extracts from it a closed form.[34] But from this there results a new question. Does limitation constitute an essential moment of the aesthetic—or is it not rather the boundless that presents a true aesthetic value? Does not precisely the thought of the unlimited, indeed of the illimitable, also in its way contain a factor with fundamental aesthetic meaning? The concept of the sublime provides the answer to this question. For the impression of sublimity in fact arises wherever we confront an object that surpasses any and all means by which we may conceive it, and which we hence are unable to bring together into a bounded whole either intuitively or conceptually. We call that "sublime" which is absolutely great—here it may be a matter of the magnitude of sheer extension or of power: of the "mathematically" or "dynamically" sublime. A relation of this sort cannot be given in objects as such, for all objective measure and estimation of size is nothing but comparison of magnitudes, in which, according to the basic standard of measure applied, the content can be called now small, now large, and thus magnitude itself is always to be taken as just a pure expression of a mental relation, never as an absolute quality and as an equally inalterable aesthetic essence. This latter determination enters in, however, when the standard of measure is transferred from the object to the subject, if it is no longer sought in

34. See above, pp. 313 f.

an individual, spatially given thing, but in the totality of the functions of consciousness. If now this totality encounters something unmeasurable, we then no longer face the sheer infinity of number, which at bottom means nothing but the power of numerical repeatability and thus an indeterminate progression, but the cancellation of all limits has yielded us a new positive determination of consciousness.

Thus the infinite, which as soon as theoretical consideration tried to grasp it as a given whole evaporated into a dialectical Idea, attains a felt totality and truth. "That is sublime [is Kant's own explanation] in comparison with which all else is small. Here we readily see that nothing can be given in Nature, no matter how great we may judge it to be, which, regarded in some other relation, may not be degraded to the level of the infinitely little, and nothing so small which in comparison with some still smaller standard may not for our imagination be enlarged to the greatness of a world. Telescopes have put within our reach an abundance of material to go upon in making the first observation, and microscopes the same in making the second. Nothing, therefore, which can be an object of the senses is to be termed sublime when treated on this footing. But precisely because there is a striving in our imagination towards progress *ad infinitum*, while reason demands absolute totality, as a real idea, that same inability on the part of our faculty for the estimation of the magnitude of things of the world of sense to attain to this idea, is the awakening of a feeling of a supersensible faculty within us; and it is the use to which judgment naturally puts particular objects on behalf of this latter feeling, and not the object of sense, that is absolutely great, and every other contrasted employment small. Consequently it is the disposition of soul evoked by a particular representation engaging the attention of the reflective judgment, and not the Object, that is to be called sublime. ...*The sublime is that, the mere capacity of thinking which evidences a faculty of mind transcending every standard of sense.*"[35]

Since in this fashion the basis of the sublime is shifted from objects to the "harmony of the spirit," since it is discovered to be not a quality

---

35. *Critique of Aesthetic Judgment*, §25 (V, 321 f.) (*Ak.* V, 250).

of being but a quality of contemplation, it is truly lifted up into the sphere of aesthetic reflection. But this sphere here no longer touches the region of the understanding and intuition, as it did in the contemplation of the beautiful, but rather that of the Ideas of reason and their supersensory meaning. While in judging the beautiful the imagination was interwoven in a free play with the understanding, in judging a thing to be sublime it is related to reason, so as to evoke a harmony of the mind "conformable to that which the influence of definite . . . ideas would produce upon feeling, and in common accord with it."[36] For Kant, however, all concord of reason passes ultimately into the one idea of freedom, and it is this which also everywhere underlies our use of the category of the sublime. What properly belongs to the feeling of ourself and our intelligible task here is transformed into a predicate of the given things of nature only through a peculiar subreption. Under deeper analysis and self-awareness this illusion also vanishes. "Who would apply the term 'sublime' even to shapeless mountain masses towering one above the other in wild disorder, with the pyramids of ice, or to the dark tempestuous ocean, or such like things? But in the contemplation of them, without any regard to their form, the mind abandons itself to the imagination and to a reason placed, though quite apart from any definite end, in conjunction therewith, and merely broadening its view, and it feels itself elevated in its own estimate of itself on finding all the might of imagination still unequal to its ideas. . . .In this way external Nature is not estimated in our aesthetic judgment as sublime so far as exciting fear, but rather because it challenges our power (one not of Nature) to regard as small those things of which we are wont to be solicitous (worldly goods, health, life), and hence to regard its might (to which in these matters we are no doubt subject) as exercising over us and our personality no such rude dominion that we should bow down before it, once the question becomes one of our highest principles and of our asserting or forsaking them. Therefore Nature is here called sublime merely because it raises the imagination to a presentation of those cases in which the mind can make itself sensible of the appro-

---

36. Ibid., §26 (V, 327) (*Ak.* V, 256).

priate sublimity of the sphere of its own being, even above Nature."[37]

To be sure, this critical solution of the problem of the sublime, when looked at more closely, carries a new critical question within itself. For through the relation of the sublime to the idea of self-legislation and the free personality the sublime seems, since it is cut loose from nature, to fall wholly into the realm of the ethical. Its special aesthetic character and its independent aesthetic value, however, would be erased equally thoroughly in either case. In fact, the execution of Kant's analysis reveals how near we are to this peril. For the psychology of the sublime leads us back to that basic emotion of awe, which we have already recognized as the universal form in which the consciousness of the moral law presents itself to us. In the phenomenon of the sublime we again recognize that mingling of pleasure and pain, of resistance and freely willed submission which constitutes the peculiar character of the feeling of awe. In it we feel ourselves at once overwhelmed, as physically finite subjects, by the grandeur of the object, while at the same time we feel exalted above all finite and conditioned being through the discovery that this grandeur is rooted in the consciousness of our intelligible task and in our faculty of Ideas. But since the sublime is founded on the same feeling as the moral in general, we thereby seem to have overstepped the boundaries of disinterested delight and to have passed into the domain of the will. The difficulty lying herein can only be removed when one sees that the subreption through which in the sublime we think a determination of ourselves as a determination of the natural object does not vanish when it is recognized as such. Our intuition remains aesthetic only when it views the self-determination of our mental faculties not in and for themselves but equally through the medium of the intuition of nature; when it reflects the inner in the outer and vice versa. Such a mutual mirroring of the ego and the world, of feeling of self and feeling of nature, comprises for us both the essence of aesthetic contemplation in general and also the essence of that contemplation which finds its expression in the sublime. Here a new form of the investment of nature with soul is advanced, ulti-

37. Ibid., §§26, 28 (V, 327 f., 333 f.) (*Ak.* V, 256, 262).

mately leading on beyond the shape of nature as it is symbolically copied in the appearance of the beautiful—and yet which on the other hand perennially leads back to nature because it can be grasped only in this very opposition. Only therein does the infinity of nature, which previously was a mere thought, receive its concrete felt truth, because it is seen in light reflected from the infinity of the self.

The proposition from the introduction to the *Critique of Judgment,* which says that in it the "ground of the unity of the supersensible that lies at the basis of Nature, with what the concept of freedom contains in a practical way" is to be demonstrated, is now made completely determinate. And henceforward we can also understand the reason for attaching the limitation that the concept indicating this unity itself affords neither any theoretical nor any practical knowledge of this unity; hence it has no proper domain, but only makes feasible transition from the mode of thinking governed by the principles of the one to that according to the principles of the other.[38] As to how the unity of the "supersensory ground" is able to differentiate itself so that it is presented to us now in the guise of nature and again under the image of freedom and the moral law, we are not once granted even a hint, much less a theoretical explanation. But even if we refuse to speculate on this topic, there still remains an undeniable phenomenon in which the contemplation of nature and that of freedom undergo a totally novel relation to one another. This phenomenon is that of artistic perception. Every genuine work of art is completely determined in the sensory respect and seems to desire nothing more than to remain in the circle of the sensory, and each nonetheless necessarily extends beyond this circle. It contains a portion of a purely concrete and personal life, and still it reaches back into a depth where the ego feeling turns out to be the feeling of the whole as well. Looked at conceptually, that might be called a miracle, but in all supreme creations of art (one need think only of the highest examples of Goethe's lyrics) this miracle is truly accomplished, so that the question of its possibility is silenced. In this respect—but only in this respect—the actual existence of art, if we do not shatter it by abstract hairsplitting,

---

38. See *Critique of Judgment,* introduction, II (V, 244) (*Ak.* V, 176).

points to a new unity of the sensible and the intelligible, of nature and freedom; indeed, it is itself the expression and the immediate guarantee of this unity. Thus the route by which we here arrive at the thought of the supersensory in every respect fits the general critical orientation, for we do not begin with the essence of the supersensory, so as then to dissect it into its individual expressions, but rather its idea arises in us, since we bring together the basic directions given in consciousness itself and make them intersect in an imaginary perspective, a point beyond possible experience.

Accordingly, the doctrine of the "supersensible substrate" of nature and of freedom is not about a primal *thing*, but about the primal *function* of the *spiritual*, which is disclosed for us with novel meaning and profundity in the aesthetic. For the universal communicability that every real aesthetic judgment claims for itself points us to a basic agreement, to which the subjects as such belong, independently of their contingent individual differences, and in which therefore not so much the intelligible ground of objects as rather the intelligible ground of humanity is presented. Kant concludes this discussion thus: "This is that intelligible to which taste . . . extends its view. It is, that is to say, what brings even our higher cognitive faculties into common accord, and is that apart from which sheer contradiction would arise between their nature and the claims put forward by taste. In this faculty judgment does not find itself subjected to a heteronomy of laws of experience as it does in the empirical estimate of things—in respect of the objects of such a pure delight it gives the law to itself, just as reason does in respect of the faculty of desire. Here, too, both on account of this inner possibility in the Subject, and on account of the external possibility of a nature harmonizing therewith, it finds a reference in itself to something in the Subject itself and outside it, and which is not Nature, nor yet freedom, but still is connected with the ground of the latter, i.e., the supersensible—a something in which the theoretical faculty gets bound up into unity with the practical in an intimate and obscure manner.[39]

This "obscure manner" is known at least to the extent we can

39. [*Critique of Aesthetic Judgment*, §59 (V, 430) (Ak. V, 353).]

precisely designate the general higher concept on which the connection rests. Once again it is the concept of autonomy, of the self-legislation of the spirit, that manifests itself as the center of gravity of the Kantian system. Because this concept receives fresh confirmation and illumination in the aesthetic, it leads us to a deeper level of the intelligible. From the autonomy of the pure understanding and its universal laws came nature as the object of scientific experience—from the autonomy of the ethical proceeded the idea of freedom and the self-determination of reason. These two, however, do not stand in isolation but are necessarily related to each other, for the world of freedom ought to have an influence on the world of nature, ought to execute its demands in the empirical world of men and things. Nature must hence at the very least be thinkable "so that the lawfulness of its form may at least agree with the possibility of ends working within it according to the laws of freedom." But every attempt actually to think it in this way perpetually collides, in the purely theoretical area, with the antinomy between causality and freedom. No matter how much progress we may make, we finally confront the tremendous gulf between the realm of the concept of nature as sensible and the realm of the concept of freedom as supersensible.[40] Only artistic insight discloses a new path to us. Even if the objective agreement of nature and freedom remains a never-completed task, even if the paths of the two intersect only at infinity, their full subjective unity is actualized within the sphere of concrete consciousness itself, in the feeling of art and the creating of art. Here, in the free play of the powers of the mind, nature appears to us as if it were a work of freedom, as if it were shaped in accordance with an indwelling finality and were formed from the inside out—while on the other hand the free creation, the work of artistic genius, delights us as something necessary and therefore as a creation of nature. Thus here we wed what simply, as existent, is distinct and must remain so with a new manner of contemplation, the special content of which continues to exist for us only if we resist the attempt to interpret it as an independent mode of theoretical cognition of the actual. The supersensible substrate the judgment of

40. See *Critique of Judgment,* introduction, II (V, 244) (*Ak.* V, 175–76).

taste points us to is hence impossible to display conceptually from appearances as objective phenomena of nature, but it is immediately confirmed in a peculiar relation of consciousness itself, which is as sharply and characteristically distinct from all relation to knowledge through concepts and laws as from any relation to the pure determination of the will. Once this relationship is clearly and unambiguously seated in the subject, this consequence has a reverse effect on the image of objective reality. The harmonious play of the mind's powers is what endows nature itself with the content of life: aesthetic judgment passes over into teleological judgment.

5

The result of the *Critique of Judgment* thus far can be summed up by saying that the concept of an end has now undergone that transformation corresponding to the Kantian revolution in thinking. The end is not an objectively acting power of nature in and behind things but is a mental principle of union that our judgment applies to the totality of experiences. As a principle of this sort, it manifests itself to us in the idea of formal purposiveness as well as in that of aesthetic purposiveness. We encounter formal purposiveness when we analyze nature into a system of particular laws and particular natural forms, but for the critical enterprise it constitutes less a new factor in appearances themselves than a concurrence of the appearances with the demands of our understanding. Aesthetic creation was also introduced directly into reality itself, but the more deeply and purely it was grasped, the more clearly it could be seen that the unity of being presented to us neither wants to be nor can be anything other than a reflection of the unity of the mood and the feeling which we experience in ourselves. But now the question arises whether these alterations in the idea of an end also exhaust its sphere of application in its entirety. Is there not some perspective in which the end not only expresses a relation of the given appearance to the beholder, but in which it is to be seen as an objectively necessary moment of the appearance itself? And to the extent that there is such a point of view, what is it and how can it be critically established and justified?

The idea of finality differs from all other categories in that through it, wherever it appears, a new type of unity of the manifold is asserted, a novel relation between a formed whole and its individual partial moments and conditions. Thus in the concept of formal purposiveness the substance of the particular laws of nature was thought in a way such that it presented not a mere aggregate, but a system which "specifies" itself according to a definite rule. Thus a totality of consciousness and its powers was disclosed in the aesthetic feeling, preceding and underlying all dissection of consciousness into individual faculties contrasted with each other. From each of these two standpoints the whole here under consideration is regarded not as if it were made up of its parts but as if it were itself the origin of the parts and the basis of their concrete determinateness. But this whole itself was purely ideal nature: it was a presupposition and requirement which our reflection saw itself compelled to apply to objects, although without entering directly into the formation of these objects and combining indissolubly with them. There is, nevertheless, one area of facts and problems in which this peculiar transition is actually made, where purpose seems to confront us not as a mere principle of subjective contemplation but as the very creature and substance of nature itself. Wherever we do not conceive nature as an aggregate of mechanical causal laws arranged in a hierarchy from the universal to the particular, but rather as a whole of life forms, this step is taken. For life is conceptually distinguished precisely by the assumption of a type of actuality proceeding not from plurality to unity but from unity to plurality, not from the parts to the whole but from the whole to the parts. An event in nature becomes a life process for us when we think it not as a mere flux of miscellaneous individual things, one following the other, but when all these particular entities are for us expressions of *one* occurrence and one essence, which reveals itself in them only in manifold structures.

A movement toward this sort of unity of being, as distinguished from a mere stream of events all of equal importance, is what constitutes for us the character of "development." Where true development is present, a whole is not formed *out of* parts, but it is contained *in* them, as a guiding principle. Instead of a uniform passage of temporal before and after, where every previous moment is swallowed up by the present and its existence is lost, in the phenomenon of life we think a mutual interpenetration of the individual moments, such that the past is conserved in the present and in both the tendency toward future formation is active and knowable. We conventionally signify this sort of connection by the concept of organism. In an organism, according to the explanation early given to it by Aristotle, the whole precedes the parts, because the former is not possible through the latter, but rather the latter only through the former. A particular stage of life receives its meaning only from the totality of the expressions of life to which it belongs; we conceive it not by divorcing it from the event as a causal condition, but by regarding it as a means, which is a means "to" that totality. "In such a natural product as this every part is thought as *owing* its presence to the *agency* of all the remaining parts, and also as existing *for the sake of the others* and of the whole, that is as an instrument, or organ. But this is not enough—for it might be an instrument of art. . . .On the contrary the part must be an organ *producing* the other parts—each, consequently, reciprocally producing the others. No instrument of art can answer to this description, but only the instrument of that nature from whose resources the materials of every instrument are drawn—even the materials for instruments of art. Only under these conditions and upon these terms can such a product be an *organized* and *self-organizing being*, and, as such, be called a *natural end*."[41] Since the idea of the end now is not referred to the relation between our cognitive powers and other powers of the mind but is immediately intuited concretely and objectively, there arises the idea of organism: "things as ends of Nature are organized beings."

However, this purely objective view ought not to seduce us into a misunderstanding. We are not here involved in a metaphysic of nature, but in a critique of judgment. The question, therefore, is not whether nature acts purposively in some of its products, whether its creative activity might be guided by a conscious or unconscious intention, but rather whether our judging is compelled to posit and assume

41. *Critique of Teleological Judgment*, §65 (V, 451 f.) (*Ak.* V, 373-74).

a special "thing-form" distinct from that of the bodies of abstract mechanics and going beyond them. And it must first of all be established, in accordance with the transcendental method, that this postulation, whatever the ultimate decision as to its justification may be, is undeniably a simple fact. We are as unable to blot out of our conception of nature the thought of organic life as to dispense with the fact of will or of aesthetic intuition and creation in our view of spiritual being. The distinction between the two ways of operating—mechanical-causal and inner-purposive—belongs to the image of nature itself, which we have to sketch according to the conditions of our knowledge; however we may answer the metaphysical question, it presents a state of cognitive consciousness demanding recognition and explanation. The contrast between the sort of events we find in a clockwork and those presented to us in a living body is immediately demonstrable in the phenomenon and as a phenomenon. "In a watch one part is the instrument by which the movement of the others is effected, but one wheel is not the efficient cause of the production of the other. One part is certainly present for the sake of another, but it does not owe its presence to the agency of that other....Hence one wheel in the watch does not produce the other, and, still less, does one watch produce other watches, by utilizing, or organizing, foreign material; it does not of itself replace parts of which it has been deprived, nor; if these are absent in the original construction, does it make good the deficiency by the subvention of the rest; nor does it, so to speak, repair its own causal disorders. But these are all things which we are justified in expecting from organized Nature. And organized being is, therefore, not a mere machine. For a machine has solely *motive power*, whereas an organized being possesses inherent *formative* power, and such, moreover, as it can impart to material devoid of it.... This, therefore, is a self-propagating formative power, which cannot be explained by the capacity of movement alone, that is to say, by mechanism."[42]

Thus a tree produces another tree by a known law of nature and hence reproduces itself in accordance with its species; secondly, how-

---

42. [Ibid., §65 (V, 452) (*Ak.* V, 374). Cf. also §64 (V, 447 ff.) (*Ak.* V, 369 ff.).]

ever, it produces itself as an individual, insofar as it enlarges and renews its individual parts in an orderly way. Although customarily we just call this latter activity "growth," we must nonetheless not lose sight of the fact that it is totally different from every other increase in size governed by merely mechanical laws, for the matter added in the growth process is used in a specifically characteristic creativity, and thus constitutes both a recreation of its species and a further development, not a mere enlargement of its mass and its quantity.[43] The natural object, which was determined as a magnitude through the basic principles of pure understanding, substantiality, causality, and reciprocity, only here receives a quality peculiar to it and which distinguishes it from all other formations; this quality, however, is not so much a property of its being as a property of its becoming, and it designates the individual direction of this becoming.

Thus the individual appearances of nature here achieve a new meaningfulness, enriching and deepening their own substance, but unrelated to an alien end lying outside them. For as was done previously in the founding aesthetics, once again the idea of purposiveness without a purpose is strictly and thoroughly worked out. This task is all the more pressing since Kant at this point once more sets himself consciously in opposition to his era. The whole teleology of the Age of Enlightenment is characterized by the thoroughgoing confusion of the idea of finality with that of general utility. The profounder elements of the Leibnizian concept of purpose were degraded by Wolff into an insipid utilitarian outlook and calculation. The universal metaphysical ideas of theodicy had here become lost in a narrow and pendantic pettiness, which sought to detect in every single feature of the course of the universe the advantage of mankind and hence the wisdom and goodness of the Creator. Wolff even bestows on sunlight a teleological justification of his kind: "The light of day," he once remarked, "is very useful for us, for with it we can conveniently carry on our duties, which cannot be done in the evening at all, or at least not so handily and with difficulties."[44] In German literature Brockes

43. Cf. ibid., §§64 and 65 (V, 448 ff.) (*Ak.* V, 369 ff.).

44. Cf. Josef Kremer, *Das Problem der Theodizee in der Philosophie und Literatur des 18. Jahrhunderts mit besonderer Rücksicht auf Kant und Schiller* (Berlin, 1909), p. 95.

became the poet of this outlook and orientation. Even when a young man, however, Kant combated it with serene and abundant irony, having been attracted by the problem of natural teleology and occupied with it since the *Universal Natural History and Theory of the Heavens*, and he had a predilection for referring to Voltaire's sarcastic saying that God surely had given us noses so that we—might put spectacles on them.[45]

The *Critique of Judgment* recurs to this authority (without naming him), but no less clearly and definitively it vanquishes the basic positive intuition of Voltairean deism. The world no longer is a clockwork mechanism finding its ultimate explanation in the hidden, divine "watchmaker," for the metaphysical form of the cosmological proof of God's existence is seen to be as fallacious as that of the teleological proof. From now on if the finality of nature is to be discussed, this cannot mean a signpost pointing to an external transcendent ground on which nature depends, but only a reference to its own immanent structure. This structure is purposive—so long as the *relative* finality for mankind or any other created being is kept clearly separate from *inner* finality, which possesses no point of comparison other than the appearance itself and the structure of its parts. As to the former, relative finality, it is clear without further ado that its demonstration remains dubious in every case. For even if we assumed that we had proved an individual phenomenon of nature or nature as a whole to be necessarily for the sake of another and teleologically constrained, what is our guarantee of the necessity of this other? If we wanted to designate it as its own end we would introduce a completely new yardstick, inadmissible and futile. The concept of something which is its own end belongs, as the establishment of the Kantian ethics has shown, not to the realm of nature but to that of freedom. If we remain within the bounds of nature, there is no escape from the circle of relativity. "We can easily see that the only condition on which extrinsic finality, that is, the adaptability of a thing for other things, can be looked on as an extrinsic physical end, is that the existence of the

---

45. Cf. "The Only Possible Basis of Proof for God's Existence," pt. 2, Observation 6, §4 (II, 138) (*Ak.* II, 131).

thing for which it is proximately or remotely adapted is itself, and in its own right, an end of Nature. But this is a matter that can never be decided by any mere study of Nature. Hence it follows that relative finality, although, on a certain supposition, it points to natural finality, does not warrant any absolute teleological judgment."[46] Strictly construed, the idea of self-purpose, like that of self-value, is restricted to the sphere of the ethical, to the idea of the subject of willing; but in the domain of objective existence it possesses a symbolic counterpart in the phenomenon of the organism (as previously in that of the work of art). For all the parts of an organism are oriented as if to a single center; this center, however, lies in itself and is related only to itself. The existence of the organism and its individual form interpenetrate each other: the one seems to be there for the sake of the other.

Here, however, there begins a new question, in contrast to the whole of aesthetic contemplation. No conflict can occur between the concept of natural beauty and that of natural lawfulness, for the validity each claims is of a totally different sort. Aesthetic consciousness creates its own world and elevates it beyond all intercourse and clashes with empirical actuality, since it constructs it as a world of play and of semblance. But this way out is denied to teleological judgment, which we apply to nature and its products, for its object is one and the same as that of judgment of experience and cognitive judgment. But can nature in general mean for the critical philosopher anything but the object of experience, presented under the form of space and time as well as the categories of magnitude and reality, of causality and reciprocity, and which is exhausted in the totality of these forms? It is impossible—so it seems—either to haggle away any of this determination of the object of experience or to add anything to it. What does it thus signify if now the idea of purpose comes forward claiming to justify or to fulfill the idea of causality? We recall that the basic premise of causality in the critical sense means nothing but the unavoidable means of objectifying the temporal succession of appearances. The causal connection of phenomena is not inferred from their temporal order, but the reverse: only by applying to a given sequence of

46. *Critique of Teleological Judgment*, §63 (V, 446) (*Ak.* V, 368–69).

perceptions the concept of cause and effect, of condition and the conditioned, can the objective time order determine its elements un-ambiguously.[47] If we hold fast to the result, we see immediately that there is no possibility of exempting any particular realm of nature whatsoever from the all-encompassing validity of the causal princi-ple. For that would instantly banish it from the one objective temporal order as well; it would no longer be an "event," in the empirical sense of this word. Hence, since the development which we attribute to the organism is truly and permanently such an event, it must also be thought as unqualifiedly subject to the fundamental law of causal connection. Every particular emergent formation in a developmental series must be explicable from what precedes and from the conditions of the environment. All determination of what is now given by a future something not yet given must remain excluded; what is earlier conditions and posits what succeeds it, because generally only in this form of conditioning is the objective phenomenon of an unambiguous temporal order constituted. In this view of nature there is no place for the assumption of a special class of purposive forces, because no gap exists into which the new idea could be inserted.

The result of this connection is that for Kant purpose cannot enter into the picture as a special principle of the explanation of natural phenomena, be they inorganic or organic. There is only one principle and one ideal of natural scientific explanation, and this is defined by the form of mathematical physics. A phenomenon is "explained" when it is known and determined in all its individual moments as magnitude and when its existence can be deduced from universal quantitative laws, and similarly from knowledge of certain constants that characterize the particular instance. That this deduction can never really be done completely, that every individual case and every individual form comprises in itself an unlimited complexity, is equally true. For where the analysis of mathematical physics has not yet been actually completed it must nevertheless be regarded as completable—if the object in question is not to fall outside the realm of nature as bounded by the universal law of conservation and its

47. See above, pp. 184 ff.

corollaries. The reduction of all events to comparisons of magnitude, and the transformation of "organism" into "mechanism" is thus set up as an unconditional demand at the very least, even in the face of all the limitations of our present knowledge. The *Critique of Teleological Judgment* leaves no doubt whatsoever concerning this result. It begins with the premise that in the "general idea of Nature," as the ensemble of sense objects, there is no basis at all for the assumption that things of nature serve each other as means to ends and that this sort of causality renders their possibility sufficiently comprehensible. For this can neither be demanded nor predicted a priori, nor can experience ever show us such a form of causality "save on the assumption of an antecedent process of mental jugglery that only reads the conception of an end into the nature of the things, and that, not deriving this conception from the objects and what it knows of them from experience, makes use of it more for the purpose of rendering Nature intelligible to us by an analogy to a subjective ground upon which our representations are brought into inner connexion, than for that of cognizing Nature from objective grounds."[48]

But were this the final result, the inquiry would have gone in a circle. For this was the very question thrust upon us after the analysis of the aesthetic finality of the powers of the mind and after the discussion of the formal finality among our concepts; namely, whether the idea of an end did not at least mediately participate in the building up of our experiential world and its objects, and to this extent possess some sort of objective validity. If the latter is denied to it, then the teleology of nature poses no new problem in the critical sense. There would be only one way to make compatible the seemingly irreconcilable demands of the purposive principle and the causal principle. If the causal principle is to remain the sole constitutive basic concept of nature and experience—and if on the other hand the idea of purpose is nonetheless to possess an independent relation to experience, this is conceivable only if this relation is itself effected and established through the mediation of the causal concept. Then and only then would a new field of activity for the concept of an end be found, if this

48. *Critique of Teleological Judgment,* §61 (V, 438) (*Ak.* V, 359–60).

concept is not to oppose causal explanation but is to foster and guide it. It is in fact here that its true and legitimate use lies. The final principle does not have a constitutive but rather a regulative meaning; it serves not for the conquest of the causal interpretation of phenomena, but rather the reverse, for its deepening and its universal application. It does not resist this interpretation but paves the way for it, since it points out the appearances and the problems to which the causal principle should address itself.

That such a preparation is fruitful, indeed indispensable, in the phenomena of organic nature is easy to show. For here the direct application of the causal principle and the universal causal laws, far from being thought of as conflicting with purpose, finds no content whatsoever on which it might be exercised. The laws of mechanics and physics do not concern the "things" of nature as they are presented to direct observation; they speak instead of "masses" and "mass-points." The object must be stripped of all its erstwhile concrete determinateness, reduced to the pure abstractions of analytical mechanics, if there is to be a possibility of subjecting it to those same laws. Where we are concerned, as in the appearances of organic nature, with matter not as mass in motion but as the substrate of the phenomena of life, where the natural form in its full complexity is our particular interest—there, before the causal deduction of the singular can be undertaken, the whole toward which the inquiry is directed must as a rule first be designated and brought out purely descriptively. Out of the general stuff of spatiotemporal being, in which everything can be basically related to everything else, some sort of specifically determined individual series must be extracted, in which the members show a particular form of affinity with one another. This is the function fulfilled by the concept of an end. Finality, unlike the fundamental concepts of mathematical physics, does not assist deduction but induction, not analysis but synthesis, for it initially sets up the relative unities which we subsequently can dissect into their individual causal elements and causal conditions. The visual process in all its particularities must be explained causally, but the structure of the eye is studied from the point of view and under the assumption that the eye is "determined for seeing," though not intentionally so

constructed. Thus teleological judging is justifiably connected, prob-
lematically at least, with research into nature, for the concept of teleological relations and forms in nature is at any rate *"one more principle*
for reducing its phenomena to rules in cases where the laws of its
purely mechanical causality do not carry us sufficiently far. . . .But this
is a different thing from crediting Nature with causes acting *de-
signedly,* to which it may be regarded as subjected in following its
particular laws. The latter would mean that teleology is based, not
merely on a *regulative* principle, directed to the simple *estimate* of
phenomena, but is actually based on a *constitutive* principle available
for *deriving* natural products from their causes: with the result that the
conception of a physical end no longer exists for the reflective, but for
the determinant, judgment. But in that case the conception would not
really be specially connected with the power of judgment. . . . It
would, on the contrary be a conception of reason, and would introduce a new causality into science—one which we are borrowing all
the time solely from ourselves and attributing to other beings, although we do not mean to assume that they and we are similarly
constituted."[49]

   That is the critical distinction that Kant wields in the old battle for
and against finality. The received metaphysical interpretation of the
concept of purpose is in fact the *asylum ignorantiae* that Spinoza said it
was, but in its purely empirical use it is more the means to an ever-
richer and more precise knowledge of the connections and the structural relations of organic nature. As a "maxim of the reflective judgment" assisting knowledge of natural laws in experience it does not
serve to "institute the intrinsic possibility of natural forms, but to
become acquainted with Nature in accordance with its empirical laws."[50]
At this point the guide to research and the principle of the explanation of particular natural phenomena diverge. One must keep firmly
in mind that no trace of that mystical aura surrounding the insistence
on and the longing to penetrate "into the heart of nature" clings any
longer to the concept of the explanation of nature as Kant conceives it,

---

49. Ibid.
50. See ibid., §69 (*Ak.* V, 385 f.).

but rather it designates an inevitable and decisive but nonetheless individual, logical function of knowledge. All causal explanation of one phenomenon by another ultimately reduces to the determination of one's spatiotemporal location by the other. In this the "how" of the transition from one to the other is not conceived; only the fact of the necessary conjunction of the elements in the empirical sequence is indispensable.

The principle of finality, when it is used in the critical sense, also renounces the task of unriddling the secret of this transition, but it orders the phenomena around a new center and thereby offers a different type of mutually interrelating form. As far as causal derivation can penetrate and as much leeway as we give it, it can never shoulder this form aside and render it dispensable. For within the phenomena of life it can of course be shown purely causally how one member of the development arises from its predecessor, but we eventually arrive, however far we may trace it back, at an initial condition of organization which we must accept as a presupposition. The causal point of view tells us the rules by which one structure is transformed into another; however that such individual "seeds" exist, that there are primitive formations specifically different from one another which are the basis of the development, cannot be made further intelligible but must be assumed as a fact. The antinomy between the concepts of finality and causality thus disappears, as soon as we think of the two of them as different *modes of ordering,* through which we try to unify the manifold of phenomena. Opposition between two basic metaphysical factors of events is supplanted by agreement between two maxims and demands of reason which complement each other. "If I say: I must *estimate* the possibility of all events in material Nature, and, consequently, also all forms considered as its products, on mere mechanical laws, I do not thereby assert that they *are solely possible in this way,* that is, to the exclusion of every other kind of causality. On the contrary this assertion is only intended to indicate that I *ought* at all times to *reflect* upon these things *according to the principle* of the simple mechanism of Nature, and, consequently push my investigation with it as far as I can, because unless I make it the basis of research there can be no knowledge of Nature in the true sense of the term at all. Now this does not stand in the way of the second maxim... that is to say, in the case of some natural forms (and, at their instance, in the case of entire Nature), we may, in our reflection upon them, follow the trail of a principle which is radically different from explanation by the mechanism of Nature, namely the principle of final causes. For reflection according to the first maxim is not in this way superseded. On the contrary, we are directed to pursue it as far as we can. Further it is not asserted that those forms were not possible in the mechanism of Nature. It is only maintained that *human reason*, adhering to this maxim and proceeding on these lines, could never discover a particle of foundation for what constitutes the specific character of a physical end, whatever additions it might make in this way to its knowledge of natural laws."[51]

The consequent reconciliation between the principles of finality and mechanism binds both to the condition that they aspire only to be different and specific ways of ordering natural phenomena, and that they renounce any dogmatic unfurling of a theory of the ultimate origin of nature itself and the individual forms in it. In such an undertaking, both the concept of purpose and that of causality would be shipwrecked. For the concept of a being which, by virtue of its purposive reason and will, is the primal ground of nature is possible in the formal, analytical sense, to be sure, but indemonstrable in the transcendental sense, for the reason that since it cannot be abstracted from experience nor is it required for the possibility of experience, its objective reality can in no way be secured. To this extent, where research into nature is concerned, the concept of an end remains "a stranger in natural science" threatening to erase the steady progress of its methodology and to detach the very concept of a cause, which designates a *relation internal to appearance*, from this its basic meaning.[52] On the other side, however, the causal idea also, if it remains aware of its essential task of "spelling out appearances so that we can read them as experiences," must renounce the claim to be the means to a true insight into the first and absolute grounds of organized life.

51. Ibid., §70 (V, 465 f.) (*Ak.* V, 387–88).
52. Cf. ibid., §§72 and 74 (V, 467 ff., 474 ff.) (*Ak.* V, 389 ff., 395 ff.).

For within phenomena themselves, the infinite complexity which every organic natural form possesses for us points also to the limits of its powers. "It is, I mean, quite certain that we can never get a sufficient knowledge of organized beings and their inner possibility, much less get an explanation of them, by looking merely to mechanical principles of Nature. Indeed, so certain is it, that we may confidently assert that it is absurd for men even to entertain any thought of so doing or to hope that maybe another Newton may some day arise, to make intelligible to us even the genesis of but a blade of grass from natural laws that no design has ordered. Such insight we must absolutely deny to mankind. But, then, are we to think that a source of the possibility of organized beings amply sufficient to explain their origin without having recourse to a design, *could* never be found buried among the secrets even of Nature, were we able to penetrate to the principle upon which it specifies its familiar universal laws? This, in its turn, would be a presumptuous judgment on our part. For how do we expect to get any knowledge on the point? Probabilities drop entirely out of account in a case like this, where the question turns on judgments of pure reason."[53] We can try, of course, here as well, to make the lines which diverge for us intersect in the supersensible; we can assume that the transcendent ground on which the world of appearance rests is so constituted that a thoroughly purposive order of the universe must proceed from it, according to universal laws and hence without the intrusion of any sort of willed intent. In this direction—for example, in Leibniz's metaphysics of preestablished harmony—lies the attempt to reconcile the realm of final causes with that of efficient causes, the concept of God with the concept of nature.

For Kant, however, the "supersensible" here means less the substrate and the ultimate explanatory ground of things than the projection beyond the bounds of experience of a goal unattainable in experience. No theoretical certainty as to the absolute genesis of being is asserted thereby; there is merely the indication of a direction we have to keep to when applying our basic cognitive methods. The possibility of reconciling mechanism and teleology in the supersensible asserts

53. Ibid., §75 (V, 478 ff.) (*Ak.* V, 400).

one thing above all: that we ought unswervingly to utilize both modes of procedure for experience itself and for investigation into the connection of its phenomena, since each is necessary and, within its own area of validity, irreplaceable. To explain the purposiveness of nature, metaphysics had involved now inanimate matter or a lifeless God, now living matter or a living God; from the standpoint of transcendental philosophy, however, the only thing left for all these systems is "to break away from all these *objective assertions,* and weigh our judgment *critically* in its mere relation to our cognitive faculties. By so doing we may procure for their principle a validity which, if not dogmatic, is yet that of a maxim, and ample for the reliable employment of our reason."[54] In this sense it is the case here also that the union of the principles of finality and causality "cannot rest on one basis of *explanation* setting out in so many terms how a product is possible on given laws so as to satisfy the *determinant* judgment, but can only rest on a single basis of *exposition* elucidating this possibility for the *reflective* judgment."[55] Nothing is said as to whence nature, regarded as a thing in itself, comes and whither it is going, but we establish in this way the concepts and cognitions indispensable for comprehension of the totality of phenomena as a self-contained and systematically articulated unity.

Thus that very principle which above all seemed destined to reach into the primal transcendent ground and the origin of all experience only probes more deeply into the structure of experience, and illuminates, instead of this primal ground, only the richness and the content of appearance itself. The reality which, under the idea of causality and mechanism, appears as a product of universal laws, is integrated into a whole of life forms for and through the principle of finality. In this consists both the connection and the contrast holding between the idea of purpose as coined in aesthetics and in natural teleology. Aesthetic judgment implied a complete reversal from the reality of the pure understanding and its universal laws; through it a new form of being was revealed and grounded in a new function of

54. Ibid., §72, note (V, 470) (*Ak.* V, 392).
55. Ibid., §78, (V, 491) (*Ak.* V, 412).

consciousness. But the domain thus granted its independence conserved this independence and insularity of character; it was separated
off from the world of empirical realities and empirical ends as a self-
sufficient world of play, centered only on itself. In the teleological
view of organic nature, however, this sort of separation does not
occur; there a stable reciprocity holds between the concept of nature
advanced by the understanding and that put forward by the teleological judgment. The principle of finality itself calls in the causal principle and instructs it in its tasks. We cannot regard a structure as purposive without becoming involved in research into the grounds of its
origin; for the assertion that it owes its genesis to intention on the part
of nature or of providence is meaningless, since it is purely tautologi-
cal and only restates the question.[56] So the attempt, at least, must be
made to hold to the idea of mechanism and to follow it as far as
possible, although we are sure, on the other hand, that we will never
thus arrive at any ultimately valid answer to the question. For knowledge means just this continuous extensibility of its own fruitfulness.
Thanks to this procedure, the secret of organic life is never solved in
an abstract and purely conceptual fashion, but the knowledge and the
intuition of the individual forms of nature are steadily broadened and
deepened by it. More than this, however, the "maxim of the reflective
judgment" may not do, nor does it desire anything more, for its goal
does not consist in a solution to the "riddle of the universe" in the
sense of a metaphysical monism, but in continuously sharpening
one's eyes for the wealth of the phenomena of organic nature and in
penetrating ever further into the particularities and the individualities
of the phenomenon of life and its conditions.

Having arrived at this point, Kant may then once again, with
the utmost methodological acuity and sensitivity, contrast his philosophical principle with the principle of the received metaphysics.
The opposition between discursive and intuitive understanding, to
which the *Critique of Pure Reason* had already called attention, is
here given a new and even more comprehensive meaning. For an
absolutely infinite and absolutely creative understanding—such as

56. See ibid., §78 (V, 489 ff.) (*Ak.* V, 410 ff.).

that from which metaphysics derives the purposiveness of the forms and order of nature—the contrast between the possible and the actual, which binds us in all our cognition, would drop away, since for such a mind the mere positing of an object in thought and in will would imply its existence. The distinction between being that is thought and being that is actual, between contingent and necessary being, would be nonsensical for such an intellect; since in the first member of the sequence of being it contemplates there would be comprised for it the sequence as a totality as well as the whole of its structure, both ideal and actual.[57] For human understanding, on the contrary, the notion of such a survey signifies a completely unattainable Idea. For it is not given to human understanding to grasp the whole and to raise it up before itself except through a progressive composition of parts. Its proper locus is not the cognition of the primal, original grounds of being, but the comparison of individual perceptions and their subordination to universal rules and laws. And there too, where it pursues the path of pure deduction, seeming to move from the universal to the particular, it invariably achieves no more than the analytical universality proper to concepts as such. "It is, in fact, a distinctive characteristic of our understanding that in its cognition—as, for instance, of the cause of a product—it moves from the *analytic universal* to the particular, or, in other words, from conceptions to given empirical intuitions. In this process, therefore, it determines nothing in respect of the multiplicity of the particular. On the contrary, understanding must wait for the subsumption of the empirical intuition—supposing that the object is a natural product—under the conception, to furnish this determination for the faculty of judgment. But now we are also able to form a notion of an understanding which, not being discursive like ours, but intuitive, moves from the *synthetic universal*, or intuition of a whole as a whole, to the particular—that is to say, from the whole to the parts. To render possible a definite form of the whole, a *contingency* in the synthesis of the parts, is not implied by such an understanding or its representation of the whole. But that is what our understanding requires. It

57. Cf. above, pp. 278 ff.

must advance from the parts as the universally conceived principles to different possible forms to be subsumed thereunder as consequences. . . . How then may we avoid having to represent the possibility of the whole as dependent upon the parts in a manner conformable to our discursive understanding? May we follow what the standard of the intuitive or archetypal understanding prescribes, and represent the possibility of the parts as both in their form and synthesis dependent upon the whole? The very peculiarity of our understanding in question prevents this being done in such a way that the whole contains the source of the possibility of the nexus of the parts. This would be self-contradictory in knowledge of the discursive type. But the *representation* of a whole may contain the source of the possibility of the form of that whole and of the nexus of the parts which that form involves. This is our only road. But, now, the whole would in that case be an effect or product the *representation* of which is looked on as the *cause* of its possibility. But the product of a cause whose determining ground is merely the representation of its effect is termed an end. Hence it follows that it is simply a consequence flowing from the particular character of our understanding that we should figure to our minds products of Nature as possible according to a different type of causality from that of the physical laws of matter, that is, as only possible according to ends and final causes. In the same way we explain the fact that this principle does not touch the question of how such things themselves, even considered as phenomena, are possible on this mode of production, but only concerns the estimate of them possible to our understanding. . . .Here it is also quite unnecessary to prove that an *intellectus archetypus* like this is possible. It is sufficient to show that we are led to this idea of an *intellectus archetypus* by contrasting with it our discursive understanding that has need of images (*intellectus ectypus*) and noting the contingent character of a faculty of this form, and that this idea involves nothing self-contradictory."[58]

All the lines previously established by the critique of reason here converge in a single point; all its concepts and presuppositions unite

---

58. *Critique of Teleological Judgment*, §77 (V, 486 f.) (*Ak.* V, 407–08).

to determine unambiguously and precisely the position occupied by
the idea of an end in the whole of our cognition. The inquiry here
passes into depths which are genuine and ultimate, into the very
foundations of the Kantian conceptual structure. Schelling said of
these propositions from the *Critique of Judgment* that perhaps never
before had so many profound thoughts been crammed into so few
pages as here. At the same time, however, all the difficulties surrounding Kant's doctrine of the "thing in itself" and his conception of
the "intelligible" are presented afresh. The principal conclusion to be
drawn from this whole consideration is that the *methodological* orientation points out the distinction between the *intellectus archetypus* and
the *intellectus ectypus*, between the understanding which is primal and
that which is secondary and craves images. The two members of this
contrast are not opposed to each other in their existence, nor do we
look in them to a difference in actual things. But through them two
systematic orientations are to be created, lending themselves to a
supportive relation with the nature of our specific means of cognition,
and its meaning and its validity. This task can be facilitated by ranging the systematic orientation beside the historical. In the history of
metaphysics, the concept of an end encounters two opposing basic
viewpoints and evaluations. On the one hand there is the doctrine of
Aristotle, on the other that of Spinoza: in the former case teleology is
the highest form of adequate cognition of being and insight into it; in
the latter it is a special "human" way of knowing, which is put into
things themselves and their formation only through a deception of
the imagination. For Aristotle the end means the τὸ τί ἦν εἶναι: the
ultimate intelligible ground of all being and change; for Spinoza it is
merely an imaginative frippery that smirches and obscures the pure
image of being, the image of substance that produces the totality of its
modifications with geometrical necessity. Between these two ex-
tremes the entire evolution of metaphysics moves. The inner freedom
Kant achieved with respect to the results of this evolution is shown
anew by the way he eschews in equal measure both typical solutions
that had been offered for the problem of finality. For him the end is
neither the basic concept of the *intellectus archetypus*, as it was for
Aristotle, nor, as for Spinoza, a creature of the *intellectus ectypus* that
falls short of the true vision of being. The teleological way of thinking

arises instead through a new *relationship* that ensues when our conditioned and finite understanding responds to the demand of the unconditioned; thus its basis is an opposition which is possible only from the standpoint of our mode of cognition, but which on the other hand is shown to be unavoidable and necessary under its previously established presuppositions.

An end is accordingly no more a product of absolute thinking than a purely anthropomorphic type of representation, which in the highest knowledge we leave behind as a mere subjective deception. Rather, its "subjectivity" itself has a universal nature: the conditioned state of human reason itself finds its expression herein. The concept of finality issues from the mirroring of experience in idea, from the comparison of the form of our categorical thinking with that other type of understanding that the demand or reason for systematic unity and perfection in use of the understanding shows us. Its nature and the particularities of its methodology are here similarly misconstrued if we relax our hold on either of the members of this correlation. If we take our stance with the absolute and archetypal understanding, the ground is cut away from under every application of the concept of an end. For purposiveness is, according to Kant's definition, the "lawfulness of the contingent"; for such an understanding, however, the concept of the contingent would be empty. That which comprises the part and the whole, the particular and the universal, in one indivisible mental gaze, the contrast between possibility and actuality, to which we are bound thanks to the basic laws of our mode of cognition, would be obliterated; there would exist for it only the absolutely unitary series of being, which would tolerate the thought of nothing in addition to and outside of itself. The survey of a set of possible cases, which is the presupposition of every judgment of finality, would also drop away here; where the insight that the whole of reality can be nothing other than what it in fact is holds sway, the assertion of some particular preferential end of this specific being loses its meaning and validity.[59] On the other hand, to say this is

59. At this point, therefore, Kant indirectly completes his criticism of the Leibnizian conception of the concept of purpose and the metaphysic Leibniz founded on it. In Leibniz's theodicy, it is God's understanding which chooses among the infinite number of "possible worlds" and "permits the actualizing" of the best of them. The

absolutely not to say that the concept of *empirical* actuality, that our thinking about *phenomena,* either must or even could be renounced in applying the concept of finality. For this thinking is stimulated precisely by that dualism of logical and intuitive conditions that is the basis for the application of this concept and cannot escape this duality without surrendering itself. Its locus is the antithesis of the universal and the particular and yet it feels itself compelled to progressively conquer that antithesis. The form of this conquest, a never-ceasing, never-completed pursuit which yet is feasible to the end, is the concept of purpose. Hence it is unavoidable for us; in no way does it go beyond the ensemble of our methods of cognition, but rather it is

---

basic flaw in this conception, according to Kant, consists in the false hypostatization of a "subjective" antithesis which attaches to the form of our cognition, and attribution of it to the Absolute itself. The basis for the fact that for *us* the possibility of things does not coincide with their actuality is that, in our mode of cognition, the sphere of the understanding and that of intuition, the realm of what is thought and what is given, are not identical in their scope, so that here something can be *thought* as possible which finds no correlate in intuition and no instance of actualization. For the "intuitive understanding," however, whose thinking is seeing and whose seeing is thinking—even if we only admit the idea of such an understanding—the distinction between the potential and the actual must be regarded as canceled out. "This means that if our understanding were intuitive it would have no objects but such as are actual. Conceptions, which are merely directed to the possibility of an object, and sensuous intuitions, which give us something and yet do not thereby let us cognize it as an object, would both cease to exist. . . . To say, therefore, that things may be possible without being actual . . . is to state propositions that hold true for human reason, without such validity proving that this distinction lies in the things themselves. . . . An understanding into whose mode of cognition this distinction did not enter would express itself by saying: All Objects that I know *are,* that is, exist; and the possibility of some that did not exist, in other words, their contingency supposing them to exist . . . would never enter into the imagination of such a being. But what makes it so hard for our understanding with its conceptions to rival reason is simply this, that the very thing that reason regards as constitutive of the Object and adopts as principle is for understanding, in its human form, transcendent, that is, impossible under the subjective conditions of its knowledge" (*Critique of Teleological Judgment,* §76). Here, as can be seen, the Leibnizian theodicy is vanquished, since the critical attack is directed not so much against its result as against the very basis of its way of posing the question. The Leibnizian application of the concept of purpose, in the idea of the "best of all possible worlds," is taxed by Kant for being an "anthropomorphism"; however, it is not an anthropomorphism of a psychological but of a "transcendental" kind that he discovers in it, and which he therefore thinks can at last be unseated through the whole of his transcendental analysis and its conclusions.

valid just precisely for this ensemble itself, though not for that "absolute" being which metaphysics in its received form treats of. The idea of an end and that of organic life are what initially give to our experience and our knowledge of nature the immanent infinity proper to them; it converts conditioned and isolated experiences into a totality, into the intuition of a living *whole*, but it simultaneously points to the limits of this whole since it comes to know it as a whole of phenomena. "If at last I rest in the ultimate phenomenon," Goethe once said, "this is but resignation; but still there is a great difference whether I submit to the bounds of human nature or to a hypothetical restriction of my limited individuality." For Kant the appearance of organic life, and also the idea of purpose in which it is expressed for our cognition, is such an ultimate phenomenon. It is neither the expression of the absolute itself nor of a merely contingent and dispensable subjective restriction of judgment, but it leads to the limits of human nature itself, so as to grasp them as such and to accommodate itself to them.

From the totality of these abstract reflections, however, we are plunged straight into the midst of the realm of intuitive contemplation, as soon as Kant goes on to make secure the basic insight he achieved in his critique of the concept of purpose in the facts of nature and in their detailed interpretation. The synthesis of the principle of finality and the principle of mechanism, and the reciprocal conditioning between the two that is to be assumed within experience, present themselves with concrete immediacy and clarity in Kant's concept of evolution. Evolution is itself a purposive concept, for it posits an "imprinted form," a unitary "subject" of the phenomena of life, which conserves itself in all changes, while it is transformed as well. But it must at the same time be explained purely causally in all its individual phases, so these truly compose a temporally ordered whole. The requirement stands inviolable for Kant from the beginning, because it was in the world of *cosmic* phenomena, the world of mechanism itself, that the full meaning of the idea of evolution first came upon him. In his initial youthful attempt to crystallize the whole of his natural scientific view of the world, the universal *theory* of the heavens had been transformed for him into the universal *natural his-*

tory of the heavens. This standpoint bore fruit not only in a fullness of new, detailed results, but, what is decisive in the philosophical sense, in a new ideal of knowledge clearly and consciously opposed to the ruling technique of systematic classification of existing natural forms, as carried out, for instance, in Linnaeus's doctrine. "Natural history, which is almost nonexistent for us," as Kant characterized this ideal in a later work on the diversity of the races of men, "would teach us about the changes in the figure of the earth, and as well the earthly creatures (plants and animals) which have changed through natural migrations and the deviations from the archetype of the basic species which have arisen in them therefrom. It would probably trace back a host of apparently diverse types of races to one and the same genus, and change the scholastic system of the description of Nature which is presently too widespread into a physical system for the understanding."[60] The basic notion is here already being advanced that nature initially comprises for the understanding a clear and surveyable unity, when we do not grasp it as a rigid entity of juxtaposed forms, but pursue it in its continuous becoming. The *Critique of Judgment* gives this thought new breadth and depth, since in the principle of formal purposiveness it erects its universal critical foundation. Here it is shown that we only understand any particular manifold insofar as we think it as proceeding from a principle which "specifies" itself, and that such a *judging* of the manifold from the standpoint of our faculties of cognition constitutes the inevitable means of making its structure conceivable and transparent. If we apply this logical result to the consideration of *physical* existents, we then immediately arrive at a new concept of nature, which, unlike that of Linnaeus, does not just dispose species and genera in ranks, separated one from the other by fixed, unchangeable characteristics, but rather tries to make the coherence of nature comprehensible through the transformation of species.

Now we can understand that it is not at all an *aperçu* of genius but a necessary consequence of his methodological presuppositions when Kant assumes this postulate in the *Critique of Judgment,* and when he

60. See "On the Various Races of Men," §3, note (II, 451) (*Ak.* II, 434).

attempts to carry it out over the entire realm of natural forms. He begins with the universal requirement for every "natural explanation," which for him is already posited through the concept and the form of scientific experience itself. "It is of endless importance for reason to keep in view the mechanism which Nature employs in its productions, and to take due account of it in explaining them, since no insight into the nature of things can be attained apart from that principle. Even the concession that a supreme Architect has directly created the forms of Nature in the way they have existed from all time, or has predetermined those which in their course of evolution regularly conform to the same type, does not further our knowledge of Nature one whit. The reason is that we are wholly ignorant of the manner in which the supreme Being acts and of His ideas, in which the principles of the possibility of the natural beings are supposed to be contained, and so cannot explain Nature from Him by moving from above downwards, that is, a priori."[61]

On the other hand, the preceding discussions have established the equally necessary maxim of reason that the principle of ends in the products of nature is not to be ignored, because, although it makes it no more comprehensible how these products have arisen, yet it is a heuristic principle with which to investigate the particular laws of nature. Even if the two principles are mutually exclusive as basic premises of explanation and deduction regarding a given thing in nature, they are nonetheless thoroughly compatible as basic premises for discussion. Our cognition has the authority to explain all the products and events in nature, even those which are purposive, as mechanical, so far as it is in our power, and indeed that is its vocation. But it must be resigned to arriving ultimately at a primordial "organization" of them for which no mechanical "why" can be seen, but only a teleological "why." Since, however, prior to this point no impediment to the question is permissible, it is praiseworthy to go through the great creation of organic nature with the aid of a "comparative anatomy" to see whether something like a system, and indeed one governed by the genetic principle, can be found. "When we consider

61. *Critique of Teleological Judgment,* §78 (*Ak.* V, 410).

the agreement of so many genera of animals in a certain common schema, which apparently underlies not only the structure of their bones, but also the disposition of their remaining parts, and when we find here the wonderful simplicity of the original plan, which has been able to produce such an immense variety of species by the shortening of one member and the lengthening of another, by the involution of this part and the evolution of that, there gleams upon the mind a ray of hope, however faint, that the principle of the mechanism of Nature, apart from which there can be no natural science at all, may yet enable us to arrive at some explanation in the case of organic life. This analogy of forms, which in all their differences seem to be produced in accordance with a common type, strengthens the suspicion that they have an actual kinship due to descent from a common parent. This we might trace in the gradual approximation of one animal species to another, from that in which the principle of ends seems best authenticated, namely from man, back to the polyp, and from this back even to mosses and lichens, and finally to the lowest perceivable stage of Nature. Here we come to crude matter; and from this, and the forces which it exerts in accordance with mechanical laws (laws resembling those by which it acts in the formation of crystals), seems to be developed the whole technic of Nature which, in the case of organized beings, is so incomprehensible to us that we feel obliged to imagine a different principle for its explanation.

"Here the *archaeologist* of Nature is at liberty to go back to the traces that remain of Nature's earliest revolutions, and, appealing to all he knows of or can conjecture about its mechanism, to trace the genesis of that great family of living things. . . .He can suppose that the womb of mother earth as it first emerged, like a huge animal, from its chaotic state, gave birth to creatures whose form displayed less finality, and that these again bore others which adapted themselves more perfectly to their native surrounding and their relations to each other, until this womb, becoming rigid and ossified, restricted its birth to definite species incapable of further modification. . . .Yet, for all that, he is obliged eventually to attribute to this universal mother an organization suitably constituted with a view to all these forms of life, for unless he does so, the possibility of the final form of the products of the animal and plant kingdoms is quite unthinkable. But when he does attribute all this to Nature he has only pushed the explanation a stage farther back. He cannot pretend to have made the genesis of those two kingdoms intelligible independently of the condition of final causes."[62]

We must follow these Kantian propositions—as widely known and renowned as they are—just as far as they will lead us, for aside from the fundamental natural scientific insights anticipated in them, they express once more the whole essence of Kantian thinking. Kant's keen eye for detail and his synthetic power of imagination, his acuteness of intuition and his critical wariness of judgment, all these appear here as though brought to a focus. The idea of a unified derivative and evolutionary series of organisms appeared to Kant as an "adventure of reason"; but he was, like Goethe, barred from entering boldly on this adventure so long as in so doing he had to commit himself to the compass of the critical philosophy. He conceived the bounds set to the journey even before he began it; he saw the Pillars of Hercules, that betokened *nihil ulterius*,[63] clearly and steadily before him from the start. For Kant evolution is no metaphysical concept, which pushes back into the transcendent source of being and enfolds in it the secret of life; it is the principle by means of which the whole fullness and coherence of the phenomena of life might be presented for our cognition. We are not accustomed to ask whence life stems when we see before us in intuitive clarity and conceptual order only the totality of its forms and its arrangement in stages. In this conclusion one of the most profound factors of the Kantian doctrine speaks out once again from a new direction. The *Critique of Judgment* holds fast to the dualism of the "thing in itself" and "appearance"; but again this dualism is mediated by the idea that the "thing in itself," *regarded as an idea*, is what first brings the reality of experience to true completion. For only the idea is what ensures the systematic perfection of the use of the understanding, in which the objects are given to us not as disparate singular things, and hence as fragments of being,

62. Ibid., §80 (V, 497–99) (*Ak.* V, 418–20).
63. Cf. *Critique of Pure Reason*, A 395 (III, 661).

but in their concrete totality and in their thoroughgoing, unbroken interconnection.

Thus the *Critique of Judgment* adheres to the basic presuppositions of Kantian thought, while on the other hand it far transcends their previous sphere of application. The trial of precritical metaphysics launched by Kant comes to its close here: the *Critique of Judgment* confirms the verdict that the *Critique of Pure Reason* and the *Critique of Practical Reason* had pronounced on dogmatic metaphysics. And yet the critical philosophy now enters into another relationship with metaphysics. For the former has pursued the latter in its most central domain and has taken its measure by deciding and solving precisely those fundamental problems which from ancient times have seemed to be the peculiar property of metaphysics. In doing all this Kant's doctrine has not exceeded the ramifications of "transcendental philosophy": the general task of analyzing the contents and means of knowledge. As the content of the ethical could only be established by exhibiting the necessary and universally valid principles of all moral judgment, so this analysis could approach the problem of art, indeed that of life itself, only through the mediation of a critique of aesthetic and teleological judgment. But now it can be seen yet more clearly that this course, which is rooted in the essence of Kantian methodology, does not abort the wealth of intuitive actuality and water it down into a system of flimsy abstractions, but that, on the contrary, Kant's original concept of knowledge has undergone an extension and deepening that only now makes it feasible to survey the *whole* of natural and spiritual life and to conceive it as intrinsically a single organism of "reason."

VII LAST WORKS, LAST BATTLES. *RELIGION WITHIN THE LIMITS OF REASON ALONE,* AND THE CONFLICT WITH THE PRUSSIAN GOVERNMENT

If we turn aside from the structure and development of the Kantian system and consider Kant's outward life after the completion of the *Critique of Judgment,* we find it precisely at the point where we left it a decade before. Nothing in his way of life or in his relation to the world and his surroundings had changed during this epoch, which was so fertile and inwardly active. It is as if every occurrence and all progress were devoted purely and exclusively to his labors and withdrawn from him as a person. Since he had consciously and methodically set the style of his outward existence, he adhered to it with scrupulous exactness and regularity down to the smallest detail. In 1783 he changed his dwelling place for the last time: he moved to the house on Schlossgraben, where he lived until his death. Kant's first biographers depicted the arrangement of this house. It had eight rooms, of which Kant kept for himself only two, a study and a bedroom. "When one entered the house," Hasse tells us, "a serene calm reigned. ... When one climbed the steps, ... one went left through the entirely plain, unadorned, slightly dingy entrance hall into a larger room, which led to the parlor, but where nothing showy was on display. A sofa, some chairs with linen covers, a glass-fronted cupboard with some porcelain, a bureau which held his silver and ready cash, a nearby thermometer and a pier table ... were all the furniture, which took up one portion of the white walls. And thus one pushed through a quite shabby door into the equally shabby 'Sans-Souci,' which one was invited to enter, upon knocking, by a cheerful 'Come in!'.... The entire room breathed simplicity and quiet detachment from the hurly-burly of the city and the world." Two tables, which usually were covered with books, a plain sofa, some chairs, and a chest of drawers comprised the total furnishings of the space, its sole decoration consisting of a portrait of Rousseau, which hung on the wall.[1] Kant was more than ever confined to his house, since in 1787 he had decided to give up the lunch table in the inn, which had been almost the only diversion of his years as a young man and *privatdozent*, and to establish a group of his own. He had not renounced his pleasure in companionship in so doing; almost every day he had at table several of his friends, with whom he spent the luncheon hour in lively and stimulating conversation. This intellectually diverting round table remained unforgettable to the younger members of Kant's circle in particular. Poerschke, Kant's student and later his colleague at the University of Königsberg, says about it that Kant here lavished an immeasurable wealth of ideas, that he uttered a myriad of genial thoughts, of which he was scarcely conscious afterward. "In him," Poerschke adds, "one saw how childlike innocence and brilliance interacted with each other; his mind bore, along with the most marvelous fruits, numberless flowers, which often amused and served but for a moment."[2] A profusion of the richest personal ideas and hints were thus confined to a very narrow circle, for Kant was very particular that, in accordance with a maxim of sociability, the number of his companions at table amount to no less than three, but no more than nine. Although he felt at that time no brooding, melancholy inclination toward solitude, by conscious intent he strongly protected himself from the press of the outside world. He himself set the limits of his own involvement in and consideration of it, since this was an area in which he put to the test his basic rule of autonomy in the smallest and most intimate things.

1. See Johann Gottfried Hasse, *Letzte Äusserungen Kants von einem seiner Tischgenossen* (Königsberg, 1804), pp. 6 ff.

2. Cf. ibid., pp. 39 f.

This tendency comes out most conspicuously in Kant's mode of existence in relation to the new element that had come into his life since the middle of the 1780s. Only now had literary fame in its full extent fallen to Kant's lot, along with all the demands and burdens. Since Reinhold's "Letters on the Kantian Philosophy" ("Briefe über die Kantische Philosophie"), which appeared in 1786 and 1787 in Wieland's *Deutscher Merkur*,[3] and since the founding of the *Jenaische Allgemeine Literaturzeitung* by Schütz and Hufeland, which soon evolved into the special organ of the critical philosophy, the victory of Kantian philosophy in Germany was settled. A long struggle against misunderstandings and attacks from opponents of all kinds was still to follow, but these battles would only undergird and confirm anew the place it henceforth assumed in the entire intellectual life of Germany. All the forces of tradition were now summoned up once more against it. Almost no manner and almost no degree of polemic were not met with here. From Nicolai's flat jokes to the objections (at least intended to be profound) of the Wolffian philosophical school, which had created for itself a special literary organ in the *Philosophisches Magazin* in Halle, founded by Eberhard and Maas, every variety of criticism was to be found. The Berlin Academy of Sciences' orientation toward popular philosophy and popular science, in its fight against the Kantian doctrine, was at one with the "adepts" and fanatical minds with new metaphysical revelations; "sound human understanding" and the outlook of philosophical "intuition" closed ranks to ward off the "presumptions" of the transcendental philosophy. Even as the Kantian doctrine spread and even with its greater and greater influence, this countermovement ran unaltered through it all. The Kantian philosophy prevailed, although it itself rapidly disintegrated into various warring parties, each of which claimed for itself the sole correct and valid interpretation of the fundamental ideas of the First Critique.

With this development, however, more and more demands from outside were laid on Kant, which tended to force him out of his self-chosen circle of life, away from his plans for philosophical writ-

3. [These appeared in book form in two volumes in 1790–92.—Tr.]

ing, and declare himself definitely in the battle going on around him. In general, Kant remained chilly toward all these efforts: he saw too clearly before him the road he had to traverse and the positive task he still had to accomplish to let himself be held back by mere repetition and interpretation of his old books. Where, as in the case of Feder's and Eberhard's criticism, he believed he saw a conscious distortion of the root intention of his philosophy, he pursued it with a ruthless and unembittered keenness. On the whole, though, he held firmly to the conviction that once the discussion was guided to the right point, the sense of the main critical problems would grow increasingly more clear out of the welter of interpretations. Besides, he had only a very limited feeling for the struggle for personal fame in the present and the future, so unshakable was his consciousness of the content and value of his philosophy. "Author's itch," which he had avoided so perseveringly during the long gestation and ripening of the *Critique of Pure Reason*, still held no power over him. It looked almost as though he simply could not see himself in the role of celebrated writer that now fell to him. Those marks of childlike innocence, which Poerschke emphasizes in his portrait of Kant and which he found to be intimately related to the basic traits of Kant's genius, often come to the fore in a surprising way. When Schütz dealt with him about his participation in the *Jenaische Literaturzeitung*, he could not be astonished enough at Kant's modesty; not only did he profess his voluntary renunciation of the author's honorarium, but he even begged that he wanted to work out his review of Herder's *Ideas* only as a trial, and that the decision between their respective views of society, which were the basis on which the *Literaturzeitung* had been founded, be abandoned.[4] "Kant," Poerschke explains over again in a letter to

4. Cf. Schütz's letters to Kant of August 23, 1784, and February 18, 1785 (IX, 257, 260) (*Ak.* X, 372, 374). "Your review of Herder," Schütz writes in the latter, "you will by now probably already have seen in print. Everyone who is an unbiased judge regards it as a masterpiece of precision.... My God, and you could believe that a review like yours might not be acceptable! It brought involuntary tears to my eyes when I read that. Such modesty in a man like you! I cannot describe the feeling that I had. It was joy, horror, and indignation all in one, particularly the last, when I think of the immodesty of so many learned men of this *seculum*, who are not worthy to unloose the latchets of a *Kant's* shoes."

Fichte, "is a model of a modest writer, of all human souls he feels his greatness the least; I often hear him judging an opponent magnanimously, only they must not attack him personally and like monks."[5] Such a nature was not to swerve one step from its road by reason of success or failure: in the whole of Kant's career as an author no sign can be found that worry over it ever upset him and that it interfered with his intellectual development in any way whatsoever.

This is not the place for us to trace out the universal effect on history wrought by the Kantian theory and the transformation it underwent in the process. Only certain personal witnesses, who inform us as to the impact of the new philosophy on individuals, might be referred to briefly. Fichte's famous saying, that he had the Kantian philosophy to thank not only for his basic convictions but also for his character, nay, for the effort to will to have a character of that kind, is typical in this regard: it expresses most pregnantly a feeling which, especially after the appearance of Kant's ethical works, spread abroad and became more and more intense. Kant's correspondence offers the most numerous evidences for this. In a letter of May 12, 1786, the twenty-year-old physician Johann Benjamin Erhard tells how he immersed himself in Kant's writings, led in the first instance by his wish to refute the Kantian philosophy, until, on pressing further, he had been completely taken captive by it. "Six months ago, awakened by the call to do it, I began to read your Critique. No other book have I taken in hand with such bitterness; to enter the lists against you was my warmest wish and prayer. My pride was in fact to blame for my blindness, for as long as I had the idea that it is Kant who frustrates in me the hope of my own system to come, my inmost being revolted against you, but as soon as I became aware that Truth had chosen as my lot to lead me out of a stormy land where I wanted to build on unfirm ground a palace to protect myself, into a paradisiacal region where a perpetual springtime did not compel me to seek safety under a heap of stone, I pressed it to my bosom and am certain it will never leave my hand. . . . Your metaphysics of morals, however, quite made

5. Immanuel Hermann von Fichte, *Johann Gottlieb Fichtes Leben und literarischer Briefwechsel* (Seidel, 1830–31), vol. 2, p. 447.

me one with you; a sensation of bliss streams through all my limbs, as often as I recall the hour when I read it for the first time."[6] In his autobiography as well, Erhard admits that he had Kant's ethical works to thank for a "rebirth of his whole inner man."[7] For Reinhold, too, this was the moment that forever bound him to Kant. Although in his later writings he tried above all to define the highest theoretical principle of the transcendental philosophy, still it was practical and religious motives that originally led him to it. Here that "concord of head and heart" which he had hitherto sought in vain was born in him. And even a man like Jung-Stilling, who was certainly not driven to the Kantian theory by any deeper speculative need, found his way into it under the viewpoint and the influence of Reinhold's "Letters on the Kantian Philosophy"; the token of its powerful and universal effect is that even this simple and modest mind dared to say that the Kantian theory would soon have effected "a far greater, more blessed, and more universal revolution than Luther's Reformation."[8] It is obvious on all sides how Kant's philosophy, even before it was fully accepted and taken over in the theoretical sense, was immediately felt to be an inescapable new force in life. Because this foundation of the critical philosophy stood firm amid the strife of the Kantian schools, which seemed more dangerous than any attacks by opponents, its essential historical power remained unweakened. The aim of the system was put forward clearly in the transcendental doctrine of freedom: people believed they could hold fast to it, even if the path supposedly leading to it seemed ever and again to be lost in darkness and in dialectical confusion.

For Kant himself there was no such separation between his results and his method, between the critical theory and its applications. For him, within the system, every part conditioned and supported the other, and the convenient and traditional division of theory from practice, with which German popular philosophy tried to mitigate the "rigorism" of its ethics, he opposed yet again as keenly as possible in

6. See Kant's correspondence (IX, 299) (*Ak.* X, 422).

7. K. A. Varnhagen von Ense, *Denkwürdigkeiten des Philosophen and Arztes Johann Benjamin Ehrhard* (Stuttgart & Tübingen, 1830).

8. See Jung-Stilling's letter to Kant, March 1, 1789 (IX, 378) (*Ak.* XI, 7).

a treatise in reply to Garve dating from 1793.[9] But still, after the theoretical foundations of his system had been completed with the conclusion of the *Critique of Judgment,* he turned once more by preference to the immediate questions of life that were exercising his era. It is now primarily political problems that press into the center of his interest, more than before. Kant used the essay against Garve to develop a complete outline of his politics and his theory of civil law, as an appendix to the particular question with which he set out. Kant's shorter treatises, too, which in this period appeared in the *Berlinische Monatsschrift,* are advanced with an eye to the specific political relations and situations of that time. The critical philosopher, who had just completed the whole of his theoretical edifice, turns journalist. He is not content to lay down abstract doctrines and claims, but is driven to become involved in the tasks of the day and to enter directly into the shaping of concrete actuality, although only by way of providing enlightenment and theory. Looked at from this perspective, Kant's literary activity during this period, which at first glance seems as conflicting as it is multifarious, immediately takes on a fixed and integral focus. Kant allies himself with the Berlin school of enlightenment philosophy, whose main organ was the *Berlinische Monatsschrift* managed by von Biester, in order to take up in concert with it the fight against political and intellectual reaction in Prussia, the portents of which he recognized earlier and more clearly than anyone else. Whatever in his basic philosophical outlook set him off from this enlightenment movement became minor for him in the face of this new common task. As early as 1784, in "An Answer to the Question: 'What Is Enlightenment?',", he had gathered up all the threads clustering around the name of this party, and endeavored to define their one most profound integrating tendency. Here the concept of enlightenment is recast by means of the critical conception of autonomy, and grounded and secured in it. "Enlightenment is man's release from his self-incurred tutelage. Tutelage is man's inability to

9. "On the Common Saying: 'This May Be True in Theory, but It Does Not Apply in Practice'" ["Über den Gemeinspruch: 'Das mag in der Theorie richtig sein, taugt aber nicht für die Praxis'"], sect. 1 (VI, 355 ff.) (*Ak.* VIII, 273 ff.).

make use of his understanding without direction from another. Self-incurred is this tutelage when its cause lies not in lack of reason but in lack of resolution and courage to use it without direction from another. *Sapere aude!* Have the courage to use your own reason!—that is the motto of enlightenment."[10] On the strength of this idea and this motto, Kant opposed all efforts to put the critical philosophy in the services of an irrationalism which, in making feeling and faith an element also of all *theoretical* knowledge, threatened in the end to demolish the foundations of the theoretical concepts of truth and certainty themselves. He turned sharply and definitively against Friedrich Heinrich Jacobi's philosophy of faith. And here too he directly combined his conceptual analysis, in which he disclosed the difference between Jacobi's concept of faith and his own doctrine of rational faith, with a political view and a political admonition. The epistemological exposition ends with a personal warning and apostrophe. "Men of intellectual abilities and broad sentiments! I respect your talents and love your feeling for mankind. But have you also considered well what you are doing, and where your attacks on reason are leading? Doubtless you want the *idea of freedom* to be preserved in sound health; for without that there would soon be an end to your free flights of genius.... Friends of the human race and of what is most holy to it! Assume what seems to you most worthy of belief, upon careful and sincere examination, be it facts, be it the grounds of reason; only do not contest reason in what it makes the highest good on earth, namely, the privilege of being the ultimate touchstone of truth! Otherwise, unworthy of this freedom, you will certainly forfeit it too, and drag down this misfortune on the head of those who are innocent, who otherwise would be fully minded to serve freedom in accordance with law, and thereby also for the purpose of the best of all worlds!"[11] Kant's style rose but seldom to that kind of urgent personal feeling: we sense in these words, written in the year in which Frederick the Great died, how lucidly Kant saw the coming of the new regime, which soon thereafter found its voice in

10. "An Answer to the Question: 'What Is Enlightenment?'" (1784) (IV, 169) (*Ak.* VIII, 35).

11. "What Is Orientation in Thinking?" (1786) (IV, 363 ff.) (*Ak.* VIII, 144-47).

naming Wöllner as minister and in the promulgation of the Prussian edict concerning religion.

Thus for the man of almost seventy, after a decade of the most comprehensive and most profound productivity, there was not a moment's respite; he saw himself straightway embroiled all over again in fresh battles, which he had to wage on diverse fronts. On the one side, it was important to ward off misunderstandings and distortions of his philosophy, which threatened its essential content and specific worth. While the reigning academic philosophy had seen in Kant primarily the "all-destroyer," as Mendelssohn had honestly felt and said, this opinion gradually gave way to another feeling and a different tactic. The initial impression of sheer negativity made by the critical theory had to lessen in the degree that its positive content emerged more and more distinctly, at least indirectly, in its *effect*. Now the attempt had to be made to conceive this content, little as people might relevantly and truly assimilate it, at least by given *historical* categories and models. In the same way that on its first appearance the First Critique was compared with Berkeley, just as Hamann hailed Kant as "the Prussian Hume," now the voices that drew attention to the relationship between Kantian and Leibnizian idealism grew louder. But Leibniz's idealism was not understood in its genuine universality and depth; rather it was seen through the medium of Wolffian philosophy and in the light of the recognized handbooks of metaphysics stemming from the Wolffian school of thought. When the Kantian results were translated back into the language of these handbooks, they seemed at first to shed their strangeness and to be incorporated into the circle of accepted ideas. But surprise was growing at what strange forms and formulas the transcendental philosophy, taken as a result already known in its essential points, had been tricked out in. All the basic methodological distinctions of the First Critique: the contrast between sensibility and understanding, the difference between analytic and synthetic judgments, the opposition between a priori and a posteriori, were affected by this view of them. Since as individual moments they were disengaged from all the systematic relations and connections to which they belong and only in which do they have their peculiar foothold and their meaning, they were thus stamped with the character of particular bits of doctrine, for which an analogue and counterpart could easily be pointed out in an alien world of ideas. The critical studies undertaken by Eberhard and Maas regarding the basic question of the First Critique, in the *Philosophisches Magazin* for 1788/89, are entirely slanted this way, despite the semblance of scientific strictness and thoroughness given to them.

Kant set his face against this procedure with a sharpness and bitterness that recalls his polemic against Feder. He, in whose mind the critical philosophy was conceivable as a living, methodical whole and only as such a whole, could see in this willful and disjointed way of treating it nothing but its "almost deliberate" falsification and misconstruction. In this, regarded simply from the psychological aspect, he doubtless did his opponents injustice; he was so little able to transport himself into the scholastic and disciplinary limitation of their way of thinking that he was inclined to attribute this fault to their will rather than to their intellect. But now he felt all the more forced, in his declaration of war against Eberhard, to set before the reader all the essential leading ideas of his system yet once more in a comprehensive survey, and to illuminate them reciprocally each by the other. In this respect, the treatise "On a Discovery by Which All New Critique of Pure Reason Is to Be Made Unnecessary by an Older One" presents an outline which in its clarity and significance stands directly alongside the *Prolegomena*. The specific nature assigned to sensibility in distinction from the understanding, the methodological peculiarity of the pure forms of space and time, the meaning of the a priori and its contrast with the innate, all this comes out once again with maximum specificity, and this yields, as if spontaneously, the proof of that singularly decisive originality of his system, an originality measurable not by the sum of its results but by the power and the unity of its creative conceptual motifs. [12]

Though in the essay he wrote in reply to Eberhard the total energy of Kant's polemical style is once more displayed, his defense against

---

12. "Über eine Entdeckung nach der alle neue Kritik der reinen Vernunft durch eine ältere entbehrlich gemacht werden soll." (See VI, 3–71) (*Ak.* VIII, 185–251).

an attack of Garve's, which followed shortly, is pitched in a milder tone. It was the fate of this man, noble and lovable though a very mediocre thinker, to cross Kant's trail at every point. Kant had forgiven him the part he played in the notorious review of the First Critique in the *Göttingische Gelehrte Anzeigen* the moment he explained it openly and candidly. But the *Foundations of the Metaphysics of Morals* necessarily aroused Garve's opposition afresh: the austerity of Kantian ethics ran counter to his reconciling nature, averse to any mordancies and oppositions, just as much as it affronted the commonplace ideas of his popular philosophy. Hence he turned, not so much against the principle of ·critical ethics directly, as against its unrestricted realization. He conceded the rule willy-nilly, so as at once to demand and to plead exceptions to it. For Kant, however, there was no weakening and no compromise on this question—and even silence would seem a compromise to him. Goethe wrote to Schiller on a later occasion, "I like the fact that the old man was always willing to keep reiterating his principles and to hammer at the same mistake at every opportunity. The younger practical man does well to take no notice of his opponents; the older theoretician must not let slip an untoward word to anyone. We will adhere to that in the years to come, too."[13] Kant took up the platitude about the difference between theory and practice as such an "untoward word." In the supposed relativity of the empirical possibilities for applying the moral law there is no deliverance from the unconditional nature of the moral claim raised by the categorical imperative. "In a theory founded on the *concept of duty*, any worries about the empty ideality of the concept completely disappear. For it would not be a duty to strive after a certain effect of our will if this effect were impossible to experience (whether we envisage the experience as complete or as progressively approximating to completion). And it is with theory of this kind that the present essay is exclusively concerned. For to the shame of philosophy, it is not uncommonly alleged of such theory that whatever may be correct in it is in fact invalid in practice. We usually hear this said in an arrogant, disdainful tone, which comes of presum-

13. Goethe to Schiller, July 27, 1798.

ing to use experience to reform reason itself in the very attributes which do it most credit. Such illusory wisdom imagines it can see further and more clearly with its molelike gaze fixed on experience than with the eyes which were bestowed on a being designed to stand upright and to scan the heavens. This maxim, so very common in our sententious, inactive times, does very great harm if applied to matters of morality. . . . For in such cases, the canon of reason is related to practice in such a way that the value of the practice depends entirely upon its appropriateness to the theory it is based on; all is lost if the empirical (hence contingent) conditions governing the execution of the law are made into conditions of the law itself, so that a practice calculated to produce a result which *previous* experice makes probable is given the right to dominate a theory which is in fact self-sufficient."[14]

This unshatterable claim of pure theory over against all particular conditions stemming from the concrete empirical material in which it is applied is shown in three directions: in relation to subjective ethical reflection, which in fact is directed to establishing valid maxims for the individual's moral behavior; in relation to the imperative of obligation toward political life and the political constitution; and finally in the cosmopolitan sense, which extends the idea of legal and moral organization to the totality of nations and states, and thus broadens it into the ideal of a universally valid law of nations. In the first regard, the exposition only needs to repeat the specifications given in the *Foundations of the Metaphysics of Morals* and the *Critique of Practical Reason* as to the relation between the "matter" of desire and the pure "form" of the will. But now it makes a further stride into the area of concrete and individual psychological problems, insofar as it takes into consideration not only the pure validity of the moral law as such, but also the factual effectiveness of its application to individual cases. And here the distinction entirely in favor of form as against matter, in favor of pure idea over against the empirical feeling of pleasure and striving for happiness, is also shown to vanish. To the concept of duty

14. "On the Common Saying," introduction (VI, 359) (*Ak.* VIII, 276–77).

belongs not only the sole truly normative meaning, but also the only effective motivating force. It is, "in its full purity," not only incomparably simpler, clearer, more comprehensible and more natural for everyone's practical use, and more natural than every motive derived from happiness and mingled with consideration for it, but also in the judgment of the most ordinary human reason it is far stronger, more urgent, and more promising of result than any grounds of motivation borrowed from the latter principle.[15] But if Kant's basic ethical ideas are extended into the area of pedagogy, an actual broadening of his general theoretical horizon can also be seen at the point where Kant turns his consideration to political life. Here he confronts a new decision in principle: the question of the relation of "theory" to "practice" is transformed into the particular question of the relation between ethics and politics.

In his basic political outlook Kant's feet are planted firmly on the soil of those ideas which found their theoretical expression in Rousseau, and their visible practical efficacy in the French Revolution. Kant sees in the French Revolution the promise of the actualization of the pure law of reason. For to him, the peculiar problem of every political theory consists in the question of the possibility of unifying diverse individual wills into one total will: nonetheless, this does not nullify the autonomy of the particular wills, but its validation and acknowledgement is achieved in a new sense. The intent of every theory of right and of the state, philosophically considered, can be nothing other than the solution of the task of how the freedom of each individual has to limit itself, under the necessity of a recognized law of reason, in such a way that it permits and confirms the freedom of everyone else in so doing. Thus Kant's theory of right and of the state consistently adheres to the universal presuppositions of the eighteenth century: the idea of the inalienable fundamental rights of man and the idea of the social contract. Friedrich Gentz said, not unjustly, about Kant's essay in reply to Garve that it contained "the complete theory of the rights of man, so copiously praised and so

15. Ibid., sect. I (VI, 369) (*Ak.* VIII, 286).

little understood, . . . which issue in a modest but complete form from
the calm and incisive reasoning of the German philosopher."[16] Indeed, Kant has no doubt that if he succeeds in unifying the theory of
civil law and political practice, if he achieves the conformation of
actual political life with the idea of the social contract, the methodological dualism between being and obligation is not erased. The
theory itself is here a pure theory of obligation, capable of seeing
always but a conditioned and relative prominence in empirical being,
perfect as we may think it. Only the *claim* to actualization is unconditioned and unfettered by any temporal and contingent limitations,
while its fulfillment remains forever incomplete.

Hence even the concept of the social contract does not signify
something factual, done in any sort of past time or to be done in any
sort of future time, but rather in fact a task, which still is to be used
and held onto as a yardstick for every judgment of what is factual. A
coalition of individual wills, as is conceptually assumed here, need
never have occurred in such a way that to consider a civil constitution
like this as binding it would have to be proven from previous history
that a people did once actually perform an act of that kind, and an
indubitable spoken or written record of it left for us. "It is in fact
merely an *idea* of reason, which nonetheless has undoubted practical
reality; for it can oblige every legislator to frame his laws in such a
way that they could have been produced by the united will of a whole
nation, and to regard each subject, insofar as he can claim citizenship,
as if he had consented within the general will. This is the test of the
rightfulness of every public law."[17] Where, on the contrary, this rule
is not fulfilled, where the sovereign arrogates rights to himself, rights
which are incompatible with the rule, then the individual possesses
as little right to opposition by force as does the people as an empirical
totality. For to concede such a right is to destroy the factual basis on
which every political order as such rests. The autonomy of the head of
state must continue unimpugned in its concrete existence; pure

16. Friedrich Gentz, "Nachtrag zu dem Räsonnement des Herrn Prof. Kant über
das Verhältnis zwischen Theorie und Praxis," *Berlinische Monatsschrift*, December, 1793.
   17. "On the Common Saying," sect. II, conclusion (VI, 381) (*Ak.* VIII, 297).

theory, however, and the universally valid ethical principles can insist that nothing stand in the way of their unhindered exposition and discussion. The opposition that is justified against the power of the state, but against it under certain circumstances both necessary and called for, is thus of a purely intellectual kind. In every commonwealth obedience to the mechanism of the constitution under laws that compel is what must rule, but at the same time also a spirit of freedom and hence of public criticism of things as they are. The right to opposition, which many theories of civil law arrogate to the citizen, thus dissolves for Kant into mere freedom of the pen; this however must remain inviolable by the sovereign, as "the sole palladium of the rights of the people."

We see in this once more the double nature of the struggle in which Kant was involved during this whole period. He begins with defending the purity and the unrestricted validity of his conception of duty, but this defense drives him back to the general question of the relation of ethical theory to practice. Previously it was not clear and unambiguous which of the two opposing moments here is the standard of measurement and which the one that is measured; the question of whether the actual serves as norm for the idea or the idea for the actual is not forwarded by a single systematic step. The substance of this division, however, is fixed for Kant on the basis of his first critical presuppositions. Just as in the theoretical realm knowledge does not conform to the object, but rather the object to knowledge, so pure obligation provides a universal rule with respect to what is empirically present and actual. Since in fact Kant upholds in this fashion the unlimited applicability of theory as such, this at the same time definitely circumscribes the scope of its means. Theory remains within its own territory: it renounces all use of force as means for the practice of opposition and resistance, so as to make use of rational means alone. This at the same time indicates the role science has in the life of the state, in its positive as well as its negative aspect. Science, in all forms of its public existence and organization, cannot avoid the power of the state and its guardianship, but it submits to the latter only under the condition that the state for its part leaves unchallenged the right of science as the principal examiner and critic of all the institutions of the state. Thus the general task broadens for Kant: from an inquiry into the basic questions of his system and a defense of the purity of his method, he is led to question the place of philosophical theory in the whole of intellectual culture, of which science and religion, civil life and the life of justice, are but individual parts. The need to indicate the bounds of the unique faculty of consciousness all over again, and to keep watch over its exact confines, merges with the relevant particular motives provided Kant by the political situation at that time. We have here anticipated Kant's reply to Garve, which appeared in 1793, because as the culmination of a certain development of thought it indicates most plainly that whole trend. Now, however, we must turn back, to follow closely the course Kant's actions as philosopher and journalist had taken since the death of Friedrich II.

Two years after Friedrich's death, Zedlitz was removed from his post as minister of cultural and educational affairs. The post was entrusted "by particular confidence" of the new king to Johann Christoph Wöllner, a man whom Friedrich had once described, in a short note to a file copy of one document, as a "swindling, scheming parson." Wöllner launched his official activity by decreeing the famous religious edict, which was followed shortly by the issuance of a censorship edict and the institution of a special censorship commission for all printed matter appearing in Prussia. The state considered it important to prosecute the battle of orthodoxy against freethinking and enlightenment with all the means within its power. The religious edict pledged to the subjects toleration of their religious convictions "so long as each quietly fulfills his duties as a good citizen of the state, but keeps his particular opinion in every case to himself, and takes care not to propagate it or to convert others and cause them to err or falter in their faith." Two years later, on December 9, 1790, it was supplemented by a rescript which was issued to the consistories and subjected the examination of candidates in theology to a meticulously prescribed schema.[18] The personal creed of the candidate was to be

---

18. For more on the religious edict and Wöllner's regime, see Dilthey, "Der Streit Kants mit der Zensur über das Recht seiner Religionsforschung," *Archiv für Geschichte*

determined by rigorous questioning, and each of them was to give his oath, sealed by a handshake, not to go beyond the bounds of this creed in the conduct of his office as teacher and preacher.

To get fully and clearly in mind the impression all these measures made on Kant, one must recall the position he had adopted toward all confessions of faith and toward the essence of the church from his youth on, since he had arrived at a firm and independent conviction regarding religious matters. When Johann Caspar Lavater in 1775 besought him as to his view of Lavater's essay on faith and prayer, Kant answered him with the utmost decisiveness and candor: "Do you then know," Kant wrote him, "to whom you are applying on this score? To someone who knows no means which stands the test at the final instant of life other than the purest rectitude in regard to the most secret sentiments of the heart, and who, with Job, deems it a sin to wheedle God and to make inward confessions which may have been extorted by fear and which the mind does not assent to when believing freely. I separate the *teaching* of Christ from the *report* we have about Christ's teaching, and to discover the former in its purity, I try first of all to extract the moral teaching, in distinction from all the legalisms of the New Testament. This is surely the basic teaching of the Gospel, the rest can only be a doctrine which is added on. . . . But when the doctrine of righteous conduct and purity of heart (with faith that God will fulfill the rest . . . *without the so-called worshipful supplications which have perennially constituted the religious delusion* in a fashion which is emphatically totally unnecessary for us to know), is sufficiently widespread so that it can survive in the world, then the scaffolding must crumble when the building is finished. . . . Now I frankly confess that in the historical respect our New Testament documents will never be able to be brought to such authority that we might dare to surrender ourselves to every part of them with unbounded confidence and thus mainly weaken our attention to the one thing needful, namely, the moral faith of the Gospel, whose excel-

der Philosophie, vol. 3; E. Fromm, *I. Kant und die preussische Zensur* (Hamburg and Leipzig, 1894); and Emil Arnoldt, *Beiträge zu dem Material der Geschichte von Kants Leben und Schriftstellertätigkeit in Bezug auf seine "Religionslehre" und seinen Konflikt mit der preussischen Regierung*, *Gesammelte Schriften*, vol. 6, ed. Otto Schöndörffer (1898).

lence consists just in the fact that all our striving for purity of our hearts and conscientiousness in righteous conduct of our lives is bound up with it. In this way the holy law is always before our eyes and makes every falling-away from the divine will, even the least, an incessant reproach to us as if we were judged by a stern and just judge, *against whom no confessions of faith, invoking holy names, or attention to worshipful observances can help at all.* . . . Now it is very clearly seen that the apostles regarded the side-doctrine of the Gospel as its fundamental teaching, and . . . instead of extolling the practical religious doctrine of the holy Teacher as essential, they preached reverence for the Teacher himself, and a kind of ingratiation by flattering and by eulogizing him, something against which he spoke so explicitly and often."[19]

Such a "religion of ingratiation," which he had branded as the immemorial, peculiar delusion of religion, Kant now saw expressly recognized and demanded by the state, and in the given circumstances the tangible, political and practical sense of "ingratiation" threatened to be ranked alongside the transcendent sense. From now on he unwearyingly lodged in every quarter the sharpest protests against this, which he felt to be both a religious and a political corruption. Almost all the brief essays which he submitted at this time to the *Berlinische Monatsschrift* are related, directly or indirectly, to this fundamental, overriding theme.[20] Reference to the Book of Job, already found in his letter to Lavater, seems to have been frequently on his lips in this connection: now he elaborates it further, since he sets in contrast to the honorable doubt and honorable despair over insight into the divinity of the world order, which is Job's hallmark, the portrait of the "wheedler of God," and gives this portrait traits that obviously are taken from those in power in Prussia at that time, and aimed at them. "Job," it is said in the essay "On the Failure of All Philosophical Attempts at Theodicy" ("Über das Misslingen aller philosophischen Versuche in der Theodizee"), "speaks the way he thinks and the way he is expected to, and speaks as probably every man in his situation would be expected to do; his friends speak in the

---

19. To Lavater, April 28, 1775 (see IX, 138 ff.) (*Ak.* X, 171 ff.).

20. Arnoldt in particular has drawn attention to this relation (*Beiträge zu dem Material der Geschichte von Kants Leben*, pp. 107 ff.).

opposite way, as if they were being covertly overheard by the Mighty One, whom they are justifying and to stand in whose favor is, in their judgment, dearer than to be truthful. This malice of theirs in saying, for the sake of appearances, things which they still had to confess they did not understand, and in shamming a conviction which they in fact did not have, contrasts with Job's straightforward courage and frankness, which is so far removed from false flattery that it almost borders on presumption, much to Job's advantage." And the reference to contemporary relationships concealed in this antithesis is increasingly unveiled as the essay goes on. "Job would most probably have experienced a nasty fate at the hands of any tribunal of dogmatic theologians, a synod, an inquisition, a pack of reverends, or any consistory of our day (with one sole exception).[21] Thus only sincerity of heart, not superiority of insight, the sincerity to openly confess his doubt, and disgust at counterfeiting a conviction not felt . . . : these are the marks which distinguished the superiority of the honest man, in the person of Job, in relation to the religious wheedler, in the words of the divine Judge." A "Concluding Remark," clearly referring to Wöllner's examination order and the oath of orthodox belief it specified, was then directed against the *tortura spiritualis* in things which by their nature are never amenable to theoretical, dogmatic conviction. In such matters he who makes an affirmation of faith simply because it is required of him, without even having glanced into himself, whether he in fact makes this asseveration deliberately or even intentionally to some degree—"he *lies* not merely the most outright falsehood in the face of his own heart's repudiation, but also the most impious, because it undermines the foundation of every virtuous intention: sincerity. How quickly such blind and superficial *creeds* (which very readily become compatible with an equally untrue inward creed), when they provide the basis for employment, can bit by bit bring the commonwealth to a certain falsity in thinking, is easily to be seen."[22] A more definite and unrestrained declaration on Kant's part about the new direction he saw taking over the common-

21. An allusion to the Berlin Upper Consistory, which under Spalding's leadership had raised energetic resistance to Wöllner's actions.

22. On all of this, see "Über das Misslingen aller philosophischen Versuche in der Theodizee" (1791) (VI, 132 ff.) (*Ak.* VIII, 265 ff.).

wealth was scarcely possible: only Wöllner's name, which was immaterial, was suppressed here, while the aim and the consequences of
his politics were erected as danger signals so plain that in this regard
not the slightest doubt nor any misunderstanding could prevail.

On this ground, conflict between Kant and the ruling circles of the
Prussia of that period was inevitable, and foreseeable long before it
broke out. The government had spared Kant in the beginning; it
probably shied away from attacking the famous author, who moreover enjoyed the personal confidence of the king, and had been especially singled out by him at the coronation ceremonies in Königsberg.
Kiesewetter, who had been dispatched from Berlin to Königsberg
especially to study Kantian philosophy, acted upon his return to the
court as tutor for the king's children, and displayed a lively enthusiasm for the universal propagation of the critical doctrine, which,
as a matter of fact, he understood and lectured on only in a popular
and dilute form. But the real opposition was pressing ever more
strongly toward a clear decision. A proposal to prohibit Kant's literary
activity altogether—according to a rumor that Kiesewetter mentions
in a letter to Kant, and which he himself in fact believed to be
unreliable—was submitted to the king in June, 1791, by the *Oberkon-
sistorialrat* (High Ecclesiastical Councillor) Woltersdorf. "He is feeble
now, in body and soul," Kiesewetter writes about the king; "he sits
and weeps for hours at a time. Bischofswerder, Wöllner, and Rietz are
the ones who tyrannize the king. A new edict on religion is expected,
and the commoners are muttering that they will be compelled to go to
church and to communion; as to this, they feel for the first time that
there are things which no prince can require, and one has to be
careful not to ignite the spark."[23] However, when Kant's essay "On
the Radical Evil in Human Nature" was submitted to him, the censor
appointed by Wöllner, Gottlob Friedrich Hillmer, could not immediately decide to refuse permission to print it; he allowed it to
appear in the April number of the *Berlinische Monatsschrift*, while he
contented himself with the thought that "only deep thinkers read
Kant's writings." But the continuation of this treatise, the essay "On

23. See Kiesewetter's letter to Kant of June 14, 1791 (X, 77) (*Ak.* XI, 252).

the Struggle of the Good Principle with the Evil for Mastery over Mankind," which this time also had the theological censor Hermes as coreader, since its content was regarded as belonging to biblical theology, offended the latter, and its publication was forbidden. A complaint by the editor of the *Berlinische Monatsschrift,* Biester, to the board of censors and to the king went in vain. It was necessary for Kant to see to publication in some other way, if he did not want to give it up altogether, and since he supplemented the two essays written specifically for the *Monatsschrift* with two further pieces, he had the whole appear as an independent book: *Religion within the Limits of Reason Alone (Religion innerhalb der Grenzen der blossen Vernunft),* at Easter of 1793. He had previously asked the theological faculty at Königsberg if it regarded the book as belonging to "biblical theology," and hence if it claimed the right of censorship;[24] as the reply proved negative, in order to obtain an expert opinion about the book from a scholarly body, he turned to the philosophical faculty of the University of Jena, whose dean at the time, Justus Christian Hennings, issued the imprimatur.[25]

If we look at the substantive content of the work, before we go into its further fortunes, it must first of all be stressed that Kant's book on religion cannot be measured by the same standards as his fundamental, principal critical works. It is not on a par with the writings on the foundation of his system, with the *Critique of Pure Reason* or of *Practical Reason,* with the *Foundations of the Metaphysics of Morals,* or the *Critique of Judgment.* For one thing, the Kantian system does not in general recognize the philosophy of religion as a fully independent member of the system, as a way of looking at things that is idiosyncratic and rests on autonomous and independent assumptions. The kind of validity which Schleiermacher later claims for the philosophy of religion is foreign to Kant, for the substance of his philosophy of religion comprises for him only a confirmation of and a corollary of the substance of his ethics. Religion "within the limits of reason

---

24. On this see Kant's letter to Stäudlin of May 4, 1793 (X, 205) (*Ak.* XI, 414).

25. It was Arnoldt (*Beiträge zu dem Material der Geschichte von Kants Leben,* pp. 31 ff.) who first proved the issuance of permission for printing by Hennings.

alone," which thus does not need to take heed of the concept of revelation and is not allowed to do so, has no essential content other than that of pure morality; it only expounds this content from a different viewpoint and in certain symbolic dress. Religion is for Kant the "knowledge of our duties as divine commands." Here, too, the concept of duty stands at the center; but contemplation of its origin and of the basis of its validity takes another direction from what was the case in the foundation of ethics. Instead of regarding the concept of duty purely as to its meaning and what it commands, we here join the substance of the demand with the idea of a supreme being, which we think as the creator of the moral law. Such a change is humanly inevitable, for every idea, even the highest such as that of freedom, can be grasped by man only in an image and by "schematization." We always require a certain analogy with nature to make the supersensible properties conceivable to us, and cannot avoid this "schematism of the analogy."[26]

In this, what governs is not only a peculiarity of our sensitive and intuitive nature, which even has to present everything spiritual in a spatiotemporal metaphor, but at the same time—and this has become fully clear to Kant only since completion of the *Critique of Judgment*—a basic tendency of our pure *aesthetic* consciousness.[27] Although the

26. *Religion within the Limits of Reason Alone* [Religion innerhalb der Grenzen der blossen Vernunft], pt. 2, sect. 1, note (VI, 205 f.) (*Ak.* VI, 64 f.).

27. This point of view comes out especially clearly when Kant opposes his own standpoint as to rational ethical faith to the standpoint of a mere religion of feeling, for according to him feeling has a positive and constructive significance only for the construction of the aesthetic world. The consequence of this for him was the possibility of a mediation which does not unconditionally reject the new factor—one especially fertile and contrary to the eighteenth-century enlightenment, which was contained, for example, in Jacobi's philosophy of feeling—but gives it an altogether different interpretation and application. "But why is there all this conflict," he concludes his essay "On a Condescending Tone Recently Raised in Philosophy" (1796), "between two parties which at bottom have one and the same good intent, namely, to make mankind wise and righteous? It is much ado about nothing, disunion out of misunderstanding, in which no reconciliation is required, but only mutual clarification. . . . The veiled goddess, before whom we both bend the knee, is the moral law within us, in its inviolate majesty. We hear its voice, to be sure, and also understand its command well enough, but we are in doubt, as we hearken, whether it proceeds from man, from the perfection of the power of his own reason, or whether it comes from some other being, unknown

powers conducive to natural and to positive religion are not only psychologically understood thereby, but also critically justified, a careful lookout must be kept so that they presume to no false independence. The preface to the first edition of *Religion within the Limits of Reason Alone* already says that morality, insofar as it is founded on the concept of man as a being who is free, but for that very reason binding himself by his reason to unconditional laws, neither requires the idea of another being superior to him to know his duty, nor any motive for observing the law except the law itself. At least it is man's own fault if such a need is found in him, for which there is no other remedy, because what does not spring from himself and from his freedom does not compensate for deficiency in his morality. Morality "thus in no way needs religion for its own service (objectively, as regards willing, as well as subjectively, as regards ability), but in virtue of pure practical reason it is sufficient unto itself."[28] Where this is misunderstood, where the religious way of thinking is permitted even the slightest influence on the essential basis of morality, then

---

to him, and which speaks to man through this reason of his. Fundamentally, we would do far better to desist from this inquiry of ours, since it is purely speculative and what we are obligated to do remains (objectively) always the same, whether the one or the other principle is used to support it: only the didactic process of making the moral law in us conceptually clear by a logical kind of instruction is purely and simply *philosophical*, but that process of personifying that law and making a veiled Isis out of reason as it commands us morally (whether we attribute to this any other properties than those discovered by this method) is an aesthetic mode of thinking this very same object. We can well make use of the latter, when the principles are purified by the former, so as to enliven these ideas by a sensory exposition, though it is only analogical, yet always with the danger of lapsing into muddleheaded visions, which is death to all philosophy" (VI, 494 f.) (*Ak.* VIII, 405). The major difficulty in giving religion a truly independent role in the whole of the transcendental critique is manifested quite characteristically here. By its content it ought, as rational religion, to merge with pure ethics, from which it is distinguished only by its form: the "personification" of just this content. But this form itself does not belong essentially to it; rather, it goes back—even if the universal, purely *theoretical* meaning of the transcendental "schematism" is disregarded—to the basic *aesthetic* function of consciousness. Accordingly, the religious appears under Kantian presuppositions not as a proper *domain* of consciousness with its own laws, but only as a new *relation*, in which the domains and faculties previously defined and demarcated with respect to each other come closer together.

28. *Religion within the Limits of Reason Alone*, preface to the 1st ed. (VI, 141) (*Ak.* VI, 3).

something happens not only to the pure fundamental ideas of ethics, but also to those of religion itself—then worship is subverted into idolatry.

Ever since he had expressed this thought in correspondence with Lavater, Kant held steadily to it. This book also calls it the peculiar "delusion of religion" when man supposes that he can do something else, apart from the good conduct of his life, to become acceptable to God; however, our action can only be called good when it is based purely on the principle of autonomy and when in thus recognizing the law as such the particular relation to the "legislator" is disregarded. No contortion of external behavior, whatever form it may take, helps to overcome a deficiency in this basic temper. "Once one has gone over to the maxim of worshipping supposedly to please God for his own sake, and also to placate Him, but to a worship which is not purely moral, among the ways of worshipping Him mechanically, so to speak, there is no essential difference which would give preference to one or the other way. They are all of equal worth (or rather worthlessness) among themselves, and it is sheer affectation to regard oneself as more elect by reason of a more subtle deviation from the sole intellectual principle of genuine reverence for God than by something making one guilty of a forgivable gross lapse into sensuousness. Whether the hypocrite makes his legalistic visit to church or a pilgrimage to the shrines of Loretto or Palestine, whether he brings his prayer formulas to the heavenly authorities by his lips or, like the Tibetan . . . does it by a prayer wheel, or whatever kind of surrogate for the moral service of God it may be, it is all worth just the same. It is here a matter not so much of difference in the outer form, but entirely of the acceptance or abandonment of the sole principle, of becoming pleasing to God either through moral conviction alone, exhibited in a living way in actions as its epiphany, or through pious gewgaws and passivity."[29]

The difficult methodological problem bound up with religion, and the special dialectic it raises, comes to the fore in just this connection.

---

29. Ibid., fourth part: "Of Worship and Idolatry under the Mastery of the Good Principle, or of Religion and Priestcraft," pt. 2, §2 (VI, 320 ff.) (*Ak.* VI, 170–73).

On one side stands the sensory "schematism" of the essence of religion, inseparable from it and at the same time unavoidable: religion would cease to be what it is if it wished to renounce that. On the other side, though, this very factor means for religion a continuing threat to its deepest and most basic content; as soon as religion surrenders itself to it uncritically, it sees itself necessarily perverted into the opposite of its fundamental tendency. We see ourselves faced with the alternative of either dissolving religion purely into ethics, and thereby allowing it to disappear as an independent form, or maintaining it by the side of ethics, but in that way also in opposition to ethics. For the deduction and substantiation of the moral law suffers any sensory support as little as it does any transcendent "supplement": every heteronomous element which we permit must necessarily unhinge this foundation. For Kant, the solution to this antinomy lies once again in the strict separation of the empirical and the intelligible, the given and the commanded. The conversion of pure rational religion into pure ethics is required, but in the world of historical appearances it is never completed; yet it is at any time capable of completion therein. The point of juncture we are looking for and to which we must hold fast lies at infinity. But it does not become in any way an imaginary point for that reason; rather, it strictly and precisely points out the direction from which religious development must not deviate, if it does not wish to miss its goal. Religion, where it appears in historical actuality, must take on the forms which are alone appropriate to this actuality. To be communicable, it must clothe itself in the sensuous signs of communication; it requires, in order to affect the life of the community, the firm outer rules and bonds of this community life. Thus in its empirical existence it necessarily becomes a church. But it submerges itself, on the other hand, in this form of existence only so as to continually transcend it and to ask what is beyond. Ever anew the idea of what religion is purely "in itself" must be contrasted with its particular and limited temporal modes of appearance; ever anew its special fundamental teaching must be affirmed over against the mere "side-doctrine" and elevated to authority. Thus the struggle between the infinite content to which it is directed and the finite modes of presentation in which alone it can be understood in fact resides in every one of its stages and phases; but it is just this struggle that gives it its historical life and its historical effectiveness. In this sense, Kant, like Lessing, regards "positive" religions as moments and transitional points in the education of mankind; in this sense he demands of them that they recognize the standard of rational ethical religion for themselves, instead of rigidifying into a narrow dogmatism, and hence indeed preparing their own overcoming and dissolution.

The general theme of the Kantian doctrine of religion is thus indicated, while the clear execution and realization of this theme, in *Religion within the Limits of Reason Alone*, is beset with many limitations. These reside mainly in the particular nature of the book, which in no wise claims to give a complete exposition of Kant's basic ideas on the philosophy of religion, but only to set forth, by the example of a specific, presupposed dogmatism, how an embodiment of purely rational basic ethical truths is obtained from a system of given articles of faith by deepening and interpreting those articles. But on the other hand, quite definite boundaries are set by reason of this link to the critical approach. Not that Kant in using this approach in general shows any desire to renounce its principle, but he now exercises this principle in a material which is accepted as given from outside. *Religion within the Limits of Reason Alone* thus has from beginning to end the character of compromise. It selects one particular dogmatic state in order to peel it away and expose in its purity the moral kernel lying hidden in the dogmatic husk. Everything that seems discordant with this central message is either eliminated from the essence of the doctrines of faith under consideration as a subsequent, falsifying accretion, or interpreted in a sense such that it harmonizes in some fashion or other with the overall method of treatment.[30] In this way, not only is an arbitrary and accidental baseline set for the treatment, but it seems, as a result of this dependence on one given set of dogmas, that a scholasticism is also suffered and reintroduced, which could be thought finally and definitively overthrown by the theoretical foun-

30. This compromise which is characteristic of *Religion within the Limits of Reason Alone* has been emphasized particularly acutely by E. Troeltsch, to whose detailed exposition I refer here: "Das Historische in Kants *Religionsphilosophie*," *Kantstudien* 9 (1904), pp. 57 ff.

dations of the First Critique. One must, though, be wary of wanting to explain this defect, which as such is unmistakable, all too quickly by the purely accidental limitations of Kant's personality and character. It was not in the least mere intellectual timidity that restrained him here. His outward consideration for the political and ecclesiastical authorities may have led to much vagueness and many instances of camouflage in his expression, but this did not disturb the core of his thought. Kant stood in opposition to traditional religion in the main no differently from the way he opposed traditional metaphysics.

Here, however, it was a matter of a different task set him: for the "fact" of a definite religion is given in a vastly stricter sense than that of metaphysics, in which each successive system seems to negate its predecessor; it is given as a relatively enduring historical datum and as one that is stable in its main outlines. He who strives to overcome it theoretically must also reckon with this empirical factuality. Idealization joins hands with the given, not to justify it at any cost, but to indicate that point in it from which it can surpass itself, because of the unfolding of the proper rational germ presupposed in it. Kant is here only following a method used by the whole Enlightenment in full subjective sincerity. He displays that cleverness in separating the exoteric and esoteric which Lessing, in his analysis and critique of Leibniz's theology, had expressly emphasized and raised in the latter. He too sought to strike fire from the flint, but he did not conceal his fire in the flint.[31] In this sense *Religion within the Limits of Reason Alone* does not so much belong to Kant's purely philosophical works as it does to his pedagogical works. Here he was speaking as educator of the people and of the government as well, and hence he had, at the very least, to begin with the form of popular faith as much as with the form of the dominant state religion. In the process, the critical mode of thought did not directly change into a dogmatic form, but it did become "positive" in a special sense: it stopped tearing down, since it could not succeed in doing that, so as instead to build up what was

31. See Lessing, "Leibniz von den ewigen Strafen," *Werke,* ed. K. Lachmann and E. Muncker), vol. 9, pp. 461 ff.

there just as it stood, in order to gradually reform it from the inside out in such a way that it took on a new form, concordant with the requirements of pure reason. In this project, Kant was personally full of that optimism toward the historical that was true of Lessing and Leibniz also. The very preservation of Christianity through the centuries proved to him that in Christianity there must reside a factor of absolutely universally valid significance, for without the creative force of the fundamental motive of pure rational ethical religion, its endurance and existence would be inconceivable.

Thus we confront at the same time a second factor in the Kantian doctrine of religion, in which the breadth of its original plan is revealed equally with the narrowness of its execution. The religion of reason, as Kant thinks of it, in its relation to the historical and empirical from the start is in no way pointed toward or restricted to any specific form in which religion appears in history. Biblical theology, in the field of the sciences, stands opposed to a philosophical theology, which in order to confirm and elucidate its assertions makes use of the history, languages, and books of all peoples, among which the Bible is included but always as just one outstanding example.[32] Along with it, the Vedas, the Koran, and the Zendavesta can also be named without hesitation, and the same right to consideration and study is granted to them. But this is for Kant only a matter of a theoretically granted right, which in his particular practical carrying-out of the basic conception comes to nothing. For at bottom Kant values the collective religious literature outside of Christianity in the anthropological sense only, not in the ethical and religious. His stance toward it is that of the connoisseur, one who shows interest in every strange phenomenon, but he is not inwardly stirred by it. Toward Judaism in its entirety and toward the Old Testament, Kant has all along so strongly subjective a prejudice that he can see in the religion of the prophets and in the psalms nothing more than a collection of statutory laws and usages. In this, however, quite apart from the substantive right and worth of such individual judgments, an essential methodological circle, contained in Kant's view of the philosophy

---

32. *Religion within the Limits of Reason Alone,* preface to the 1st ed. (VI, 147) (*Ak.* VI, 9).

and history of religion, is revealed immediately. The ethical measuring rod is help up to the specific forms of religion as a universally valid and objective criterion, but in the way it is applied subjective feeling and outlook unmistakably play a role. Because he had been certain of the moral *effect* of the New Testament scriptures from his youth on, the question of their unique and incomparable *content* is settled for Kant from the start. Rational analysis was here only to confirm and explicate in detail what, as an overall result, was already sure for him in advance.

The power of the initial pietistic impression of his youth is shown nowhere so clearly as in Kant's book on religion. For it had been Pietism, to be precise, which had brought into undeniable currency once again that principle of "moral" written interpretation on which Kant's theory of religion is also based. As early as the Middle Ages, in fact, this form of interpretation, among others, was well known and current. Thomas Aquinas already makes a systematically acute and specific distinction between the *sensus allegoricus,* the *sensus anagogicus,* and the *sensus moralis* or *mysticus* of a scriptural passage. In Pietism, this kind of biblical interpretation had then taken on that specifically Protestant cast in which it affected Kant. Filled with the idea of the unconditional primacy of practical reason, he now sought out the exclusively ethical meaning behind every religious symbol familiar to him. The whole set of Protestant dogmas—the dogma of the Fall and redemption, of being born again and of justification through faith—is traversed with this intent. Kant has unqualified subjective confidence that the fundamental and leading idea of his rational religion must be capable of having dominion over this set of dogmas and conforming to its actuality; but for exactly this reason he does not strive beyond it, since he is sure that he can fully demonstrate in it the universal application of his principle.

In fact, the whole analysis and critique of the dogmas that runs through his book on religion concentrates from the outset on one point. Kant's theory of "radical evil" in human nature, like his conception of the doctrine of the personhood of Christ, the interpretation that he gives to original sin and to the idea of justification, his concept of the kingdom of God, and his opposition between the purely moral and the statutory laws—all this is related to one single basic philosophical question, and only in that does it find its true unity. Everywhere in this theory it is for Kant a matter of particular moments and particular interpretations of the *concept of freedom*. Freedom and the opposition between heteronomy and autonomy, between the sensory and the intelligible worlds, is the original fact to which all fundamental religious doctrines point in a veiled and symbolic form. The method of the Kantian philosophy of religion is consistently aimed at making this connection evident. Attempts have been made to draw a sharp line between Kantian philosophy of religion and Kantian moral philosophy, so that the concept of redemption can be called the specific substance of the former, but it has rightly been maintained to the contrary that the motive of redemption means for Kant's philosophy of religion nothing but a specified limitation of the problem of freedom. He knows and allows no "redemption" in the sense of a supernatural, divine interference, which takes the place of the moral subject's own act; rather, he sees in it only the expression for the intelligible act itself, in virtue of which the self-legislation of the pure will and of practical reason wins mastery over the empirical sensuous drives.[33] Thus, even for the Kantian theory of religion, freedom remains at the same time the sole mystery and the sole principle of explanation. It illuminates the essential meaning and aim of the doctrine of faith, but there is no further theoretical "explanation" of it itself—on grounds given in the critical ethics. All we can do with respect to it consists in conceiving it precisely in its inconceivability.[34] But in establishing and acknowledging the bounds of our theoretical knowledge in this way, we are not led into a mere mystical darkness, for little as any question can be raised about "why," about a further ground of freedom, yet freedom itself and its content are given in the unconditional demand of the ought as something absolutely certain and necessary. Religion and ethics both, each

33. On this, see Kuno Fischer, *Geschichte der neueren Philosophie,* 4th ed., (Heidelberg, 1914), vol. 5, pp. 289 ff., and the objections Troeltsch ("Das Historische in Kants Religionsphilosophie," pp. 80 ff.) raises to Fischer's interpretation.

34. See above, pp. 261 ff.

in its own language, express this content; but basically it remains one and the same, so truly is the moral law in its essence only one thing, however many the forms and symbols we may try again and again to express it by.

Thus, despite all its complications, the Kantian philosophy of religion shows that it is governed by a basic, integral systematic idea, while in Kant's *book* on religion this unity is presented in only a qualified and inadequate way. Hence it is understandable that the initial effect wrought by *Religion within the Limits of Reason Alone* was ambiguous through and through. The two poles between which judgment oscillated are visible as soon as we set Schiller's assessment against the impression Goethe received from the work. Goethe recoiled indignantly from the book, in which he could see merely a concession to ecclesiastical orthodoxy and dogmatism; he remarked bitterly in a letter to Herder that Kant has disgracefully "slobbered on" his philosopher's cloak "with the blot of radical evil, so that even Christ would be enticed to kiss its hem." Schiller, in contrast, whose feeling about the Kantian doctrine of radical evil was at first no less antagonistic, in the end let himself be captured by the Kantian definition of and argument for the concept, since he was forced to recognize in it, though oddly disguised, the fundamental idea of the Kantian doctrine of freedom, to which he had for a long time been inwardly devoted. He too expressed his concern, in contrast to Körner, that Kant's basic tendency would be misunderstood: while Kant's intention had only been not to throw away what had been attained, and to that end he was especially adept at relating philosophical thinking to reason still in leading strings, the dominant dogmatism would straightway seize it all and exploit it for its own ends—and thus in the long run Kant would have done nothing other than "shore up the rotting edifice of stupidity." Sceptical as his estimate of the Kantian doctrine of religion was, he believed himself clear on its essential content. He believed he could ascertain in Kant a completely independent intellectual attitude toward the stuff of dogmas: Kant bypassed them, just as the Greek philosophers and poets had treated their

mythology.[35] As far as the church orthodoxy itself is concerned, it
could not be deceived for an instant as to the unbridgeable gap between the Kantian persuasion and the system favored and required
by the state. Yet the government tried to avoid open conflict. Even
when Kant published in book form the essay banned by the censor, it
did not bestir itself immediately. However, Kant's essay in reply to
Garve in September, 1793, which moved in a threatening way from
general ethics to encroach on the theory of the state, and which asserted not only religious freedom of conscience but also freedom of
the pen as the sole palladium of the rights of the people, deducing
this from the basic concepts of natural right, inevitably aroused anew
the suspicion and concern of the political powers.

Kant foresaw the conflict that would necessarily ensue, and, little
as he sought it, he was disdainful of the timid holding back that could
still perhaps have averted it. "I hasten, esteemed friend," he wrote to
Biester in May, 1794, when he sent him his essay "The End of All
Things" ("Das Ende aller Dinge"), "to send you the promised
treatise, rather than bring an end to correspondence between you and
me. . . . I thank you for the information you shared with me, and
convinced of having acted in every case scrupulously and lawfully, I
look forward calmly to the end of these singular events. If new laws
command what is not contrary to my principles, I will conform to them
immediately; that will happen even if they should merely forbid that
my principles be made public, as I have done heretofore (and which
in no sense do I regret). Life is short, especially what is left after 70
years have passed; to bring it to an untroubled close, some corner of
the earth can be found, I suppose."[36] Certainly these words are not
an expression of a fighting mood, but still this man of seventy, who
by all his habits and by his whole pattern of life was totally rooted in
his native city, and who two decades earlier had called it an instinct of
his physical and mental nature to avoid every external change, now
was even ready to give up his teaching post and his right to live in
Prussia, his homeland, if he could safeguard his independence in no

35. Goethe to Herder, June 7, 1793; Schiller to Körner, February 28, 1793.
36. To Biester, May 18, 1794 (X, 240 f.) (*Ak.* XI, 481 f.).

other way. As far as the essay Kant sent to Biester is concerned, it contains such clear references to the current situation, and such bitter disquisitions against the Prussian rulers, that these could scarcely overlook them. "Christianity," it says, "above and beyond the greatest respect which the holiness of its laws infuses, has something else in it which is worthy of love. . . . If now some type of authority is added on to Christianity to ensure this, be the intent thereof ever so well meant and the aim thereof ever so good, its lovableness has vanished. For it is a contradiction to *command* someone not only to do something but also that he should do it gladly. . . . Thus it is the *free* way of thinking—equally distant from the slave's outlook and from anarchy—from which Christianity expects its teaching to be effective, by which it has the power to win over the hearts of men to itself, men whose understanding is already illuminated by the idea of the law of their duty. The feeling of freedom in choosing one's ultimate goal is what makes the giving of the law lovable to them. . . . Should it once happen that Christianity stops being lovable (which could indeed occur were it armed with imperious authority, instead of its gentle spirit), then rejection and rebellion against it would inevitably come to be the dominant way of thought among men, because there is no neutrality in moral things (still less a combining of opposing principles). . . ; thereupon, however, since Christianity is *destined* to be the universal religion of the world, but it would not be *favored* by fate to become so, the (erroneous) *end of all things* as regards morality would occur."[37] These sentences are written in the baroque style of Kant's old age, but their essential meaning and thrust were nonetheless unmistakable. The government was forced into the decision to take action against the embarrassing remonstrator who was gradually edging more and more out of the circle of "deep-thinking scholars," where they at first thought him safely enclosed, and who now turned against them with the weapons of mockery and satire in particular. Thus there was issued to Kant, on October 1, 1794, the famous letter signed by the king personally, in which he was reproached for having

---

37. "The End of All Things" ["Das Ende aller Dinge"] (VI, 422–24) (*Ak.* VIII, 337–39).

"misused" his philosophy over a long period of time "for the distortion and debasing of many principal and basic teachings of Holy Scripture and of Christianity," and in which he was instructed, to avoid the royal disfavor, henceforth to be guilty of nothing similar: "otherwise you can unfailingly expect, on continued recalcitrance, unpleasant consequences."[38]

Kant's attitude toward the reproaches and threats leveled against him is well known. In writing his defense, he first rejected the accusation that he as a *teacher of the young*, that is, as he understood it, in his academic lectures, had ever mixed in any judgment on the Bible and Christianity, and he made reference on this score to the nature of Baumgarten's textbooks, which he squarely based his lectures on and which of themselves ruled out any such connection. Also, in his book he had not in any way spoken as a "teacher of the people," but exclusively intended a "discussion among the scholars of the faculties," so that it must needs be an incomprehensible and closed book to the general public. Further, his book on religion could not contain a "debasing" of Christianity and the Bible, for the reason that in it the sole theme was the evolution of pure rational religion, not the critique of definite historical forms of belief; moreover, so far as he had dealt with the specific content of Christianity, he had left no doubt that he recognized in it the fullest historical product of pure rational faith. "As concerns the second point," Kant's explanation concludes, "I will henceforth be guilty of no distortion and debasement of Christianity of the (alleged) kind: thus to prevent even the least suspicion on this score, I hold it as most certain herewith, cheerfully to declare myself Your Royal Majesty's most faithful subject: that I will refrain entirely in the future from all public discourses concerning religion, natural or revealed, in lectures and in writing alike."[39]

In his reply to the royal rescript, Kant thus gives in to the government's demands on practically all points; in the process, he tries to find a justification for this retreat only in that, by a mental reserva-

---

38. See the wording of the letter in the preface to *The Contest of Faculties* (VII, 316) (*Ak.* VII, 6).

39. See *The Contest of Faculties*, preface (VII, 317–21) (*Ak.* VII, 7–11).

tion, he limits it to the reign and the lifetime of Friedrich Wilhelm II. The addition that "as His Majesty's most faithful subject" he pledged himself henceforward to silence in religious matters, as Kant himself later explained, explicitly contained this meaning. This reservation has often been harshly censured, but these reproaches have at best not touched the essential, decisive point. If Kant, being conscious of and sensitive to the philosophical life's work still lying ahead of him—he himself never regarded this work as finished, and in his eighties still complained that important parts of it were yet incomplete—had resolved to renounce the battle against the Wöllner regime because this fight would have robbed him of the best part of the strength to live and work still remaining to him, it would be narrow-minded and petty to wish to take him to task on this score. It is the basic right of a genius to determine for himself his own path and his own tasks out of his personal necessity, which is at the same time the highest impersonal necessity; and it is always shortsighted and unproductive to want to substitute an external, abstract and doctrinaire measuring rod for this internal one.

If Kant therefore had now sacrificed his activity as publicist or had put it off to a more favorable time, in order to gain room and leisure for accomplishing the other problems that still awaited him, all complaint about this would be baseless. But in fact there is a sign in his attitude toward the government's writ of accusation that shows he now, in full inner freedom, no longer opposed settlement of the conflict he so clearly foresaw and so resolutely went forth to meet. Indeed, he thrust the idea of a merely apparent retraction from him with all his strength of mind. "Retraction and betrayal of one's inward conviction," runs one of his notes from this period, "is base; but keeping silence in a case like the present one is the duty of the subject; and even if everything one says is necessarily true, there is no duty to utter all truth publicly." Even here he thus weighed the scope and extent of individual duties carefully against each other, in his strict and methodical way; but in all this, quite apart from the personal privileges he granted himself with respect to the ruling political authorities, he at least underestimated the personal power he actually possessed against them. "When the strong men of the world," he wrote to Karl Spener about this time, "are in a state of intoxication, whether it originates from a breath of the gods or from noxious vapors,[40] it is advisable for a pygmy who is fond of his skin not to meddle in their quarrel, even by the gentlest and most respectful persuasion; mostly because, while they wouldn't listen to him, he would be misunderstood by others who are tattletales. Four weeks from today I enter on the seventieth year of my life. What particular thing can someone this old still hope to effect with men of spirit? And with the common masses? Labor thus employed would be labor lost, indeed labor harmful to him. In this half a life that is left, an old man is well advised that *non defensoribus istis tempus eget* [these defenders are not short of time] and to consider the extent of his powers, which allows for almost no wish beyond that for peace and quiet."[41] The ironic undertone in these sentences is unmistakable; but on the other hand, they reveal the full native timidity and self-consciousness of the lonely scholar and thinker, who feels a deeper and deeper aversion to every development in the "squabbles of the world." It was not fear of losing his post that was crucial for Kant in all this; he had already reckoned in advance with the possibility that he would have to resign from it, without any effect on his attitude. Even more foreign to him was any false esteem for rank and eminence as such: all reports about his personal communication with King Friedrich Wilhelm II, whom he had to welcome as rector of the university at the coronation ceremonies in Königsberg, celebrate the unaffectedness and natural frankness he displayed then. But Kant has a modest enough opinion of the role the individual might play in the polity as a whole, under an absolutist government. Here he was held back by that scepticism that caused him to renounce early on any directly practical activity of reform. As concerns the *theories* of morality, religion, and civil right,

40. [Kant's word here translated as "noxious vapors" is *Mufette*, derived from the French *mofette* or *moufette*. It is hard to say precisely what Kant had in mind in using it, since in older chemistry *mofette* stood for any nonrespirable gas, while Buffon used it to apply to the firedamp or chokedamp found in mines and also to a Mexican mammal, the *ysquiepail* (perhaps the skunk), which emits a foul smell. In addition, its German adaptation can mean "bad wine." Kant would certainly have been familiar with its scientific meanings, and may well have had them in mind here.—Tr.]

41. To Spener, March 22, 1793 (X, 197 f.) (*Ak.* XI, 402 f.).

he believed them to have been taken to the point from which they could, progressing gradually and step by step, gain their increasingly extensive influence on "praxis." But he did not feel called upon to lay his own hand directly and actively to this. Objectively, he doubtless did have too low an opinion of the influence his personality could have exercised, because he was utterly incapable of surveying and assessing what his philosophy already meant as an ideal force in the whole life of the nation. In this, perhaps, lies the essential defect and error in Kant's attitude toward the rescript of the Prussian government: but to avoid it he would have had to feel himself elevated above his historical setting in a totally different degree than in fact he felt; he would have had to ascribe to his individual self an immediately influential force that he never credited it with.

Within the confines of philosophical speculation, however, Kant's thinking remains, as before, oriented toward basic political problems, which now undergo a fresh expansion and deepening. From the constitution of the individual state, the question trenches onto the idea of a "federation of nations," the indispensable empirical and historical prerequisites of which Kant tries to found and establish in his work *Perpetual Peace* (*Zum ewigen Frieden*) (1795). In the methodological sense, however, the whole series of ideas connected with this once again leads back to one indivisible foundation, which heretofore had had no independent and creative treatment in the critical system. The Kantian conception of the state rests on his conception of the idea of freedom, but the idea of freedom in itself alone does not suffice to constitute the concrete concept of the state. If the state, in its ideal task, points to the sphere of freedom, in its factual existence and its historical actualization it belongs to the sphere of coercion. This places it in a contradictory position, to mediate which is precisely one of its most essential definitions. The "Idea for a Universal History from a Cosmopolitan Standpoint" had already hinted at this connection, but a most important factor was still missing in it, through which alone the conflict between force and freedom, and the link between the two, is brought to its sharpest and most exact conceptual expression. In the concept of force lies the necessary preparation and prerequisite for the concept of right. For precisely what distinguishes moral duty from the duty of right, according to Kant, is that the former asks not only about action but at the same time and above all about its subjective maxims and motives, while the duty of right abstracts from every consideration of that sort, so as to judge action as such merely with respect to its objective circumstances and execution. It is sheer agreement or disagreement of an action with the laws, without regard to its motives, that constitutes its legality, while its morality is only assured when it is established that it proceeds from the idea of duty as its sole motivating ground. It is the latter agreement which, since it relates to something purely inward, simply is *commanded;* the former is what can at the same time be *demanded.* The external coercibility of an action is hence joined with the concept of right itself. "Right in its strict sense," in which any contribution of moral concepts is disregarded, can and must "be envisaged as the possibility of a general and reciprocal coercion consonant with the freedom of everyone in accordance with universal laws." "For just as the only object of right in general is the external aspect of actions, right in its strict sense, that is, right unmixed with any ethical consideration, requires no determinants of the will apart from purely external ones; for it will then be pure and will not be confounded with any precepts of virtue. Thus only a completely external right can be called right in the *strict* (or narrow) sense. This right is certainly based on each individual's awareness of his obligations within the law; but if it is to remain pure, it may not and cannot appeal to this awareness as a motive which might determine the will to act in accordance with it, and it therefore depends rather on the principle of the possibility of an external coercion which can coexist with the freedom of everyone in accordance with universal laws ... thus right and the authority to apply coercion mean one and the same thing. The law of reciprocal coercion, which is necessarily consonant with the freedom of everyone within the principle of universal freedom, is in a sense the *construction* of the concept of right: that is, it represents this concept in pure a priori intuition by analogy with the possibility of free movement of bodies within the law of the *equality of action and reaction.* Just as the qualities of an object of pure mathematics cannot be directly deduced from the concept but can only be discovered from its construction, it is not so much the *concept* of right but rather a general, reciprocal and uniform coercion, subject to universal laws and harmonizing with the concept itself, which makes any representation of the concept possible."⁴²

It is this exposition Kant tries to provide in the *Metaphysical Elements of the Theory of Right* (*Metaphysische Anfangsgründe der Rechtslehre*), which appeared at the beginning of 1797. It forms the final book belonging wholly to the sphere of the great chief systematic works and having their nature, since it sets up a universal principle for a specific, objective and intellectual cultural field, intended to explain the nature and the necessity of its construction. This already is no longer the case to the same degree in the *Metaphysical Elements of Virtue* (*Metaphysische Anfangsgründe der Tugendlehre*), which follows in the same year. For the principle of ethics here is laid down in advance, as something already firmly based: now it is only a matter of how to trace it through a wealth of applications, in which Kant's discussion frequently loses itself in a laborious schematism and a thorny casuistry. Even the development of the concept of private right, which is laid out in the first part of the *Metaphysical Elements of the Theory of Right,* with its division of rights into personal, real, and real personal, is not free of this increasingly overpowering tendency toward a schematic, by which the detailed questions are frequently classified and to which they are subordinated. Kant's construction of honor as a real personal right is especially typical in this regard.

His treatment only rises to a greater freedom of overview when it applies itself to the questions of public right: political right and international right. What Kant had earlier put forward separately in his short treatises now is substantiated by and deduced from a single fundamental idea. The questions of the sovereignty of the ruler and its origin in the sovereignty of the people, the division of powers flowing from this and the delimitation of their rights with respect to each other, are discussed with systematic completeness and together

---

42. *Metaphysical Elements of the Theory of Right,* introduction, §E (VII, 33 f.) (*Ak.* VI, 232 f.); cf. introduction, III (VII, 19) (*Ak.* VI, 218).

with their latent relation to empirical historical detail. The method
Kant relies on in doing this seems at first glance not to differ at all
from the natural right point of view governing the philosophy of right
of the whole Enlightenment and revolutionary period. The theory of
the social contract—especially in the form Rousseau gave it—is here
assumed to hold throughout. But yet once more the tendency already
apparent in the essay against Garve on the relation between theory
and practice puts in an appearance, lending its special hallmark to
Kant's overall view, as within the evolution of the conception of
natural rights. The social contract is raised from the sphere of the
empirical and the specifically historical into the sphere of the "Idea."
"The act by which the people constitutes a state of itself, or more
precisely, the mere idea of such an act (which alone enables us to
consider it valid in terms of right), is the *original contract*. By this
contract, all members of the people (*omnes et singuli*) give up their
external freedom in order to receive it back at once as members of a
commonwealth, that is, of the people regarded as a state (*universi*).
And we cannot say that men within a state have sacrificed a *part* of
their inborn external freedom for a specific purpose; they have in fact
completely abandoned their wild and lawless freedom, in order to
find again their entire and undiminished freedom in a state of lawful
dependence (i.e., in a state of right), for this dependence is created by
their own legislative will."[43] Thus the intelligible in the idea of freedom guarantees for Kant the intelligible in the concept of the state
and of right, and guards it against being confused with something
purely factual, which is founded exclusively in the actually existing
relationships of power and rule.[44]

The community of the body politic, into which the individual is
assimilated and to which he gives himself as an individual without
reservation, however, includes by its own ideal nature a totality of
ideal conditions, which can be summed up in the proposition that
what the whole people cannot decide concerning themselves, no
legislator can decide either.[45] This universal spirit of the original con-

43. Ibid., §47 (VII, 122) (*Ak.* VI, 315–16).
44. On all of this, cf. above, pp. 223 ff.
45. *Metaphysical Elements of the Theory of Right,* General Remarks on the Legal Consequences of the Nature of the Civil Union, §C (VII, 135) (*Ak.* VI, 327). On Kant's

tract furnishes the guiding principle and norm for all particular types and forms of government, which is "to alter the mode of government by a gradual and continuous process... until it accords *in its effects* with the only rightful constitution, that of a pure republic. The old empirical (and statutory) forms, which serve only to effect the *subjection* of the people, should accordingly resolve themselves into the original (rational) form which alone makes *freedom* the principle and indeed the condition of all *coercion*. For coercion is required for a just political constitution in the truest sense, and this will eventually be realized in letter as well as in spirit."[46]

While here it is a matter of the most universal basic questions concerning the philosophy of right and of the state, in his next work Kant returns once more to his personal experience with the existing political powers in regard to his literary and philosophical activities. This relation scarcely comes to the surface, save in the preface to the work, but it clearly forms the motive from which its basic ideas arose and which explains its whole structure. Once again it is the system of the sciences and the connection and order of its chief components that Kant undertakes to establish here: but instead of inquiring into the content and the pertinent presuppositions of the sciences, he now takes hold of them exclusively from the perspective of their relations with the state and its administration. It is not so much their logical status as their disciplinary activity that is in question here, and for which a fixed principle is required. On the strength of this turn of consideration, the quarrel between the sciences has become a contest between the faculties. For the state needs to take notice of the sciences insofar as they confront it as specific associations with settled boundary lines with respect to one another, as independent corporations based on historical right. Only as externally organized in this way does the state recognize them as members of its own organization, for which it assumes a right of supervision as well as a duty of protection. From this point of view, a whole discipline is considered and

theory of right, cf. esp. Erich Cassirer, *Natur- und Völkerrecht im Lichte der Geschichte und der systematischen Philosophie* (Berlin, 1919).

46. Ibid., §52 (VII, 148 f.) (*Ak.* VI, 340 f.).

evaluated only according to its place within the entire political hierarchy, so the scholar can count on a hearing only insofar as he is able to show that he is at the same time a representative and *official* of the state. This is the manner of framing the question which Kant adheres to throughout *The Contest of Faculties* (*Streit der Fakultäten*); but in the midst of the dry profundity with which he pursues it, one detects clearly a sportive humor which once again reminds us of the style of Kant's youthful works. And here too, as in those other books, the humor is the expression and reflection of an inward philosophical self-liberation. This self-liberation, as was fitting and natural to Kant, consists in his converting his personal conflict with the administration of the state into a conflict of method, and in his trying to settle it that way. Since he places himself entirely at the standpoint of the political practitioner, intentionally narrowing his political horizon, he tries to demonstrate the right and the inalienable freedom of philosophical theory and of science from precisely that perspective. Through the attitude and aim of the politician, which he has assumed, the true outlook and conviction of the critical thinker gleams at every point, and this duality is what gives *The Contest of Faculties* that amalgam of cheerful, reflective irony and dogged, businesslike solemnity which comprises its peculiar character.

The ironic undertone becomes audible as early as the first section, wherein Kant, in alliance with tradition, distinguishes the "higher" theological, juristic, and medical faculties from the "lower" philosophical faculty. The genesis of this received distinction is, as he comments, readily recognizable: it stems from the government, with which it is, indeed, never a matter of knowledge as such, but simply of the effects on the people that the government expects from knowledge. On this basis, it sanctions certain theories, from which it promises itself a useful influence, but it does not condescend to propose any kind of definite theory itself. "It does not teach, but only gives orders to those who do (as for truth, that has to look out for itself), because on taking up their posts they came to an understanding by the agency of a contract with the government. A government which busied itself with theories, thus also with the spread or the improvement of the sciences, and hence wished to play the scholar itself in the shape of its highest personage, would only bring shameful attention on itself by such pedantry, and it is beneath its dignity to lower itself to the level of the vulgar (to its scholarly class), who don't understand jokes and who mold everybody involved with the sciences into the same shape."[47] In this sense it obliges the individual disciplines to specific statutes, on the strength of its authority as magistrate, since "truth" cannot exist for it except in the form of such a statute, and does not need to exist. The Bible is prescribed to the theologian, the universal law of the land to the jurist, to the physician the system of medical regulation, as rule and guide. Punctilious adherence to this rule is what ensures theology, jurisprudence, and medicine their place in public life, and what elevates them to the dignity and rank of a "higher" faculty.

Only one thing: knowledge purely for the sake of knowledge, is left empty-handed in this allotment and division, because no essential potentiality for directly practical ends is to be expected from it. If one still wants to assign a place to it, too, it must then content itself tamely with the rank of a "lower faculty." In it, reason remains free and independent of governmental orders, but for that very reason it remains ineffective, and must be meek, devoid of influence on the course of affairs. What its inalienable prerogative is, viewed objectively, allots to it the lowest place in conventional estimation. The philosophic faculty as such stands quite outside the circle of command and obedience, and it is human nature "that he who can command, though he be also a humble servant of another, still thinks himself superior to someone else who, to be sure, is free but has nobody to order around."[48]

Out of this difference in the basis of the rights of the faculties, there now results a "lawful controversy" between them: a conflict which is grounded in their very being and which hence cannot be eliminated through any sort of compromise, but must continue and be fought out. As parts and members of the political hierarchy, the higher faculties continue to be defined as much by their appetite for power as by

47. *The Contest of Faculties,* First sect., introduction (VII, 329) (*Ak.* VII, 19).
48. [Ibid. (VII, 330) (*Ak.* VII, 20).]

their desire to know, while the philosophical faculty, to the extent
that it wants to remain true to its task, has to receive all its directives
from this latter. Thus its natural role is that of opposition, but an
opposition of a kind requisite and unavoidable for the prosperity and
the positive progress of the whole itself. The philosophical faculty
wages the eternal conflict of the "rational" against all that is merely
"statutory," of scientific reason against power and against tradition.
In this its basic function, it may not be hampered and confined, even
by the state, insofar as it understands its own needs and its own
vocation. All that the state may require of it is this: that it not trench
directly on state administrative activities. The training and education
of men of practical affairs, whom the state needs for its ends, is left to
the higher faculties, which for this reason are subject to its legitimate
oversight. But it may also be expected, conversely, of the members of
the higher faculties that they not overstep the boundaries drawn for
them. If the biblical theologian refers to reason for any one of his
statements, "he thus leaps over (like Romulus's brother) the wall of
the faith of the church, which alone confers salvation, and goes astray
in the open meadow of judging for oneself and of philosophy, where
he, having fled spiritual government, is exposed to all the perils of
anarchy."[49] Just so the jurist, as an appointed judicial officer, has
simply to apply the existing legal decrees, and it would be preposterous if instead before doing so he demanded or wished to prove them
to be reasonable. Only the philosophical faculty, as guardian of pure
theory, can never regard itself as exempted from this proof. It can
happen that a practical doctrine is followed out of obedience, "but
thereby to assume it to be true because it is commanded, is totally
impossible, not only objectively (as a judgment which *ought* not to be)
but also subjectively (as a judgment which no man *can* pass)."[50] Accordingly, if the quarrel is over truth and falsity, not about the utility
or harmfulness of a theory, there is no higher principle than reason:
to limit its autonomy in any way at all is nothing other than to destroy
the essential concept of truth itself.

49. [Ibid., first sect., I, sect. IA (VII, 334) (*Ak.* VII, 24).]
50. Ibid., first sect., I, sect. II (VII, 337) (*Ak.* VII, 27).

What consequences issue from this for the contest between rational religion and church faith, between the pure philosophy of religion and biblical orthodoxy—this *Religion within the Limits of Reason Alone* has already expounded. What *The Contest of Faculties* does in this connection is only to supplement and confirm the earlier expositions, in which memory of the specific phases of the personal battle Kant had to wage echoes everywhere. However, reflection takes a new turn when—in the form of the exposition of the conflict between the juristic and philosophical faculties—it takes into its attack the question of the relation between the natural right and the positive right foundation of the constitution. Is all right simply the expression of actual empirical power relationships, and can it be resolved into them, as its essential basis, or does an ideal factor cooperate in it, which asserts itself slowly and steadily as a political effective factor as well? The answer to this question includes, according to Kant, nothing more trifling than the judgment as to whether human history and the human race are conceived as ascending and progressing steadily toward the better, or whether both persist at the selfsame stage of perfection, with minor oscillations, or even are as a whole exposed to decay and retrogression. If one tries to decide this from the standpoint of pure reflection on happiness, the upshot can be nothing but negative: Rousseau's pessimism toward culture holds here absolutely correctly. Eudaimonism, with its sanguine hopes, seems to be untenable and to promise little in support of a "prophetic history of mankind" which bears on continuing further progress on the road toward the good.[51]

But here immediately there intervenes the methodological consideration that the problem in general cannot be brought to clarification and solution in a purely empirical way. For to raise the question as to the moral progress of mankind is already a paradox. It is a matter herein of predicting something about the inquiry that of its nature cannot and ought not be predicted. The fate of the human race is not a fate imposed by any sort of blind "nature" or "providence," but it is the outcome and the handiwork of humanity's own free self-

51. Ibid., second sect., §3b (VII, 394) (*Ak.* VII, 82).

determination. But how is one to trace and to make visible the course
and path the intelligible determination takes, in the empirical, causal
running of events, in the sheer flux of appearances? The two realms
are nowhere actually congruent, thus a relation of this kind is only
possible in that the world of appearance, that is to say, the continuance of historical occurrences in the world, at least contains a
symbolic event whose interpretation leads us back to the realm of
freedom necessarily and of itself.

Is there such a historical sign, to which the hope and expectation
that the human race as a whole is conceived to be continuously progressing may be joined? Kant answers this question by referring to
the French Revolution, which is to be understood here not in its
empirical course and outcome, but exclusively with regard to its ideal
meaning and its tendency. "The occurrence in question does not involve any of those momentous deeds or misdeeds of men which
make small in their eyes what was formerly great or make great what
was formerly small, and which cause ancient and illustrious states to
vanish as if by magic, and others to arise in their place as if from the
bowels of the earth. No, it has nothing to do with all this. We are here
concerned only with the attitude of the onlookers as it reveals itself *in
public* while the drama of great political changes is taking place: for
they openly express universal yet disinterested sympathy for one set
of protagonists against their adversaries.... Their reaction (because
of its universality) proves that mankind as a whole shares a certain
character in common, and it also proves (because of its disinterested-
ness) that man has a moral character, or at least the makings of one.
And this does not merely allow us to hope for improvement; it is
already a form of improvement in itself, insofar as its influence is
strong enough for the present. The revolution which we have seen
taking place in our own times in a nation of gifted people may succeed, or it may fail. It may be so filled with misery and atrocities that
no right-thinking man would ever decide to make the same experiment again at such a price, even if he could hope to carry it out
successfully at the second attempt. But I maintain that this revolution
has aroused in the hearts and desires of all spectators who are not
themselves caught up in it a *sympathy* which borders almost on en-

thusiasm, although the very utterance of this sympathy was fraught with danger. It cannot therefore have been caused by anything other than a moral disposition within the human race."[52] It is the certainty of this disposition on which is founded the hope of the evolution of a condition of natural right in the relation of the individual to the state and in the relation of separate states to each other. A phenomenon such as the French Revolution was, will never be forgotten, because it has revealed a capacity for the better in human nature, the like of which no politician would have rationalized from the course of things till now, and which alone unites nature and freedom in accordance with the inner principles of right in mankind.

Now it is shown that the ideal of the state, as the great social theoreticians have regarded it—as the the ideal of a constitution concordant with the natural rights of man—is no empty chimera, but rather the standard for every civil constitution in general. And with this insight "perpetual peace" ceases to be a mere dream: for the establishment within a nation of a constitution strictly democratic and republican in spirit also offers the external guarantee—as the book *Perpetual Peace* had already put forward—that the intent of unjustly oppressing one nation by another, and likewise the means of realizing this intent, are progressively weakened, so that approximation to the "cosmopolitan" condition is also progressively fulfilled in the history of nations.[53]

With its prospect on this goal of human history, in which the idea of freedom is to find its concrete fulfillment and its empirical political actualization, Kant's philosophical activity comes to a close. The idea of freedom forms the terminal point of his philosophy, just as it had formed its beginning and middle. What Kant's activity as writer adds to those discussions is only a sparse literary gleaning, adding no further dimension to the essential substance of his philosophical system. The final section of *The Contest of Faculties*, which treats of the contest of the philosophical faculty with the medical faculty, is only

52. [Ibid., second sect., §6 (VII, 397 ff.) (*Ak.* VII, 85).]
53. For the whole of this, see VII, 391–404 (*Ak.* VII, 79–94). Cf. *Perpetual Peace* (VI, 427–74) (*Ak.* VIII, 341–81).

superficially hooked on: this treatise, "On the Power of the Mind to Control Its Feelings of Illness by Sheer Willpower," is concerned only with a number of dietetic precepts, loosely arrayed, that Kant had tested out on himself personally and with methodical self-observation. Even the *Anthropology* of 1798 cannot in any sense take its place beside the essential main systematic works by virtue of its content and structure: it compiles merely "in a pragmatic respect" the rich material on human history and anthropology that Kant had assembled over a long lifetime from his own observations and from odd sources, and had enriched over and over by the notes and studies for his lectures.

On the other hand, that work in which Kant's entire inner concern was wrapped up during this period, and which he himself saw as belonging intimately to the whole of his systematic labor, never came to maturity, as untiringly as Kant devoted himself to its continuance on into the closing years of his life and until the complete expiration of his physical and mental powers. With a perpetually renewed effort of will he applied himself to this book, "The Transition from the Metaphysical Principles of Natural Science to Physics" ("Übergang von den metaphysischen Anfangsgründen der Naturwissenschaft zur Physik"), which was to lead to a complete and concluding survey of the "system of pure philosophy in its coherence." His biographers unanimously bear witness to the affection he attached to this work, about which he was wont to speak "with veritable animation" and which he many times declared to be "his most important work."[54] He often thought that he had reached the conclusion of this *chef d'oeuvre;* he believed that only a brief editing of the manuscript was needed to be able to publish it, "his system as a complete whole."[55] Was it simply a natural self-deception on the part of the old man that misled him into this judgment? We are tempted to suppose that, when we look at the superficial form of the manuscript.[56] The same sentences and ex-

54. See Reinhold Bernhard Jachmann, *Immanuel Kant geschildert in Briefen an einen Freund,* Third Letter, pp. 17 f.; E. A. C. Wasianski, *Immanuel Kant. Ein Lebensbild nach Darstellungen der Zeitgenossen Jachmann, Borowski, Wasianski* (Halle a.S., 1902), p. 95.

55. Cf. Hasse, *Letzte Aüsserungen Kants von einem seiner Tischgenossen,* pp. 21 ff.

56. Parts of the manuscript were published by Rudolf Riecke in the *Altpreussische Monatsschrift,* 1882–84, under the title, "Ein ungedrucktes Werk Kants aus seinen

pressions recur over and over in innumerable repetitions; the important and the trivial tumble over each other in a motley jumble;
nowhere is there to be found a realized systematic arrangement and
strict structure and movement of thought. And yet, the further one
reads, the more it becomes evident that the real defect is not so much
in the ideas themselves as in their exposition. It is as if his original
creative power of thought lingered longer in Kant than the lesser
powers of arrangement and division. His power of recall breaks
down; his memory is not sufficient for him to recollect the beginning
of a sentence when he writes the end of it; stylistic periods get confused; and yet there gleam forth from time to time in the midst of this
chaos individual ideas of astonishing power and depth—ideas which
are devoted to illuminating once again the whole of his system and
exposing to view its ultimate foundations. In particular, information
can be found here about the methodical meaning of the opposition of
the "thing in itself" and "appearance" the equal of which one might
seek for in vain in the earlier works. The attempt to coin in detail the
intellectual handiwork of his old age seems, in view of the state of the
manuscript, probably doomed to remain forever vain—thus the deeper one immerses oneself in the samples from the book published so
far, there well up only pangs of regret that it was not granted to Kant
himself to recover this treasure.

In 1795 Wilhelm von Humboldt could still advise Schiller, following information he had gotten from Memel, that Kant was carrying a
monstrous host of unworked-out ideas in his head, which he intended to elaborate in a certain order, so that he reckoned the life
span remaining to him more in accordance with the size of that stock
of ideas than by the usual probability.[57] Schiller himself found in the
"Proclamation of the Approaching Conclusion of a Treaty of Perpetual Peace in Philosophy" ("Verkündigung des nahen Abschlusses
eines Traktats zum ewigen Frieden in der Philosophie"), aimed at
Schlosser, which Kant published in 1797, a fresh and genuinely
youthful character, which might almost be called aesthetic, as he

---

letzten Lebensjahren." For the substance of the entire work, now cf. esp. Erich Adickes's exposition, *Kants Opus posthumum* (Berlin, 1920).

57. Humboldt to Schiller, *Briefwechsel*, ed. A. Leitzmann (Halle, 1908), p. 153.

added in a letter to Goethe, if one were not plunged into embarrassment by the drab style, which might be called a philosophical officialese.[58] The young Count von Purgstall reports, from his personal association, the deep impression he received from Kant's lectures in April, 1795, and the brilliance and clarity they shed over the whole of his thought; and Kant's colleague Poerschke testifies in a letter to Fichte in 1798 that Kant's mind was not yet gone, although he no longer possessed the capacity for continuous intellectual labor.[59] Even in the conduct of his personal affairs and in carrying on the business of his post, Kant repeatedly showed in this period that his old force of will and energy had not left him. He had indeed given up his lectures as of the summer of 1796: on July 23, 1796, he seems to have mounted to his lecture-desk for the last time.[60] He even refused the post of rector when it was offered to him again in 1796, referring to his age and his physical feebleness.[61] But two years later, when the attempt was made to restrict his functioning in the university senate and substitute in his place an "adjunct," who was to safeguard his rights for him and conduct his business, he rebelled against such a request in powerful language and terse legalistic argumentation.[62] The painful feeling of "a total end to his counting for anything in matters concerning *all* of philosophy" hung before his eyes, and the sense of no longer being able to reach this goal never left him from this time on; he himself called it, in a letter to Garve, a "sorrow of Tantalus."[63] Despite the inward inclination that drove him forcefully again and again back to the basic and main theme of this period, the problem of the "transition from metaphysics to physics," he now fended off questions about his philosophical labors, for the most part with clear awareness and lack of pretense. "Oh, what it is like *sarcinas*

58. Schiller to Goethe, September 22, 1797.

59. *Fichtes Leben und literarischer Briefwechsel*, vol. 2, p. 451.

60. On this question, see the material in Arnoldt, *Beiträge zu dem Material der Geschichte von Kants Leben und Schriftstellertätigkeit*, and also Arthur Warda, *Altpreussische Monatsschrift* 38:75 ff.

61. Letter to the Rector, February 26, 1796 (*Ak.* XII, 461).

62. To the Rector, December 3, 1797 (X, 330 f.) (*Ak.* XII, 463).

63. To Garve, September 21, 1798 (X, 351) (*Ak.* XII, 254).

colligere [to pack for the journey]! That is all I can think about now,"
he often said to his friends, by Borowski's account.[64]

It is a signal literary dispensation that we are so precisely and fully
informed about no other portion of Kant's life as we are about this last
one. In the reports of his faithful friend and nurse-companion Pastor
Wasianski, poignant in their simplicity and calm objectivity, we can
trace the distinct phases of his complete decline from year to year,
almost from week to week. We do not need to go into the details of
these reports here, though, since they do not transcend a mere record
of illness. Wasianski reports the statement of a "passing scholar,"
who sought Kant out some two years before his death, that he had
not seen Kant, but only Kant's shell.[65] Increasingly now Kant himself
felt the pressure of such visits, to which more and more people were
tempted, partly through personal interest, partly through sheer
curiosity. "In me," he was wont to reply to the compliments of such
visitors, "you see an old, decrepit, and feeble man, who has lived out
his life." In December, 1803, he could no longer write his name, nor
comprehend any expression of sociability; ultimately he began to fail
to recognize those around him. Only the basic traits of his character
remained true to him, even as his intellectual powers crumbled, and
one can give all the more unqualified credence to what Wasianski tells
us about this since his account overall is pitched in the tone of plain
truth, scorning all decorative rhetorical trappings. "Every day," he
recounts concerning his intercourse with Kant in the last years, "I
profited; for daily I discovered one more lovable facet of his good
heart; daily I received new assurances of his trust. . . . Kant's greatness as a scholar and thinker is known to the world, I cannot evaluate
it; but no one has had such opportunity as I to observe the finest
traits of his unassuming good nature." "Ever and again there were
some moments when his great mind, though it no longer shone as
blindingly as before, was nonetheless visible, and when his kind
heart was even more luminous. In the hours when he was less bur-

---

64. Ludwig Ernst Borowski, *Darstellung des Lebens und Charakters Immanuel Kants*
(Königsberg, 1804), p. 184.
    65. Wasianski, p. 202.

dened by his weakness, he acknowledged every measure that alleviated his fate for him with heartfelt thanks to me and active thanks to his servant, whose extremely burdensome labors and unwearied loyalty he rewarded with considerable gifts.''

There is a particular incident from the final days of Kant's life, preserved by Wasianski, that makes the retention of the fine human traits in Kant's personality more clearly visible than any merely indirect reference might. ''On February 3,'' roughly a week before Kant's death, ''all urge to live seemed to be entirely slackened and to wane completely, for from this day on he ate essentially nothing. His existence seemed to be only due to a kind of momentum of a motion which had been going on for eighty years. His physician had arranged with me to visit him at a certain hour, and wished my presence close by. . . . When he arrived, Kant being almost unable to see any longer, I said to him that his doctor had come. Kant stands up from his chair, extends his hand to his doctor, and talks about *posts*, repeats the word frequently in a tone as though he wants to be helped out. The doctor calms him by saying that everything is taken care of about the posts, because he takes this utterance for a delusion. Kant says: 'many posts, troublesome posts,' then quickly: 'great kindness,' shortly thereafter: 'thankfulness,' all this disjointed, yet with increasing warmth and a certain degree of consciousness of himself. I guessed his meaning quite well, however. He wanted to say that with his many and troublesome posts, especially that of Rector, it was very kind of his doctor to visit him. 'Exactly right' was Kant's reply; he was still standing, and about to collapse from weakness. The doctor requested him to sit down. Kant hesitated uncertainly and uneasily. I was too familiar with his way of thinking to have made any mistake about the real cause of the delay, why Kant did not change his position which was fatiguing and weakened him. I made the doctor aware of the true cause, to wit Kant's courteous way of thinking and civil manners, and assured him that Kant would sit down just as soon as he, the stranger, had first taken a chair. The doctor seemed dubious about this reason, but he was quickly convinced of the truth of my statement and moved almost to tears when Kant, having collected his powers with main force, said: 'The sense of humanity has not yet abandoned me.' That is a noble, refined, and good man! we cried to each other as one."

It is a chance utterance, arising from a particular situation, we are told of here, but it has a universal and symbolic value, seen in the context of Kant's personality. Kant's biographers say that at a time when it was very difficult for him to follow ordinary, everyday speech, his grasp of general ideas was retained undiminished: one needed only to turn the conversation to a general philosophical or scientific topic for him to be moved immediately to lively participation. Just as this trait testifies to the force and durability of fundamental theoretical ideas in Kant's mind, the uninterrupted controlling guidance of his will is again mirrored in what is told us about the expressions of his character in the last years. He was and he remained, as Wasianski puts it, "the man of determination, whose feeble foot often tottered, whose stern soul never." As difficult as it often was for him to grasp a simple decision relating to a present concrete situation, he persevered in his resolution, even under what were for him the most difficult circumstances, as soon as he had once laid hold of it and safeguarded it by a consciously formulated maxim.

Together with this energy and consistency of will, the essential tenderness of his personal nature came to light more and more as well. Charlotte von Schiller said about Kant that he would have been one of the greatest phenomena of mankind in general if he had been able to feel love; but since this was not the case there was something defective in his nature.[66] In fact, even in Kant's relation to people in his immediate surroundings, in all the sympathy and all the selfless devotion of which he was capable, a certain limit set by reason was never crossed, and this rational control, where one thinks himself justified in expecting and demanding a direct expression of emotion, can easily arouse the illusion of an impersonal coolness in reflection on human things and relationships. Actually, all emotions of the "softhearted kind," as he himself called them, were alien to Kant's disposition and nature. But all the more richly and delicately de-

66. On this and the following, cf. Otto Schöndörffer, "Kants Briefwechsel," *Altpreussische Monatsschrift* 38:120 ff.

veloped in him was the emotion which he himself regarded as the fundamental ethical emotion, and in which he thought he recognized the motive force for all concrete ethical behavior. His relationship to individuals was guided and ruled by universal respect for the freedom of the moral person and his right of self-determination. And this respect was no abstract demand, but it acted on him as an immediately living motive, determining every particular utterance. By this disposition Kant acquired that "courtesy of the heart" which, if not precisely the same as love, is nonetheless related to love. His "sense of humanity," which he held fast to and guarded until the last days of his life, was divorced from every merely sentimental subsoil. It was precisely in this respect that his particular special quality prevailed against his times and his environment, against the Age of Sensibility. Kant's attitude toward mankind was defined by the pure and abstract medium of the moral law; but even in this law itself he recognized and at the same time honored the highest force of human personality. Therefore the idea of humanity and of freedom was not for him a politico-social and pedagogic ideal, but it became the lever by which he displaced the entire intellectual and spiritual world, and lifted it from its hinges. The idea of the "primacy of practical reason" implied a transformation of the basic conception of theoretical reason itself: the new feeling and the new consciousness of humanity led to a universal "intellectual revolution," only in which did it find its final and decisive footing.

On the morning of February 12, 1804, Kant died. His funeral turned into a great public ceremony, in which the whole city and the inhabitants of all quarters of it took part. His body had been laid out in his home previously, and a great host of people "of the highest and lowest condition" streamed in to see it. "Everyone hastened to seize the last opportunity . . . for many days the pilgrimage went on, every day. . . . Many came back two and even three times, and many days later the public had not yet fully satisfied its desire to see him." The obsequies were organized by the university and by the students, who were intent on showing special honor to Kant. Amid the tolling of every bell in Königsberg, young students came to Kant's house to take up his body, from whence the innumerable procession, accompanied by thousands, wound to the university cathedral. Here it was laid in the so-called professor's vault; later a special hall, the Stoa Kantiana, was erected on this spot.

But splendid as its external forms were and great as was the participation in Kant's funeral, and however much "the clearest marks of universal reverence, ceremonial pomp, and taste," in Wasianski's phrase, were united in it, Kant himself had become almost a stranger to his environment and his native city when he died. In 1798—six years before his death—Poerschke had already written to Fichte that Kant, since he did not lecture any more and had withdrawn from all social intercourse save that in Motherby's house, was gradually becoming unknown even in Königsberg.[67] His name shone with the old luster; but his person had begun to be increasingly forgotten. The historical effect of his philosophy waxed greater and greater and the most distinctive part of his philosophy was being spread abroad by entire hosts; but in the final years of his life his personality already seemed to belong more to memory and to legend than to the actual historical present. And this, too, reveals a typical trait essential to Kant's life and significant for it. For the greatness and power of this life did not consist in all the personal and individual factors of Kant's mind and will achieving an ever-richer unfolding, but in its putting itself always more definitely and exclusively in the service of relevant demands, ideal problems, and tasks. The personal forms of life and of existence here had no independent worth purely as such; their whole significance is merged into their becoming the stuff and means of the life of abstract thinking, which moves according to its own law and by the force of its immanent necessity. On this relation of person and thing is founded the entire form and structure of Kant's life, is founded that which constitutes its profundity and that which might appear to be its peculiar limitation and narrowness. Full devotion to purely impersonal goals seems eventually to have as its inevitable consequence impoverishment of

67. Poerschke to Fichte, July 2, 1798; see *Fichtes Leben und literarischer Briefwechsel*, vol. 2, p. 451.

the concrete substance and the individual fullness of life, but on the other hand, it is only here that the full, compelling power of the universal emerges—that universal expressed equally as a theoretical and as a practical idea in the world of Kant's thought and of his will.

We recall with what power and freshness, with what immediate subjective vivacity Kant's fundamental orientation speaks even at the outset of his activity as philosopher and writer, in *Thoughts on the True Estimation of Living Forces*. "I have already marked out the road ahead," the young man of twenty-two wrote, "which I intend to follow. I shall embark on my course, and nothing shall hinder me from pursuing it."[68] Kant's thought had traversed this road in a far more comprehensive sense than his youthful enthusiasm could have foreseen. The path from detail and the particular to the whole, from the individual to the universal, had been trodden in the most diverse directions. His reflection had begun with the problem of cosmology and cosmogony, with the questions of how the world arose and how it is ordered. What was most important in that was to establish a new standpoint for judgment. It was not only necessary to go beyond direct sensory perception, which remains bound to spatiotemporal particularity, to the respective here and now, but also to supplement and deepen the mathematical scientific world-picture of Newton, since it took up the question of the temporal origin of the cosmos and at the same time created a new dimension of reflection. Only then did the empirical terrestrial horizon expand into the truly comprehensive and universal horizon of astronomical conception and judgment. An analogous broadening of the concept of human history then took place, in Kant's researches into the foundation of a physical geography and an empirical anthropology, since history was classified as a special case of the general problem of organic evolution and subordinated to it.

Kant's critical period retains this basic tendency, but it shifts the center of gravity from the "natural" to the "mental," from physics and biology to the realm of logic and ethics. Here too, by the indica-

68. See above, p. 31.

tion of their universally valid a priori foundations, the full force and depth of the authority of judgment and action are first brought into clear consciousness, but at the same time the boundaries that the application of these principles cannot overstep without becoming lost in the void are fixed. Both moments, that of establishing and that of limiting, are for Kant directly implied in each other, for only in binding the understanding and the will by a universal and necessary law is the objective order of the worlds of the understanding and of the will, on which their essential content rests, produced.

In the famous parallel he draws between Plato and Aristotle in his history of the theory of colors, Goethe compared two basic types of philosophic reflection with each other. "Plato comports himself in the world like a blessed spirit, whose will it is to sojourn in it a while. For him it is less a matter of learning to know the world, because he already assumes it, than of sharing with it as a friend what he brings with him and what it needs so sorely. He presses into the depths more to fill them with his own being than to explore them. He moves longingly to the heights, to participate once again in his source. Everything that he utters is related to an eternal One, Good, True, Beautiful, whose demands he strives to enliven in his bosom. . . . Aristotle, on the contrary, stands in the world like a man, an architect. He is just here, and is going to work and to produce here. He studies the earth, but no farther than until he strikes hard ground. From there to the center of the earth the rest is all the same to him. He traces round a monstrous circle for his foundation, gathers materials from all sides, sorts them, piles them up, and thus ascends to the heights like a pyramid, in a geometric form, while Plato reaches for the heavens like an obelisk, indeed like a pointed flame. When two such men, who apportion human nature between them to a certain extent, appeared as distinct representatives of glorious qualities which are not easy to combine, when they had the fortune to educate themselves fully, to utter their education completely, not in short laconic sentences like oracular sayings but in exceptional, extensive, numerous works; when these works for the best part remain to mankind and are more or less continuously studied and reflected on: it naturally follows that the world, insofar as it is regarded as feeling and thinking, was obliged to devote itself to one or the other, to acknowledge one or the other as master, teacher, leader."

It is indicative of the scope and depth of Kant's philosophical genius that, as regards the fundamental orientation of his mind, he is an exception to the universal contrast in intellectual history that Goethe expresses typically here. The alternatives posed here held no force and validity for him. In place of this struggle between philosophy's intellectual motivations in world history up to the present, in him there enters a unification that is novel in the world. If Plato and Aristotle seem to be divided into representatives of separate qualities in mankind, Kant, in his philosophical achievement, erects a new total conception of what man can do and attain in conceiving and performing, in thinking and doing. Perhaps in this lies the peculiar secret of the historical effect his doctrine has exercised. For in Kant the basic tendencies Goethe contrasted in his portrait of Aristotle and Plato join and fuse, and both are in such perfect equilibrium that one can hardly speak any longer of a contrary preeminence of one over the other. Kant felt himself a Platonist specifically in the foundations of his ethics, and in the *Critique of Pure Reason* he declared himself forcefully and decisively for the correctness of the Platonic "Idea" and against all objections to it stemming from the "vulgar appeal to so-called adverse experience."[69] But then a current of passing fashion tried to substitute for Plato the dialectician and moralist the mystical theologue, lauding Plato as a technician in this sense, as the philosopher of the supersensuous and of "intellectual intuition"; whereas Kant no less vigorously attached himself to the "worker" Aristotle, on whom that "philosophy with a condescending tone" thought it could look down. "It can occur to no other than the philosopher of *intuition*, who does not prove himself by the herculean labor of self-knowledge from below, but rather from above, soaring on high, by an apotheosis which costs him nothing, to give himself airs: because he speaks from his own insight and therefore is obligated to be called to account by no one." In contrast, the philosophy

69. See above, p. 253.

of Aristotle is hard work, for Aristotle's aim as metaphysician is directed in every instance toward division of a priori knowledge into its elements and toward its reconquest and reassembling from these elements, no matter whether and by what means he accomplishes it.[70]

The dual orientation of Kant's conception of philosophy is here indicated in a few words. The critical philosophy also strives from the empirical and sensory to the "intelligible," and it finds its fulfillment and its true conclusion only in the intelligible of the idea of freedom. But the path to this goal leads "through the herculean labor of self-knowledge." Accordingly, no "flights of genius" and no appeal to any sort of intuitive flashes have any weight here, but strict conceptual demands and necessities rule; here no immediate feeling of evidence, psychological or mystical, decides, but methodically performed scientific analysis and the "transcendental deduction" of the basic forms of knowledge. The genuine intelligible, which underlies experience, is only attained in the strengthening and securing, in the full critical understanding, of precisely this experience itself. Even this endeavor which leads on beyond experience to the supersensuous and to the Idea pulls back all the more deeply into the "fertile lowland of experience" to do this. It is even a proof of the power of the Idea and of idealism that both, in raising themselves beyond experience, only achieve complete understanding of the form of experience and the law of its structure in thus elevating themselves. The Idea strives into the absolute and unconditioned, but the critical attitude finds that the true unconditioned is never given, but is always imposed, and that in this sense it is one with the demand for the totality of conditions. Hence, to step into the infinite it suffices to penetrate the finite in all its aspects. Fully developed, the empirical itself guides us to "metaphysics"—as metaphysics, in the transcendental sense, should be presented and expressed as nothing else than the whole stuff of the empirical. The endeavor toward the unconditioned is innate and native to reason, but the total system of

70. See "On a Condescending Tone Recently Raised in Philosophy" (1796) (VI, 478, 482) (*Ak.* VIII, 390, 393).

conditions of theoretical and practical reason itself is shown to be the
ultimate unconditioned to which we can advance. In this sense, the
concepts of "what can be investigated" and "what cannot be investigated" are demarcated and defined in Kant's doctrine. Something
that cannot be investigated remains unknown; it is no longer a mere
negation, however, but rather it becomes the rule of knowledge and
action. It is no longer the expression of an impotent and hopeless
scepticism, but it aims to point out the path and the direction in which
inquiry has to move and by which it has to unfold itself comprehensively. Thus, in the truly intelligible, in the intelligible of reason's
task, the world of being is transformed into a world of deed. In this
new relation between the conditioned and the unconditioned, between the finite and the infinite, between experience and speculation,
Kant has wrought a new type of philosophical thinking in contrast to
that of Plato and Aristotle: in him, the specifically modern conception
of idealism, inaugurated by Descartes and Leibniz, achieves its systematic perfection and fulfillment.

INDEX

Abstraction, concepts obtained by, 102–03
Action and reaction, Newton's law of, 222–23, 291
Actuality, 192, 193, 208
Adickes, Erich, 94
Aesthetics, 219, 278, 284, 308–34, 337, 340, 342
Alembert, Jean Le Rond d', 51; *Essai de Dynamique*, 30
Analogies of Experience, 182–88, 206, 222
Analytic of the Beautiful, 310–26
Analytic of the Sublime, 326–34
Analytic universal, 350
Anaxagoras, 289
Anselm, Saint, 65
"Answer to the Question: 'What Is Enlightenment?' An," 223, 227–28, 367
Anthropology, 55; Kant's lectures on, 53
Anthropology, 19, 408
Anticipations of Perception, 178, 180–82
Aquinas, Saint Thomas, 389
Arcana coelestia (Swedenborg), 79, 81
Aristotle, 27, 130, 169, 207, 276–77, 281, 282, 286, 336, 352; physics of, 67; and Plato compared, 417–20; ten predicaments, 169, 173–74
Arithmetic, viii, 157–58, 161, 180; antilogicist analysis of, xii; a priori concept of, xi; contrasted with geometry, 158
Arnoldt, Emil, 21

Art, 307–08
Atomism, 44
"Attempt to Introduce the Concept of Negative Magnitudes into Philosophy," 44–45, 74, 81, 105
Augustine, Saint, 68; *Soliloquies,* 7
Autonomy, concept of, 224, 243–44, 251, 333, 362, 384
Axioms of Intuition, 180

Bacon, Francis, 9, 218
Baumgarten, Alexander, 69, 84, 284, 303–04, 325, 394; *Metaphysica,* 69, 111
Beautiful, the: perception of, 310–34, 340. *See also* Aesthetics; Analytic of the Beautiful
Beck, Johann Sigismund, 294
Berkeley, George, 194, 195, 369
Berlin Academy of Sciences, 55, 65–66, 77, 232, 363
Berlinische Monatsschrift, 223, 367, 378, 380–81
Biester, Johann Erich von (editor of *Berlinische Monatsschrift*), 367, 392–93
Borowski, Ludwig Ernst, 12, 21, 26, 32, 33, 39–40, 53–54, 137, 411
Boscovich, Ruggiero Giuseppe, 42
"Boundaries of Sensibility and Reason, The," 123
Broad, C. D., xi